When Baseball Returned to Brooklyn

When Baseball Returned to Brooklyn

The Inaugural Season of the New York–Penn League Cyclones

ED SHAKESPEARE

FOREWORD BY CARL ERSKINE

McFarland & Company, Inc., Publishers
Jefferson, North Carolina, and London

Photo credit is given to the following persons and institutions: Associated Press Worldwide Photos, pages 5, 8; Baseball Hall of Fame Library, 38, 44, 84, 85, 87, 91, 92, 93, 95, 98, 99, 101, 102, 106, 116, 122, 123, 213; Brooklyn Public Library — Brooklyn Collection, 4, 88, 103, 108, 117, 119, 210, 306; Dodgertown, 226, 308, 309, 310, 311; Gary Thomas/ *The Brooklyn Papers*, 6, 12, 23, 48, 50, 57, 61, 62, 69, 126, 127, 132, 144, 145, 147 top and bottom, 148, 149, 150, 157, 158, 160, 162, 167, 182, 184, 186, 219, 230, 244, 253, 258, 259, 264, 266, 270, 272, 273, 277, 280, 285, 297, 302, 307, Jim Riggs, Post-Journal (Jamestown, New York) Sports Editor, 130.

LIBRARY OF CONGRESS CATALOGUING-IN-PUBLICATION DATA

Shakespeare, Ed.
　　When baseball returned to Brooklyn : the inaugural season of the New York–Penn League Cyclones / Ed Shakespeare ; foreword by Carl Erskine.
　　　　p.　　cm.
　　Includes bibliographical references (p.) and index.

　　ISBN 0-7864-1459-6 (softcover : 50# alkaline paper)

　　1. Brooklyn Cyclones (Baseball team)　2. Baseball — New York (State) — Brooklyn (New York)　3. New York–Penn League (Baseball league)　I. Title
　　GV875.B69 S53　2003
　　796.357'64'0974723 — dc21　　　　　　　　　　　　2002151779

British Library cataloguing data are available

Cover photograph: KeySpan Park (Coney Island)

Manufactured in the United States of America

McFarland & Company, Inc., Publishers
　Box 611, Jefferson, North Carolina 28640
　www.mcfarlandpub.com

To the fans and players of Brooklyn baseball —
from the days of the Brooklyn Dodgers
to the return of the Cyclones.

Wait till next year? Next year is now.

Acknowledgments

For my family, and for my friends — both old and new. This book is the result of the contributions of many persons. These contributions are through friendship, advice, encouragement, and shared memories.

For the Shakespeare family: Mom and Dad; for David and Ellen; Jenny, Laura and Craig. For Glenda Randy, Lisa, Will and Bev Hoppe. For Barbara Carr and Ann. For Kent and Kathy Zerby, Mike and Nathalie Quinn, Joe Reilly, Tom Vona, Dennis Flynn, Barbara Schweitzer, Norma Christiansen, Jeannie and Don Wilcox, John Morrison, Jerry Shaw, Maureen McBurney, George Vischer, Fred Swearingen, Carmen Russo, and Bob D'Amato, Bob Taylor, C.K., L.G., Diane Fisher, John Tague, Rick Zuvich, Bob Zuvich, and the Slugs. For Jim Mavroleon, and all the softball Grads from 1968–2003. Diane Fisher, Eileen Kennedy. Special remembrance of friends Jack Kuhnert, Cal Wilson, John Fisher. Bill Hart, infielder, Brooklyn Dodgers.

For all the Cyclone players, especially for the insights provided during interviews with: David Bacani, David Byard, Anthony Coyne, Noel Davarez, Lenny DiNardo, Matt Gahan, Justin Huber, Mike Jacobs, Forrest Lawson, Wayne Lydon, Brett McGinley, Robert McIntyre, Rylie Ogle, Angel Pagan, Matt Peterson, Edgar Rodriguez, Francisco Sosa, John Toner, Ross Peeples, Mike Jacobs, Angel Pagan, Robert McIntyre, Jeremy Todd, Brian Walker, and Joel Zaragoza. For the special insights provided by numerous interviews with: Jay Caligiuri, Frank Corr, Mike Cox, Harold Eckert, Vladimir Hernandez, Joe Jiannetti, Brett Kay, Ross and Junior Peeples, Tyler Beuerlein, and Luz Portobanco. For R.C. Reuteman, Dave Campanero, Marty Haber, and Rick Johnson, of the Brooklyn Cyclones for their help and for their comments during interviews. Great appreciation to Shoni and Phil Soffer for word processing and manuscript preparation.

For June Harrison for her valuable assistance with photos. For Gary Thomas, photographer extraordinaire, for his help in providing access to his many photos and permitting their use in the book. For Gersh Kuntzman for his help all during the 2001 season and for the insights provided by his columns in *The Brooklyn Papers*. For Mike Dolan and Mark Healey for their ideas and company. For Tom Gilbert of the Associated Press Photos. A special thanks to librarians Judy Walsh and Susan Aprill at a wonderful treasure — the Brooklyn Collection at the Grand Army (Main Branch) of the Brooklyn Public Library. Heartfelt thanks to the National Hall of Fame in Cooperstown, New York, with special thanks for photo help to Bill Burdick and for help with research questions from Russell Wolinsky. Thanks to the staff of the Upper Shores Branch, in Lavallette, of the Ocean County, N.J. Library. Much appreciation for the folks at Dodgertown for the friendly assistance and for the use of their photos. Thanks to the New York Mets Minor League Complex for their help in many matters. Thanks to talented clubhouse man Kelly Sharitt for his help throughout the project. Thanks to Noah Diethrick of the Jamestown Jammers for his cordial reception on my visit to Jamestown Kudos to Reggie Armstrong for his observations. For Vin Dimiceli, senior editor of *Brooklyn Papers*. For Jack Bowen, Gary Carter, Tony Cincotta and Joe G., Joe Blackburn, Jason Day and Jason Klein, umpires.

Special to Brooklyn Dodgers Joe Pignatano, Clem Labine, Duke Snider, Clyde King, Johnny Podres, Ralph Branca, Tommy Holmes, and Al Gionfriddo for their generous interviews. To Betty Erskine for her kindness. Appreciation to the fans of Brooklyn baseball: Chuck Monsanto, Nick Cunningham, Ed Gruber, Steve Gruber, Robert Martin, Sam Cosola, Walter Bentson, Bob Berardelli, Gail Block, Don and Donna Byrnes, Steve Sommers, Burnley Duke Dame, John Davenport, Eric Montague, and Herm Sorcher.

Special thanks to friend and writer Kevin Coyne for his extensive help. Kevin was on the team at the start, and he provided advice and encouragement all along. Great appreciation to Robert McCord as friend, editor, and agent. Robert shaped the outline for the book and was instrumental in bringing the book to publication. Thanks to Sharon Rose Scire-Chianetta for her editing. Thanks for the shared memories of Rudy Riska, Tom Knight and Marty Adler. Appreciation to Edgar Alfonzo, Bobby Ojeda, Howard Johnson, and Mike Herbst for their help. To Guy Conti for all his help, insight and kindness.

Thanks to Mayor Rudolph Giuliani, Fred Wilpon and Jeff Wilpon. Baseball was taken away from Brooklyn. They brought it back! Many thanks to Carl Erskine for his foreword, his observations and his inspiring encouragement. To Mark Lazarus, friend, fan and raconteur. Hats off to friend Warner Fusselle for his recollections through hours of interviews, and the generous use of his scorebooks and interview tapes.

Thanks to all.

Contents

Foreword

There seems to be a certain chemistry in life that at times causes events to come together in a natural, yet unique, way. These special times then are marked forever in their time in history.

That's my feeling about the city of Brooklyn and the ten baseball seasons I spent there as a Brooklyn Dodger player. The borough itself was, and is, mostly residential, and richly mixed with a variety of ethnic groups. It was the ideal place for Branch Rickey to introduce Jackie Robinson as baseball's first black player.

It was also an ideal place for young families, and we, the Brooklyn Dodgers of the 1940s and 1950s, were young families. The norm in Brooklyn was close families, and we were adopted by the neighborhoods. Manhattan, with Broadway, had its glitter; the Bronx had its sophistication; Brooklyn had its Dodgers. This post–World War II team won the National League Championship in 1947, '49, '52, '53, '55, and '56. That brought a new respectability to the borough. The team's departure in 1958 was a serious blow.

Would baseball ever come back to Brooklyn? The answer, some forty plus years later, is yes.

What a refreshing experience to go back to Coney Island and watch real professional baseball at KeySpan Park. Young baseball talents are starting their careers in Brooklyn. Any of us who played for the Dodgers in Brooklyn can certainly relate to that.

It's only fitting, then, for a talented writer named Shakespeare to write eloquently about Brooklyn baseball, then and now.

You are in for a rich and rewarding experience in the pages that follow.

Carl Erskine #17
Brooklyn Dodgers 1948–1957

1

Prologue

"Past is prologue"
— *The Tempest* (William Shakespeare)

Before the Beginning

Brooklyn—February 23, 1960

A huge wrecking ball, painted to resemble a baseball, swings from a metal chain. Before a small crowd of dignitaries, including former Brooklyn Dodgers Carl Erskine and Pee Wee Reese, and a sprinkling of Brooklyn's devoted fans, the wrecking ball sweeps back into the air, hanging from its chain like the ball in a pitcher's hand. The wrecking ball starts forward, as if it's a pitch heading toward home plate, but the target for this ball is a section of the upper deck of Ebbets Field, a ballpark intact since the final Brooklyn Dodger home game on September 24, 1957. The ball flies toward beloved Ebbets Field and hits with a *Smash!*

Vero Beach, Florida—April 26, 2001

Smash! The baseball explodes off the bat of Michael Jacobs and rocks toward the gap in right-center. Jacobs, a powerfully built, left-handed hitting Met catcher, churns his legs and swings his arms in an all-out dash around second. As the Dodger pitcher backs up third base, Jacobs raises dust as he slides in with a triple. A sacrifice fly drives him in for the game's first run. Today, Dodgers are playing baseball at Dodgertown in Vero Beach, where they have held spring training camp since 1948. But today's game at Field Two is not played by major leaguers; instead, it is performed by young minor leaguers in the Mets' and Dodgers' systems.

The Dodgers departed Brooklyn for Los Angeles following the 1957 season, but the Dodgers never left Vero Beach. The baseball fans in Vero never had to suffer the wrenching removal of a beloved team; the Dodgers merely showed up in 1958 with the letters LA replacing the letter B on their royal

3

Ebbets Field — intact, circa 1950s.

blue caps and went right on training at their East Coast home. After Brooklyn lost the Dodgers, many of their fans eventually switched their allegiance to the Mets, who began in the 1962 season. In June, the Mets are bringing a Class A minor league team to Coney Island in Brooklyn, where professional baseball will return to the borough after an absence of 44 years; the new Brooklyn team will be called the Cyclones, and they will play at the newly constructed KeySpan Park, where right field juts up against the Parachute Jump at the boardwalk.

Here, at Vero Beach, on Field Number Two, a field without grandstands, scoreboard, lights, and concessions, before a group of four fans, members of the future Brooklyn team play farm team members of the former Brooklyn team, as teams — and time — collide.

Sanford, Florida — March 3, 1946

Jackie Robinson reports to his first Dodger spring training. While Moses Fleetwood Walker and his brother Welday were in the major leagues in 1884, Robinson is the first black to be signed by a major league team in the twentieth century. He is attempting to make the roster of the Montreal Royals, the top

Ebbets Field and Carl Erskine — the wrecking ball slams into the wall —1960.

Dodger farm club. The white players of the Brooklyn Dodgers and Montreal Royals stay at the lakefront Mayfair Hotel, while Robinson and his wife board with a prominent local black couple, Mr. and Mrs. David Brock. On March 5, the Robinsons and John Wright, the second black player to sign with Brooklyn, are having dinner at the Brocks' home. The Dodgers call the Robinsons and Wright, directing them to leave the house at once because the

KeySpan Park (Coney Island).

Dodgers have been informed of an imminent hostile march on the home by white racists. The Robinsons and Wright flee to Daytona Beach.

Vero Beach — Spring 1948

After conducting their 1946 spring training in Florida, in both Sanford and Daytona Beach, Branch Rickey, part-owner and the general manager of the Dodgers, conducts the 1947 spring training in Cuba and Panama, opting to leave the United States in order to train in more accepting racial climates.

In 1948, the Dodgers arrive in Vero Beach as a result of an invitation from Bud Holman, a local businessman, for whom the Dodgertown stadium is now named. Rickey had been searching for a permanent training center that would be exempt from southern segregationist laws called Jim Crow. When the Naval Air Station in Vero Beach was given to the city of Vero Beach, Holman and Rickey made their move.

In Jackie Robinson's first game at Vero Beach, before the largest crowd to see a baseball game there, a crowd about half black, Robinson bats first for Brooklyn and hits a home run.

Vero Beach, Florida — April 26, 2001

To visit Dodgertown is to wander into a time warp. While Ebbets Field was wrecked and replaced with a high-rise housing project, Dodgertown has remained essentially unchanged. Bordered by orange groves and containing its own nine hole golf course, the grounds include 6,500 seat Holman Stadium, three other baseball fields, two half fields, a convention center, a swimming pool, a lake, tennis courts, ten batting cages and numerous pitching mounds and plates. The Dodgers' offices and other buildings on the grounds are one story, flat-roofed structures of beige cement with wood trim. Most housing was built during the late 1940s and 1950s and has the look of Florida architecture of a half-century ago. On 64 acres, Dodgertown feels spacious, with woods, lots of flowers, palm trees, and lawns. It's a campus for baseball, and it remains quaint. Its streets and walkways are still lined with street lamps whose glass globes are painted as baseballs. Near Field Two, a small bridge crosses a stream, and the mind flashes back to photos of Brooklyn Dodgers like Gil Hodges and Carl Erskine crossing the same bridge 50 years ago.

Near the Dodgertown bridge is Holman Stadium, with its 17 rows of pastel seats that slope from a hill down to the field. Within the stadium, flowers and trees give the area a noncommercial feel. There are open-air dugouts like those of the early 1900s, and the players are in full view while they are seated on wooden benches. Behind the home plate screen is the 1950s style press box, two rows of seats in a cement block building. The press box was built without doors; one just enters. Behind the press box is a souvenir stand. Along with Los Angeles Dodger memorabilia are remnants, nearly antiques, from Brooklyn Dodger days. A Jackie Robinson teddy bear, dressed in Brooklyn uniform with "1955" in blue stitching, sells for $250. There is also a ceramic plate, with an autographed photo of Brooklyn Dodger great Roy Campanella, that retails for $400. These artifacts seem like treasures discovered in the attic of a family's summer bungalow, with Ebbets Field as their abandoned and razed primary residence, and Dodgertown as the summer cottage that the family never left.

From Holman Stadium, a short walk past the bridge brings spectators to the Dodgertown Convention Center, a building both utilized by the Dodgers and rented to the public for business conferences. A one-story building matching the simple 1950s look of all the Dodgertown structures, it has a restaurant, a bar, offices, and large conference rooms named after former Brooklyn Dodgers like Jackie Robinson, Pee Wee Reese, and Gil Hodges. The décor is timeless and the Convention Center could be almost brand new, if this were 1955. Huge black and white framed photos decorate the halls, some photos as large as four feet high and ten feet wide. In one photo, an almost life-sized Jackie Robinson is sliding home; in another large photo, Roy Campanella makes a tag at the plate. Pee Wee Reese and Carl Furillo, they're all there, vibrant ghosts of springs past.

Outside, private streets and walkways in the complex are marked with small wooden street signs, like arrows, that show these pathways named for former Brooklyn Dodgers. One can ramble down Jackie Robinson Avenue, walk on Pee Wee Reese Boulevard, or drop over to Don Drysdale Drive. There

Johnny Podres clinching Brooklyn's World Series, 1955.

is even an intersection, like pathways in a park, where Vin Scully Way (named after the former Brooklyn Dodger and current Los Angeles Dodger broadcaster) intersects with Jaime Jarrin Avenida (named for the Dodgers' Spanish language announcer, the first such in the major leagues).

In the fall of 1956, long before any Japanese played in the majors, the Dodgers made a postseason tour of Japan. They played a memorial game on November 1 in Hiroshima. Fastened to the cement wall of the outside of the Holman Stadium press box is a bronze plaque, with the engraved names of many members of the Dodger organization, including Dodger captain Pee Wee Reese and owner Walter O'Malley. The plaque reads:

> "Dedicated to the victims of the bombing of Hiroshima.
> May their souls rest in peace."

Vero Beach, Florida — April 26, 2001

Korean guest pitching coach Young-Soo Kim is showing his pickoff move to several Spanish speaking Dominican pitchers. They stand in the shade under oak trees in back of third base on Field Two. Because Kim and his pupils lack a common language, most of his teaching is done nonverbally.

Kim moves his feet quickly, jumping from an imaginary mound, and makes a pretend throw to second base. The young pitchers practice the move, with Kim continuing to demonstrate. It's teaching baseball by mime, and the protégés quickly adopt Kim's technique.

Meanwhile, the game on Field Two continues. The teams in this game are in extended spring training. Their parent clubs and the other minor leaguers departed spring training almost a month ago. The players remaining in Florida are awaiting the start of short season leagues that begin in mid–June and end soon after Labor Day. Until joined by signees from baseball's annual June draft of high school and college players, after which the teams begin regular season play, squads of about fifty players remain in Florida in a state of limbo, practicing and playing preseason games.

In the extended spring training game on Field Two, the Dodgers have been held scoreless for two innings by Brooklyn Cyclone prospect Chad Bowen, last year's top starter for Kingsport with a record of 7–2 and a 3.00 earned run average, but the Dodgers tie up the game on a single.

Behind the Met dugout, Omar Minaya, Met senior assistant general manager–international scouting, sits on the lone small set of metal bleachers. He takes notes, constantly evaluating prospects. Many of the Met players on the field played in Kingsport, Tennessee, last year, the lowest level in the Mets' United States farm system. Impressing Minaya could help the Mets' players reach Brooklyn, the next rung up the ladder, but five rungs from the majors.

After single runs by the Dodgers in the third inning and by the Mets in the fourth, Brooklyn infield candidate Rob McIntyre, a smooth fielder who hit .296 at Kingsport, knocks in a run with a sharp single. Jacobs drives in two runs with a double. The Mets bat around in the order and score five times. In the ensuing innings, Brooklyn outfield candidate Wayne Lydon, who stole 34 bases for Kingsport, demonstrates his speed to Minaya with a seventh inning diving catch in left field. A succession of pitchers for both teams keeps each club scoreless from this point until the bottom of ninth inning when the Dodgers score three runs off Brooklyn candidate David Byard, a 6'3" right-hander from Mount Vernon, Ohio. After the ninth inning, the teams play an extra inning, for additional practice; the Mets leave the field as 7–4 victors.

Under the trees in back of third base, Kim is now demonstrating a screwball grip to several Dodgers. Kim's presence is just one example of baseball's ever expanding international ties. The Dodgers have established baseball offices in Venezuela, Mexico, Italy, Australia, and the Dominican Republic. Baseball interest is so high in the Dominican Republic that eager baseball prospects actually pay to attend baseball camps where major league scouts are present.

In addition, the Los Angeles Dodgers, in an attempt to expand their international presence, have made tentative plans to have two players from mainland China attend spring training this year. Those plans fell through, but the Dodgers' goal remains: to open China to baseball.

N.Y. Mets Complex, Port St. Lucie, Florida—April 27, 2001

The next day, Edgar Alfonzo sits outside the Mets' minor league clubhouse in Port St. Lucie, a city about 25 miles south of Vero Beach. Alfonzo, at 33, is the manager of the Brooklyn Cyclones. A former minor-league second baseman for 13 years, Alfonzo reached the zenith of the minors, Triple-A level, but he never played in the majors. Six feet tall and looking strong and trim, Alfonzo looks as if he could take the place of his 25-year-old brother, the star second baseman for the New York Mets.

"I didn't play my first official baseball game until I was 13," states the new Brooklyn skipper, who grew up in Santa Teresa, Venezuela. "I had played some baseball before that age, but I was mainly a volleyball player. I still remember my first real game. My father bought me my first glove; I had my first uniform, and we were playing on an all-dirt field. I played shortstop. And in my first real game I got up to bat five times, and I struck out five times, three times swinging and two times looking. How did I feel? I felt excited! I wasn't discouraged at all. I loved it!"

Not letting five strikeouts get him down is indicative of Alfonzo's baseball philosophy. "Of course, a player must have ability," adds the manager, "but personality is something I look for in evaluating a player. I only had half the ability of many players, and I lasted for thirteen years as a professional player, while many players with twice my natural ability were only able to last two or three years in the minors before they were out of baseball. I was able to play so long because I was always straight. I always listened, and I gave it my best."

"Three years after I started playing, I signed a professional contract; I was only 16 years old. I started with Quad Cities in the Angels' organization. I was a second baseman in the California Angels' system for eight years; then I played second base for five years in the Baltimore Orioles' system. I never played on the same team with my brother Edgardo, but back in Venezuela, he used to come to all my games, follow me around and learn."

After his playing career ended, Edgar became a hitting and infield coach with the St. Lucie Mets for the 1998 and 1999 seasons. In 2000, he managed the Kingsport Mets, the Mets' lowest classification (Rookie-A Ball).

"Last year I had to be a big brother, father, and uncle to the players," says Alfonzo. "Some were on their own for the first time and couldn't even do their own laundry or even fry an egg. The game decisions like when to bunt, hit and run, or switch pitchers, those are easy. It's dealing with the players, one at a time. That's hard. I learned that I had to treat each of the 35 players differently because they were all individuals. Yet, when I teach players how to play, I teach them all equally, whether they are a top prospect or not. I try to help them all the same and let their talent determine who will advance."

Last year, the Kingsport Mets played in an attractive rural setting before crowds of 1,000 or 1,500. Many of these same players are performing in virtual isolation at extended spring training, yet will play for expected crowds of over 6,500 if they play for Brooklyn.

"When they see the crowds, they will be nervous at first," says Alfonzo. "I am talking to them now about it. If they make an error, perhaps a fan of the visiting team will yell 'You stink!' at them, but I will teach them to ignore any bad comments and concentrate on the game."

Unlike the 1950s Brooklyn Dodgers, predominantly married men who lived in Brooklyn neighborhoods such as residential Bay Ridge, the 2001 Brooklyn Cyclones will be mainly single players in their late teens or early twenties, and Alfonzo said the Mets are attempting to find them dormitory-like housing on a former military base.

Alfonzo heads for Field Four, where he will instruct infielders as he hits ground balls to them. "I was a coach for the [New York] Mets for three weeks this season before I came down here. I was in New York, and I really liked it. Someday, maybe in eight or ten years, I would like to manage in the majors. But right now, I love working with kids."

N.Y. Mets Complex, Port St. Lucie, Florida—April 27, 2001
Later that day, the Mets play a practice game at their complex. "Buen trabajo [good work]," says Guedy Arniella to one of the Mets. Standing right behind the team's fenced-in dugout, she can be seen and heard by the players sitting just a few feet away.

A psychiatric social worker at Mount Sinai Hospital in New York City, she is at the Mets' Port St. Lucie complex as a consultant. She is the age of the players' mothers and she works with the Mets' international players, predominantly players from the Dominican Republic, Venezuela, and Mexico. During spring training, and in the regular season, she travels to the Mets' farm clubs and assists the international players in making adjustments to playing baseball in the United States. With dark hair and a friendly smile, she effortlessly switches back and forth between English and Spanish, depending on the language of her listener.

"The United States culture is more reserved than the culture of most of the international players. We are emotionally more distant here when we are in public. They are not used to that. Also, our culture is more regimented. For example, in Santo Rio, in the Dominican Republic, there are no speed limits. Things are less structured there. Here, there are many more rules and laws. So much is different for the players who come here. Even dating is different. Back home, many young men are not permitted to date a young woman unless there is a chaperone present. Here, these young men are in a

Mike Cox — Brooklyn Cyclones.

different culture, under the stress of highly competitive conditions, and they are used to a macho culture in which young men aren't encouraged to express their feelings. They're used to family and friends at their games, and here there is no one. I try to be at their games to encourage them, provide support. Many of these young men are all alone."

After some moments, Ms. Arniella brings up the recent tragic death of Brian Cole, a top Met outfield prospect. In the short interval of days between the conclusion of regular spring training and the start of the full-season minor leagues, four weeks ago, Met players were permitted to return briefly to their homes. Brian Cole was driving to his home in Texas when he died in a car accident in Georgia. "So many of the players knew Brian," said Guedy Arniella. "They were so upset over Brian's death. I came down here then." Guedy becomes silent and reflective.

Later, Carly McBride arrives and stands next to Guedy. About Guedy's age, Carly is employed by the Mets to teach English to Spanish-speaking players. Displaying an energetic personality, she watches the game, conversing with Guedy. Ms. McBride teaches four nights a week in a conference room at the Holiday Inn in St. Lucie. Many of the minor leaguers live there, and classes are in the early evening. She has written a booklet containing the translations from Spanish to English of useful baseball words and phrases as well as translations into English of everyday expressions. Players are issued the colorfully illustrated booklet, and they study it for her classes.

Some examples from her booklet include: mira el corredor (watch the runner); tira por el plado (throw strikes); bola mala (wild pitch); bateo y cordido (hit and run); dos hombres en base (two men on base); cuadrangular (home run).

A Met minor leaguer from Australia, catcher Justin Huber, wants to communicate better with the Spanish-speaking players and has asked Carly McBride to teach him Spanish. She has scheduled his lessons at the Holiday Inn. She invites a writer to sit in on her class. "The kids will enjoy it. They don't get to meet many professionals at home, and they enjoy talking to guests and trying out their English."

In 1947, Jackie Robinson's debut made national headlines. In 2001, Edgar Alfonzo becomes the first minority after the Negro Leagues to manage a Brooklyn professional baseball team, and no one even mentions it. International players, rare in 1947, have become common today, with 25.3 percent of the major league players in 2000 born outside the United States. The Mets players on Field Two, about a 50–50 mix of internationals and United States players, are driven by one goal; to be among the ten percent of minor leaguer players who reach the majors. They can climb towards the goal by first making the team that will play in Coney Island, Brooklyn.

Ebbets Field, Brooklyn — September 24, 1957

The Brooklyn Dodgers, their move to Los Angeles all but announced, play their final home game and defeat the Pittsburgh Pirates 2–0, before 6,702 mourning fans. After the game, the fans take blades of grass or dirt from the infield, souvenirs from the field of their beloved team. Organist Gladys Gooding plays "May the Good Lord Bless You and Keep You" followed by "Auld Lang Syne."

Brooklyn — April 28, 2001

This morning, for the first time since 1957, single game tickets are on sale for a Brooklyn professional baseball team. The line of eager ticket buyers stretches for blocks as over one thousand fans queue up at Kings Plaza Mall. Grandparents who have waited 44 years to see another Brooklyn game mix with grandchildren who are under the mistaken impression that Jackie, Pee Wee, Billy, Skoonj, Gil, and Campy are no longer in Brooklyn. With season box seat tickets already sold out, the Brooklyn Cyclones are a hot ticket, and as the grandchildren sit in the packed Coney Island stands this summer, they'll hear about how those old Dodgers still exist, in memory, and their grandparents, who thought there would never be any more Brooklyn players to love, will find out that there will be — for baseball is back in Brooklyn.

Introduction

Passion. Brooklyn baseball is a passion. The people of Brooklyn were passionate about their baseball teams even before there was such a thing as professional baseball. The game of baseball actually was created in the New York metropolitan area, and Brooklyn was heavily involved in baseball — in fact, Brooklynites helped to create baseball. Brooklyn's involvement in the creation of baseball led to a succession of famous amateur teams and then to Brooklyn's first professional team. The professional team eventually developed into the team known as the Brooklyn Dodgers, a team that was so loved that it didn't just represent Brooklyn — in many ways the team *was* Brooklyn. And then, after the 1957 season, the love affair ended. The Brooklyn Dodgers did the unthinkable — they left and became the Los Angeles Dodgers.

Fans of the departing Dodgers used words that exceeded mere "hurt" to describe their broken hearts. Forty-four years later, former Dodger fans described their feelings when they knew the Dodgers were leaving: Some said, "I was crushed!" or "I was devastated!" Some even said, "It tore my heart out!"

Then, in 1998 vague rumors started that professional baseball would return to Brooklyn. Rumors turned into possibilities, possibilities turned into plans, and in 1999 it was confirmed that professional baseball, in the form of a minor league team, would return to Brooklyn in 2001, the first year of the new century.

What would a gap of 44 years do to Brooklyn's love for baseball? Was the removal of the Brooklyn Dodgers the end of the passion? Would a borough of 2.7 million persons — the size of an immense city — support a minor league team in the New York–Penn League, a league predominantly designed for first year pros?

Who was left in Brooklyn to remember the old Dodgers? Author Thomas Wolfe stated, "You can't go home again." Could baseball go home again, to Brooklyn? How would baseball's return to Brooklyn be similar to the era of Brooklyn baseball of 1947 to 1957, their acknowledged greatest time? What would be different?

15

Once, before the onset of the multi-million dollar contracts of today, the Brooklyn Dodger players lived in the same neighborhoods, sometimes upstairs in the same houses, as their fans. Many of those Dodgers have passed away; Brooklyn idols Jackie Robinson, Pee Wee Reese, Gil Hodges, Roy Campanella, Carl Furillo, Billy Cox and many others can never return.

If life allowed magical wishes, a Field of Dreams, the old Brooklyn Dodgers would return, in their prime of life, to play before their fans, also 44 years younger, in Ebbets Field.

But Ebbets Field has been demolished for over 40 years — it's now the site of a housing development. The surviving Brooklyn Dodgers are mostly men in their seventies and eighties, their remaining fans mainly in their fifties to their eighties. If the clock couldn't be turned back, what would actually happen?

The new Brooklyn team would be a New York Mets' farm club, its players predominantly 19 to 22 years old. They would not be the internationally famous legends of post–World War II Brooklyn, but would be unknowns, some already in the Mets' farm system, but many still in college, not yet selected in baseball's June draft.

To what extent could the clock be turned back? Had Brooklyn's baseball passion turned to something else?

Brooklyn's beloved Dodgers, sometimes affectionately known as "Dem Bums," were now playing three thousand miles away, in Los Angeles.

The new team, the Brooklyn Cyclones, was being formed. What would professional baseball's return be like for the players, fans, front office people, announcers, and for the former Brooklyn Dodgers? What would baseball's return be like for Brooklyn?

I spent the 2001 season following the new Brooklyn Cyclones because baseball had come back to Brooklyn, and I wanted to experience its return and explain what it was like. The Brooklyn Dodgers did not return. It was not the 1950s, it was 2001. It was not Ebbets Field; it was KeySpan Park in Coney Island. How would the Brooklyn Cyclone experience be like that of the Brooklyn Dodger experience? How would it different? The Brooklyn Dodgers couldn't come back, but the Brooklyn Cyclones were about to play the first professional baseball in Brooklyn in 44 years.

This book was written to tell the story of that return.

A Bit of Dodger History

The Dodgers left Brooklyn after the 1957 season. But the start of Brooklyn baseball went back over a hundred years before that. The team that became known as the Brooklyn Dodgers had its roots in the very dawn of baseball — the 1840s in the New York metropolitan area. At that time, players could be hit with a ball when they were off a base — being hit was called being "soaked," and when one was soaked, the player was out. It wasn't as bad as it sounded. The ball was much softer than it is today. This all came from the English game of rounders — played with a pitcher, a ball, a bat, and a varying number of bases — a game whose rules were amorphous, and whose rules gradually took on a form similar to what we now know as baseball. In 1845, Alexander Cartwright codified the rules of this "New York game," and baseball took form. Using Cartwright's new rules, the first official baseball game between opposing teams took place on June 19, 1845, at Elysian Fields in Hoboken, New Jersey. The game was played between two teams from Manhattan. The New York Metropolitan area was baseball's first hotbed, and Brooklyn got right into the swing of things.

The Jolly Young Bachelors was their name and they were Brooklyn's first organized baseball team, making their debut in 1854, six years before the Civil War. Amateur baseball was a big hit in Brooklyn. Other amateur teams were formed, including the famous Brooklyn Atlantics, winner of the first baseball national championship, held at Elysian Fields in 1865. The Atlantics won several other national championships.

The Trolley Dodgers became Brooklyn's first major league team. After one year of playing in the minor leagues, in 1884 they joined the then major league American Association. The team was known as the Trolley Dodgers because of the vast trolley network that Brooklyn pedestrians had to cross while walking in the city.

The team switched to the National League in 1890 and was known for awhile as the Bridegrooms, because a number of their players were married that previous winter. This franchise, under various names and playing in first Brooklyn and then Los Angeles, has stayed in the National League ever since.

Brooklyn almost lost its team a hundred years ago, so there never would have been much of a Brooklyn Dodger history at all. In 1902, Harry Von der Horst, the majority stockholder, became ill and put his shares in the team up for sale. Ned Hanlon, the team's manager, and a former star player with Baltimore, announced his intention to buy the stock and move the team to Baltimore.

A former seller of peanuts, programs and tickets for the Brooklyn team, Charles Ebbets, had worked hard and had dedicated himself to the Brooklyn club, and he had been allowed to buy some stock in the team when he was named the club's business manager. Virtually without money of his own, Ebbets borrowed enough money to purchase the team and keep the club in Brooklyn, saving Brooklyn's team for another 55 years. Now club president, Ebbets later constructed the field named in his honor, and in 1913 the team moved from Washington Park (the second Washington Park), with its wooden stands, to the then modern facility of Ebbets Field.

Ebbets hired Wilbert Robinson as manager, and for a time the team was known as the Robins, in his honor. The team won pennants in 1916 and 1920, but lost the World Series, first to Babe Ruth's Boston Red Sox and then to the Cleveland Indians in which Brooklyn's Clarence Mitchell hit into baseball's first unassisted triple play.

After Ebbets' death in 1925, Robinson was elevated to club president. The remaining owners and Robinson could not duplicate the success the team had under Ebbets, and the team fell into decline. The team finished sixth in four straight years at the end of the 1920s. But, look who was being born around that time: Pee Wee Reese in 1918. Jackie Robinson in 1919. Billy Cox in 1919. Roy Campanella was born in 1921. Carl Furillo in 1922. Gil Hodges in 1924. Joe Black in 1924. Clyde King in 1925. Duke Snider was born in 1926. Carl Erskine in 1926. Clem Labine in 1926. Don Newcombe in 1926, Ralph Branca in 1926, Junior Gilliam in 1928, and Joe Pignatano in 1929. Finally, Sandy Amoros in 1930 and Johnny Podres in 1932 — the heroes of Game Seven of the 1955 World Series.

The team began to be known more for their foibles than for their good play. One such event was when star Babe Herman hit a double and three Dodgers wound up at third base. Such craziness earned the team the moniker "The Daffiness Boys."

There was an old story that one time a cab driver was parked outside Ebbets Field, and he yelled up to a patron inside, "How are the bums doing?"

The fan replied, "Brooklyn's got three men on base."

The cabby shouted back, "Which base?"

Casey Stengel, a former Brooklyn outfielder who would later manage the Yankees to eight World Series victories, was named manager in 1934. Stengel fit right in with the Dodger Daffiness Boys, for when he was a player he had once come to bat with a bird under his cap and doffed his hat before batting, allowing the bird to fly out. Stengel couldn't stem the tide of losses however, and he was let go in 1937. From 1922 through 1938 the team finished sixth eleven times and seventh once. They came close to a pennant only once — in 1924, the year before Ebbets' death.

In 1938, the team was losing financially as well. The Depression and mismanagement left the club over $1 million in debt, with about half of that debt owed to the Brooklyn Trust Company. Bill collectors were hounding the team and things got so bad that the phone bill couldn't be paid and the phones were disconnected. The heirs of the former owners, Ebbets and Steve McKeever, were fighting for control of the club. Through the intercession of National League president Ford Frick, Larry MacPhail, a protégé of the St. Louis general manager Branch Rickey, was appointed general manager.

Things began to change immediately. MacPhail convinced the Brooklyn Trust Company that the way to earn money was to spend money, and MacPhail was good at spending money. He obtained the colorful Leo

Durocher to manage and play shortstop. He started to buy ball players, spending the then astounding sum of $50,000 to purchase first baseman Dolph Camilli. He hired Red Barber to broadcast the games on radio and obtained lights so the Dodgers would be the first New York team to have night games.

In the next few years, MacPhail bought Hugh Casey and Whitlow Wyatt, both languishing in the minors, and traded for outfielder Dixie Walker. The team would trade for minor leaguer Pee Wee Reese and then obtain Pete Reiser. The team was on the way up. MacPhail purchased farm teams and signed working agreements with others. The stage was set.

In 1941, the Dodgers won their first pennant in 21 years, edging the Cardinals. They were to face the Yankees in the World Series. Trying to win Brooklyn's first World Series, the Dodgers trailed two games to one when they had the fourth game all but won. With a 4–3 lead and two outs and two strikes on the batter, Tommy Henrich, the next pitch was an alleged spitball that got by Dodger catcher Mickey Owen. Henrich reached first and the Yankees went on to score four runs and hold on to win the game and soon the Series.

During the years of World War II, the Dodgers kept signing young players, but MacPhail was ousted by the Dodgers' owners, particularly those representing the Brooklyn Trust Company. Branch Rickey was installed as the new general manager. Rickey developed the farm system and came up with a plan that was to rock baseball. Major league baseball had not had a black player since several blacks played before the turn of the century. Rickey decided the time was right to break baseball's unofficial ban against signing black players. Rickey signed Jackie Robinson in 1945. Robinson played at the top Brooklyn farm club, Montreal, in 1946, and then made a sensational debut with Brooklyn in 1947, breaking the segregation barrier, being named National League Rookie of the Year, and leading the Dodgers to a pennant. Once again, the Dodgers lost the World Series to the Yankees.

The Dodgers were establishing the core of the team that would be their golden era. African American players Roy Campanella and Don Newcombe followed Robinson. Carl Furillo, Duke Snider and Gil Hodges became regulars. Carl Erskine came up as a pitcher.

Going to Ebbets Field was an event. The Dodgers had their famous Symphony band. They entertained the fans and players alike with music that was more fun than it was symphonic. The loud fan in the outfield, the one with the cowbell, was Hilda Chester. Happy Felton, an entertaining figure, ran the Knothole Gang, for kids.

The Dodgers won another pennant in 1949, but again lost to the Yankees in the Series.

The Dodgers lost the pennant on the last day of the 1950 season to the Phillies and lost the 1951 pennant on the final game of a three game playoff to the Giants when Bobby Thomson hit his famous ninth inning home run, the "Shot Heard 'Round the World." Dodger fans said, "Wait till next year."

The Dodgers won pennants in 1952 and 1953, but again lost to the Yankees in each World Series. For each series lost, Dodger fans again said, "Wait till next year."

Soon Walter O'Malley, part owner, forced out Rickey.

Finally, in 1955, it happened: Brooklyn won its first World Series. They beat the Yankees in seven games and Brooklyn fans went wild. Finally, next year was here.

In 1956, the Dodgers again lost the World Series to the Yankees. In 1957, the Dodgers finished in third place, but the die was cast. Owner Walter O'Malley moved the team to Los Angeles.

The Dodgers had left Brooklyn for good. Ebbets Field lasted until 1960, when it was demolished to build public housing. Only memories remained. All the Brooklyn Dodger games were now in the past, forever unalterable, museum pieces. Professional baseball would not be played in Brooklyn for the rest of the twentieth century.

The twenty-first century was another matter.

What I Expected and What Actually Happened

When I decided to write this book, I had the following expectations:

1. The new Brooklyn team would play at a temporary stadium at the Parade Grounds, a well-known baseball site next to Brooklyn's Prospect Park, and only blocks from where Ebbets Field used to be.

2. The team would draw approximately three thousand fans per game — a level that would place them in the midrange of New York–Penn League attendance,

3. Former Brooklyn Dodgers players would be a presence at the new stadium. Many of the former Brooklyn Dodgers would be at Opening Night, and the former "Brooks" would often make appearances at the new stadium.

4. The new players would be cognizant of Brooklyn Dodger history. They would be well acquainted with Ebbets Field history. Maybe they wouldn't know the old Dodgers as did the fans who remembered them live, but the new players would be well versed on the post–World War II Brooklyn Dodgers like Jackie Robinson, Duke Snider, Roy Campanella, Carl Furillo, Gil Hodges, Pee Wee Reese, Carl Erskine, Don Newcombe, Ralph Branca, Clem Labine, Junior Gilliam, Billy Cox, Don Drysdale, Sandy Koufax, Johnny Podres, Joe Black, Sandy Amoros, and Preacher Roe.

5. The fan base of the new team would feature a mixture of former Brooklyn Dodger fans and their sons and daughters, and grandchildren. The crowd would be of all ages and races, mostly from Brooklyn today, or they would be ex–Brooklynites.

6. The new Brooklyn team would establish a rivalry with the Staten Island Yankees, the New York Yankees' New York–Penn League affiliate. This was a natural. In the fall of 2000, there was a Subway Series as the New York Mets and the New York Yankees met in the first Subway World Series since 1956, when the Yankees beat the Dodgers. How could their farms teams not be rivals, as Brooklyn was a Met farm team and Staten Island a Yankee farm club? How many years had Brooklyn played the World Series against the Yankees between the end of World War II and when Brooklyn moved? The answer is six times: 1947, 1949, 1952, 1953, 1955, and 1956. They also played each other in 1941. The Yankees won every time except once—1955, the Brooklyn Dodgers' only World Series win. The Staten Island Yankee team and the Brooklyn Cyclones were just across New York Harbor from each other. This had to be a rivalry.

7. The new Brooklyn players would live in Brooklyn and become part of the Brooklyn community. My expectation was that they would live in a military base, like Fort Hamilton, or else live as part of host families who would each take in a few players for the summer.

8. The new Brooklyn team's games would be broadcast on a New York radio station by a young announcer who would be a counterpart to the legendary Red Barber, voice of the Brooklyn Dodgers. It would be fun to listen to a neophyte announcer over the airwaves and hear the word "Brooklyn" once more used with baseball.

9. The media coverage of the team would be extensive, with New York's newspapers following the team throughout the season. *The New York Times*, *The New York Post*, and *The New York Daily News* would give daily stories, features and box scores. The smaller Brooklyn newspapers would provide even more extensive coverage.

10. The crowds of fans who came to the game would be nostalgic for the old Dodgers and would resemble in demeanor the crowd's behavior at Pittsfield, Massachusetts, the former Mets affiliate in the league. The return of baseball would be charming, almost quaint.

11. The Brooklyn Cyclones would establish regulars who would stand in comparison or contrast with their 1947–1957 Dodger positional counterparts. Fans could compare the Cyclones' shortstop with Pee Wee Reese, the second baseman with Jackie Robinson, the new Brooklyn right fielder with Carl Furillo, the pitchers with Carl Erskine (Oisk), the catcher with Roy Campanella, the first baseman with Gil Hodges, etc.

As to their on field success, I had no expectations one way or the other, since the team would be composed mainly of players drafted from college, along with a few players from the previous season's Pittsfield team and a few players promoted from the 2000 Kingsport rookie league team.

Of the 11 expectations, after the season was over I evaluated every expectations with regard to its fulfillment. Two of the expectations were fulfilled; three were not; and the other six expectations were fulfilled partially. In addition, areas of interest that I had not considered prior to the season became factors. How the above expectations turned out will be discussed as part of the book's conclusion.

That the season did not go as expected was not disappointing; in many ways, that the season was not predictable actually made it more fascinating.

There was one tragic exception to this result. The enormous exception was the September 11 attack on the World Trade Center.

While the attack deeply affected everyone associated with the Cyclones — players, staff, media, and fans — during the days preceding the attack the Brooklyn Cyclone community was, of course, unaware of the coming tragic events, and this book will relate the season as it occurred, not covering the tragedy until it happened, near the conclusion of the season.

Some Incidents

The Brooklyn Cyclones' season could aptly be described as a roller coaster, just like the Cyclone ride of the same name.

The team played 76 regular season games in 79 days. Some players played the whole season. Others were cut or demoted. Some were promoted. Two players quit. Some players were injured; others were trying to recover from injuries.

There was an intense rivalry, the "Ferry Series" that developed between Brooklyn and the Staten Island Yankees. The teams remained close in the standings, fighting for first place in the McNamara Division. Fans crossed the Verrazano-Narrows Bridge or took the ferryboat to see games at the rival's field.

There were road trips to upstate New York, New Jersey, Massachusetts, Vermont, and Ohio — road trips on a bus often driven by former ambidextrous pitcher Fred Wood, nicknamed "Fast Food Freddie" by the players. Fred Wood drove very safely, but had a penchant for trying "shortcuts" that got him lost. Very lost.

There was a winning streak that was nearly beyond belief. Actually, there were two winning streaks, sometimes running concurrently. There was a slump.

A player had escaped Cuba, hidden out in the mountains of Mexico, then joined the Cyclones, then left the team, and then changed his mind, then was sent to another team in the Mets' organization.

"Big Bird" Byard was a player who drove the team van through the streets of Brooklyn, happily waving and beeping at strangers, as he did in his small Ohio hometown.

The Cyclone ride in Coney Island.

After an apparent brushback pitch, there was a whale of a fight that caused the Brooklyn team to have a bunch of players suspended.

There was the pitcher who liked to put the radar gun on unknowing persons who threw out the first pitch of ball games and record their velocities.

A sportswriter donned the mascot gear and masqueraded as the mascot and hit his head on the dugout. The real mascot once had an opposing team threaten to "rip his head" off, which would have traumatized the young fans.

There was the pitcher who after games would wear a do rag (handkerchief) around his head and mingle with the fans outside the players' entrance.

There was a sign on the outfield wall that said, like the old Abe Stark sign did in Ebbets Field, "Hit this sign, Win a suit."

A Cyclone outfielder once came into a key game, with the score close, as a pitcher.

There was a Japanese Met player who played two games with the Cyclones and almost hustled "too much" on a ground ball.

The Zooperstars' ball field entertainers appeared and devoured the batboy, and there was the umpire who danced his way into the hearts of the fans.

One pitcher, returning to play after a serious arm injury, lived in New Jersey at home in his boyhood bedroom and had half the neighborhood come to Brooklyn for his games.

There was the player who looked, and was, as tough as Carl Furillo, and who didn't mention that he was a diabetic.

There were players who lived in converted classrooms at a Brooklyn parochial school.

A fan ran onto the field and tried to circle the bases and make it to home plate, where the Cyclones' catcher waited.

There were races of human-sized Nathan's hot dogs along the left-field line.

There was the announcer [Warner Fusselle] who worked so hard at his job that he sometimes left the ballpark as late as 4 A.M. after recording his statistics in preparation for the next game.

That same announcer [Warner Fusselle] once thought he was about to be mugged in Times Square. It turned out the voices behind him were those of friendly Cyclones just saying hello.

A player who actually hit the "Hit sign, Win suit" sign won a free suit.

There were pitchers who slept in the aisle of the bus because that was the best place to sleep if you needed to pitch the next game.

There were Cyclone players who appeared on MTV.

There was the Cyclone ticket account representative by day who became the wild "Party Marty" character at night.

Victory celebrations were held at former Dodger haunts like Lundy's, and new haunts like Peggy O'Neills and The Salty Dog.

Cyclone players appeared in *GQ Magazine*.

There were unexpected fireworks while a game was in progress at Cone Island and a sun delay at Pittsfield.

One time, in Ohio, sombreros were worn by the entire bullpen of the home team, the Mahoning Valley Scrappers.

There was a wild September series between the Cyclones and the Staten Island Yankees.

And, a few days later, there was the horror of September 11.

But when the season was beginning, no one was thinking of a terrorist attack.

People were thinking baseball.

Forty-four years is a long wait.

What I Learned

There were many things that I learned from following the Cyclones during the 2001 season. These were not only facts, but lessons about the people involved with Brooklyn baseball, past and present. What I learned isn't always easily quantifiable. Sometimes what I learned was more of a feeling that I experienced or one that players or fans related to me. Often, what I learned surprised me. What the reader learns from following this account may be different that what I learned or felt.

Along the way, while following the Cyclones, only sometimes aware that it's happening, you find yourself becoming part of a community. A community that has baseball as its heart. Why does it seem that people who love baseball make such good friends? Spend ten hours at a ballpark on many days and it starts to seem like home. Writers like Mike Dolan and Gersh Kuntzman start off as strangers and end as buddies. Radio announcer Warner Fusselle is admired for his total professionalism in June. By September, he's your friend. In June, you notice fans in and around Section 14 — the section right behind the Cyclones' first-base dugout. By August, you're friends with Mark Lazarus, the "Mayor of Section 14."

In June, it's hard to tell one player from another. As the summer moves along, you get the biggest kick out of Mike Cox's sense of humor and left-hander's view of life, so that when he pitches, he's not Mike Cox, the smallish lefty from Texas, but Mike, the bright, humorous nice guy that you talk to every day, but who goes out on that mound and becomes a bulldog every fifth day.

You talk to Harold Eckert at first because he's a Jersey guy from Edison, only a 40-minute ride from Coney Island. You talk to him more, and you find out that he's been out of baseball for two years and has had a tendon taken from his Achilles and placed into his injured pitching elbow. And he's 24, old for the short-season Single-A level. You learn how his eyes tear when he talks how much he missed playing. I learned that catcher Brett Kay dives in the dirt to practice blocking imaginary pitches, and beats writers at trivia games. I learned that infielder Jay Caligiuri looks like a choir boy off the field and a swarthy, mean dude between the lines. I learned that third baseman Joe Jiannetti had a college football scholarship that he turned down, that he's a tough guy who also has diabetes, and a grandmother who figures out his batting average for each game while she listens on the Internet. I learned that outfielder Frank Corr lived in his aunt's basement in Brooklyn, that pitcher Luz Portobanco is a former young boxer, and that Ross Peeples learned his great pitching control by throwing baseballs through a tire. I learned that infielder Vladimir Hernandez escaped Cuba so that he could come to play baseball in the United States and that Vladimir was poor of money and wealthy of character. I learned that every one of these guys loves playing baseball. And I learned that most of them aren't getting rich doing it.

While what I learned will be a topic more fully explored throughout the book and reviewed near its conclusion, one more thing that I did learn will be revealed early on.

A few blocks beyond the left field wall at the Cyclones' home park is the world famous wooden roller coaster ride called the Cyclone. You can see this still-operating ride from the ballpark; it's beyond the left field wall, and the team has taken on its name. Coney Island is far diminished from its glory days in the first half of the twentieth century. The size of the formerly immense amusement area is now only a few blocks. But the Cyclone is still going strong. And when you begin to ride the Cyclone, it initially has a long, slow ascent as you sit in the roller coaster car being pulled up to the first drop. But you get to that first drop, and everything is poised as your car momentarily is at the peak and then WHOOSH! The descent is frighteningly fast.

One thing that I learned about the Cyclones' beginning is that it was a lot like the beginning of a ride on the Cyclone. There was a long slow start. How about a 44-year slow start? There was a steady, unhurried buildup to the first game, and then WHOOSH!

Welcome to a ride with the Cyclones.

Inning 1

Spring Training

The best hitting catcher of all-time — a better hitter than any catcher who has ever played on any major league team in over 100 years of baseball history, reported to spring training in February with the New York Mets. His name is Mike Piazza, and he stands 6'3", 215 pounds of wall-to-wall muscle. Piazza, after getting his feet wet playing 21 major league games with the Los Angeles Dodgers in 1992, really broke into the majors in 1993 and was the National League Rookie of the Year. He has played eight full seasons and is an eight-time National League All-Star. He has a lifetime .328 major league batting average and will enter the 2001 season with 278 major league homers and 881 runs batted in. His face is instantly recognizable to millions of baseball fans around the world, and he is a sure Hall of Famer still in his prime.

Mike Piazza trains with the rest of the New York Mets in Port St. Lucie, Florida, a sleepy city on Florida's East Coast about an hour's drive north of West Palm Beach, which is socially cool. Port St. Lucie isn't cool. What it is, however, is quiet, at least compared to the din in more southern Florida cities like Miami, Fort Lauderdale and the Palm Beaches. But when Piazza trains, there is interest, lots of it, even in Port St. Lucie. Mike Piazza is a celebrity, a mega-star known to even non-baseball fans. The New York Mets, who appeared in last year's World Series, losing out to the New York Yankees, have other stars, almost as well known. There is Al Leiter, a 16-game winner in 2000, and Edgardo Alfonzo, 2000 All-Star second baseman who hit .324 last season with 25 home runs and 94 RBI, and an additional cast of talented enough to win the pennant.

These Mets' players attract plenty of interest from the press, and from the fans — some of whom plan their vacations around the Mets' spring training. The players on the Mets' 40 man roster and other invited players trying to make the 25 man opening day roster officially start training in mid–February, although many of them voluntarily report early for workouts. The informality of spring training permits fans far more access to players than does the regular season. When time permits, in between workouts, Met players talk to fans and sign autographs. The Mets will begin exhibition games on March 1, the same day that their minor leaguers report for their spring training.

March 1, 2001

The players who will play on the new Brooklyn farm team report with all the other Met farmhands on their official reporting date and arrive quietly at the Met minor league clubhouse on the opposite end of the complex from Thomas J. White Stadium. Unlike the commotion that surrounds the major leaguers, the minor leaguers, 120 of them, train on four practice fields. For them, it is a long awaited day of opportunity. But unlike the interest generated by the major league Mets, in and around White Stadium, these minor leaguers train anonymously on the back fields of the hundred acre complex.

Luz Portobanco, Ross Peeples and Michael Cox are household names essentially only in their own households. So are Matt Gahan, Bret Herbison, Harold Eckert, David Byard, and Blake McGinley — known mainly to their families, friends, and some college baseball fans or some fans of Kingsport, a Class-A affiliate of the Mets. Back home, or in their college towns, or maybe back in Kingsport, yes, people do remember these guys. But here, under the Florida sun on the complex's back fields, they are just eight of the dozens of pitchers in camp. Just eight pitchers vying for a spot on the highest minor league level they can reach.

Carl Erskine was a star high school pitcher in Anderson, Indiana, who, when his chronic arm problems allowed, was the ace of the Brooklyn Dodgers' pitching staff for most of their golden era of 1947–1957. After joining the Dodger farm system after his Navy service in World War II, Erskine rapidly moved from the Dodgers' lowest level league, D-ball, to the majors in less than two years. After starting at Danville, Illinois, for the tailend of the 1946 season, Erskine won 21 games the next year at Danville. He moved up to Double-A Fort Worth in 1948 where he pitched a half season. Then he went straight to the major league Dodgers, where he stayed for his entire career — through the last year in Brooklyn and the first 1½ years in Los Angeles. Erskine was a key factor in helping the Dodgers win five pennants in Brooklyn and one World Series, the only one the Brooklyn Dodgers ever won, in 1955. He pitched two major league no-hitters, both in small Ebbets Field; only five men in the history of baseball have pitched more than one no-hitter. He was a good friend of Jackie Robinson and fully supported Robinson's struggle in breaking the so-called color barrier. Erskine was one of Brooklyn's most popular players.

Carl Erskine was nicknamed "Ersk," which in Brooklynese is pronounced "Oisk."

Carl Erskine: "One of the things that is misleading to fans, and family and the player himself, is that here he goes to spring training, and he gets the shock of his life. He was the star of his local team, and now he looks around, and all the guys are good, and he gets a revelation. He was All-County, he was All-State, and when he gets down to the camp, here's 50, 60, 80 guys; so a shock has to settle in, and now you have to realize that it's not going to be easy anymore. Now, all these guys are my equals, more or less. That's one of the things, one of the hurdles a young player has to overcome.

"When I came here for my first spring training, the Dodgers had 26 farm teams. I never saw so many good arms, good athletes. And you just have to adjust to that and realize that the competition is really good, really stiff. And it's a whole new mindset. Now you're not the darling of the group; you're just one of many.

"And now the task is that you have to compete and to excel on this level to go to the next level. You can't just be a run of the mill ball player, you have to really excel at this level. And that's only at the Class-A level. And then the same thing applies at Double-A. You still have to jump to the majors, and that selectivity gets tougher and tougher and tougher.

"When you compare this to my day, you do have a lot more major league jobs at the top now, but one of the disadvantages today is that you can have some absolutely talented players, but the judgment of the hierarchy is, 'I don't think he can make the majors; he's probably a Triple-A player, but I don't see him as a major league player.' So the kid might be cut. Times have changed, because they are going to draft more guys, and they don't have that many guys in the minor leagues, so it's someone's judgment that his bat is a little slow and that he'll never hit major league pitching.

"I have kids call me and they've been released, and they have good records at the minor league level. And the kid may call me; they say, 'Carl, I pitched for Double-A last year, my earned run average was 3.10; I had so many strikeouts and they released me. What do you think?'

"Now I don't know what happened, I wasn't there. But I know what must have happened. Somebody said, 'He's a good kid. He's done everything we've asked him. He's got a lot of ability. He's a good Double-A pitcher. He might make it in Triple-A, but his velocity is too slow; he's never going to make it in the majors.'

"Now, they miss people like that. In my day, when we had 26 farms teams, they'd send some kid back, and they'd say, 'He'll probably make Double-A,' and now, all of a sudden, he gets a little experience, and he starts learning a little bit, and he's got good aptitude, and some coach starts helping him, and then he starts coming out of the minor leagues like a bullet. That kid today might never get that chance. That's a difference. The minors are just not the proving ground now. In the old days, when teams had lots of farm teams, teams had to fill rosters to develop talent. They would sign a lot of kids and free agents. Scouts used to say on their scout cards, 'This kid can play as high as Class-A.' And they needed these kids to fill rosters. Or they might say, 'This kid can play as high as Double-A.' But they'd miss every once in a while. Some kid that they'd think wouldn't make it would make it. Some kids they thought would make it, wouldn't make it. But today, they don't have that privilege. If the kid is deemed limited at the major league level, they'll probably cut him. If the scout or the hierarchy — the player development people — say we have to draft some people, then they have to get rid of some people. 'Our rosters are already full. We can't take on more. Who's going to go?' So they say, 'Here's Charlie. He had a good year, but you know what, his velocity is limited. When he gets up to the next level, he's not going to be able to hold his own. So we're going to have to tell him.' So with that maybe they'll trade him to somebody, or the kid gets released. And the kids says, 'I played four good years in the minors, why would they release me?' But, there's no place to put him.

"It's just the reverse of the old days when we had lots of room to put people in the minor leagues, but few jobs at the top. Now, there's the flip side. If you can hold your own through those levels, you've got lots of chances to play in the majors. There are 30 teams in the big leagues today, so a player with ability who can perform in the minors has a better chance of playing in the big leagues than in my day.

"I can see it happen the other way because a lot of kids talk to me who got released, and they had a lot of talent.

"Almost all the Cyclones' players are draft choices. Teams today invest in players more than they ever did. And what a break I got to play for the Dodgers. I could have gotten a little more money if I played for the Red Sox or the Phillies, but I wanted to play for the Dodgers.

"It's hard for me not to sound like an old-timer. It's not worse now; it's just different. We didn't have nearly as many college players then. In my day, it was rare. Jackie Robinson was a rare bird because he was a college man. And Gil Hodges had a little college. Most players from my day didn't come close to going to college. Now it's hard to find a kid that hasn't been to college, in a major league system. So that's a part of the change. And there's more major league players coaching in college. So there's a little difference in how talent is developed.

"The flip side of that is that there are fewer kids playing Little League because American kids are playing soccer, or Nintendo and doing other things. There are so many more choices."

Occasionally, some hardcore fans take a look at the minor league workouts, but mostly the minor leaguers train by themselves with the only civilian spectators usually being maybe one set of visiting parents, a girlfriend, and maybe somebody's wife. You'll probably find more people waiting for a bus than you will observing the minor leaguers.

First of all, a fact of minor league reality: Nobody wants to play in Brooklyn. Not that anybody holds anything against the borough. Some of these minor leaguers would be relatively happy to be assigned there. But every minor leaguer wants to reach the major leagues, and they want to reach the majors as soon as possible. And Brooklyn is not at the top of the Mets' minor league chain. In fact, it's closer to the bottom. So where do players want to be assigned at the conclusion of spring training, around April 1? Don't be silly. There's only one answer, and that's the New York Mets. Making the Mets would be a feat of astronomically small odds for these players, but they would like to do it. If they can't make the Mets, as almost none would ever have a chance, what's next? Let's look at how the Mets' minor league system operates.

Baseball is a game of skill. Certain high levels of hand/eye coordination, reflexes, speed and physical power are necessary for any player to become a professional baseball player, but these natural talents must be developed into refined skills, skills so refined that most baseball players require about four and a half years of minor league apprenticeship before they reach the majors; whereas professional football players, relying on athletic abilities developed into skills at big time university football programs, usually make the major league National Football League immediately after their college careers have concluded, and players in the National Basketball Association usually go from anywhere from one to four years of major college basketball right into the pros. In fact, an increasing trend is for the best high school players to skip college altogether and enter the NBA right after high school, á la Kobe Bryant of the Los Angeles Lakers. Although some baseball players skip the minors entirely, it is a miniscule number, fewer than 1 percent. Brooklyn native Sandy Koufax comes to mind. (Koufax was "forced" by the baseball rules of the time to stay at Brooklyn for two complete playing seasons after first signing a contract with the Brooklyn Dodgers because he signed for a high bonus.) Because the development of baseball's unique skills usually requires years for players to obtain enough innings for pitchers and enough at-bats for hitters to prepare them, baseball's minor leagues serve the purpose of preparing future major leaguers.

Baseball's minor leagues are not a new development. In fact, 2001 was officially recognized as the hundredth anniversary of minor league baseball, although independently run minor leagues go back far longer. For the early years of the twentieth century, baseball's lowest minor leagues were made up of teams that would sign players, generally from their geographical area, to professional contracts. Playing before the local fans, players had no allegiance to any of the big league clubs, for their contract was entirely with the local club. Players would be scouted by an informal system more like a grapevine of baseball talk and letters than any formal network. Word of particularly good players would spread, and a team in a higher-level minor league would purchase those players' contracts. As a player worked his way into higher leagues, some minor league teams were affiliated with a major league club. Major league clubs didn't own the teams, but the teams had a working agreement with the major league team in which a major league team would purchase a player from a lower minor league team and assign his contract to a team with which they had a working agreement.

So the major leagues' obtaining of talent was somewhat haphazard as they scouted the minors for good prospects at lower levels and placed them under contract and farmed these players out to a minor league team with whom they had a working agreement to train their players. It took Branch Rickey, later an owner/general manager of the Brooklyn Dodgers, to change this system when he took over the St. Louis Cardinals in the 1920s.

Rickey started buying up farm teams, and those he couldn't buy he made working agreements with, until he had established an actual farm system, a pipeline of Cardinal-owned players. Instead of relying on the lower minor leagues to sign players, develop them initially, and then have the Cardinals purchase their contracts, Rickey started to get in on the ground floor of production. He vastly increased his scouting department and began to sign hundreds of players right out of high school. This Cardinal chain had teams in all levels of the minors, from the lowest level D, on up through C, then B, then Single-A, then Double-A and then Triple-A, the highest level. Rickey brought the concept of mass production into baseball. Most of the players would never make the majors, but by the sheer mass of the number of talented players he controlled, Rickey assured that a steady stream of talent could flow to the majors. Instead of having to pay independently owned minor leagues teams for their best players, Rickey saved money by inexpensively signing players to their initial pro contract and allowing them to try to survive in a cutthroat minor league system by clawing their way to the top. Those who were good, but not great, talent, he sold to less foresighted teams and pocketed a share of the profits. Since Rickey's farm system got the jump on every other major league team, his Cardinal pipeline started to pay dividends once his early signees had developed for some years in the minors. This led to Cardinal pennants in 1926, and pennants in 1928, 1930 and 1931, and a World Series victory against the Philadelphia Athletics, and a World Series win in 1934 over Detroit. The Cards continued to win even after Rickey was fired from the Cardinals in 1942. St. Louis won pennants in 1943 and 1944, winning the '44 World Series over the St. Louis Browns.

Rickey became a part owner and general manager of the Brooklyn Dodgers in 1942, and he immediately began competing against himself. This occurred because a farm system is an investment that takes years to pay off in profitable players. So when Rickey went to the Dodgers, his farm clubs of the Cardinals, his legacy, continued for years to produce players he had signed to contracts as 18 year olds. In fact, as Rickey developed the Brooklyn Dodger farm system as he had the Cardinals, it led to the 1947 pennant race between the Rickey-developed Cardinals and his newly developed Dodgers. Rickey won out, and his Brooklyn farm system overtook the Cardinal system, leading to Brooklyn pennants in 1947, 1949, 1952 and 1953. Rickey's innovation, setting up a whole chain of farm clubs owned or controlled by the major league club, was eventually adopted by every major league team.

Baseball in 2001 still has these farm systems, but some things have changed. Players from high school or college used to be able to sign a contract with any team they wanted. They could sign with the team of their choice, oftentimes signing with the highest bidder for their services. Major league baseball instituted a draft of United States and Canadian players, and a drafted player has a year to sign with a team that drafted him before he is once again eligible for next year's draft. If a player signs a minor league contract, his rights are controlled by the major league team for a period of six years. Then the player must be on a major league roster, or he is subject to being drafted by another team.

One difference in the farm systems of today is in the number of teams. Baseball no longer has D, C, or B level teams, but these designations are more a matter of semantics. There are still basically similar levels, but the letter designations have changed. In a sense, it's the baseball equivalent of grade inflation.

The lowest level team is an A team now, which sounds a lot better to fans than a D team, but it's still the lowest level. Now the levels are, from the bottom up: A, AA, and AAA. But it's not that simple. Class A has lots of subdivisions. A is subdivided into full-season A and short-season A. Full-season teams in A ball play a schedule that runs from early April until approximately Labor Day. The Mets, like most major league teams, have two full season A teams, one in what is known in the trade as High-A and one in Low-A. The next level down contains short-season clubs. The Mets have two of these as well. One is just called Short-Season A (Brooklyn), and the other is called Rookie Short-Season A (Kingsport) in which the majority of players must be in their first year. Thus, the Met farm system, similar to most in baseball, has the following teams, with one team on each of six levels.

New York Mets Minor League System

Norfolk Tides (Virginia)	AAA	International League
Binghamton Mets (New York)	AA	Eastern League
Port St. Lucie Mets (Florida)	High-A	Florida State League
Capital City Bombers (Columbia, SC)	Low-A	South Atlantic League
Brooklyn Cyclones (Brooklyn, NY)	A (Short-Season)	NY — Penn League
Kingsport Mets (Tennessee)	A (Rookie Short-Season)	Appalachian League

The Mets also have two other teams that are included in their farm systems. The Mets have one team each in the Venezuelan Summer League, and the Dominican Summer League, in which they have prospects from these countries sign with the Mets and play for a year or two before hopefully getting a chance to play for the Mets' higher level farm chain. For the purposes of this analysis, we will consider only the stateside teams in the Met system.

The Met system is thus like a ladder to the big leagues, with most players beginning at the bottom of the ladder, Kingsport, or on the next rung up, Brooklyn. Players beginning at Kingsport are generally either players just out of high school, out of the smaller college programs, or up from one of the Mets' teams in the Dominican Republic or Venezuela. Players who will be assigned to Brooklyn are usually players who have played the year before at Kingsport and thus are being promoted, or players who are repeating a year in the New York–Penn League from the Mets' former affiliate in the league, Pittsfield. Just before the season begins is baseball's draft. High school and college players who are drafted and sign with the Mets spend a week in Florida and then join their teammates on the short-season clubs just before the season begins.

The general progression for a player who is doing well is to move up one step a year, but this is not a hard and fast rule. Players sometimes repeat a year at a level because of injury, poor performance, or inexperience. Players sometimes do so well that they skip a level, like being skipped a grade in school. Players sometimes receive a promotion partway through the season or are sent down a level in the season.

The 120 Met players who are gathered here for spring training all want to make one of the Mets' four full season clubs, because these clubs are closer to the top — the big leagues. Players have a pretty good idea of where they fit in. Most of the players who played last year at Kingsport will probably be promoted to the new Brooklyn team, but some may be sent back to Kingsport. An exceptionally good spring could enable a player to skip Brooklyn and wind up at the next level, Capital City, located in South Carolina's capital city, Columbia, and sometimes called Cap City or just Columbia. Injuries and performances by others will have an effect.

Guy Conti, the New York Mets' minor league field coordinator, is in charge of the instructional development of the entire Met farm system, the six United States farm clubs plus the two foreign affiliates. From the Mets' spring training headquarters in Port St. Lucie, he is in constant contact with the Mets' front office hierarchy and with the Met farm managers and coaches. During spring training, all of the Met farmhands are for the time being in one place. Conti, a former minor league pitcher in the Houston Colt .45's farm system, spent 12 years in the Los Angeles Dodgers' farm system as a manager, coach, and scout. Long after the Dodgers left Brooklyn, their Brooklyn influence is still passed on in the Dodger system by former Brooklyn pitcher Tommy Lasorda, and through the Dodger organization, which was permanently stamped by Branch Rickey's influence. Conti, who signed his first minor league playing contract in 1960 but hurt his pitching arm and never made it to the major leagues, is a trim man, about six-foot tall with auburn hair, and the fiery eyes of an evangelical preacher, a man whose demeanor mixes part drill sergeant, part father figure, part teacher. He is a well-spoken, good-natured fellow with a sense of humor. He also seems pretty tough, tough enough to have the respect of all 120 of these players. He's a natural instructor who explains baseball clearly and concisely and who clearly loves his job. Tom Lasorda (former Brooklyn Dodger pitcher, former L.A. Dodger manager, and current Dodger vice president) is known for his vast store of enthusiasm, but when the gods were handing out enthusiasm, Conti wasn't shortchanged either.

> **Guy Conti:** "In spring training our different clubs are in here, and we don't want to have them come in initially naming them Norfolk, Binghamton, St. Lucie, Capital City, Brooklyn, and Kingsport, so we put them initially in groups called A, B, C, D, or something like that, so that the kids who don't make a full-season team, such as the kids who don't make the Columbia roster out of spring train-

ing, don't feel that way initially. Later on in spring training, when we're formulating these clubs, we have to decide which kids have the skills and experience to make a full-season club, and which kids we think need more teaching and more work, and they go to extended spring training for six weeks to get ready to join either Brooklyn or Kingsport.

"Once we determine which kids are going to our full season, top four clubs, we have a number of kids left over, and once again, we don't say Kingsport or Brooklyn so they don't think they have no chance of making Brooklyn and are ticketed to Kingsport, so we label them Black and Orange, or Group One or Group Two, something like that so they don't feel discouraged. These kids did not make a full-season club, and they are assigned to extended spring training, and they play a schedule of games against the extended spring training squads of the Marlins, the Dodgers, the Expos, and the Cardinals. There is an extended spring training league down here of teams playing games against each other to formulate which kids are going to go to Brooklyn, which kids are going to go to Kingsport.

"These kids in June are joined by the drafted kids that we feel are experienced enough to go to Brooklyn and Kingsport based on the reports from our various scouts, and then we divide these kids up into what we call Brooklyn and Kingsport, and we send them off for their seasons.

"I have a working list of where players will be next season: We have New York, Norfolk, Binghamton, St. Lucie, Cap City, Brooklyn, and Kingsport. And right now we have the players slated tentatively for various working groups in spring training. They'll come in on these various working groups for spring training, be promoted to a higher working group, or demoted to a lower working group before we can formulate these clubs.

"For example, if someone had a good season at St. Lucie, they deserve to be on the Binghamton working group, and they deserve to get a look see by our Double-A staff, and they will either earn that position on that club, or we will say that they are just not ready, and they'll have to go to St. Lucie for a while. Those working groups change weekly.

"Our minor league kids will arrive March 1, and stay for a month until approximately April 1 or 2. They will be competing for a position on a full season club on a AAA, AA, or A roster.

"They have an idea of where they'll be, but we have to make a determination of where players will be assigned for the season. These tentative assignments are constantly changing due to trades, injuries. I have to be ready to plug in players; for example, I have to know who's our next catcher at Norfolk.

"A lot of where players are going for the next season comes out of the [fall] Instructional League of the year before. We try to formulate, 'Is this kid who played at Kingsport ready to go to Brooklyn?'

"The formulation of the first Brooklyn team started over a year ago. Right now, I'm looking at my board and I've got five pitchers penciled in on my board that won't be ready for Columbia and will start the season at Brooklyn. They will be here for spring training, then go through extended and then go to Brooklyn.

"The Brooklyn/Kingsport kids are housed in the Holiday Inn in Port St. Lucie, and we have vans that bring them to the field every day. They practice in the morning, from approximately nine until noon; they have lunch and then play a game in the afternoon. That's six days a week. They have early-work at eight in the morning. They will have post-work that is done in the afternoon or after the game. We have so many players that not all of them play in the game, so they are here at the field working on hitting, or fielding, or fundamentals or something that they need work on. They get a full day of baseball, and it's all geared toward playing the game the way the Mets want it taught. Normally, if a player plays in the game that day, he won't have post-work unless he has a bad game and needs to work on something right away. If they work here all morning and then nine innings of a game that starts at one, then they are pretty spent when that is over. The guys who do the post-work are normally the guys who don't play in the game that day.

"I have a complete schedule for every minute on what I want to get done for the day. I always have individual fundamentals on there, and I always have team fundamentals on there. I can tell you exactly what the first basemen worked on, on any day. I can tell Steve Phillips [New York Met general manager] and Jim Duquette [New York Met senior assistant general manager/player personnel] exactly what they worked on, what specific day and who worked on it. It's all organized, and I'm very accountable for the instruction that we give down here, and right-fully so. Our front office people put a lot of money into drafting these kids, and they want to make sure that the instruction is being given to them that they need to progress to the major leagues."

After the players were selected for the Mets' full season teams, includ-ing speedy outfielder Angel Pagan and left-handed pitcher Mike Cox, over 40 players remained in Florida at Port St. Lucie.

Mike Cox is a "small" left-handed pitcher from Pasadena, Texas. He is 5'11", 195 pounds. He's about average size for a middle infielder, but small for a pitcher. He has short, light brown hair and a friendly smile. He is soft-spoken and very observant. He has a Texas accent, but it's not extreme. He is in his second pro season, having played in 2000 for Pittsfield, the Mets' farm team that year in the New York–Penn League.

Mike Cox: "I went to Sam Rayburn High School. Then I went to Division I Texas Pan American. I was an outfielder in college, and then I pitched my final year. The scout liked what he saw. I was a center fielder for two years, and then the third year I got to pitch on and off. I was both an outfielder and a pitcher my third year. I was kind of a spot reliever. I wouldn't come in to pitch on the same day that I played outfield, but I might play outfield one day, and then come in to pitch in relief the next.

"I kind of knew going into the draft that I was going to get drafted. A lot of people had said that they were going to pick me up, but the Mets were a team I didn't talk to. I talked to several others, and the Mets were the last team I thought would pick me up. I talked before the draft to Kansas City and Arizona, the Texas Rangers, quite a few teams. I knew I would be picked after the tenth round and before the twentieth. I was home with my older brother, and we watched instan-taneously all the rounds as they occurred, on the computer. Before I got the phone call, I knew what round I went in. The phone call came three minutes after the draft. My older brother was a catcher in the Phillies' organization, and he played for Batavia, in the New York–Penn League. He was in professional baseball for four years. He made it as high as the Florida State League, and then he broke his ankle on a slide into second base.

"I wanted no negotiations. I wanted to sign and go. I didn't want to start off with bad blood. After I signed, I went off for a week of extended [training] and that really helped me out before I went off for Pittsfield. I had a year there that was better than expected, because I had never had much coaching in pitching. I'm really a newcomer to pitching and I have a lot to learn.

"After spring training this year, I was sent to Columbia. It was a big deal for the guys who were already there. You didn't want to go to Brooklyn after you've been in short-season already. Nothing against Brooklyn. But I've been in short-season already.

"They pretty much told me that I was going to be a long relief guy in Columbia. Some guys know going into spring training where they're going."

The players not selected in April for the full-season teams remained in another world called "Extended Spring Training," usually called by baseball people as just "Extended." Here the players would remain at the Port. St. Lucie Holiday Inn and continue to report for workouts at 9 A.M., often before 8 A.M. for "early" work. Four or five days a week, the players in extended would play a game against some of the farmhands from other relatively nearby farm teams like the Expos and the Cardinals, both from Jupiter, or the Dodgers from Vero Beach.

Luz Portobanco, a 6'3" right-hander who was born in Nicaragua and moved to Miami at age 6, is one of the pitchers vying to make the Brooklyn squad. Last year, Portobanco was 6–2 with a 2.34 earned run average at Kingsport. Luz had to sneak out to play baseball in Miami because his mother thought the area where they lived was too dangerous for Luz to go off on his own to play. Portobanco, whose name begins "Luz de Jesus," meaning "light of Jesus," is a street smart and street tough player who used to amateur box in Miami.

Harold Eckert had a promising pitching future at Florida International University when he blew out his elbow in a regional tournament. Not wanting to leave the game, Eckert continued to pitch. His team lost the game, but the Los Angeles Dodgers drafted Harold in the 19th round. A drafted player must be offered a contract, and Eckert was upfront with the Dodgers about his injury. He soon signed with the Dodgers, but because of the injury the Dodgers voided his contract, and he became a free agent. "Eck" had elbow surgery performed and was out of any form of baseball for two years. He signed with the Mets in November, and at 24 is attempting a baseball comeback.

Another pitcher looking to make Brooklyn is Ross Peeples. Last year, he broke into professional baseball by going only 1–2 at Kingsport, but he had a low earned run average of 2.61. He's a Georgia player who learned his excellent control by pitching balls into a tire hung in the backyard. He's tall at 6'3", strong at 205 pounds, is left-handed, always an advantage in baseball, and has pinpoint control. Ross Peeples throws his fastball at 85 miles per hour, which puts him in the top 1 percent of any males his age. Compared to an average young man, Peeples throws bullets. In baseball, an 85-mile-per-hour fastball is slow.

Don Zimmer and Jim Gilliam — in spring training with Brooklyn Dodgers at Vero Beach.

Joe Jiannetti looks hard-nosed and he is. A former high school football star, Joe is 6'1" and 185 pounds, seemingly none of it fat. Only 19 years old, he is out of Daytona Beach Junior College. He plays a fearless third base and uses a maple bat, his favorite wood. More the age of the players who play at Kingsport, Joe is hoping to make Brooklyn as one of its younger players. He is also diabetic and gives himself insulin injections twice a day.

At extended spring training, one or two days a week are called "camp days" in which all the players would work on fundamentals and drills at Port St. Lucie. Because the Mets' minor league complex now had over 40 players, only about half the players played against other teams on any given day — the rest remained at Port St. Lucie for morning and afternoon workouts. By now, the big league Mets had departed, as had most of the minor leaguers. The 40-plus remaining players might have felt like guests who had stayed too long at the party, after most others had moved on. Their workout area was quiet even when the big league Mets were down there.

Now, it was almost ghost-like.

And now the players' wishes had been modified. While before the start of the full-season clubs, all the players had at least the whisper of a hope to make a full-season team, even if they sensed that possibility as highly unlikely, now there became a new equation to consider. Players could make the Kingsport squad — not a desired choice for the players who had already spent a season there and wanted to move up — they could make the Brooklyn squad, a step up the ladder from Kingsport, or they could be released — the worst, by far, of the alternatives.

Among the more than 40 players were many members of last year's Kingsport Mets, all now hoping to reach Brooklyn. These candidates included Luz Portobanco and Ross Peeples. Other candidates included: David Byard, another 6'3" pitcher, much heftier than the thin Portobanco, with Byard carrying a David Wells–like 235 pounds; Wayne Ough, an Australian who, like Portobanco, can crank a fastball at 94 miles an hour; and Chad Bowen, another big right-hander, who led the Kingsport staff with seven wins.

Position players included Francisco Sosa (no relation to Sammy), a catcher from the Dominican Republic who had played a year at Kingsport after playing two years for the Mets' team in the Dominican Summer League. There was Mike Jacobs, a lefty-hitting catcher who had played last season at Kingsport with a few games at Capital City (Columbia). There was also Forrest Lawson, a powerful looking, and fast, outfielder from Seattle (who will be eternally susceptible to taunts from the stands saying, "Run, Forrest, run") and Wayne Lydon, who is so fast that people may someday say, "Look at that deer; it runs like a Lydon." Infielders included Robert "Mac" McIntyre, known for his slick fielding, who played for both Kingsport and Pittsfield last year, and Jeremy Todd, a strong first baseman who played for Pittsfield.

In the years immediately prior to Jackie Robinson's signing by the Dodgers to a minor league contract, the Brooklyn Dodgers did their spring training in Sanford, Florida, on the East Coast. Once the Dodgers inked Robinson, Branch Rickey decided that to conduct trading in racially segregated Florida would be too risky. To find a more habitable racial climate, he had to take his Dodgers farther south — so much farther south that Rickey conducted spring training mainly in the Dominican Republic and Panama. After spring training in 1946, Robinson was assigned to Montreal, the only Triple-A club the Dodgers operated outside of the United States. It was thought that Montreal would provide a better racial environment for baseball's first modern black player. Then in 1947, when Robinson's outstanding year at Montreal made his promotion in time for the start of the 1947 season likely, Rickey conducted a good portion of the Dodgers' spring training in Havana, Cuba. Once again, it was thought that by leaving the United States, the Dodgers could have a more accepting racial environment.

After Robinson's initial major league season, Rickey moved the entire Dodger spring training operation to an abandoned naval air station in Vero

Beach, Florida, that he converted into a baseball complex in time for spring training in 1948. The Dodgers, both in Brooklyn and Los Angeles, have continued to conduct spring training there every year since.

Carl Erskine's first spring training was in Pensacola, Florida, in 1947, but by 1948, the Dodgers had moved their spring training base to Vero Beach, where it has remained to this day. Carl Erskine discusses what that spring training was like.

Carl Erskine: "The minor leagues were very testy in the Dodger organization because of so much competition. Not personally testy, but testy in the sense of the fierce competition. This was in Vero Beach, Florida. Branch Rickey had made a deal with the city of Vero Beach to lease an old naval air station that was abandoned after the war. It had barracks, a mess hall. He built a baseball complex around that. It had diamonds, sliding pits, pitching strings, pitching mounds and so on. We lived in the barracks, and it had double bunks and a mess hall. It was like being back in the service because it was all contained right there. That's what basically went into Dodgertown in Vero Beach, which is now a beautiful facility, and it is scheduled to be re-done again in the next four or five years.

"I don't know exactly how many players were there at any one time, but there were something like 790 players under contract in the Dodger farm system at that time, plus there were a lot of free agents that came to spring training. You could do that at that time. Some of 'em were not decent ball players, but somebody knew somebody at the top of the Dodger organization and said, 'My son, when he gets older, can always say he went to spring training with the Dodgers.' Well, they don't do that anymore. Now there are too many good arms, too many good athletes.

"There was one room where Mr. Rickey had blackboards all around the room, 26 of them, and each had the minor league team's name at the top. And they would go in at night, the managers, the scouts and coaches. Mr. Rickey would hold forth with them, and they would discuss how to fill a roster at Albuquerque or Danville, or Fort Worth. Who can move up, etc. Then they'd post these lists daily. So guys couldn't wait to see if they got cut, or where they'd be sent, or if they were released. So, from that standpoint, I'd say it was fierce competition. Somewhere there is an old magazine cover that has a shot of all these players in one photo, all vying for these jobs. That made it extremely competitive."

February 6, 2002

Hall of Fame member Duke Snider grew up in the Dodger farm system. He is standing outside the batting cages in Vero Beach, Florida, where he is an instructor this week for the Dodgers' Adult Baseball Camp. The adult campers range in age from their twenties to the oldest camper, who is 86. Duke is asked about how first year professionals need to adjust to pro ball. The camp is held at the same Dodgertown where Duke trained 55 years ago.

Edwin "Duke" Snider was part of the New York triumvirate of center fielders — Snider, Mickey Mantle and Willie Mays — who all made the Hall of Fame and were celebrated in Terry Cashman's song "Talkin' Baseball" with the refrain "Willie, Mickey and the Duke."

Fans of the Dodgers, Yankees and Giants constantly argued over which center fielder was the best. In the 1950s, Duke Snider hit 326 home runs and drove in 1,031 runs — both more than any other player in that decade.

Duke was from Southern California and one of his boyhood heroes was UCLA star Jackie Robinson. At age 75, Duke still appears as he did years before. He's trim and is clearly recognizable as "The Duke of Flatbush."

Duke Snider: "You don't think about adjustments [to professional ball]. You have to learn how to play and how the Dodger system works. But there are no adjustments. You play the game of baseball. It's played the same. It's 90 feet to first base. It's sixty feet six inches to home plate. You just have to learn how to throw properly, how to hit the ball properly and just improve the more you play. It's probably more of a mental adjustment than anything else, because you're stepping up in levels, in the higher classification and competition play.

"We didn't think. We just tried to play, and have some fun and win. Except you're playing every day. It's amazing how good a person can get when they do something every day. How much you learn. Then it's more or less instincts. You learn by playing, not by reading. Mister Rickey used to have lectures in the auditorium. I worked out on this field, right over here. I spent hours in the batting cages working on my swing and George Sisler, a Hall of Famer, helped me. Branch Rickey was my instructor; he worked on me in different phases of my hitting. They made me a Hall of Famer. They worked with me on my strike zone. I had to learn to hit the outside pitch to the opposite field. They worked with me on different phases of hitting. What was a strike? What was a ball? They would throw me nothing but curveballs for a half-hour, and I would hit curveballs for a half-hour. One of the scouts would throw to me. He had a decent curveball. It was just repetition. That's what makes you good.

"Hitting is reaction. I don't know the players of today. The ones of today who were coachable would be fun to work with because they have a lot of talent, or they wouldn't have gotten as far as they did. Some are going to hit .220 or .240 their way. I think there's a tendency today for over-instruction by throwing too much at once at them, and they're confused. There are a lot of instructors around. And everybody has a different way to teach. You have to listen, and you have to be coachable. You may think you know how to do it, but a lot of these guys have a lot of good ideas for you. Whenever I try to teach, I don't try to throw too much at 'em at one time.

"Like the hitters at this fantasy camp. I watch 'em hit and I pick out their flaws, and I'll throw one correction at 'em at a time. Let them work on one thing rather than have four or five things on their mind. Because if they start thinking about their hands, or their hips, or their feet, or their head watching the ball, think all those things, pretty soon they're going to forget about the ball, because they're going to thinking about their hands or feet or everything else, so you throw one thing at them, then when they start doing that so that it's a reaction so that they don't have to think about it any more, it's just a reaction. Then you can throw something else at 'em. Don't confuse them. It's called the 'K.I.S.S.' method, *Keep it simple, stupid.* And if you do that, then it makes it a lot simpler for the youngsters, and I'm not saying they're stupid. It's just the less that you have to use your computer, which is your head, then the better hitter you're going to be. If you just react to the pitch and then hit it hard. [You correct] one thing — the most important thing first — whatever they're doing wrong. Then after that, you throw a little more at them, then a little more, usually not that particular day. Usually when you're teaching someone you're with them more than the week we're here at this camp.

"I'm working with a college kid in my hometown. And he was wiggling the bat, and he didn't just have the bat ready, so I've got him with a quiet bat now, holding his hands a bit higher. He goes to Stanford, and now he's doing very well. He hit over .400 in fall ball. He made the team as a freshman. Donny Lucy is his name, and he's a fine young man and coachable. He has a 4.2 grade point average. Donny can throw and hit, and he's a catcher, and he's a good athlete so he can play first, and play the outfield. The coach told him he's made the team, so he's going to play quite a bit."

Carl Erskine for ten seasons was a sort of biannual commuter, living for six months in Bay Ridge, Brooklyn, and about four and a half months in his hometown of Anderson, Indiana, and six weeks in Vero Beach.

Bay Ridge is a section of Brooklyn that borders the shores of the upper harbor to New York City. Often, eighteenth century Scandinavian sea captains made their homes in the three-story wooden houses that provided a fine view of the harbor. Later, many Italian and Irish immigrants made Bay Ridge their home.

Today, a Middle Eastern influence is established in Bay Ridge's shopping district.

People who think of Brooklyn as the "big city" would be amazed to walk Bay Ridge's many residential streets. Tree lined, with many single-family homes, often with small lawns, much of Bay Ridge has almost a small town feel to it.

Carl Erskine lived in a rented home in Bay Ridge and became a part of the community. His sons played Little League ball in Bay Ridge. Bay Ridge was the home of many Dodgers during the seasons of the 1947–1957 era. Duke Snider, from California, lived there, as did Pee Wee Reese and backup catcher Rube Walker, so did pitchers Clem Labine and Clyde King. Often the Dodgers living in Bay Ridge would car pool, not only to games at Ebbets Field, but also to Dodger away games at the Polo Grounds, and to Yankee Stadium in the World Series against the Yankees.

The Brooklyn connection between baseball and Bay Ridge runs to this day. During the 2001 season, many of the Cyclone players lived at Xaverian High School in Bay Ridge. A great National League hitter and briefly a Brooklyn Dodger, Tommy Holmes was a Bay Ridge resident. Today, Bay Ridge is the home of Joe Pignatano, former Brooklyn Dodgers catcher, later a Los Angeles Dodger, Kansas City A, San Francisco Giant and New York Met. Later, Brooklyn native Pignatano was the bullpen coach for the Mets for 14 years. He also coached for Joe Torre when Torre managed the Atlanta Braves.

A little known fact is that Pignatano caught the last innings of the final game at Ebbets field. A Brooklyn native, Pignatano signed with the Dodgers at 18 years of age, spent the next nine years trying to reach the major league Dodgers, with his minor league career interrupted by two years of army service during the Korean War. Finally, in the second half of the Dodgers' final season, 1957, he made his major league debut with Brooklyn.

Pignatano was the bullpen coach for the 1969 New York Mets World Series champions.

Joe Pignatano: "I grew up in Brooklyn and played sandlot ball, and I played high school ball in Brooklyn. The high school coach wrote the Dodgers, and the Dodgers wrote me, and I was given a tryout at Ebbets Field for a week.

"I grew up on Fifteenth Street, which is near Cropsey Avenue, and I was raised there. My house was later torn down to make way for the Belt Parkway. Where the Belt Parkway makes a right turn going to the Verrazano Bridge were three baseball diamonds, and that's where we played as kids. They're fixing it up now, and they are adding more fields now. We had to maintain the fields then. The Park Department didn't even maintain them. We had to walk all the way to Mark Twain Junior High School, which is on the other side of the Bay, going toward Sea Gate, to get a permit to play on that field. We had to get the permit every week. We ran the team ourselves. I was the youngest guy on the team. I was 14, and the other guys were all 17, 19, 20. There were no adults. Our team was called the Cyclones. We didn't play in a league. We'd call other teams and play. We'd play at Coney Island, we'd go to Sheepshead Bay, and there was a team at Bay Parkway at 60th Street; we used to go there. This is where we played. When we started playing sandlot ball, before we went to the Cyclones, we got a team together and nobody wanted to catch, so I said I'd do it, and I became a catcher. We were just neighborhood guys, and we wanted to play.

"At the time I went to high school, my school was called Specialty Trades, and it became Westinghouse Vocational. We were at the foot of the Manhattan Bridge, right across from Sperry Rand. It was an old factory building is what it was. I was a catcher there, too. When I tried out at Ebbets Field, it was a whole week tryout. We went on a Monday, and on the first day they weeded out the guys that they didn't think would make it. After the second day, they weeded out a few more. And after the week was up, they signed me. I think there were only two out of about 30 or 40. The other was a young guy, I think his name was Pete Gentile."

Joe Pignatano spent every spring training, while he was in the Dodger organization, at Vero Beach. It took him nine years, two of them in the United States Army, before he was able to make the majors in the summer of 1957, Brooklyn's last season.

Joe Pignatano: "Desire! That's how I was able to make the major leagues. (He points to his heart.) Desire! And maybe, just a little bit of talent."

Pignatano is being modest. He had a strong arm and unlike many catchers, he could run. He also had more pop in his bat than he was given credit for. But regardless of his arm, speed and power, Pignatano is right. He made the major leagues because his talent was coupled with a tenacious desire, with a work ethic that the Puritans would admire.

Pignatano was never a star. He was usually a backup catcher, but he was one of the few of the many millions of young boys who dream of a baseball career to be signed to a professional contract. He then survived seven minor league seasons to reach his dream.

During his career, he caught Sandy Koufax and Carl Erskine, played alongside Duke Snider, Gil Hodges, and Pee Wee Reese, played on the first Mets team with Hodges — one that was managed by a former Brooklyn Dodgers outfielder named Casey Stengel — and was a coach on the staffs of Hodges, Yogi Berra, and Joe Torre. Throughout baseball he is known affectionately as "Piggy," which is a name that has nothing to do with his appearance (neat) or manners (considerate), but is merely a takeoff from his last name.

Joe Pignatano was born in Brooklyn and has spent most of his life there. He still coaches there, as a volunteer at Poly Prep, a private Brooklyn high school that his grandson — a baseball player himself — attends.

Joe Pignatano — as a Brooklyn Dodger farmhand with Montreal.

He describes what it was like to be at the Brooklyn Dodgers' spring training camp in Vero Beach, Florida.

Joe Pignatano: "In Vero Beach, we went to school. They split the program up. In the first week or ten days of spring training, we took batting practice and used the sliding pits. We would throw the ball off this half-barrel and it would come off different ways, different angles; it was to quicken our hands. We went to 'school.' We did this every day. Every 45 minutes we went to a different station until we got in decent shape to play. Then, if you played a game in the morning, you did the same thing in the afternoon. Or if you did these stations in the morning, then you played a game in the afternoon. Then when you really got in shape and were ready to go you played two games a day.

"When you played in the games, if you made any mistakes they'd tell you about it. They'd say, 'Remember what we did here?'

"We did this every day until I got to the big leagues. In the morning, we'd go to every station. We'd go to about four or five stations in the morning and four to five stations in the afternoon.

"If you were playing that day, it was closer to 20 minutes each station. We did the same thing every day. Stations included batting practice, fielding practice, warming up pitchers, sliding pits, the barrels, the relay, cut-offs; we did all of this.

"We were living in barracks. If we had to use the bathroom, we had to get up in the middle of the night and use the bathroom down the hall. We had no bathroom in the room we were in. We were eight, ten, twelve guys in a room. We were living in bunk beds.

"And before breakfast every morning we used to listen to lectures in the theatre. These lectures were at about seven o'clock in the morning. Before we'd even go to the lecture, we'd go out there and run around the field three or four times, depending on how well whoever was in charge liked what we did. Then we'd go to the theatre and have our lecture. Then we'd go back to the barracks, dress in our uniforms, and then go eat breakfast. And then go out on the field. After lunch, we'd get out on the field at around 12. It would depend because they broke up the lunches, because there were at least 400 guys down there; they probably had about three lunch periods in the cafeteria. And the food was good. Meanwhile other groups were working out.

"After we were ready, we'd start to play games against ourselves, or play other minor league teams down there. Fort Pierce was near us. Toronto was a minor league club there. Everywhere around us there were minor league teams. We'd go to Orlando, wherever there was a minor league team. We had four fields to play in at Vero. When the big league club was playing at home we couldn't use that field, but most of the time they did most of their playing at Miami Stadium. They'd only play a few games at Vero Beach."

Guy Conti's experience in the Dodger organization taught him how things were run in the Brooklyn Dodger days of Branch Rickey. The New York Mets' minor league field coordinator discusses spring training then and now.

Guy Conti: "I don't think that spring training differs significantly from what Mister Rickey did with the Brooklyn Dodgers in the 1950s. Mister Rickey was the founder and the inventor of a lot of techniques that his fielders, and hitters, and pitchers used. I think the game of baseball hasn't changed much over a lot of years. Except the players have gotten bigger, stronger, and faster. Technologically, we're more advanced and we know the tendencies of hitters and pitchers, what they like to throw and when they like to throw it, but the game of baseball is still about hitting, catching, running, and throwing. Those skills are skills that can be improved upon and developed and what we're trying to do in the year 2001 is very "similar" to what they were trying to do back then.

"Mister Rickey had what he called a string in the bullpen. He had two poles with strings from them that outlined the strike zone over home plate. So the catcher sat behind these strings so the pitchers could have a little more command of the strike zone; they could see when the ball was in that strike zone or not. We do the same thing. We don't have physical strings per se, but we have mental strings when we are working on the different zones of the strike zone. Up and in, low and away, down and in, up and away.

"Our pitchers are working on their command all of their pitches and we simulate hitters being in there and we say, 'Okay, this is a two-two pitch. What do you want to do with this pitch?' or, 'It's a 0–0 pitch.' We're always putting in the minds of our pitchers that although there's no batter in there, there *is* a batter in there. And if there's somebody you're working with, there's somebody you're throwing to.

"I remember when I had Don Sutton [Hall of Fame pitcher who came up through the Los Angeles Dodgers' farm system]. He came to Bakersfield, California, and he very definitely had those thoughts in his mind when he warmed up before a game. He would actually have a right-handed hitter and a left-handed hitter stands in there when he was in the bullpen warming up. I watched him go through this and I asked him, 'Don, what were you thinking there? What was going through your mind?'

"And he told me, 'I've already pitched the first two hitters of the game in my mind. When I take the mound to start the game, I'm facing the third hitter. I know my arm is good and ready; I've thrown all my pitches, and I've got the first two hitters out already.' That's the way he did it and that's the way he was taught.

"It's very definitely a carryover from the Branch Rickey days; a lot of the things we do on turning double plays, a lot of the baserunning things we do were brought by the greats of the game like Jackie Robinson and Maury Wills. Baseball is a game of skills, and skills can be improved upon.

"Recently, I've seen such an increase in the mental side of the game, with pitching, hitting, and baserunning. People are smarter; they know what they're doing. You saw in this year's World Series, some of the things that Derek Jeter did. Those weren't taught. Those were things that he had instincts to do, and he was mentally aware and focused to do those sort of things, but a lot of today's game is really traced back to the Branch Rickey era.

"One thing that goes back to Mr. Rickey is turning the double play. There are different methods to turning the double play, the crossover, and the inside and outside ways, but I have to look at the talent of the kid we have and the teaching method to fit that kid. It's like in basketball playing a running game with guys who can't run. So we're looking at the abilities of our players and trying to find the abilities of each player and take the teaching technique to fit the player so he has more chance to be successful."

While the Cyclone candidates might feel very familiar with the Dodgers' spring training drills from their golden era, conditioning in spring training has been a revolution in the past 50 years.

Joe Pignatano tells about his spring training conditioning:

Joe Pignatano: "What we did for conditioning then was run. And we did stretching, but mostly what we did was run. We didn't do weightlifting. None. And when we ran we didn't do jogging — we sprinted. Yes sir.

"They said, 'Whatever you're going to do, do it hard.'

"So I used to take care of myself. They told me I had 'x' number of minutes to run, and I used to rope off 50, 60 yards for myself. And they used to watch us. When you finished, they'd say, 'Okay, you can go. You did your work.'

"I used to run 50, 60 yards. I'd run once, then walk back. Then do it twice; then I'd walk back. Up until I got to five times in a row. All these times I sprinted hard. Then I'd go back to four sprints in a row, then three, two, one. Then after that I'd walk for about 15 minutes. They knew who to let run on their own and who not to. They even tried to get me to run with the pitchers, but I refused. Because the pitchers will only get mad at me because I want to do what I want to do and the pitchers will tell me, 'You're crazy. You run too hard.' That's the way I was. Hey, you do what you want to do. But I was always in shape. When I got to spring training I didn't hurt like these guys."

Mike Herbst, who during the 2001 campaign was the medical coordinator for the entire Met minor league organization, explains modern conditioning. Midway through the Cyclones' season, he also became the Cyclones' trainer. A graduate of the University of Florida, Herbst has been in the minor leagues for ten years. He is a Brooklyn native, having grown up in Marine Park, an area near the bridge to the Rockaways and a residential area of many single family homes and a fine park by the same name, Marine Park, where the Torre brothers grew up and played ball in assorted leagues. Marine Park is only a 15-minute drive from KeySpan Park in Coney Island. Herbst always has a cell phone with him and a portable computer as he keeps track of all the Mets' minor league players

Mike Herbst: "There's more emphasis now in the strength and conditioning end of it in spring training. Now players don't come to spring training to get in shape, but they have to show up in shape, ready to go from the first day of spring training. We still have the same fundamental drills; we still hit, and play spring training games. We still warm up the same way; nothing's really changed in that aspect. The biggest change is that the minor league guys and the big league guys don't come to spring training to get in shape like they used to. They didn't used to do anything in the off-season. In the 1950s, they just showed up, and they still had six weeks to get ready for the season. Now, the kids have to show up in spring training ready to go from day one, because of the competition and the money, all that kind of stuff.

"We have a strength and conditioning book that we wrote, myself and New York Mets trainer Scott Lawrenson, and we also have a video. The book and video tell them what they're supposed to be doing as far as lifting is concerned, what they're supposed to be doing as far as running, how much they're supposed to run, how much they're supposed to throw, what they're supposed to eat. We give them nutritional information. The book is given to all the kids and the video demonstrates the exercises that we want them to do in the off-season. From the day they're done playing baseball at the end of the season, every single day is scripted — what they're supposed to do, how much they're supposed to run, and how much they're supposed to lift. There's one program for position players, and one for pitchers. We've had the book and the corresponding video for five years.

"We do certain conditioning tests when they arrive for spring training. We test their body fat, their height, weight; we test their grip strength, and we test their flexibility. We compare last year's totals to this year's totals. We measure their time in the 440 and their times in the 300-yard shuttle run; we see what their times are back-to-back. We time things and compare them to years past. We're all high tech now, so we're able to put all this information into computers and make a quorum decision on whether they're getting better or worse, on whether they need motivation, they need nutritional help, from every aspect of it.

"We have a grip strength meter, and we test each hand separately. We just want to look to see if a kid is maintaining his strength over time. A pitcher might come in and have a 75 one year on his right hand, and then the next year he might have a 65, so we know there's been a significant drop in his grip strength. This may tip us off to a potential nerve problem in his shoulder, or a problem in his elbow. Something that's painful that he's not able to do it as much as before, maybe he's not working out as hard as he was before, maybe he has some sort of neurological problem, something like that. We don't normally make remedies just based on their grip strength, but we use it as a baseline.

"We do blood work on every single player. So we have a baseline in case anyone has any significant problems later. We do blood work on every single player from the big leagues all the way to our minor leagues. When they first get to spring

Warner Fusselle (left) with Reggie Armstrong.

training we do a urinalysis; we do a blood composition; we do all these things when they first get to spring training so we can get a good baseline if anyone has any potential problems, such as a high glucose level or a high fat, high lipid level, if he has any problems with his blood, if there's any kind of disease going on, any kind of pathology. We test all this out in spring training so we can get a good baseline through urinalysis and blood work. We get a good baseline on how these kids are coming into spring training, and sometimes we flag certain problems. Sometimes a kid has really high cholesterol and we put him on medication. Sometimes they have really high glucose levels, which might indicate diabetes. It's a lot of potential problems that could be going on and you try to flag any problems early in spring training.

"We have a mobile X-ray unit right at the stadium; we have ultrasound stimulator machines; we have instant access to a medic center which is right there; we have a mobile ambulance unit that takes care of us. We have automatic defibrillators in case someone goes down with a heart problem — anyone on the field or one of our coaches. Those are some of the big changes that we have made over the years.

"We have a special field mapped out that has a big square and it's covered with grass and we have our own area that's fenced in just for conditioning. That's all we use it for. We used medicine balls in there, we have step up boxes, we have leg bands, we have tubing, we have cords, we have jump rope. It's right outside the weight room door when you walk outside. We do running there, we do ball drops, that kind of thing.

"We test the players on the 300 yard shuttle run, which is one of the things we do when the players first come in. We do it twice, with a three minute recovery period in between runs so we can see how the players recover.

"The players have a weight training schedule, but everybody's different depending if they're a rehabbing guy, or not a rehabbing guy. Some come in twice a week. Sometimes it depends on who was in the game that day. Sometimes it depends on which pitchers were in the game; it's all different.

"Everything is totally supervised, and their whole spring training is totally planned out before they even get there. They can't just go in the weight room and work out on their own. We have strength and conditioning experts in the weight room at all times, and they chart all the work that goes on there.

"Some of the kids come in early for work at 8 A.M. and others come in at nine. It varies depending on who is playing that day. Some players stay for post work in the afternoon. It depends."

When Joe Pignatano had an off-season, his first thought was not necessarily conditioning. Pignatano had to support himself. He needed to work, yet that work kept him in shape.

Joe Pignatano: "I went away into the army. When I came back [to Brooklyn], my mother and father had bought the house next door, so I was there until I got married. When I was in the minors, I didn't work out in the off-season because I had to work. But the work I did kept me in shape. I was a plumber's helper and when the man that was driving the oil truck couldn't make it, I drove the oil truck and did the oil deliveries. I was in the best shape I was ever in. I used to lug the hose, jump on the truck."

Guy Conti explains modern conditioning:

Guy Conti: "There's been so much research into the physical side of it. On every ball club we've got a conditioning and strength person. On every ball club we have a trainer. In the days of the Branch Rickey's, they didn't have that kind of stuff. Even when I played, our trainer was the clubhouse kid who did the laundry and sprayed out the shower at the end of the day. Well, trainers don't do that now. They're certified physical trainers from medical departments; they're a specialist because the investment is so great nowadays. You don't want to invest that amount of money in someone who can't play anymore. There's a lot of money, a lot of research, and a lot of time invested in these kids as far as their conditioning. The drills that we do are designed specifically for baseball. Obviously, football weightlifting is very different from baseball weightlifting. When our minor league kids go on the road, they are assigned to a gymnasium. We find a gymnasium every morning where they must go and condition themselves daily to keep in shape. It's more of a preventive thing during the season, but in the off-season we're monitoring it right now as we speak. We have people calling kids, finding what they're doing in the off-season. because it's so demanding now to come out and play 162 games during the year and let your body go during the off season. It doesn't happen.

"If players do weightlifting improperly and they do it to excess, they can tighten up muscles that are so valuable to baseball that they can't be tightened. We have to have a loose, flexible muscle as opposed to a beach muscle look. We don't want that look. They'll use machines and free weights. Our pitchers use free weights, but they can't lift over five pounds. Dr. Jobe has a program in L.A. that we've

Bobby Ojeda — as a Brooklyn Cyclone.

copied, that most people have copied, that says what you are to do with five and seven pound weights. When they get over that weight for a pitcher, you can do as much damage as you do good. The important thing is to educate the players that more isn't necessarily good. We want them to be controlled, and we want them to be monitored. Our strength and conditioning people put out an off-season manual that every one of them was given before they went home, and they are instructed to follow that manual. Obviously, there are some skinny ones who want to get bigger and stronger, and they do a little bit more than they should. But all of a sudden they become muscle-bound and tight, and that's not the muscles we want for baseball.

"The stretching and flexibility programs, the weightlifting programs and the off-season programs, are all different from the 1950s. I think the real Brooklyn Dodgers had an off-season. I don't think there is an off-season anymore. There's so much money in the major leagues that Leiter, Piazza and these guys hire personal trainers who are with them all year to keep them in good shape because they're trying to get one or two extra years because of the money, and it's very important to them because their physical conditioning and their shape determines their success. Edgardo Alfonzo took two weeks off. Now he has a personal trainer and he's working every day to get his back stronger so he can have a big season again because his back was injured last year.

"Players are instructed when they leave the year before not to come to spring training to get in shape, but to already be in shape because it's too short a time for you to come in to get yourself in shape when everybody else is ready. Take an arm, throwing a baseball. If you report to spring training March 1, and that's your first day of starting to get your arm back in shape, you're gonna be five or six weeks behind everybody else because everybody else is going to come here on March 1 ready to throw the ball to some degree because they've been throwing and working out. We will be very popular on January 4, down here with people from all organizations. They'll be throwing, they'll be running, they'll be catching, they'll be doing a lot of things on their own because it's in the rules that no one can be out there with them. But they will be here, the facility will be open, but they will be doing it on their own. I come down here and open the doors, and I'm around here, and the balls are available for them, and they can play catch and run. It's warm weather here; it's open. And they know it's open, so a lot of different kids come from different organizations, which I don't mind, and they're going to work out, and this is a good place to do it. The last thing I told our kids before they left the Instructional League was, 'Don't come to spring training to get in shape. Because if you do, you're going to be behind a whole lot of people. Be ready to go.'

"The players who were released probably had played at Kingsport the previous year. People who play at Kingsport this year pretty much have to make the Brooklyn club. If they're 18 or 19, then maybe they can go back and play another year at Kingsport, but we don't like to repeat that level because we're going to have 30 or 40 more kids coming June 6 to chase their jobs. So there is an element of a kid not being able to make a full-season club who goes for another year, but very seldom would he go for three years."

The 47 Cyclone players in extended went about their routine from April up until the draft in June. The current players in extended would soon be getting company.

Inning 2

The Players

The Players in Extended Spring Training

June 4, 2001

Queens is the best place in the world. Brooklyn is the second best place in the world. Kingsport, Tennessee is the third best. And home is the worst.

In the above list of preferences, the actual mileage from Flushing Meadows, Queens, to Coney Island, Brooklyn, is 15 miles — plus a world of talent, good health, good luck, hard work and about four years. Of course, what we're talking about is the favorite place in the world for the 47 Met farmhands lingering in extended spring training in Florida. And their Nirvana is a rather generic 1960s ballpark in Queens called Shea Stadium, home of the New York Mets. Facing the realities of minor league baseball, the Met farmhands know they're not going to Shea Stadium in two days, cutdown day. So they face the actual hope of going to Brooklyn, the more advanced of the New York Mets' two short season farm teams. Never have 40-plus young men been so unanimous in their preferences. Brooklyn is fifth down the ladder rungs of the Mets' farm system, but it's above the bottom rung — Kingsport.

It's not that these players particularly enjoy Brooklyn, although a few have visited there, and a few have relatives in the New York metropolitan area. But take any similar number of athletic young men and name any metropolitan area in the United States, and you'd find similar situations.

It's not that the farmhands have anything against Kingsport, Tennessee, because many of them spent last season there, and nobody's been griping about it. It's just that these young players are facing a ticking biological clock. It's not about having babies, but it is about the birth of their dream, and the biological clock is even more pressing than that facing young women of similar ages concerned about their biological clock. Women in their late teens or early twenties concerned about having children realize that they may have perhaps more than two decades before time runs out. The young ballplayers in Florida may only have one or two days before they are cut. Even if they're not cut, they may have only weeks or months to prove to the Met hierarchy that they should stay under contract to the Mets. A Met farm player is expected to advance one level per year up the six-step minor league ladder. This rule isn't hard and fast, but players must keep moving up — or they risk being moved out. A 22-year-old, just graduated college senior feels more time pressure than a 19 year old who played last year at Kingsport. Every year, the Mets are signing another 30 or 40 new players, which means that in some way 30 or 40 must leave, since the number of players in their United States farm system generally runs at about 170.

Everybody is going to Brooklyn, or Kingsport, or home. Picture how they will find out their destination. Perhaps a player envisions a quiet conference with a Mets representative. Picture that and the realities of minor league practicality haven't been absorbed. The way these 47 young men will find out their destinations, and perhaps the path to their future, is when they enter the clubhouse tomorrow and look at a bulletin board.

These players and others all wanted to be at Brooklyn. If called up higher in the system they world gladly go, but at this point the choices amounted to Brooklyn, Kingsport, or home. And nobody wanted to go home. But the players in camp weren't their only competition. Tomorrow would be baseball's annual draft. Drafted players from high schools and colleges are selected on June 5 and 6. If they agreed to terms with the Mets within a few days, they would head for Florida to join those players already at extended spring training. All would have a chance at Brooklyn.

In early June, the Mets had over 40 players in extended spring training. Tomorrow, the Mets would be participating in baseball's First Year Players Draft. Held each year in early June, this year's draft would enable the Mets to draft players whom they had been following, some for as much as five or six years, from as far back as their sophomore year of high school to their junior or senior year of college. Other players on the Mets' draft list would be recent additions, added only this year.

So the new Brooklyn team would actually come mainly from two sources: players who had played last year in the Mets' system, mainly at Kingsport, with a few having experience at Pittsfield; the other players would come from the draft. It was impossible to accurately predict the make-up of the Brooklyn team because at this late date, June 4, only 15 days before the season opener at Jamestown, many of the Brooklyn players would be selected in the draft. Some of the key candidates from the players in extended spring training to make the Brooklyn club included two catchers.

Mike Jacobs is stately in appearance. At six-foot-two and 200 pounds, he appears tall and rangy. You could picture him someday, after his baseball career, in motion pictures or television as a "movie cowboy," like former Brooklyn Dodger Chuck Connors, the former "Rifleman." Jacobs' erect bearing and dignified manner gives him a resemblance to another catcher, Hall of Famer

Carlton Fisk, catcher for the Red Sox and White Sox. But while Fisk's recent baseball goal was to get into the Hall of Fame, Jacob's is more modest. He wants to get to a full season A club. Jacobs is from Chula Vista, California, near the beach at San Diego and about as far geographically and sociologically as one can get from the gritty beachfront of Coney Island.

As a left-handed hitting catcher, he's a prized commodity in baseball, since catchers are right-handed throwers and thus most hit right-handed. Not only does Jacobs hit lefty, he does it with power. Only 20 years old, his power potential is excellent, since he should get stronger as he matures.

Another catcher vying for a spot on the Brooklyn club is Francisco Sosa. Physically, he most resembles Brooklyn's Roy Campanella, the catcher during their glory years and a Hall of Famer. Sosa is 5' 11", stocky, but not as heavy as Campanella. It's a mark of how baseball heights have increased that Campanella, at 5' 9", was considered a little short for his time, as is Sosa in his, but the heights have moved up two inches. But Campanella was small only in stature. His body was powerful, with giant forearms, a barrel chest and tree trunk legs. Campanella was built for power, and that was his game. Sosa's game is more like that of a middle infielder who bats second. In fact, Sosa sometimes did bat second, unusual for a catcher. Sosa has hit only two home runs in three years of professional baseball. Sosa's game is the bunt, the hit-and-run, hitting behind a runner, always getting the bat on the ball. And Sosa can run, stealing 18 bases in his year in the DSL and 12 last year at Kingsport. Recovering from an injured arm, Sosa seems to deserve a shot at Brooklyn since in his first three minor league seasons he has batted a combined .310.

But without much power and trying to get his arm up to 100 percent, Sosa must compete against Jacobs, Australian star Justin Huber, and any one of several catchers that the Mets will draft.

Answering a question that is always asked of him — whether he is related to fellow Dominican Sammy Sosa — Francisco says, "No, no relation." He smiles, has a quiet professional manner and is a hard working player. Sosa struggles a little with English, but he handles pitchers well and his offensive game — with all the strategy of his bunts, steals, and hit and runs — is a throwback game and fun for a fan to watch.

Of the three main candidates in extended spring training for catching positions on the Cyclones, all come from different countries: Jacobs from the United States, Sosa from the Dominican Republic and Justin Huber from Australia. In the old Brooklyn Dodgers days, practically all the player candidates were from the United States. There were a few exceptions: Sandy Amoros, an outfielder from Cuba, was one. Elmer Valo, for a brief time a Dodger outfielder, was born in Czechoslovakia, but grew up in the United States. Chico Carrasquel was from Venezuela. Back in the late 1940s and in the 1950s, baseball was a United States sport with a few exceptions. Today, it is very much an international sport.

Justin Huber comes from an area in Australia in which environmental shows are filmed. Huber is a strapping 6' 2" and looks like he would love playing American football. His speech is heavy with a charming Australian accent, and one wonders how that would sound in the midst of Coney Island. He mentions that he loves catching because he gets to call the game, to be in charge. He's got a twinkle in his eye and a puckish demeanor. He's played for the Australian National team. He's a right-handed batter who looks strong enough to develop some power. During extended spring training he's been sitting in on the English classes that a number of the Spanish speaking Mets' farmhands take. Justin does this so that as a catcher who will have to work with Spanish speaking pitchers, he will know Spanish; so, while the Dominicans and other Spanish speakers are learning English, Justin Huber is learning Spanish. It looks like it will be a close call whether Huber gets to start at Brooklyn or is sent to Kingsport. He's too good a prospect to be cut, so it's all a matter of where the Mets feel he should begin. It also depends on what catchers are drafted in the next two days and which of them sign contracts, and of the ones who sign contracts, which of them do it immediately after the draft.

At 23, infielder Jeremy Todd was one of the older Cyclone candidates. Last year, at Pittsfield, his first in professional ball, he drove in 47 runs in 63 games. Of his 53 hits, 20 were for extra bases. He hit only five home runs, but with Pittsfield's immense right-center field, it's not the best spot for a left-handed power hitter. A converted catcher coming off a knee injury, Todd would almost certainly not be going to Kingsport. That would be heading backwards. At his age, advanced for a short-season A league, Todd needed to make strides fast. Disappointed about not making a full season team, his knee still not 100 percent, Todd needed to make the Brooklyn club and then produce fast to get an in-season promotion to Capital City or St. Lucie. Physically, of the 1947–1957 Dodgers, he most resembles Gil Hodges, also a converted catcher who wound up at first base. At 23, Hodges was already in Brooklyn, playing for the Dodgers. Todd has some catching up to do, but first he must make the Brooklyn squad, and then hit his way out of the league as soon as possible. Hodges, at 6' 2", was considered a strong giant of a man and Todd, of the same size, is considered an average sized first baseman for the New York–Penn League. How times change.

David Abreu was another infield candidate for the Cyclones. At six-foot and 160 pounds, he has played four years in the Met system. Last year, he hit .288 at Capital City and .333 in limited action at St. Lucie. A second baseman, he was born and lives in San Pedro de Macoris, home of numerous major league infielders from that Dominican city. He can run, as evidenced by 29 stolen bases at Cap City and another three in St. Lucie. Nearly 22, he has a lifetime minor league batting average of .306. He seems quite capable of playing full season Class-A ball, so a year at Brooklyn would seem to be a step down for him, but yet, here he is, in extended spring training trying to make Brooklyn.

Another Dominican second baseman in extended spring training was Leandro Arias. He played in 1998 in the Dominican Summer League and in 1999 with the Mets' Gulf Coast League team, a team the Mets no longer operate as they now place most of their younger players with their teams in the Dominican Summer League, the Venezuelan Summer League, or with short season Kingsport. With the 1999 Gulf Coast League Mets, Arias had a banner year, making the league All-Star team, leading the league in triples, second in total bases, second in slugging percentage, fourth in runs scored and fifth in runs batted in. He was injured in 2000 and sat out the season and is now coming back from a season off. Still only 20, he will probably be sent to Brooklyn or Kingsport, having too good a previous record to be cut.

Another infielder at extended trying to make Brooklyn is Anthony Coyne, out of Yale University. Some former Yale baseball players decide to be president. George H. Bush batted what he termed "second clean-up" at Yale, a gentleman's way of saying that he batted eighth. Anthony Coyne doesn't have time to run for president; he's too busy trying to make Brooklyn. A shortstop and second baseman, he played last year at both Kingsport and at Pittsfield. From Huntington, Maryland, he's 22. Splitting last year between Kingsport and Pittsfield, he hit .225 at Kingsport and .208 after he was promoted to Pittsfield. He's 5' 10", a sturdy 190 pounds and a 23rd round draft pick in 2000. He asks a writer about what Brooklyn is like and says he gets the feeling that he will make the Brooklyn squad, if he makes any squad at all, because of the way he is being used and the players he is with in the intrasquad games. He is surprised to learn that the Brooklyn ballpark is right on the beach, connected to the Coney Island boardwalk. Asked about his major at Yale, he says, "It was history.... But it was really baseball."

Robert McIntyre is another infielder at "Extended" who played last season at both Kingsport and Pittsfield. Another Met farmhand signed by scout Joe DelliCarri, Robert is a 5' 10" shortstop, about the same size as Brooklyn Dodger shortstop Pee Wee Reese. Robert is from the high school that has produced many major leaguers, including former Met superstar pitcher Dwight Gooden: Hillsborough High School. From Tampa, Robert was a 13th round draft pick in 1999. He hit .304 in the Gulf Coast League in 1999, then last year played in five games at Pittsfield where he hit .176, and then hit .296 in 53 games at Kingsport. He has good speed and is smooth in the field. Robert is a black player who proudly mentioned that he has played at Jackie Robinson Ballpark in Daytona Beach. He is soft spoken, looks thin, but has strong arms and some power.

Joe Jiannetti looks tough, and he is. With a long, bull neck, he is obviously an athlete. At six-foot-one, Jiannetti has the build of a running back, and he was a former high school footballer playing in St. Petersburg who was good enough to earn scholarship offers. Joe doesn't mince words. He tells it straight and truthfully. Although Joe is a third baseman, he did play some outfield in college. The closest in demeanor on the old Dodgers to Jiannetti is Carl Furillo. Furillo was tough. If a pitcher threw at him, Carl would sometimes charge the mound. He had been known to also let his bat "slip" out of his hands after he was thrown at, the bat heading right for the offending pitcher. Furillo was also said to have once beaten up a roommate, hospitalizing him in a fight over turning out the lights. And he once was said to have almost choked Leo Durocher to death.

Joe Jiannetti doesn't have Furillo's temper, but Joe has at least his toughness. A dia-

Joe Jiannetti — Brooklyn Cyclones third baseman.

betic, Joe's condition scared off some teams, but not the Mets, who drafted Joe in 1999 and told him to go to junior college and they would try to sign him in a year, while they still retained his rights. Jiannetti dives for balls, dives into bases, dives into home, backs off from nobody and hangs in against close pitches at the plate. The question is whether he is ready for Brooklyn or whether he will begin his professional career at Kingsport.

Joe Jiannetti: "I first started baseball when I was four. I played where I grew up — in St. Petersburg, Florida. My dad pulled some strings to get me into Little League at that age. Then when I came back the next year when I was five, they said, 'How can you be moving up to the five year old category?' And my dad said, 'What are you talking about? He's only five now. It must have been a mistake.'"

"I played catcher in Little League; my dad wanted me to be a catcher. And he also told me that it was the quickest way to the big leagues. He had played catcher and he loved it. He was the coach of the team, so he always put me at catcher. My dad got me my first glove. I had a catcher's mitt that my dad had used. It was big

for me. Then my grandma bought me a glove. Then when I was ten, I started playing shortstop. And I played shortstop through high school, and then I switched
to third.

"When I was growing up, baseball kind of ran my life. I was on the traveling team,
and my family planned vacations around baseball. Everything was planned around
baseball. Even as it is now, only more so. I live now in St. Petersburg, only five
houses away from the house I grew up in as a kid. I live on Snell Isle in St. Pete.

"I was always better than most other people growing up. I was bigger than a lot
of other guys and pretty much better than them. I guess I was just born with ability. Most of the other kids played basketball and everything else. All I did was
play baseball. If I didn't have a game, I would want to go out with my dad and
play catch. I'm playing all year round and they're only playing a couple of days.

"The Mets drafted me in the fortieth round after high school. They told me I
could sign, but they said they didn't really want me to sign. I would go to junior
college for one year because they have the rights to me for 51 weeks of the year.
They said, 'We'll see how your year goes, and we'll try to negotiate with you after
the season.' So I played one year and signed around Memorial Day, which is seven
days before the next draft. We went back and forth [on the contract] and we agreed
on Saturday, and then on Memorial Day, Monday, I drove over here to St. Lucie
and signed. I was so happy when I signed. That's what I wanted to do. My parents and my sister were right there, and then I called everyone. I didn't have time
for a party or anything because I was leaving the next day. I agreed to the offer
over the phone on Saturday, and the next day I drove to St. Lucie, signed on Monday and was on the field on Tuesday.

"Extended was my first time in professional baseball, so I was real excited. I didn't
realize how much work it actually was. I wake up at six-thirty and I'm leaving for
the field at seven o'clock. Before that, in college and high school, I'm not going
to the field until three-thirty or four o'clock in the afternoon. Now I'm getting up
at six-thirty, leaving at seven, being on the field at eight all the way until three-
thirty. It's a full day's job, and I'd get home and feel exhausted. Then I'd just come
back to the Holiday Inn and lay around. I wouldn't do anything, I'm so tired.
Everyone said before I signed that it's a lot of work, that it's much harder, but you
don't realize how much work it is until you actually go through it. You can't imagine. They had two vans at the Holiday Inn, but I had my car here so I drove over.

"Some days at eight we'd field ground balls. Other days, I'd hit in the cages.
Other days, I'd work on double plays. Whatever they planned.

"After we had practiced, we'd eat chicken sandwiches, half a sub, hot dogs,
maybe; we'd eat the same stuff all the time. Then after lunch we'd go to an away
game; we'd take two vans."

Edgar Rodriguez is another third base candidate. He's 5' 11", 180 pounds,
appears thin, but he has power. He doesn't speak a lot of English and is always
brief when he responds to a question in English. But he doesn't seem to speak
a lot in Spanish either. A good fielder, he has a strong arm. This is his first
minor league season. He's from San Pedro de Macoris in the Dominican
Republic. San Pedro de Macoris seems to produce professional infielders — maybe
it's in the water. San Pedro de Macoris produces infielders as New York City
produces basketball point guards, and western Pennsylvania produces quar-
terbacks. Edgar is the cousin of New York Mets reliever Armando Benitez,

and Edgar lives with him in the off-season. If he can learn to hit his cousin, Edgar can hit in the majors. For Edgar, it's Kingsport or Brooklyn.

Joel Zaragoza can field at any infield position, but he has yet to show he can hit well enough to get out of short season A ball. A 5' 10", 180-pound, smooth-moving defensive specialist, he hit only .155 at Kingsport in 1999 and .178 at Pittsfield in 2000. Fluent in both Spanish and English, Zaragoza bridges the language gap on the team, serving as an impromptu translator for players in either language. Not a complainer despite his rather limited playing time in his first two years, Zaragoza is the solid character type of player who may stay in an organization for years. At 20 years of age, he still has some time on his side, but he must soon start to show he can hit.

Angel Pagan never played high school baseball, but instead played on nonscholastic teams. A center fielder, his biggest asset, both on offense and defense, is his speed. He is still learning to become a switchhitter and is still becoming comfortable from the left side, his newer side. At six-foot-one and 175 pounds, he may increase his low power as he matures, since he's only 20 years old. While trying to steal, he gets thrown out, but the Mets want him to continue to steal so that he stays aggressive and develops his technique. He's from Puerto Rico; the Mets drafted him in the fourth round in 1999. In his first professional season at Kingsport, he hit .361 in 72 at bats, but hit only one home run and had only six extra base hits. He's seemed to prove what he can do at Kingsport and seems at least ready for Brooklyn, if not Capital City.

Noel Devarez is a right fielder with power. Devarez wraps the bat high around his head as he stands in the box, and he handles fastballs well, but curves give him trouble. At six foot, he's a solid 175 pounds, from San Pedro de Macoris, in the Dominican Republic. He has good speed and goes back on balls well. In addition to a weakness against curveballs, another weakness is his tendency to be thrown out on the base paths, either trying to stretch a hit or trying to advance on a base hit. His upside is his power, and teams stick a long time with players that exhibit the kind of power Devarez has. Devarez broke in with the Mets' Gulf Coast League team in 1999 and hit .286 with four home runs, and then last season he hit .305 at Kingsport with nine home runs in 197 at bats. Off the field, he doesn't feel too comfortable speaking English and generally speaks with the other Spanish speaking players on the team. He also listens to his Walkman headphones a lot and is pretty quiet.

Michael Piercy is an outfielder who has been bouncing around the minor leagues for years. A left-handed batter, he's 25, ancient by the standards of short-season baseball; he is trying to hook on with Brooklyn. At his age, Kingsport is out, so if Piercy is not cut, the team he'll make will be Brooklyn. A religious man, Piercy has an engaging personality and a lot of enthusiasm. He loves to hit and he loves to talk. At 25, the odds are against his even making the Brooklyn team, let alone reaching the majors, but stranger things have happened and every so often a 30-year-old rookie breaks into the big leagues, so hope springs eternal. Piercy could go to play in an independent league, but feels he will better his chances of someday making the majors if he sticks to a team in "organized baseball."

Forrest Lawson is a 6' 3", 195-pound outfielder from Federal Way, in the State of Washington. He was the Mets' eighth round pick in the 1999 draft. In his third year in the Mets' system, he hit .271 at Kingsport and seems ready for Brooklyn — the next level. He's an excellent defensive outfielder at any outfield position, and he hustles and backs up plays every time. He's only 20 years old and has a chance to just keep developing as he progresses through the Met organization. He runs well and stole 12 bases in 60 games at Kingsport.

Wayne Lydon isn't fast. He's at the next level of speed above fast — rocket-like. A former high school football star in Pennsylvania, Lydon is an outstanding athlete who never played as much baseball in the Northeast as many teammates from the warmer weather South and from California played, so he has a bit of catching up to do. The upside of that is that he is nowhere near his potential because he is still so raw. Just 20 years old, he's six-foot-two and 190 pounds. He hit only .183 at the Gulf Coast League Mets in 1999 and .203 at Kingsport in 2000. He's now learning to hit left handed so that he can switch hit. His potential means he will play somewhere, but he would like to move up to Brooklyn.

Luz De Jesus Portobanco is an enigma. At 6' 3" and 205 pounds, he can throw a fastball at 94 miles per hour. Portobanco is religious and credits God for his success. On the other hand, Portobanco doesn't turn the other cheek too much; he's pretty good with his fists. He was born in Nicaragua and moved to Miami, Florida, when he was five. He learned to box at a young age and was in several fights. Portobanco was drafted with the Mets' 36th pick in the 2000 draft. He was 3–3 at Kingsport last season with a 4.89 earned run average. He needs to work on his curve and change-up. He has already been told by the Mets that he will begin the season at Brooklyn. He speaks both English and Spanish.

Luz Portobanco: "Yeah, I'm bilingual. I started school here since I was small and I have fun. Before I wasn't even into sports. One day there was a guy, I was playing basketball and he saw me. He knew I wanted to play baseball; I told him I wanted to try out to play baseball and he got me into it for free. That's where I started everything. I was a third baseman, a hitter, and a good batter at Little League. That's where everything started and everybody saw me that day. The guy gave me a challenge. He changed it a little by little, and I still got to learn more.

"My first name, 'Luz', means light and my middle name is De Jesus, so my name means 'Light of Jesus'. My last name is Portuguese. Nobody else has that last name, so somebody who has my last name must be related to me. I came to the United States from my country, Nicaragua, and I haven't been back to my country in 15 years. I grew up all my life here — in Miami."

Luz Portobanco and Tyler Beurelein, Brooklyn Cyclones players.

Harold Eckert has to make a comeback. He hasn't pitched in two years, not in an official college or professional game. While pitching in the NCAA Regional Tournament in 1999, Eckert injured his elbow and has been out of organized baseball competition for two years. The six-foot-three-inch right-hander was pitching in what turned out to be his final college game when he tore the ligament in his elbow. He was drafted by the Los Angeles Dodgers and although Eckert made them aware of the injury, they were required by baseball's rules to offer him a contract. Eckert first signed with the Dodgers, and eventually was signed by the Mets as a free agent in December of 2000. He is recovering from "Tommy John–type surgery in which a ligament from Eckert's ankle was transplanted to his elbow. Eckert signed without a bonus, just wanting a chance to prove that he can pitch. His status is up in the air, and if he makes a team, it will be either at Kingsport or at Brooklyn.

Harold "Eck" Eckert: "I had a full scholarship to Florida International. In my senior year, we were playing Florida Atlantic in a regional tournament. I had talked one day to [scout] Camilo Pascual of the Dodgers just once before the draft. Sometimes there were ten, fifteen, twenty scouts at the games. A lot of the scouts talked to me all the time.

"I thought maybe the Indians or the Mets would pick me. I knew the draft was coming, and I thought I had a shot. In the quarterfinals of the conference tournament, we were playing South Alabama. I was feeling great; I had a bad first inning and there were some errors, but after that we started scoring and I struck out twelve or thirteen in a row; I struck out sixteen guys. And we won. Then after that,

I felt some tightness, but not pain. Then later that week I couldn't throw in my midweek workout because I hurt. And I couldn't pitch without pain, right from the first warmup pitch right in my humor bone. It was in the inner elbow. No matter what type of pitch, it felt as if someone were stabbing me. That whole day I felt as if I was in some kind of a dream. I felt it was my job to get them into the winners' bracket. We've never won a regional before. I was only throwing around 82, 83 when normally I threw 88 to 92, 93. I just knew from the first pitch. I won that game. I pitched like four and two thirds innings. I went as far as I could go. I felt if I threw another one that I would pass out. I would tie my shoe after almost every batter just to get me some time to recover between pitches. I allowed, I think, one hit and one run, and I struck out nine guys. It took the

Harold Eckert — Brooklyn Cyclones pitcher.

most concentration I ever had in my life. It felt like I was on a bubble, on a cloud on the mound. I remember even praying, saying, 'Please let me throw another pitch.' Between innings, I took Tylenol to help the pain. There were tears in my eyes because of the pain, frustration, and the fear. Then I threw a fastball and it went seventy something miles an hour, so that was it. The coach came to take me out.

"I thought when I threw the last pitch that this pitch may be the last pitch I ever threw. We were winning like 4 to 1, and I remember sitting on the bench in the dugout and tears were coming down. You realize that baseball isn't the most important thing in life, but at that moment, it is. Your whole future isn't the most important thing in life, but at that moment, it is. Your whole future rides on how well you do and which team drafts you, and in what round.

"The next day I still hurt, and the doctor took me over to his hospital. At first, he tested it and it's supposed to move one millimeter only, but mine moved five point five millimeters. Then, the following day, he took me to the hospital; we were playing another game, and if we won this we would be going to the regional championship, and if we lost, my college career would be over. The only time he could get me in the hospital was during when the game was going on, and I was thinking this could be my last college game, and I'm not even there to hug any of my friends or to say thanks to the coach. I got my MRI at the hospital, and I called up the trainer, Jill, and I said, 'How are we doing?' She said, 'We're down 1-0, there's a guy on second base and two down.'

"The doctor came in and said there's a full tear on the ulna collateral ligament. And that was it.

"Then Jill said, 'So and so's at bat,' then I heard the ping of the bat, this is college, and Jill said there was a line drive caught. So my college career was over, and I was told about the injury — all in about a few seconds.

"One or two days later, the draft came, and the Dodgers drafted me. We had a meeting the next day, and I told the Dodger guy. I couldn't pretend I was all right when I wasn't. They said they had been planning to send me up to Vero Beach to pitch in the Florida State League, right away.

"I lost out on playing professional baseball, and I lost out on playing up a couple of levels in baseball, and I lost out on any money I was going to get for signing.

"I had the surgery on August 26, 1999, three months after all this happened.

"That was the fall semester of what would have been my fifth year in school. They took a tendon out of my left leg and put it in my elbow. They try to take it out of your left wrist first. But some people don't have that tendon or it's very small. I had it, but it was very small. The next spot is the plantaris longis, in your left leg, in your calf. They took that out, but it didn't fit. They didn't like it, so then they took a piece of my Achilles off. It's called an Achilles graft. They put a piece of your Achilles, which is like the strongest tendon in your body, and they put that in my elbow. This is called Tommy John surgery.

"That next spring, I rehabbed it. It takes a year to rehab it. I could have not signed with he Dodgers, and they would have owned me for the whole year, or I could have signed and let them release me, and then I'd be a free agent. The rules are that if you are a free agent, then they have to offer you a contract. So I chose to sign, and I'd see what they'd do. Once they draft you, they have to send you a contract. Now the ball was in their court. They brought me down to Vero Beach where I saw a doctor who verified what was wrong with my arm. And then they released me, and I became a free agent.

"At first, my arm was in a soft cast. It took a couple of months just to get my arm to straighten again. Getting a new tendon in your arm felt like there was a piece of plastic in there. And when the trainers who were helping me at college were bending my arm, it almost felt like the piece of plastic would break. I rehabbed it all fall, winter and spring.

"After a lot of rehab, I tried to make a comeback in June of 2000. They had pro tryouts at the school. Five days before the tryout I was hitting 90 on the gun, and the day of a bullpen tryout I didn't pitch well, and then my arm felt terrible, and I thought I blew it out again. Luckily, it was just a strain, and I had to start over again. So I had now missed another short season. So I came home in the fall of 2000.

"I came home to Edison [New Jersey] and dedicated myself to working out. That's all I did. I didn't work or anything.

"In fall of 2000, it's called scout day, around the middle of November, I flew down to Miami, and I worked out with Florida International's team, just like I was a member of the team. Then in two innings of a tryout I struck out six, with one hit. I was 86 to 90 or 91 on the gun.

"Only one scout came down to talk to me after that, and it was Joe Salermo of the Mets. He wanted my phone number, and he said he'd talk to his boss. That was around November 20; you only need one guy to give me a shot. They talked to me for a while, and then they called me at home in Jersey. Then they said I had to send in all my medical papers to this place. On December 17, 2000, they called me up and said they were going to give me a contract. I was at my best friend's house, Eddie Hebert's, when they called. I felt like something was lifted off me. I was crying. From May of '99 until December of 2000 was the hardest period of my life. Then I called my parents and I kept saying, 'I can't believe it!' I should have been in my third season, but at least I had a shot. My parents started crying when I told them.

"Then I had a reason to work out for the Florida spring training on March 3. I was hoping to make a full season squad, but then I didn't, and I had to stay for extended.

"I had a little tendonitis at first, but by the end of regular spring training I was getting better and pitching well. I was just hoping I wouldn't get cut."

Ross Peeples is slow. Too slow, say some. Oh, he's a bright young man; he's not slow there. And he can run all right, not real slow there, but nobody much cares about that since he's a pitcher. But the 6' 4", 196 pound lefthander is slow because he can only throw a baseball at 85 miles an hour. Go to the pitching tent that almost all minor league teams now have in their ballparks and buy three throws for a dollar and try your own arm. See the young 20-year-old studs try the same thing. Usually, nobody in the ballpark comes anywhere close to throwing a ball at 85 miles an hour. But in professional baseball, 85 miles an hour is slow, so Peeples relies on exquisite control. He was a 46th round pick by the Mets in 2000 and was 1–2 with a sparkling 2.61 earned run average at Kingsport in 2000. He's proved what he can do at Kingsport, so Brooklyn looks like his next chance to prove that radar guns don't always prove who's a winning pitcher.

Matt Peterson was a second round draft pick in 2000, but he signed too late to play during the 2000 season. Second round picks get high bonus money, and they get lots of attention. Only 19 years old, Peterson is a 6' 5" right-hander, thin at 185 pounds. He pitched at Rapides High School in Alexandria, Louisiana. Second round picks don't get cut, so it's a matter of where to start Peterson's career, Kingsport or Brooklyn.

David Byard, known as "Big Bird", is a big guy at 6' 3" and 235 pounds. A relief pitcher, he went 2–1 with a 4.05 ERA at Kingsport last season. A 35th round draft pick out of Mount Vernon Nazarene College, he's just turned 21. He's one of the few married Cyclones candidates. Funny off the mound, he's one of the most popular players in camp, but he's all business on the mound and has been pitching really well in "extended."

The Players from the Draft

Professional baseball is about to hold its annual draft. The draft, held in 56 rounds, is akin to the drafts held in basketball, football, and hockey.

Yet, each sport has its own draft procedures. In baseball, players are drafted from high schools and colleges in the United States and Canada. High school seniors are eligible, as are college juniors and seniors, and any junior college player.

There are many complicated rules and procedures, but without going into exceptions, the basic procedure is that major league baseball teams draft in each round in inverse order of their previous year's record. Any player who is drafted has his rights held by the club that drafted him for a year. If he doesn't sign until a period of week before the following year's draft, a player is free to be drafted by any team, or if not drafted, is a free agent able to sign with any club.

Jack Bowen is one of the New York assistant directors of amateur scouting. His grandfather was an assistant to Branch Rickey. Jack Bowen coordinates the scouting of Met prospects. He helps to supervise 29 members of the Mets scouting staff, including 3 regional supervisors, 18 area supervisors and 8 part-time scouts.

Jack Bowen: "I saw Cox pitch at Pan Am last year. I saw DiNardo. I saw Olson up in the Cape League. I saw Portobanco in high school. I saw Walker this year at Miami. I saw Bacani at Fullerton. I saw Jiannetti down at Daytona Beach Junior College, I've seen McIntyre, and I saw Corr, Lawton, Pagan and Kay."

"We have sixteen area scouts and they bring myself and Gary LaRocque [Mets' assistant general manager/amateur scouting] in to see their best prospects. So I can compare Michael Cox with Lenny DiNardo with another left-hander from Minnesota. A player is constantly being evaluated by the coaches, the scouts. Sometimes later, if a player doesn't work out, we look back and try to figure out why. It's not real scientific; we know we're going to be wrong. We try to just minimize the mistakes. Sometimes, if it doesn't work out, it's physical. Sometimes it's mental. The kid just doesn't put forth the effort.

"The character of the kids we draft is one of our priorities. If you're investing money in a kid, his off-field character is important. That's why after we've seen all these kids play in the spring in their high school or college seasons, we've got a big board in New York where we line 'em up by ability. When it comes time for the Mets' turn to select, we know this guy is number one, this guy number two, sometimes up to five hundred names on our draft board. That's how we select them. It's not much different from the NBA, or the NFL or the NHL as far as how you line 'em up on the board, and in our sport you have to take in the high school and the college guys. That's a little tough.

"Say you go down to Arkansas, and you see a shortstop facing a pitcher who's throwing maybe 75 miles an hour, tops, and then you've just seen David Bacani playing in California against top-flight college guys throwing in the 90s. It's difficult, but I've been doing this for 17 years now. You have to see a high school shortstop facing well below average pitching and compare him to a college shortstop who's facing pitchers with a major league average fastball. It is difficult; that's why we're wrong more than we're right.

"We're talking about drafting kids in the first and second rounds. That's where the big money is. Our area scout has known this kid since his sophomore or junior year in high school. He files a report with the New York Mets' Scouting Department that he really likes the player for a first or second round number. Then, we'll bring in the regional cross-checker and get his report, and we'll see whether it backs it up or whether it disagrees with it. After the regional cross-checker sees the kid, that's when myself, or Gary LaRocque, or Fred Wright, our other regional cross-checker, sees the kid. Then we'll give our opinion. Some kids, up in the high rounds of a draft, we might give seven or eight opinions on. And we may have multiple looks at that player. We want to get those first few round picks right. We want to make sure the money is spent right in the first few rounds of the draft. The guys down in the lower rounds of the draft we may have only one report on. So it varies. The higher the pick, the more opinions you're going to get."

Duke Snider has been a Hall of Fame player, a minor league manager and a major league broadcaster. Few fans may know that he was also a scout.

Duke Snider: "It's very difficult to scout because you have to take a player apart and say what he can't do. Some of the things he can do you take for granted. Like a lot of kids in high school will excel because physically they're better, and the other kids haven't developed as much yet. But you have to size up and see the parents; so you have to size up the parents because usually the kids are going to be built like the father or the mother. You have to size up the parents to see what this kid is going to look like when he's 25 or 30.

"If you're a good baseball scout you can see how they're going to develop. Branch Rickey was the greatest baseball man I ever met, and he called in Gil Hodges and me into his office one day, this was when we were both rookies on the Brooklyn Dodgers in 1947, and he said, 'In a couple of years, you two guys are going to become two of the top home run hitters in the National League.' We walked out of his office and we thought, 'I'm the sixth outfielder and Gil's the third string catcher — how does he know this?' And lo and behold, we became that."

The Brooklyn team will be made up mostly from players from three sources: One source consists of players who played in the New York–Penn league last year and who will play at this level again. They could be in extended spring training in Florida now, or playing at a full-season club now, most likely the step above Brooklyn at Capital City (Columbia, South Carolina). This source amounts to usually only a handful of players. The second source is players who played last season at short-season Kingsport and who will move up to Brooklyn, and who are now in extended training. This traditionally in the New York–Penn League will be about eight to twelve players. The next source is players from college, another ten to fourteen players. The total roster may not exceed thirty players.

Players who sign contracts with the Mets within a few days of the draft join the other farmhands already in extended spring training, where the drafted players have about a week to break in until the roster is picked. Players who don't sign right away go to Florida after the short-season teams have been picked, and stay in Florida about a week before the reassignments.

In the first round the Mets selected Aaron Heilman, a left-hander senior from Notre Dame. First round picks can command top money, often over a million dollars for a signing bonus. At 6' 5", Heilman is considered an advanced prospect with years of big-time college experience. If he signs, the Mets' hierarchy has decided to send him to a full-season club, probably High-A Port St. Lucie.

In what is known as a "sandwich pick" (a pick between the first and second round awarded for other teams signing major league free-agents), the Mets selected David Wright, a third baseman from Hickory High School, in Chesapeake, Virginia. If Wright signs quickly, he will probably be sent to Kingsport because he is just out of high school. In the second round, the Mets selected Alhaji Turay, an outfielder from Auburn (Washington) High School. If he signs, because he is out of high school, he too will probably be sent to Kingsport. A supplemental pick after the second round was William "Corey" Ragsdale, a 6' 4" shortstop, and noted basketball star from Jonesboro, Arkansas.

In the third round the Mets selected Lenny DiNardo, a 6' 4" lefty from Stetson University. DiNardo is hot stuff, having pitched for Team U.S.A. He can command a good bonus and may not sign immediately. If he signs, Brooklyn is his likely destination.

The fourth round selection was yet another lefty, Brian Walker, from Miami University. He is from the recent College World Series winner and can also command a substantial bonus. If and when he signs, Brooklyn is his likely destination.

The Mets' fifth round selection was Danny Garcia, from Pepperdine University. A converted center fielder now playing second base, Garcia can do all the things that baseball people love: he bunts, he can hit and run, he can steal, he hangs in at second on the double play and he takes out other infielders as he breaks up double plays. He is an advanced player and if he signs with the Mets, he may begin his career at Brooklyn. In the sixth round, the Mets picked Jason Weintraub, a right-handed high school pitcher from Tampa.

Another college selection in the draft for the Mets was Tyler Beuerlein, a catcher from Grand Canyon, full of muscles and a switch-hitter.

In the eighth round the Mets selected Brett Kay, another catcher and a relative of an NFL player. His father was a linebacker for the Los Angeles Rams. From Cal State Fullerton, Kay also played in the College World Series. He was the highest Met pick to ink a contract in time to attend extended training.

Brett Kay: "I was always a catcher in college. In high school, I was both a catcher and a center fielder. When I was growing up I was always one of the key players and in high school I got a lot of accolades, that kind of stuff. I always felt I was good. When I was a little kid, other kids were jealous and didn't like me too much because I was good. In college, we had a bunch of superstars, but I always thought I was as good as they were. I never told everybody I was good; it was just the sort of thing that happened.

"Growing up, in addition to baseball, I played basketball and football in high school. I was a point guard in basketball and in football I was a tight end/ wide receiver/linebacker.

"I first heard [about being drafted] as we were on our way to play the Cardinal for Cal State Fullerton ... and I heard I was a draft pick by the New York Mets and I was actually surprised because I had a thumb injury that was healing. I was out 17 games, so I was really ecstatic and happy. I really hadn't heard that much from the Mets ... I was excited when I signed my contract. I had thought money was going to be an issue, but money's money. I know I made the right decision to sign. The area scout, Fred Mazuca, came over to my house with the contract. I was real happy, and I celebrated quietly with my girlfriend and my family."

Jay Caligiuri signed as a 13th round pick. The second cousin of Paul Caligiuri, a soccer player who had played on the United States National Team, Jay Caligiuri played third base at Cal State–Domingas Hills. Caligiuri is listed as 6' 0" and 190 pounds, not big for a third baseman, who in baseball as a corner infielder (first or third base) is supposed to provide power numbers. But Caligiuri showed power at Cal State–Domingas Hills.

Jay Caligiuri's mother talks about Jay's first baseball coach — herself.

Barbara Caligiuri: "We lived in Valencia, California. He was a little guy, about 5 years old. He played on the Phillies, and it was a little T-ball team. A friend of mine had this little boy, same age, and he loved baseball just like Jay, and she asked me, 'You want to coach?' And I said, 'Sure, let's do it.' So Jay's very first baseball team, little T-ball team, I coached first and the other gal coached third. Some of the dads on the team weren't too sure about us, and they were concerned. 'How can two moms coach a team?' Well, Jay's team ended up being the undefeated team of the league. So that was kind of cool to be his first coach."

Jay's dad, Lynn Caligiuri, tells about the family's baseball background.

Lynn Caligiuri: "Oh yeah, our whole family. I grew up with baseball. My dad's a big baseball fan. Actually, he was a big Brooklyn fan at the time, grew up in Wisconsin, then went on the Navy and ended up in the Los Angeles area. I grew up playing baseball. Played all the way through Little League, played college ball, the University of San Diego, tried out for the Kansas City Royals, didn't make it."

Barbara Caligiuri relates her son's best day in college baseball.

Barbara Caligiuri: "The stadium [at Point Loma, California] kind of overlooked water, like this stadium [KeySpan] does. The wind was really not a factor at the time when he was hitting. He got up the first time and took a good swing and out it went. It was kind of like, well okay, you know, no big deal, it went out. Well then, we're sitting there, we're all chatting, and he gets up again, swings, out it goes. Okay, okay, okay. Everybody was really kind of cool and calm. Lynn and I were sitting there. We try not to get too excited because it can go ... he can strike out the next time you're up, right? We're looking at our friends over in the stadium, and they're just going nuts. So then he gets up again, and the third one goes out. Then the next one, he gets up and the fourth one goes out, and everybody is just going nuts. We're just sitting there all looking at each other going, 'We don't believe this.' We just put our heads in our hands and go, 'Unbelievable.' It was a moment in time that it kind of sits still and ... it's something we'll remember and he'll remember too."

Lynn Caligiuri: "Right after he hit four, a couple of weeks later at Cal State Domingas Hills ... three in a row, three at bats in a row and then his fourth at bat, he got beaned. They weren't going to allow him to do it twice in a row in the same season."

Jay Caligiuri's father tells about the day Jay was drafted.

Lynn Caligiuri: "Well, about 10:00 I was in my office working and trying to get the draft actually, on the radio on the Internet. He came in and said, 'Well, see you later.' I said, 'Where are you going?' He said, 'I can't sit around and I'm going to Magic Mountain.' So he did. He went to Magic Mountain with his buddies. About noon, we got a call, from a different team actually, who said, 'We're getting close to tenth round, we're thinking about taking Jay. Will he sign?' I said, 'I'm sure he will.' So our other son was home; we had to go pick up a car that was at the repair shop, and then we came back. There was a message from one of his friends saying, 'Gee, Jay, bet you're out getting a New York hat right now, congratulations.' So then I looked it up right away. The New York Mets had picked Jay on the thirteenth round, and it was real exciting. We were going to make him wait. Well, in this age of cell phones and pagers, I'm sure somebody was going to get hold of him before we did. So I called him and said, 'Hey, I got a couple of phone calls.' So then I told him. He was real excited."

Jay Caligiuri: "Actually, I was at Magic Mountain in California. I couldn't be home. It was too nerve wracking. I went out with my friends, had a good time. When it happened, my dad called me on my cell phone in Magic Mountain and it was pretty exciting. I had a good time for the rest of the day there. Then I came home and had a big party at my house with my family and friends.

"Growing up, I was always on All-Star teams, right from my first year in Little League, but a lot of guys on my Little League All-Star teams weren't as good later as they were when they were younger. In my sophomore year in high school, I sort of took off, and I started playing with older guys. I was always All-League or All-County.

"Then I started playing in 'scout leagues' in Southern California. We played with wooden bats. I was getting experience playing in front of pro scouts and college coaches and getting them to tell me, 'You're good.' At that point, I started playing against guys two and three years older than I was, and I was holding my own with them, if not playing better than they were. I started realizing that I had the talent to take me a lot of places, and it's taken me to my education and it's taken me to professional baseball."

Jay Caligiuri — Brooklyn Cyclones infielder.

Frank Corr doesn't look like an outfielder. He looks like a catcher, which he was earlier in his baseball career, when he was in his first year of college, and before that, in high school. He's 5' 9", very strong, but stocky. Most outfielders, if they're much less than six feet, are the base-stealing kind, the ones who slap the ball, bunt, steal bases, and are often leadoff men. Frank Corr isn't a candidate for leadoff. He's not super fast. He's a power hitter whose height in the 1950s would be considered slightly short. But baseball heights have advanced by about two inches in 50 years. So Frank Corr in 2001 terms is considered very short, and he didn't fit the mold. He has an energetic personality, a friendly smile and light brown hair. He has expressive wide eyes and seems to do everything with gusto. He loves playing ball and goes all out.

Frank Corr: "Throughout my career, everybody always said, 'He's too short.' Out of high school, everyone said, 'You're not the prototype size for a major league baseball player, so you won't be drafted.' And I was drafted in the ninth round out of high school. Then in college, I had real good stats and everybody said again, 'You're not the prototype size of a major league player, you won't be drafted,' and I was drafted in the seventeenth round. I just go out there and give a hundred and ten percent every day, man, and whether I'm leading the league in home runs or leading in strikeouts, as long as I can look in the mirror and say, 'I gave it my all today,' then that's all I care about.

"Joe DellaCarri [a Met scout] said to me, 'I don't care how tall you are. I've seen you play. I know you can play. All you gotta do is prove it to everybody else.'

"My dad is a real strong guy. I get a lot of genetics from my dad. My dad is short and stocky. Strong. And I look exactly like my dad; I'm the spitting image."

Frank Corr tells about the draft call.

Frank Corr: "I was at my house in Daytona, Florida, with my folks and a couple of family members. I got the call maybe about eight-thirty or nine at night, and I was ecstatic, to tell the truth. As a senior in college, it's not about the round. It's all about if you want to play the game of baseball, and if you love it enough. All I really wanted was to play.... They asked me when I wanted to leave and I said, 'As soon as possible.'"

Jack Bowen: "Our area scout went to see Lenny DiNardo, a high profile teammate of his, pitch, and Frank Corr was playing left field. Frank was what we call a 'gut feel' guy of the area scout. That means that the scout has a gut feeling about this player and that's what Joe DelliCarri had about Frank Corr. DelliCarri signed Zaragoza, he signed DiNardo, he signed Corr, and he signed McIntyre. Joe knew we were there to see Lenny pitch, but he always told us, keep an eye on the left fielder, Corr. He said, 'You're not going to get a good first impression because he's stocky and doesn't have the build you look for, but the big kid does something every time I go see him.' I saw him and he had a so-so game for me, and then Gary LaRocque [New York Met assistant general manager/amateur scouting] saw him, and he kind of had the same feeling that Joe did. So you can see, you get three or four opinions even on a guy like Frank Corr, who wasn't a high profile guy. He was a later round pick, a college senior who just wanted a chance to play. Every organization wants those good character guys that show ability with the bat, or speed or something that lets us give them a chance to get into pro ball. A lot of it is the kind of day they have when we're there to see them. If they have a good day, then we're going to like 'em. If they have an off day, our opinion's going to be less of them. A lot of it's luck. When Joe DelliCarri sends me to Florida to see a particular guy, if he has an off day that's all I can go on 'cause I don't know the guy as well as Joe, who's seen the guy play maybe 25 times. So a lot of it is luck in being in the right place at the right time — as far as being the right guy who's there on the day the player does business for you. Our chance of success is better than if he has an off day when the Yankees are there. Their opinion is going to be different than ours because they saw him on an off day, and we saw him on one of his better days.

Guy Conti: "Joe DelliCarri drafted Joe Jiannetti out of high school in St. Petersburg. And Joe Jiannetti was what we call a draft-and-follow. That's a kid that you draft late. Your intentions aren't to sign him. Your intentions are to let him go to a junior college, play a lot of games, scout him under our control — if you draft out of high school and he goes to a junior college, he's under control of the Mets up until about a week before the draft. At that time we can negotiate with him, his contract is our property — and we can come to an agreement as we did with Joe this year. Joe DelliCarri drafted him in the 45th or 46th round out of high school. He played at Daytona Beach Community College. We all went in to see him play at Daytona this year, and we liked him and we came to an agreement with him before the draft. We did some research with a doctor who does some research with diabetes and other conditions that are so prevalent today, and he said with the advances of medicine today it can be controlled-don't worry about it. You know about it, you do the research, and you go with what your medical people tell you. Scouts are selling their players to us. They like these kids."

Other draftees that signed with the Mets included: Blake McGinley, a 6' 1" lefty out of Texas Tech by way of California, in the 21st round, a stylish thrower who seems to throw without effort; and David Bacani, a 5' 8" second baseman from Brett Kay's school at Cal State Fullerton, of Philippine ancestry, an aggressive, but small, table-setter.

Also signing was John Toner who's 6' 3" and looks like L'il Abner, or like Joe Hardy, the baseball player from the musical *Damn Yankees*. He looks like his muscles have muscles. He's an outfielder from Western Michigan University.

Joe Jiannetti, the new 19-year-old third base candidate out of Daytona Beach Community College, explains: "Two days before we left camp to go to Kingsport or Brooklyn, they asked us if we were going to drive or fly. I told 'em, 'If I'm going to Kingsport, I'm going to drive; if I'm going to Brooklyn, I'm going to fly. Soon as I find out, I'll let you guys know.' The list was going to be put up after the last regular practice. Then the next day we'd have an early practice and then leave. They would put the names on a bulletin board. If your name is on the Brooklyn list, then you're going to Brooklyn; if you name is on the Kingsport list, then you're going to Kingsport; if your name isn't on either list, then you're released.

"There was one kid that I met the two weeks that I was here; he thought he was going to Brooklyn, and his name wasn't on the list, and he was really upset. Just one or two guys were released. Some guys were nervous about where they were going, but they kind of kept it in, you could tell. Nobody wants to run around saying, 'I hope I go here, I hope I go there.' You just want to go out there and do your best.

"Everyone wanted to go to Brooklyn. Some guys knew when I met them, they were already told, they said, 'I'm going to Brooklyn,' or 'I'm going to Kingsport.' But some guys were fighting for jobs."

Who Made the Team?

It's June 14. The seasons for the Mets' full season teams have been going on since early April. The Brooklyn season begins with the season opener on June 19 at Jamestown, New York. Rosters have to be formulated. The Brooklyn team may carry 30 players on its roster, not including any players on injury rehabilitation. Twenty-five may dress in uniform for each game. Brooklyn doesn't want to carry the full 30 right away because it needs to leave room for some just-drafted players who may sign contracts in the next few weeks. The Mets don't want to bounce players around too much; it could hurt their confidence to start the season with Brooklyn and be sent down to Kingsport in a few weeks to make room for a new draftee, so Brooklyn will probably go with about 25 players to start the season.

The list is posted in the clubhouse. On the first Brooklyn roster in 44 years are the following:

Pitchers (11)	Pos.	Age	B — T	Yrs.	Hometown	School	2000 Club
Bowen, Chad	RHP	19	R — R	1	Hendersonville, TN	Gallatin H.S	Kingsport
Byard, David	RHP	23	R — R	1	Mt. Vernon, OH	Mt. Vernon Nazerene	Kingsport
Cabrera, Yunir	LHP	20	L — L	1	San Pedro de Macoris, Dominican Republic	S.P. de Macoris	Kingsport
Gahan, Matthew	RHP	25	R — R	0	Agonewaban, NSW, Australia	S. Cross Univ., NSW	—
Herbison, Brett	RHP	24	R — R	5	Elgin, Ill	Burlington Cent. H.S.	Injured
McGinley, Blake	LHP	22	L — L	0	Bakersfield, CA	Texas Tech	
Ough, Wayne	RHP	22	R — R	1	Vinceni Township, Australia	Trinidad St. JC	Kingsport
Peeples, Ross	LHP	21	L — L	1	Cordele, GA	Middle Georgia Coll.	Kingsport
Peterson, Matt	RHP	19	R — R	0	Alexandria, LA	Rapides H.S	
Portobanco, Luz	RHP	21	R — R	1	Granada, Nicaragua	Miami Dade CC	
Sherman, Chris	RHP	21	R — R	0	Apios, CA	San Jose State	

Catchers	Pos.	Age	B — T	Yrs.	Hometown	School	2000 Club
Jacobs, Mike	C	20	L — R	1	Chula Vista, CA	Grossmont JC	Cap/Kings.
Sosa, Fransisco	C	20	R — R	1	Esperanza, PR		Kingsport

Infielders	*Pos.*	*Age*	*B — T*	*Yrs.*	*Hometown*	*School*	*2000*
Abreu, David	2B	21	S — R	2	San Perdo de Macoris, DR		
						Gaston P. Deligne	Cap. City
Arias, Leandro	2B	20	R — R	1	Santo Domingo, DR	Melida Giral	Injured
Coyne, Anthony	INF.	22	R — R	1	Huntington, MD	Yale University	Kings./Pitts
McIntyre, Robt.	SS	20	R — R	1	Tampa Fl	Hillsborough H.S.	Kings./Pitts
Rodriguez, Edgar	3B	21	R — R	0	San Perdo de Macoris, DR		
Zaragoza, Joel	INF.	22	R — R	1	Bayamon, PR	Bethune-Cookman	Pittsfield
Todd, Jeremy	1B	23	L — R	1	Maylene, AL	Southwestern, IL	Pittsfield

Outfielders	*Pos.*	*Age*	*B — T*	*Yrs.*	*Hometown*	*School*	*2000*
Corr, Francis	OF	22	R — R	0	Daytona Beach, FL	Stetson Univ.	
Devarez, Noel	RF	19	R — R	2	S.P. de Macoris, DR		Kingsport
Lawson, Forrest	OF	20	R — R	1	Puyallup, WA	Rogers H. S.	Kingsport
Piercy, Michael	OF	25	L — L	2	Hillside, NJ		
Toner, John	OF	21	R — R	0	St. Joseph, MI	Western Michigan	

Field Staff	*Pos.*
Alfonzo, Edgar	Mgr.
Johnson, How.	Coach
Ojeda, Bobby	Coach
Montague, Eric	Trainer

How does this roster compare with the players who played on the 1957 Brooklyn Dodgers, the last previous Brooklyn professional team?

For one thing, the Brooklyn Cyclones are taller. Of the 17 players who pitched for the Dodgers that year, five were under 6' 0". On the Cyclones, no pitcher on the opening roster was under six foot.

Of the '57 Dodgers position players that year, 10 of 18 were under six feet tall. Roy Campanella was 5' 9", Sandy Amoros was 5' 7", Pee Wee Reese was 5' 10", Junior Gilliam was 5' 10", John Roseboro 5' 11", and Joe Pignatano 5' 10". The tallest regulars were Duke Snider at 6' 0", and Carl Furillo at 6' 0", and Gil Hodges, considered a very tall man in his day, at 6' 2".

Only six of the Cyclones 17 opening day position players were under six feet, with all of the under six footers at 5' 10" or 5' 11", except for Frank Corr at 5' 9". Outfielders John Toner and Forrest Lawson are both 6' 3", three inches taller than any regular outfielder on the 1957 Dodgers.

The Cyclones aren't considered exceptionally tall by modern standards. Their arch rivals, the Staten Island Yankees, feature sluggers like 6' 5" Shelley Duncan, 6' 3" Jason Turner, and 6' 3" Aaron Rifkin. How do they compare height-wise to 1957 Yankees like 5' 10" Mickey Mantle, 5' 8" Yogi Berra and Moose Skowron, at only 5' 11"? The modern Brooklyn player as a minor leaguer is on average taller than his major league counterpart of the 1947–57 Dodgers.

The Cyclones are also more racially diverse than the 1957 Dodgers, who were in the vanguard of racial opportunity. Five members of the '57 Dodger roster were African American; out of 36 who played that year. On the Cyclones, nine out of 25 on the opening day roster were black or Hispanic.

The Cyclones continue the modern trend of geographical diversity, as nine of the Cyclones were born in foreign countries, plus one from non–U.S. mainland Puerto Rico. The Cyclones had six players from the Dominican Republic, two born in Australia, one from Nicaragua, and one from Puerto Rico. The '57 Dodgers had two players born outside mainland U.S., in Sandy Amoros, from Cuba, and Elmer Valo, born in Czechoslovakia.

Another modern trend exhibited on the Cyclones was the number of players from the West or South. The 1957 Dodgers had Campanella and Furillo from Pennsylvania, Joe Pignatano and Sandy Koufax from Brooklyn, Don Newcombe from New Jersey and Johnny Podres from New York State.

Now players are more often from California and Florida. The opening roster of the Cyclones had two players from Florida — Corr and McIntyre — and four from California: pitchers McGinley and Chris Sherman, catcher Jacobs, and infielder Caligiuri. The third and fourth round draftees were from Florida — left-handed pitchers Lenny DiNardo and Brian Walker — the draft-and-follow, Joe Jiannetti, was from Florida, and the 22nd pick, David Bacani was from California, as was its eighth pick, catcher Brett Kay. The only players from truly northern areas on the opening roster were Michael Piercy from New Jersey, and the rehabbing Brett Herbison, from Illinois.

On the 1957 Dodgers, the only significant player who spoke Spanish was Amoros. On the Cyclones, Sosa, Arias, Abreu, Devarez, Rodriguez, and Cabrera were Spanish speaking, Zaragoza and Portobanco were bilingual.

Many Cyclones had attended college. Nine Cyclones on the opening day roster had completed at least three years of college, and other college educated draft picks were negotiating contracts. Most of the Brooklyn Dodgers of the 1950s did not attend college, with Ralph Branca, Clyde King, Jackie Robinson, Sandy Koufax, and Gil Hodges being a few of the exceptions.

Most of the Brooklyn Dodgers of the golden era were married — men such as Reese, Robinson, Campanella, Snider, Furillo, Erskine, Hodges, and Branca. The Cyclones were mostly single, with David Byard as a married father being one of the exceptions.

The Cyclones were younger, with their opening day roster averaging a shade over 21 years of age, and the Dodger rosters of the post–World War II period averaging about 30 years of age.

The Brooklyn Cyclone roster exhibited trends typical of the changes in baseball in the past 50 years. Their roster had a higher percentage of players from outside the U.S., they were taller, had more college, and tended to come, if from the United States at all, more from areas outside the Northeast, particularly Florida and California. The modern Cyclone players spoke more Spanish, were mainly single and were typically the age of a college junior or senior.

Who made it, and who didn't? Let's start with the catchers. Mike Jacobs, the stately catcher who has at 20 already played for Columbia, made it, as did Francisco Sosa, the good-hitting catcher overcoming a sore arm.

One who didn't make it was Justin Huber, who in his first professional season has high promise but no United States professional experience. He was sent to Kingsport, where he could be a regular catcher.

In the infield, it's Todd at first base, back for his second year in the league. At second base are Abreu, in his fifth minor league season, and Arias, coming back after sitting out last season with an injury. For shortstop, it's McIntyre, smooth fielding and quick, and Anthony Coyne, athletic and from Yale; at third base is Joel Zaragoza, also back in the league after playing last season at Pittsfield, Jay Caligiuri, from Division II California State, Domingas Hills and Edgar Rodriguez, from the Dominican Republic.

Also not making Brooklyn was Joe Jiannetti. Joe is only 19 and a year out of high school, playing last year at Daytona Beach Community College. With Caligiuri and Rodriguez at third base, the thinking on Jiannetti seems to be to let him get his feet wet at lower level Kingsport.

In the outfield, Brooklyn kept the minor league veteran Piercy and two members of last year's Kingsport team: power-hitting Devarez and all-around talented Forrest Lawson. Brooklyn also took power-hitting draftee Frank Corr.

Not making the Brooklyn team was the extremely fast Wayne Lydon, who was sent back to Kingsport. Lydon would be learning to switch-hit so that he could take better advantage of his electric speed by batting left-handed against right-handed pitching. Lydon felt hurt that he was not promoted with the other outfielders from last year's Kingsport team. The Mets' thinking was to let him learn to switch-hit at a lower classification than Brooklyn. Lydon took the decision respectfully and professionally, but he took it hard, feeling like a kid that's been left back when the rest of the class was promoted.

Guy Conti: "The team that went to Brooklyn was selected in several ways. Number one, after the June draft, we bring the players that signed from that draft down to a mini-camp in St. Lucie, and we work them out and we try to place them according to age and skill level. We want the first-year players to have a chance for some success. Then there were also kids in extended spring training, kids who didn't make a full season club coming out of spring training, and they stayed in St. Lucie for about a month or two months, so that the June draft kids joined the extended spring training kids, and we assembled a team and sent it up to Brooklyn."

Harold Eckert: "Nobody knew who was going where, but I generally was working out with Brooklyn, and they called me in and I thought they were going to tell me I would start the season in St. Lucie because of my age and the fact that I had recently been pitching well. Yator [Lyle Yates, the Kingsport pitching coach] had a smile on his face. They said. "You're going to Tennessee, and they'll make you into a starter. They said we'll try to get you up here to St. Lucie.""

Guy Conti: "Harold Eckert had not pitched because of an arm injury. We got him in extended spring training, and he was throwing very well, and this was his first chance in some time throwing in competitive situations. We had him in

Kingsport to start him out at a lower level because we wanted to make sure he was healthy. That was the main thing. We fit him in where we feel he can compete and not be overmatched, but we had to check on his health first.

"Luz Portobanco was selected for Brooklyn basically because of age. He's a talented kid, but he's a young kid, so we took him to extended, let him work with Ojeda, and we took him to Brooklyn."

"We wanted Ross Peeples to work with Ojeda and we wanted him to be a starting pitcher. "We already had kids playing at the full-season level. There are people in places already, so we don't want to move them unnecessarily. Brett Kay came from a high level college program, so he's ready for short season A ball, as was Caligiuri, who also came from a top-level college program.

"Kingsport is basically made up of high school players and signees from Latin America. Brooklyn is basically made up from players in extended and college players from the June draft. You'll have special kids like Heilman, who are high draft picks and go to a higher level right away.

"Jiannetti is a tough kid. When we signed Jiannetti, we sent him to Kingsport because we hadn't seen enough of him. As soon as he got to Kingsport, he overmatched the pitchers. There was no sense in leaving him there. We had to move him to where he's challenged. We found out he can really hit.

"Frank Corr was similar to Caligiuri and Kay. Paul LoDuca [now a Los Angeles Dodger star who is about the same size as Corr] caught, played first, third, and the outfield when he first came up to the majors. Corr is about the same size as LoDuca, and Corr might do some catching, too.

"To select the Brooklyn squad, a high school draft kid is going to go to the lower level, Kingsport. An older June draft kid will get a chance at a higher level, like Brooklyn. At the meetings to select players will be the farm director, the roving instructors, and myself. We meet every day to select players, and we list them tentatively every day.

"Wayne Lydon was sent to Kingsport to learn to bat left-handed. This was his first year switch-hitting. He was demoralized by being in Kingsport because all the other extended guys got sent to Brooklyn. He felt he was left behind.

"Walker and DiNardo came into the season with tired arms after pitching a long college season."

They were then sent to Brooklyn.

Between Innings

Warner Fusselle, noted announcer, is the lead radio voice of the Brooklyn Cyclones. In 1970, he began announcing baseball games for the minor league Spartanburg Phillies. He has worked as the voice of the national television shows *This Week in Baseball* and *Major League Baseball* and has done *Major League Baseball Magazine,* as well as other television work. He has also been innovative in creating many baseball record albums and CDs.

Warner Fusselle: "I grew up in Georgia. I was born in Louisville, Kentucky, but I never lived there. I grew up, basically in Georgia; most of my childhood was in Gainesville, Georgia, a small town in the mountains about 50 miles outside of Atlanta.

"While we lived for a while in Virginia, in first grade, a boy about two years older lived across the street, and he taught me how to read the box scores and read the standings, and I've been interested in sports ever since. I played baseball and basketball. At a young age, you wanted to play in sports, but if I couldn't, I wanted to be something like a general manager.

"I played center field, first base and pitched in high school baseball at Gainesville High School and also played basketball there. The baseball team was undefeated my senior season until the playoffs. So after I completed college at Wake Forest University, I went to a broadcasting school in California, and that's how all this started.

"After I finished broadcasting school, I wrote letters to a hundred small radio stations and included a postcard where they could reply, and it was one of my first rude awakenings to the real world when only about thirty radio stations requested tapes. One station in South Carolina wanted somebody to do news, and if things worked out I could sometime do sports. Marty Breneman, who wound up doing the Cincinnati Reds' games, was there as well as others who wound up doing major league games. Then I went to Spartanburg, South Carolina, and replaced John Gordon, who was called to Baltimore to do the Orioles, so if I were willing to go there and replace him and do basketball games, who knows, something might work out for the baseball minor leagues.

"The night before I was to break in at Spartanburg, I had never done a game before, so I went to Atlanta and did a basketball game for practice, speaking into my fist — it's called hand miking. You've got to speak the words out loud, otherwise it's no good. You just can't think the words because you can think a lot faster than you can speak and that kind of practice won't help you. John Gordon told me about that, and it helped me at basketball. So I applied for the baseball job, and the Spartanburg Phillies had a new general manager, and he was a big shot, so he said, 'Look, I want you to do this, but you have to give me something on tape.' So I said, 'I don't have anything.' So he said, 'Tomorrow, Clemson is opening its baseball season against Louisville. Just go down there to Clemson and do two or three innings on a tape recorder so I can see that you have a clue as to what's going on. It doesn't have to be great. Just do something, so I know you can do it.'

"So I got my little tape recorder, and the press box was right next to the dugout, and I was embarrassed because there were people coming in and out, so I did a little hand miking, and I said I'll wait until the last few innings to record some play by play. And it got to the last two or three innings and the same thing happened. People were there and I felt like I couldn't do it, so I got my little recorder, and I went down to the right field line and stood down there where there's nobody there, and as soon as I got there all these cross country runners who were around came over and stood right there to watch the game, and so I couldn't do it. So I thought, 'I blew it. My career is over before it even has started. My life is shot. It's my own fault.'

"I went to the general manager, Red Berry, and I said, 'I couldn't do it. I was self-conscious. There were people everywhere. I couldn't do it and I'm sorry.' He said, 'I just need to see that you can do it. Go out to Spartanburg High School tomorrow, and if your tape is okay, you have the job.'

"So the next day, I go out to Spartanburg High School, and the same thing happened. I'm sitting in the stands and I can't do it. So I went out behind the center field fence, and the same thing happened. Some cross-country runners came by and stood right by me, but they left. I did one or two decent innings and I got the job.

"In my first professional game, I was nervous about doing the announcing and keeping a scorebook at the same time, and I was hoping for an easy game to score, like a 1–0 game — and the Spartanburg Phillies beat the Gastonia Pirates that day by a score of 16–2. And Dave Wallace was the pitcher for Spartanburg, who later became the general manager for the Los Angeles Dodgers. So on my first road trip, we lost a game and the manager *knew* I was there and waiting to catch the bus. I had to phone the newspaper and do my post game show, and they *left me there*. And I had all my equipment, and the umpires were driving home, and they stopped, and gave me a ride home to Spartanburg that night.

"I was there in Spartanburg from 1970 through 1974. It was a six-team league. The longest trip for a couple of years was fifty miles, so there were no overnight trips.

"Clint Courtney was the manager of the Greenwood Braves while I was with Spartanburg, and Greenwood would win practically every game. Plus, the rumor was that he would water the field all night to get a rainout and save his pitching. Even on a sunny day, he would get a rainout if he needed it.

"The reason I was interested in this Brooklyn job was because it was baseball, of course, and it's Brooklyn. I've not applied for any other minor league jobs because I've done television and all these major league baseball things. But I read all the books about Red Barber and how he came from Mississippi and Florida, and I thought, 'What must that have been like to be doing major league baseball in Brooklyn, New York when you're from the South?' Then I became friends with Ernie Harwell, and he's from Georgia, as I am, and his first major league job was with the Brooklyn Dodgers. So the Dodgers sent a back-up catcher to the Atlanta Crackers for Ernie Harwell, who later went over to the Giants and did the television of the famous 'shot heard round the world.'

"When I started out, I wrote Red Barber a letter. Then, after my job ended in Richmond [later in his career, Fusselle announced games for the Triple-A Richmond Braves], I wrote Red Barber for advice. He said, 'Keep in mind that life is a marathon, not a sprint, and that the one thing to keep in mind when applying for a job is if the guy doing the hiring likes you.' Which is basically true. Before he died, I did a story on Red in Tuscaloosa, and he got to like me and gave me extra time, and I heard his stories and all. When I heard about baseball coming back to Brooklyn, I always thought what it would be like to broadcast baseball in Brooklyn. And even though this is a different team, and a different era, I would still like to do this. It could be a great experience. So I thought, how do I go about doing this? I called the Mets and the fellow I spoke to knew who I was, and he said, 'You would do that?' And I said, 'Sure.' And I said the same thing to R.C. Reuteman, [Brooklyn Cyclone vice president] and he said, 'You'd be willing to do this?' and he knew who I was. So it worked out, and I got the job.

"R.C. said there's a small radio station at Kingsborough Community College and there's also this simulcast thing, where the games would be on television with just the audio, like listening to radio on television. In addition, Ed Randall would be doing some games on television. Many of the Brooklyn TV sets would be able to pick up the games. After all this, a guy from Madison Square Garden called, and they sent someone to help announce the games, and it turned out to be Reggie Armstrong, and it worked out fine. I guess my résumé got me the job because they all knew I'd done *This Week in Baseball*, and *Major League Baseball Magazine* and been the voice of *Major League Baseball* and all that, and they seemed to be pleased that I was doing their games. But the Brooklyn thing, and being from the South, and reading about, and knowing Ernie Harwell and Red Barber ... when I saw the ballpark, I said, 'This is incredible.'

"I went out to see the park in March or April, and then I thought this will really be the place to be in June and July. I thought it would be great, and it was. I think it was cooler to be at Brooklyn than at any major league place because the city had gone so long without baseball."

Bobby Ojeda Becomes a Pitching Coach

Bobby Ojeda won 115 games in the Major Leagues, pitching mostly for the Boston Red Sox, the New York Mets, and the Los Angeles Dodgers. He is resuming his baseball career as the pitching coach with the Brooklyn Cyclones, rejoining former Met teammate Howard Johnson, the Cyclones' batting coach. Ojeda and Johnson were part of the Mets' 1986 World Series Champions. Ojeda was 18–5 that year as the Mets' mound ace.

Bobby Ojeda: "I was interested in getting back. I first had the thought in December, and then I talked to my good buddy, Jay Horwitz [the Mets' director of media relations], and the Mets were just then putting the staff together at Brooklyn, and I went in and talked, and it just came down to, 'Do I want to do it?' I had been out of baseball for seven years. I love baseball, and that's what I know. I wanted to get back, and I said to myself, 'Let's see what happens. If I don't like it, then it's only a six months' commitment.'

"I live in New Jersey, and it's only a ride of a little over an hour to the ball park, depending on traffic. I would be going off to Florida for three and a half months, but then I would be coming home. It wasn't as if I was going off to Iowa or something like that. Then I would be back home, and that was nice because then I could be at home and still be back in baseball.

"Twenty-three years ago I pitched in the New York–Penn League for Elmira, in the Red Sox system. I have some good examples to give the kids on my pitching staff here in Brooklyn because when I was in this league I did awful, but I worked hard, and I turned things around.

"The one thing I try to instill in my guys is confidence and belief in themselves. I think that's the most important thing. Their abilities have gotten them to this point, and after that it's their belief, confidence, hard work and desire to get there that's going to take them all the way. I don't really remember anyone else from that league who later made the majors because I was just so scared the whole time and I was just trying to stick around, and I didn't really notice.

"Hojo [Howard Johnson, the Cyclones' batting coach in 2001] and I go back to 1979 in the Florida State League. He was with the Detroit Tigers' farm team, the Lakeland Tigers, and I was with the Boston Red Sox team, the Winter Haven Red Sox. We go way, way back. We just enjoy being at the ball park, and we have fun.

"I feel fortunate, and Hojo feels fortunate, that the careers we had made us satisfied with what we've accomplished. There's no feeling like, 'Gee, I might have, I could have, I should have.' So we had fun while we played, and we're having the same amount of fun now that we're coaching and passing on our knowledge to these guys. So far it's been a wonderful experience. And having Hojo here gives me the comfort level of having a teammate.

"I actually have a picture of myself and Hojo in my office at home, him sitting on my lap in my locker after we won the big one [the 1986 World Series with the Mets]. It's a tremendous picture, and we just have this look on our faces, not so much the elation craziness, but the champagne was flowing, and the cigars were lit, and it was a just a little reflection with all the chaos around us.

"I found out I was traded to the Mets when I was playing golf back home in California, and I guy came driving up to me on a golf cart, all out of breath, and he said to me, 'Bobby, you've just been traded to the Mets. I said, 'All right,' and I just continued to play golf. Little did I know that basically Met history was just born for me at that point.

"When Hojo and I were on that '86 team, we just had an attitude that we were taking no prisoners. I mean you're talking about a year where everything just comes together. We were just adamant about winning. We went out with the sole purpose to beat that other team. Nothing else mattered. That was our goal and that's what we were all about, and that's what we did.

"I'm proud of these guys on our Brooklyn pitching staff. In extended in Florida, they had a 3 to 1 strikeout/walk ratio. That's excellent. I don't want them thinking of pitching to corners. These guys have responded. When they get out there, it's not about me; it's about their concentration. The reason you win 2–1 ball games is because you don't give up seven or eight walks. If you give up eight hits — try walking seven with that and see what happens. These kids have it in their brains that 'you have to hit me to beat me,' and that's just what I like."

INNING 3

Brooklyn

Brooklyn Baseball History

Baseball and Brooklyn. As a pairing, this is nothing new. In fact, the linkage of baseball and Brooklyn goes back to the very beginnings of baseball itself. Baseball and the Dodgers was a glorious combination, but the roots for the love affair with the Dodgers go back to before there was such thing as professional baseball and before Brooklyn was a borough. The roots go back to when Brooklyn was a city, and the Civil War was in the future.

Brooklyn didn't just adopt baseball; it helped to create it. For example, the first pitcher to throw a fastball was from Brooklyn. The first pitcher to throw a curve was from Brooklyn. The first game that charged admission was held in Brooklyn. The first baseball box score was created by a Brooklyn newspaperman and printed in a Brooklyn paper, and the first baseball professional is thought by some historians to come from Brooklyn. The first recognized national baseball championship was won by a team from Brooklyn. Let's go back to the beginning.

Baseball didn't spring into existence as the creation of any one individual. Games played with a stick hitting a ball, in many forms, go back thousands of years. Baseball's roots in the United States go back to the mid–1700s when the English game of rounders, an offshoot of cricket, came to this continent.

Rounders was a very informal game. There were anywhere from two to five bases used. The number of players on each team depended on the number available to play. The ball was tossed underhanded, and after hitting the ball, a player ran from base to base, eventually trying to score a run. The base runner could be put out by being "plugged" or "soaked" with the ball; that is, the runner was hit with the ball while he was not on a base. This is not as bad as it sounds because the ball at that time was bigger than today's baseball and had India rubber at its core and soft rags around the core, so that the ball was much softer than today's ball.

Forms of rounders were played throughout the eastern United States, but each area had distinct preferences for playing rules. Sometimes the game of rounders was called "round ball" or "soak ball," or sometimes even "base ball."

In 1845, in New York City, a bank teller and volunteer fireman named Alexander Cartwright was the founder of the Knickerbockers Base Ball Club of New York. It was a group of young men who played base ball on Sundays, and Cartwright would constantly come up with new rules for each week's contest. What Cartwright did was to adopt rules from other areas of the country, add to them the local rules, add a few new rules that he created, and eventually devise the first set of rules that could actually be considered baseball. Cartwright didn't like New York's custom of using five bases; he preferred the custom of the Philadelphia area, which used four bases in a diamond shape. Cartwright adopted the Philadelphia diamond, and then lengthened the bases to 90 feet. He abolished the "soaking" rule and substituted tagging the runner or getting the ball to the base ahead of the runner. Cartwright standardized the number of players at nine, and he formalized the batting order. He decided there would be "three strikes and you're out" and three outs per inning.

The Knickerbocker Base Ball Club found playing areas in Manhattan hard to come by, and so they rented, for $75 a year, a playing area in Elysian Fields, in Hoboken, New Jersey. Elysian Fields, on Hoboken's northern shore, is only a short ferry ride from mid-town Manhattan. The Knickerbocker Club played several intramural games at Elysian Fields and even played a Brooklyn team featuring several star cricket players, on October 21, 1845, defeating the Brooklyn team by a score of 24–4.

By 1846, Cartwright had finished his experimenting, and he publicized a set of 20 rules for Base Ball. Then, after a few intramural games at Elysian Fields using his new rules, what is now generally recognized as the first baseball game took place. It was a game on June 19, 1846, between Cartwright's Knickerbockers and a team called the New York Nine. The New York Nine won this first ever baseball game, at Elysian Fields, by a score of 23–1. Exactly 155 years later, on June 19, 2001, the Brooklyn Cyclones would play their first game, but baseball and Brooklyn had over a century and a half of games before that.

Cartwright's new rules caught on like wildfire, and the new rules spread first throughout the New York metropolitan area, and then to other eastern cities. By 1851, the Knickerbockers found some official competition as they began to play matches against New York's Washington Club. In the fall of 1852, a third New York team was formed; the Eagles.

Where was Brooklyn in all of this? As usual, right in the thick of things. Baseball continued to be played, and by 1854, the Knickerbockers Club played several matches against the Gotham Base Ball Club (formerly the Washington

Club). By the end of the season, two other base ball clubs in greater New York had been formed; the Empire Club, based at Elysian Fields, and the Jolly Young Bachelors Base Ball Club of Brooklyn, later to be called the Excelsiors.

By 1855, the Excelsiors played intramural matches while the other clubs played in a loosely organized informal competition. That same year saw an explosion of new base ball teams. The Putnam Club was organized with their home grounds in Williamsburg, Brooklyn. Base ball clubs, up until this time usually composed of white collar young men, now added some clubs composed primarily of "working men." The Atlantic Base Ball Club, playing from Brooklyn's Capitoline Grounds, and the Eckford Club, based in Brooklyn's Greenpoint, were formed.

In 1858, admission was charged for the first time for a base ball game. It involved all-star teams made up of players from Brooklyn and New York and was held at the Fashion Racetrack, in Long Island. Admission charge: 50 cents.

Four years later, Brooklyn then had another baseball first when Brooklyn's Union Grounds became the first enclosed base ball park. The Union Grounds regularly charged admission, becoming the first grounds to do so, another baseball first. Charging admission led naturally to players asking for a share of the gate, and it is believed by some historians that the first paid players were in Brooklyn, albeit their payments were "under the table" because of the amateur rules of the time.

There's a dispute among baseball historians about this, but the very first paid player was believed by some researchers to be James Creighton, who achieved fame while pitching for Brooklyn's Excelsiors. But why did Creighton get his surreptitious payments? Simply because he was baseball's first great pitcher.

Playing from 1857 to 1862, when all baseball players were considered amateurs, Creighton pitched when all pitches were delivered in a stiff-wrist underhand delivery. Creighton added an illegal, but unnoticeable, underhanded wrist snap, which added speed to the pitch. So, in a sense, he had invented the fastball. Then he began to change speeds on his pitches, in effect adding the change-up. In 1860, baseball added the called strike, so for the first time, a batter could not endlessly wait for a pitch he wanted. This vastly increased the value of a pitcher. So if Creighton accepted under the table payments to pitch for the Brooklyn Excelsiors in 1860, he gave Brooklyn baseball three firsts in baseball history: the fastball; the change-up, and the paid baseball player. But modern baseball theory has it that a pitcher usually needs at least three pitches to reach top effectiveness, and another Brooklyn player would provide that next pitch.

Candy Cummings pitched for the Brooklyn Excelsiors and the Brooklyn Stars in the amateur baseball of the 1860s. As a member of the Brooklyn Stars in 1867, he is credited with inventing the curveball. He claimed he came

W. A. "CANDY" CUMMINGS

PITCHED FIRST CURVE BALL IN BASEBALL
HISTORY. INVENTED CURVE AS AMATEUR
ACE OF BROOKLYN STARS IN 1867. ENDED
LONG CAREER AS HARTFORD PITCHER IN
NATIONAL LEAGUE'S FIRST YEAR 1876.

Candy Cummings — inventor of the curveball.

up with the idea while throwing seashells on a New England beach as a 14-year-old. Later, he played professionally for several clubs in the major league National Association and in the National League, and was elected to the Baseball Hall of Fame in 1939, credited as the curve's inventor.

While all this was going on, another Brooklynite, one transplanted from England, Henry Chadwick, was writing about it. After falling in love with baseball upon seeing an 1848 game at Elysian Fields, Chadwick began writing about baseball and eventually became baseball's first full-time baseball writer. He wrote for New York papers like the *New York Clipper*, and the *New York Herald*, and of course he wrote for his city's paper, the famous *Brooklyn Eagle*.

Brooklynite Chadwick is credited with inventing baseball's box score.

But Brooklynites were not just inventing aspects of baseball, they were winning at it. In 1860, the Excelsiors embarked on the first great baseball tour. They toured New York State, returned to Brooklyn to face the Atlantics and then left to continue the tour in Baltimore and Philadelphia. Thus, a Brooklyn team can be said to have invented the road trip.

The Civil War helped to spread baseball, and while the war was raging, Brooklyn achieved another baseball first. The Atlantic Club of Brooklyn played the first international match ever recorded as they beat the Young Canadian Club of Woodstock, Ontario, 75–11.

After the Civil War ended, in 1865 Brooklyn added another first as it won the first "grand match" for the championship of the United States when the Brooklyn Atlantics defeated the Mutual Club of New York 13–12 in a game at Elysian Fields that was called in the sixth inning because of rain.

The next year, the Atlantics kept Brooklyn in the news by winning a three game series between the Atlantics and the Athletics of Philadelphia, for the championship of the United States.

In 1867, another Brooklyn team almost won a national championship as the Uniques of Brooklyn lost to the Excelsiors of Philadelphia 42–17 for the "Colored Championship" of the United States.

Baseball became openly professional with the Red Stockings of Cincinnati paying their players in 1867. Then in 1871, baseball's first professional league, the National Association of Professional Base Ball Players, was formed. The eight-team league did not have a Brooklyn club at the start, but in its first season the Fort Wayne Kekiongas dropped out of the league and were replaced by the Brooklyn Eckford team. The National Association also featured the New York Mutuals, who played their games in Brooklyn. The National Association lasted only five years, and the National League replaced it in 1876. Playing in the league were the New York Mutuals, of Brooklyn.

The Dodgers major league history actually began as a member of the American Association, a new major league, in 1884. Nicknames at the time were informal names conferred upon the teams by fans and newspaper writers, and the names were easily subject to change. In its earliest years the team carried various names, and in 1888 four of the players were married, so in 1889 the team's nickname became the "Bridegrooms," a name the team had, among others, for two decades. In 1890, the team jumped leagues to the rival

Emmett Kelly as a "Bum."

National League. In 1891 the second Washington Park burned down, and the team moved to Eastern Park, which had trolley lines on two sides of it. By this time, Manhattanites called people from Brooklyn "Trolley Dodgers" because of Brooklyn's vast array of trolley lines — and the name Trolley Dodger stuck for years. That was soon shortened to Dodgers to fit limited newspaper space. The team was still sometimes called the Bridegrooms. When Wilbert Robinson was the manager, the team name became the Robins, in his honor. It was also known as the Superbas for a time. In 1930 the name officially was changed back from Robins to Dodgers, and it's been Dodgers ever since.

Charles Ebbets was a ticket seller for the Brooklyn team who worked his way up to business manager. His loyalty and hard work was rewarded when owner Harry Von der Horst sold Ebbets several shares in the team, eventually allowing Ebbets to buy an interest in the club. In 1902, Von der Horst became ill, and he announced his intention to sell the team. Manager Ned Hanlon announced that he wanted to buy the club and move it to Baltimore. Ebbets vowed to keep the Dodgers in Brooklyn, but he had no money. But he eventually found a loan for enough money to buy the stock and keep the team in Brooklyn.

The Dodgers played in a park called Washington Park, a wooden edifice. Ebbets dreamed of a modern park that would seat over 25,000 fans. Ebbets bought land in what was called "Pigtown," so called because it was a dump where farmers brought their pigs to feed. Ebbets' goal was thought of as foolish, but he persisted, and construction began in March of 1912. A reporter suggested that the field be named after Ebbets; Ebbets gave in, and history was made. Under Ebbets' direction, and with Wilbert Robinson as field manager, the Dodgers won a pennant in 1916. They lost in the World Series to Babe Ruth's Red Sox. Then they won another pennant in 1920 and lost the World Series to the Cleveland Indians.

But Ebbets died in 1925, and the other club officials chose Wilbert Robinson to be club president as well as manager. It didn't work. Robinson couldn't transfer his managerial skills to the front office, and the Dodgers started to flounder. The players took advantage of Robinson. Players became night crawlers, and play on the field suffered. The Dodgers finished in sixth place the last four years of the 1920s.

During the last part of Robinson's reign as manager, the Dodgers became known as the Daffiness Boys. They featured players like outfielder Babe Herman, who, while a fine hitter, was less than stellar on the field and on the bases. He was once hit by a fly ball, not on the head as legend has it, but on the shoulder. Once he hit into a double play as Brooklyn wound up with three runners on third base — one going back to third, one on it, and Herman chugging into it.

The Dodgers were mired in bad baseball, but they were also mired in

Charlie Ebbets — constructed Ebbets Field.

ever-increasing debt. They owed a total of over $1 million, about half of that to the Brooklyn Trust Company. Their telephone bill hadn't been paid, and their telephones were shut off. Desperately trying to avoid going out of business, the club asked National League President Ford Frick for help, and Frick in turn asked Branch Rickey of the St. Louis Cardinals for advice. Rickey suggested a longtime friend and associate, Larry MacPhail, formerly general manager of the Cincinnati Reds. The Dodgers hired MacPhail, who acted like a whirlwind.

MacPhail first painted the ballpark and improved the bathrooms. Then he set about improving the club on the field. He borrowed $50,000 to buy Dolph Camilli to play first base. The sum shocked baseball as it was astronomical in the days when baseball's best seats sold for under $3.

Then MacPhail, who had started night major league baseball with the Reds, charged $72,000 worth of lights to General Electric and put in lights at Ebbets Field. He hired Red Barber from Cincinnati to be the Dodgers' announcer on radio, breaking an agreement of the Dodgers, Giants, and Yankees not to broadcast games on radio. MacPhail didn't bring radio to Brooklyn halfheartedly. He put the Dodger games on WOR, a 50,000-watt station. He then hired Branch Rickey's son, Branch Jr., to run the farm system.

MacPhail obtained Leo Durocher from the Cards to play shortstop and named Durocher manager in 1938.

MacPhail picked up pitcher Hugh Casey from the minors in 1939, got pitcher Whitlow Wyatt from minor league Milwaukee, picked up veteran outfielder Dixie Walker, and paid $75,000 for Louisville shortstop Pee Wee Reese. In 1940, he obtained Pete Reiser from the Cardinals' chain when the commissioner freed many players from Branch Rickey's "chain gang." He got Ducky Medwick from the Cards, paid $100,00 for pitcher Kirby Higbe from the Phillies, and Branch Rickey sold him catcher Mickey Owen from the Cardinals for $60,000. MacPhail paid $90,000 and two minor leaguers for All-Star second sacker Billy Herman from the Cubs.

The Dodgers kept improving, and in 1941 they were in a dogfight of a pennant race with the St. Louis Cardinals. Durocher had placed Pete Reiser in center field, and he led the league in hitting at .343, played great defense and ran wild on the bases. The Dodgers clinched the pennant against the Boston Braves and rode the train home to a rousing celebration at New York's Grand Central Station, where they were greeted by thousands of delirious Brooklyn fans.

The Dodgers faced the Yankees in the World Series that year, the first of seven Fall Classic meetings between these two teams from 1941 to 1956.

The Yanks won the first game, and the Dodgers, behind the pitching of Whitlow Wyatt, won the second. In the third game, the Dodger starter, Freddie Fitzsimmons, was hit on the knee with a line drive and had to leave the game with a broken kneecap, and the Yankees scored two runs off Hugh Casey to win.

In the fourth game, Casey was on the mound in relief holding a 4–3 lead in the top of the ninth. Casey retired the first two batters and had two strikes on Tommy Henrich when Casey threw a pitch that Henrich swung at and missed, but the pitch got by catcher Mickey Owen. Henrich raced to first base on the strikeout. The Yankees'

Hilda Chester — famous Dodger fan.

Joe DiMaggio then singled, and the Yankees kept hitting, scoring four runs, and then held the Dodgers in the ninth. Brooklyn fans were crushed to be one pitch from victory and then lose the game to the Yankees. The Yankees wrapped up the Series the next day with a 3–1 win. Losing a starter with a broken kneecap and then losing after striking out the last batter in the next game made Brooklyn's fans feel snake bit. It wouldn't be the first time.

On December 7 came the attack on Pearl Harbor, and the United States was at war. Dodger infielder Cookie Lavagetto enlisted in the Navy in February, and many of the Dodgers' younger players would soon be drafted or enlist. But while the Dodgers still had the core of their team, they led the league at one point in July by 13 games. Pete Reiser had his average up to .383, and Dodger fans were anticipating another World Series, but in a July game, Reiser raced back to center field and fractured his skull in crashing into the wall in an attempt to catch a ball hit by the Cardinals' Enos Slaughter. Reiser came back before he was ready, hit under .200 for the rest of the season, as his average shrank to .310, and the Dodgers lost the pennant to Branch Rickey's Cardinals. Reiser would never be the same.

Under pressure from the Brooklyn Trust Company to increase profits, the volatile MacPhail resigned near the end of the 1942 season. After MacPhail resigned, the Dodger ownership wanted to obtain a more stable leader to run the team. Dodger stockholder Jim Mulvey asked Commissioner Ford Frick for advice, and Frick suggested the Dodgers go after Branch Rickey. In the fall of 1942, a group consisting of Rickey, John L. Smith (a Brooklyn chemical manufacturer, and an attorney representing the Brooklyn Trust Company), and Walter O'Malley each bought 25 percent of the Dodgers. Dearie Mulvey, daughter of former Dodger owner Steve McKeever, and her husband, Jim Mulvey, held the other 25 percent.

Rickey immediately went to work to build up the Dodgers' farm system. Meanwhile, the talent on the Dodgers was entering the military service as Pee Wee Reese, Hugh Casey, Pete Reiser, Johnny Rizzo, Billy Herman, and Kirby Higbe all went into the service in 1943. Rickey almost at once traded or released many of the Dodgers' older players, such as Paul Waner, Whitlow Wyatt, Dolph Camilli, Joe Medwick and Fred Fitzsimmons.

Rickey was really competing against himself. He had revolutionized baseball's minor leagues by establishing a farm system for the St. Louis Cardinals. Instead of buying players from existing independent minor league teams, Rickey with the Cards had instituted a pipeline, signing hundreds of players at young ages and letting them try to climb through a system of Cardinal owned or controlled minor league teams to reach the Cardinals. Such a system requires years to pay off, and when Rickey first went to the Dodgers, the Cardinals continued to win pennants because their team wasn't hit as hard by the military draft as the Dodgers, and because Rickey had established a solid Cardinal team that was still being fed by undrafted players from his outstanding farm system. Rickey began signing talented players like college pitchers Ralph Branca and Clyde King, but it wasn't enough to overcome his earlier groundwork when he ran the Cardinals.

The Cardinals won pennants in 1942, '43, and '44. The Dodgers slipped to seventh in 1944 and fifth in 1945.

In the meantime, Branch Rickey had yet another revolution planned for baseball. Baseball had been racially segregated since the 1884 season when black player Moses Fleetwood Walker played for the Toledo Blue Stockings, a team in the then–major league American Association. Other black players played in various minor leagues. But before an exhibition game against the Blue Stockings in 1883, Cap Anson, manager and first baseman for the Chicago White Stockings, protested that he didn't want to play against Toledo because of the presence of Walker, its catcher. Anson's protests were ignored, and he finally agreed to play when informed that his team wouldn't be paid unless they played. The game was played, but apparently Anson's protests helped to lead to baseball's adoption of its "Color Line" after the 1884 season, when Toledo was dropped from the American Association meetings. After that, Major League Baseball solidified its opposition to black players and this unwritten, but real, ban continued through World War II.

Denied access to the white major leagues, blacks developed their own leagues, both major and minor. Stars like Josh Gibson, called the "black Babe Ruth" for his prodigious home runs, and great pitcher Satchel Paige played in Negro Leagues for years

In earlier years, several attempts were made to break the bar. New York manager John McGraw tried to pass black second baseman Charlie Grant as a Native American, but when African-American supporters packed the stands for an exhibition game, McGraw's ruse was detected, and Grant had to leave the Giants before he could play in any official games.

Later, maverick owner Bill Veeck had concocted a scheme in which he attempted to stock his Philadelphia Phillies as an all-black team, using players from the Negro Leagues, but Veeck's plan was revealed and squashed before he could implement his idea.

Throughout the 1945 season, Rickey had his scouts comb the Negro Leagues looking for a player who could be the first to break baseball's "Color Line" since 1884. To provide cover for his scouting, Rickey announced plans for a new Brooklyn baseball team to be called the Brown Dodgers.

The racial climate in the country was changing. African-American Joe Louis was a national hero in boxing. Blacks were already playing pro football. Blacks had served with distinction in the U.S. armed forces in World War II, and increased political pressure was on baseball to integrate.

It became apparent to players in the Negro Leagues that the question of baseball integration was not a matter of "if," but a question of "when." Privately, black players speculated about who would be the first to break the barrier. Many figured the first black player would be Satchel Paige or Gibson, both of whom had been playing in postseason exhibition games against white major leaguers for years, more often than not beating the major leaguers. Paige's pitching was considered on a par with that of baseball superstar Bob Feller, and Gibson's home runs were legendary. But both black players were past their athletic prime. In 1945, Gibson was 37 years old and Paige, who was very indistinct about his true age, was thought to be at least 43 years old.

Rickey researched the players' private lives as well and decided that the person to integrate baseball was Jackie Robinson. Robinson was a world-class athlete who was better known for his exploits in other sports than for his baseball prowess. At UCLA, he was a halfback who helped lead UCLA to the Rose Bowl. He later played semi-pro football in Hawaii. He was also a track star and was UCLA's leading scoring on its basketball team, as a 5' 11" forward. He had only played one season of Negro League baseball and was not considered as even the best player in the league at his position — shortstop Willie Wells was rated as superior.

Rickey signed Robinson to a contract, and it was announced in October of 1945 that Robinson had signed with the Dodgers and would begin the 1946 season at Montreal, one of the Dodgers' top farm clubs. Montreal was chosen because its racial climate was more accepting of integration than that of the Dodgers' other top farm clubs, which were in the United States.

But Rickey didn't stop breaking the racial barrier with Robinson. Soon after Robinson had inked a Dodger pact, Rickey signed catcher Roy Campanella to a contract. Campanella had been playing in the Negro Leagues since he was 16. At 24, he was an eight-

Jackie Robinson and Branch Rickey.

DODGERS
CLUB HOUSE

KEEP OUT

Jackie Robinson about to join the Dodgers.

year professional veteran. Campanella also played winter ball in the Caribbean and Mexico, so he was very experienced. Next, Rickey signed big Don Newcombe, from New Jersey, who had been successful pitching for the Newark Eagles team in black baseball. Campanella and Newcombe were both sent to play for Nashua, New Hampshire, down the ladder from Montreal in the Dodgers' chain.

The signing of Robinson created national headlines. At the start of spring training, Robinson reported to spring training with John Wright, a black pitcher signed by Rickey. Robinson and Wright joined the over 600 players that Rickey had at Sanford, Florida. There was racial pressure from the local community, and Robinson and Wright were forced two days later to go to Daytona Beach, Florida, to train with the rest of Montreal's team.

Robinson, under enormous scrutiny and pressure, struggled in spring training. Rickey's plan all along was to start Robinson at Montreal and bring him to the majors the next season.

After spring training ended, Robinson and Wright were assigned to Montreal. Montreal's first regular season game was away, at Jersey City, New Jersey — just across the Hudson River from New York City.

Robinson was playing second base, his projected major league position. In his debut, Robinson silenced all doubters, as he rocked four hits, including a home run, stole three bases and led Montreal to a win.

As Robinson was tearing up the International League, the Dodgers were once again battling St. Louis for the pennant, but Brooklyn came up short. The Dodger lineup included players like: Carl Furillo, back from the war; fellow rookie outfielder Gene Hermanski; Reese, back from the service; and a talented young catcher named Bruce Edwards.

Dodger line-up, from left, Jim Gilliam, Pee Wee Reese, Duke Snider, Jackie Robinson, Roy Campanella, Gil Hodges, Carl Furillo, Billy Cox, and Carl Erskine; behind team, Walter Alston.

The teams battled back and forth all summer for the league lead and finished in a dead heat. There was to be a best-of-three game playoff.

In the first game, the Dodgers' Ralph Branca pitched well, but the Cardinals won, and in the second game the Cardinals had an 8–1 lead going into the ninth inning. The Dodgers' bats came alive, and they scored three runs and had the bases loaded, with the potential tying run coming up. Howie Schultz pinch hit. He hit a shot down the third base line, just foul. Then the count went to 3–2, and Schultz struck out swinging, ending the Dodger season.

The next season, the Dodgers held spring training both in Havana, Cuba, and for some time in Panama because they thought the racial climate would be easier on Robinson there than in the United States. Rickey kept Robinson with the Montreal team, but played him at first base. This was done mainly to keep Robinson away from the take out slides that a second baseman must endure — slides whose severity might be increased from the players on opposing teams who resented Robinson's presence as a black man integrating baseball. Robinson played well as Montreal held daily exhibitions against the Dodgers. Rickey had thought that by showcasing Robinson against the Dodgers there would be a groundswell of support from the team to add Robinson to the Brooklyn roster. In fact, the opposite happened. While most Dodgers accepted Robinson at once, a few circulated a petition asking that Robinson not be added to the Dodgers. That was big trouble for Rickey, but Rickey and Durocher made it clear to the players that Robinson would play on the team if they wanted him to, whether those players wanted Robinson or not.

After the previous season, there were rumors that manager Durocher would join his former boss Larry MacPhail, now directing the Yankees. Durocher had constantly been in hot water over his alleged association with known gamblers. Durocher brought the situation to a boil by accusing MacPhail of having gamblers as his guests at a ball game in Havana against the Dodgers. The baseball commissioner, Happy Chandler, was concerned about Durocher's conduct, which had included Durocher's beating up a fan, as well as Durocher's various wild ways and associations. MacPhail asked for a meeting to confront Durocher, but even though MacPhail and Durocher settled their differences, Chandler felt Durocher's conduct merited a suspension, and Durocher was suspended for the entire upcoming season. Branch Rickey then hired Burt Shotton to manage.

The Durocher suspension came on April 10, on the day that Rickey had planned for Durocher to announce that the Dodgers wanted Robinson on their team. The next day, Rickey made the announcement that Robinson was being added to the Dodgers' roster in time for the opening of the 1947 season.

Robinson was hitless in his Major League debut, but he fielded flawlessly at first base and scored a run. After an initial rough few days, he started hitting, and the Dodgers started winning. Pete Reiser was in the outfield; Carl Furillo was turning heads as a right fielder or centerfielder. Ralph Branca was pitching up a storm, eventually winning 21 games. Robinson was terrific. He hit .323, stole a league-leading 29 bases and was voted the National League Rookie of the Year. The Dodgers pulled away from the pack and won the pennant easily. In the World Series that year, they were once again to face Yankees.

The Yankees were winning the Series 2–1. The fourth game was in Ebbets Field. The Yankee pitcher, Bill Bevens, was pitching a no-hitter going into the ninth inning, and the Yankees led 2–1, the Dodgers having scored their run after a walk, an error, and a sacrifice fly. The Dodgers' Furillo walked, and Al Gionfriddo ran for him. Gionfriddo stole second, and the Yankees then intentionally walked pinch-hitter Pete Reiser. Eddie Miksis ran for the already injured Reiser, and then pinch-hitter Cookie Lavagetto hit a double off the right field wall to break up the no-hitter and win the game. The teams split the next two games, and the Yankees won the seventh game 5–2 to beat Brooklyn once again.

The next year, 1948, Durocher was once more installed as the Dodger manager. The team was struggling, and the catching was a problem because Bruce Edwards had injured his arm the previous winter. Durocher was pressuring Rickey to bring up Campanella from the American Association, which Rickey had integrated with Campanella. Campanella came up to the Dodgers in July. He was made the regular catcher, and Durocher moved the third-string catcher, Gil Hodges, to first base. Both moves were instant successes. But the Dodgers' play was not up to 1947 standards, and attendance fell. Walter O'Malley and his new ally, owner Robert L. Smith, put pressure on Rickey to fire Durocher. The Dodgers sank to last place. Realizing that O'Malley would probably find a way to get rid of Durocher eventually, Rickey arranged a deal in which Durocher went to the New York Giants, replacing Mel Ott as manager, and the Dodgers brought back Burt Shotton. The Dodgers battled back, and within a month went into first place. Carl Erskine was brought up from the minors and pitched well, but they finished the year in third place, seven and a half games behind Boston.

In 1948, Robinson had had another outstanding year, and Campanella's debut was outstanding as he had 9 home runs and 45 RBIs in just 83 games. For the 1949 season, the Dodgers added another black player, powerful pitcher Don Newcombe. Thus the Dodgers' set line-up for the glory years emerged.

At first base was Hodges, at 6' 2" considered a giant of a man with huge hands. Hodges was an excellent fielder and a powerful right-handed home run hitter. At second was Robinson, in his prime, a man who could beat teams with his running, his power, his fielding, his bunting, his fire. At shortstop was Pee Wee Reese, the Dodger captain, an All-Star. At third was Billy Cox, one of the best fielding third basemen of all-time, an acrobat.

Don Newcombe — Dodger pitcher.

In the outfield was Furillo in right, with his powerful arm and his skill at playing balls hit off the right field wall. Snider was in center field, the "Duke," the Dodgers' main left-handed threat and a great fielder. In left, the Dodgers used Gene Hermanski. Left field would be the one position that wasn't stable for the Dodgers for the rest of the time in Brooklyn. Later, Andy Pafko would hold the job for a while, but left field was generally a revolving door for the Dodgers.

The catcher was Roy Campanella. This lineup, absent left field, remained virtually unchanged through 1957. After 1952, Robinson had slowed in the field and was moved to left field and third base. Junior Gilliam took over at second. Billy Cox and Robinson shared third for a time until Cox was traded. Later, Robinson retired after the 1956 season, but this was the Dodgers' set lineup for years.

In 1949, the Dodgers won the pennant on the last day of the season on a Duke Snider single against the Phillies, and once again Brooklyn entered the World Series against the Yankees. The Yankees won this Series by four games to one.

The next year, John L. Smith died, and his will named his wife and the Brooklyn Trust Company as executors. When Walter O'Malley and Mrs. Smith formed an alliance, O'Malley controlled the Dodgers and was able to force Rickey out of his Dodger ownership, although through some deft, complicated maneuvering, Rickey made O'Malley pay dearly for Rickey's stock. After the 1950 season, Rickey was out, and O'Malley replaced manager Burt Shotton with Charlie Dressen.

On the field, for the second year in a row, the pennant came down to the final day of the season. The Dodgers overcame a nine-game Philadelphia lead, and on the final day of the season the Dodgers had to play at Philadelphia. If the Dodgers beat the Phillies, both teams would play a best of three playoff for the National League pennant. This was one of the most famous games in Dodger history. The game was tied at 1–1 in the bottom of the ninth. The Dodgers had no outs with Cal Abrams (who grew up in Brooklyn) on second and Pee Wee Reese on first. Snider singled to center and Abrams tried to score and was thrown out on the play. The Dodgers failed to score that inning, and eventually lost the game in the tenth when Dick Sisler hit a three-run homer for the Phillies, and they held on to win 4–1. Once more, the Dodgers seemed snake-bitten as Abrams and third base coach Milt Stock were reviled for the play as being reckless because if Abrams had stopped at third, the Dodgers would have had the bases loaded with none out and needing only a run to win, with the heart of the Dodgers lineup due up. It was a bitter loss and Brooklyn fans were crushed.

The next year, the Dodgers started with a vengeance. They opened a 13½ game lead over their arch rivals, the New York Giants. From mid–August, the Giants began gaining on the Dodgers. With one game remaining for each team, the Giants and Dodgers were tied for first place. For the third consecutive year, the Dodgers were to play Philadelphia with the pennant on the line. In the third inning, it was announced that the Giants had won their game. Jackie Robinson made a sensational game-saving catch of a line drive in the 12th inning, and then Robinson won the game with a home run in the 14th.

The Giant-Dodger rivalry was the greatest rivalry in baseball. Back in the days of the eight-team National League, teams played each other 22 times a year. Dodger fans would travel to the Polo Grounds for games, and Giant fans would come to Ebbets Field. No other city had teams in the same league. A fan could travel to the visiting ballpark for the price of a subway token.

The rivalry began early in the century. In the off-season, in 1934, Giant manager Bill Terry was asked about Brooklyn's chances for the coming season. When he answered, "Is Brooklyn still in the league?" his remark heightened the animosity between the clubs.

When Leo Durocher took over as Giants manager, he encouraged the Giant pitchers, like Sal "The Barber" Maglie, to brush back the opponents' batters, and Durocher was even more encouraging when it came to the Dodgers — he had a point to prove against his former employers and didn't get along too well with some of the Dodgers such as Carl Furillo and Jackie Robinson, and his pitchers kept them loose. Durocher's pitchers sometimes engaged in brushback contests with the Giants' hurlers, and the contests were more like a war — in some games numerous players were hit by pitches.

The 1957 Dodgers-Giant playoff series went down to the last game, played at the Polo Grounds. The Dodgers, with starter Newcombe pitching, held a 4–1 lead going into the bottom of the ninth inning. Alvin Dark led off with a single and Don Mueller followed with another single to put Giant runners on first and second. After Monte Irvin popped out, Whitey Lockman doubled, scoring a run. Mueller broke his ankle sliding into third and left for a runner. The next batter was Bobby Thomson. The tying runs were on second and third. The Dodgers had Carl Erskine and Ralph Branca warming up in the bullpen and brought in Branca to pitch to Thomson. After a called strike, Thomson hit the next pitch into the short left-field stands, and Russ Hodges, the Giants' radio announcer, said 13 times, "The Giants win the pennant! The Giants win the pennant!"

This is now the summer of 2001, 50 years later. But to some Brooklyn fans, it was like yesterday.

Guy Conti, the New York Mets' minor league coordinator, constantly observes the Mets' six statewide farm clubs, usually spending five days in a row so that he can see the complete starting rotation — in each visit. He was driving to a Cyclones' away game at Augusta, New Jersey — where the ballpark's outfield goes up to a corn field — a rural spot like the Iowa ball field in the movie *Field of Dreams*.

Guy Conti: "I was driving to the game here [Brooklyn at New Jersey], and I stopped on the highway at a small diner for breakfast. I was on my cell phone talking at my table and I guess from my conversation on the phone that it was pretty obvious that I worked for the Mets. After I was done talking, a man at the table next to me said, 'I couldn't help hearing your conversation. Are you with the Mets?'

"I explained that I was, and we got to talking. He mentioned that he was originally from Brooklyn and had been a big Brooklyn Dodger fan. I mentioned that I was in the Dodger organization for 12 years. Then the guy starts talking about the famous playoff game in 1951, and he's talking about it like it's yesterday. He goes through the whole situation; he knows Branca and Erskine were in the bullpen; he goes through both lineups. He goes through the whole ninth inning. Each play. He's talking about this game like it was yesterday. And he's getting upset, right there in the diner, all over again that the Dodgers lost. And it was 50 years ago!"

When the Dodgers lost to the Yankees in the World Series, or to the Giants for the pennant, it wasn't like a city where there was only one major league team. Dodger fans had to live with their defeats throughout the year, and the years. And not all people living in Brooklyn were Dodger fans. Most were, but there were Giant fans in Brooklyn, and Giant fans maybe where one worked, or a fan's cousin in the City (Brooklyn's name for Manhattan) was a fan of the Giants or the Yankees. They were around. And as a Dodger fan you had to live with this. Year after year.

Bobby Thomson hits that homer off Branca, and Branca, a great young pitcher at the time, never hears the end of it, either. Dodger fans keep saying, "Wait till next year." It became their mantra. The closest thing to being a Dodger fan in the early 1950s is being a Red Sox fan today. The last time the Red Sox were World Champions was in 1918 when they beat the Chicago Cubs in the Series. Bill Buckner boots a grounder in the '86 World Series, and the Mets win, and Buckner,

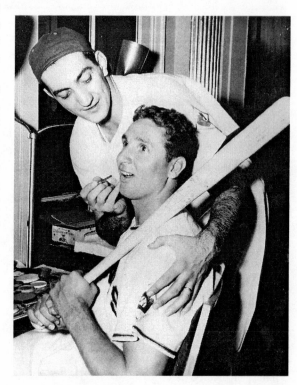

Ralph Branca and Bobby Thomson.

an outstanding ball player for years, never hears the end of it. Year after year, the Red Sox fans listen to the abuse, as others call their team "choke artists."

Duke Snider: "I don't like the word 'choke.' The reason why people sometimes don't perform under pressure is not because they 'choked.' It's because they tried *too* hard."

Next year was 1952. The Korean War was on, and the Dodgers' pitcher, Don Newcombe, was drafted into the service. Newcombe had won 56 games in his first three major league seasons. The Dodgers replaced him with rookie pitcher Joe Black, who had pitched for years in the Negro Leagues. Black was outstanding and was named the National League Rookie of the Year. The Dodgers clinched the pennant on September 21 and earned the right to meet — you guessed it — the Yankees in the World Series. This would be the third time in six years that the Dodgers had faced the Yankees. Since the Dodgers faced and lost to the Yankees in 1941, it was the fourth time in a row that the Dodgers' World Series opponent was the Yankees.

The Yankees no longer had the retired Joe DiMaggio, but they had Yogi Berra, Mickey Mantle and Phil Rizzuto, and a strong pitching staff. The

Joe Black walks past the Yankees.

Dodgers took a three games to two lead, and it looked as if the Dodgers would finally win their first World Series. The Dodgers' Billy Loes was pitching in the sixth game, and held a 2–1 lead in the seventh inning. He dropped the ball out of his hand while he was standing in the pitching rubber, and a balk was called, advancing the Yankee base runner to second. The next batter, pitcher Vic Raschi, hit a bouncing ball toward Loes that Loes lost, and the tying run scored. In the next inning, Mantle homered, and Loes and the Dodgers had lost. Later, Loes said that he lost Raschi's bouncing grounder "in the sun." It sounded ridiculous, but knowledgeable fans knew that at Ebbets Field in the late October afternoon, a high bouncing ball could be lost in the sun streaming through the stands from behind home plate. It was true. Loes lost a ground ball in the sun, and the Dodgers had to play a seventh game in Ebbets Field. Mickey Mantle homered to put the Yankees ahead 3–2, and the Yanks held on to win another Series. Once more, the Dodgers had come so close.

The Dodgers entered the 1953 season with what had become their pat lineup. Hodges was still at first, Robinson second, Reese short, Cox third, Furillo right, Snider center, Campanella catching and someone to fill left field. But then their manager, Charlie Dressen, decided that Robinson's range at second base had diminished. Robinson, who had entered the majors as a 28-year-old rookie, was now 35 years old and had put on weight. Dressen decided to switch Robinson to third base and put rookie Junior Gilliam, another player signed from the Negro Leagues, at second base. Robinson hurt himself in the first regular season game, and for the rest of the year Dressen used Robinson and Cox at third and also frequently used Robinson in left field. The Dodger lineup was devastating. The Dodgers won 105 games (losing only 49) and headed to the World Series where, once again, their nemesis, the Yankees, awaited.

The Yankees jumped out to a two-game lead. Then the Dodgers, behind an incredible 14-strikeout effort by Erskine, won Game 3: Brooklyn tied the Series in Game 4, and in Game 5 a Mantle grand slam led the way for the Yankees. Down three games to two, the Dodgers lost in the bottom of the ninth as Billy Martin hit a chopper up the middle for the Yankees' Series win. The Dodgers had now been in five World Series from 1941 to 1953. All of the World Series were against the Yankees, and the Yankees won them all. Once again, Brooklyn fans said, "Wait till next year."

At the end of the season, Dressen wanted a multiyear contract and O'Malley didn't want to give it to him. O'Malley won this battle and named Walter Alston as the new manager. There was another major change. Red Barber, who had done so much in his broadcasts to popularize the Dodgers, had been working the World Series games for a low payment. Barber asked for a negotiated sum rather than merely an amount Gillette, the television sponsor, deemed acceptable. O'Malley refused to back Barber and when Barber,

Three sluggers — Roy Campanella, Duke Snider, and Gil Hodges.

feeling that O'Malley failed to support him, left for the Yankees, O'Malley made Vin Scully the Dodger's lead announcer, where he remains to this day.

The Dodgers had an off season under Alston in 1954, and the Giants won the pennant and then swept Cleveland in the World Series. Teams from New York City had now won the World Series every year from 1949. Unfortunately for the Dodgers, these teams had been the Yankees for five years in a row and then the Giants.

Time seemed to be running out on the Dodgers. Their marvelous everyday lineup, remarkably stable for nearly a decade, was getting old. Robinson and Reese would enter 1955 as 37 year olds. Campanella was 36, Furillo 35, and Hodges 31. The pitching staff was relatively young, as Erskine was only 28, Johnny Podres was only 22, Clem Labine was 28 and Brooklyn's own Sandy Koufax was 19. The Dodgers' veterans hung on and the pitching stayed tough, and the Dodgers breezed through the season to win the pennant by 13½ games.

The Dodgers' Series opponents naturally were the Yankees, who took a two games to none lead in the Series. The Dodgers won the next three games, and the Series returned to Yankee Stadium. The Yankees hammered the Dodgers in Game 6. Johnny Podres, who won the second game, started Game 7 for Brooklyn, and the Yankees started lefty Tommy Bryne. Playing the percentages, Alston during the year had often juggled his lineup, with switch hitter Junior Gilliam playing second base against right-handers with lefty-swinging Sandy Amoros in left field — and Gilliam switching to left field against lefty pitching with right-handed hitter Don Zimmer at second.

With lefty Bryne pitching, Alston had Gilliam in left and Zimmer at second. The Dodgers scored a run in the fourth on a two-base hit by Campanella, who

Sandy Amoros makes "the Catch."

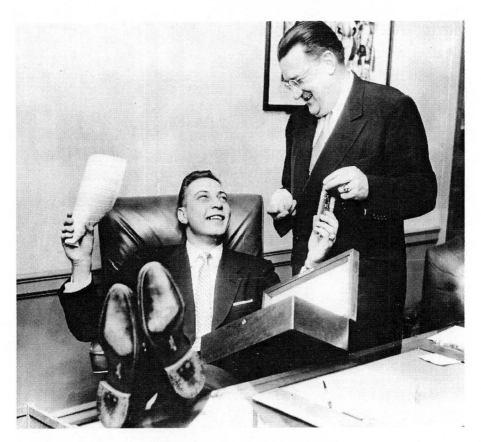

Johnny Podres and Walter O'Malley.

was singled in by Hodges. In the sixth inning, leading only 1–0, the Dodgers loaded the bases. When right-hander Bob Grim, a Brooklyn native, came in to pitch, Hodges scored a run with a sacrifice fly, and a walk to third base-man Don Hoak reloaded the bases. Alston pinch hit the lefty-hitting George Shuba in place of righty Zimmer. Shuba flied out. Now Alston had to replace Zimmer at second base. He decided to put Amoros in left and move Gilliam in to second base. This turned out to be the key decision of the Series.

In the sixth inning, the Yankees had one out when Billy Martin walked, and Gil McDougald bunted safely for a hit. Yogi Berra was up. Podres was still on the mound for the Dodgers. Podres' fastball seemed to be slowing as he tired, and the Dodgers moved Amoros away from the left field line, figur-ing the left hand hitting Berra, normally a dead pull hitter, would really be able to pull Podres. Podres threw an outside pitch, and Berra slapped the ball late, and hit it toward the left field foul line. The left-handed Amoros raced toward the line. Nearing the warning track, he reached out with his right (gloved) hand and just managed to grab the ball. Had the right-handed Gilliam been in the same spot in left, it was highly unlikely he could have made the catch since his glove hand would have trailed the play. Amoros' spectacular grab was turned into a double play, as Amoros threw to Reese who threw to Hodges at first base to double McDougald.

It was the game turning point. In the Yankee eighth, the Yanks put on two runners, but failed to score. With the Dodgers still leading 2–0, the Yankees batted in the bottom of the ninth. After retiring the first two batters, Podres faced Elston Howard. Howard hit an easy grounder to Reese at short. Reese threw to first, the ball bounced in the dirt, but Hodges scooped it out, and the Dodgers had won their first World Series.

Pandemonium broke out in Brooklyn. People were dancing in the streets. Impromptu parties sprang up all over the borough. Finally, next year was now.

And yet, in that winter of the Brooklyn Dodgers' greatest glory, the talk over Brooklyn was that if the Dodgers didn't get a new ballpark, they might move. O'Malley scheduled seven regular season home games to be played in Jersey City's Roosevelt Stadium, one game against each of the other seven National League teams. The action was a kind of unspoken threat that, in effect, said, "Build me a new stadium. See, I can take our games out of Brooklyn for seven games a year. I could do it for all of them."

The next year, Brooklyn made another run at the pennant and edged out the up-and-coming Milwaukee Braves. Once more, the Dodgers would play the Yankees in the World Series. The Dodgers won the first two games at Ebbets Field, and the Yankees won the next two games at Yankee Stadium. In the fifth game, Yankee starter Don Larson pitched against the Dodgers' Sal Maglie. After a Mantle homer and another Yankee run, the Yanks led 2–0 in the sixth. Don Larson still hadn't allowed a base runner. He was pitching a perfect game, something that had never been done in a World Series. Larson continued his perfection into the ninth inning and struck out pinch-hitter Dale Mitchell to win the game with the first, and still only, perfect game in World Series history.

In the next game, the Dodgers' Clem Labine and the Yankees' Bob Turley each pitched ten scoreless innings and in the 11th Jackie Robinson singled in Brooklyn's winning run. Once again, the two teams went to a seventh Series game.

The Dodgers' Newcombe started Game 7 and allowed home runs to Berra in the first and third innings, and to Elston Howard in the fifth. Relief pitcher Roger Craig gave up a grand slam homer to the Yanks' Skowron in the seventh, and the Yanks went on to win 9–0.

Jackie Robinson had decided to retire after the season, and he accepted a $10,000 payment from *Look* magazine to announce his retirement in an upcoming issue. Meanwhile, O'Malley traded Robinson to the Giants. Robinson held back on his announcement until the magazine was issued. The old Dodgers were beginning to change.

In 1956, O'Malley was increasing pressure to get New York City to build him a new Brooklyn ballpark. O'Malley had been talking about a new ballpark for years. He wanted several sites, one of them over the Long Island Railroad Station in Brooklyn. The New York politicians, most noticeably Robert Moses, wouldn't give it to him. O'Malley began secretly courting Los Angeles.

O'Malley arranged a trade of minor league franchises with Phil Wrigley, of the Wrigley Gum Company, who owned the Chicago Cubs and who owned the Los Angeles Angel (Cub franchise) in the Pacific Coast League. Because Wrigley held the Pacific Coast franchise, he held rights to the territory O'Malley wanted. O'Malley swapped the Dodger minor league franchise in Fort Worth for the Cub franchise in Los Angeles. A steal for O'Malley.

Next, O'Malley knew that the other baseball owners wouldn't approve a move to the West Coast if only one team went there. The cost of flying there for just one series of games wouldn't be worth it. O'Malley needed an accomplice, and he found it in New York Giant owner Horace Stoneham, who arranged to take his Giants to San Francisco. Stoneham had already been planning a move of the Giants to Minneapolis, site of their top farm club. O'Malley and Stoneham both received National League permission for their move and the deal was set. They would both move to the West Coast at the conclusion of the 1957 season.

During the 1957 season, rumors abounded about the Dodgers' move. That year the Dodgers played eight National League games in Jersey City. Campanella was hurt and was getting old. He was 37 and had been playing professionally for over 20 years, and his body was worn down. Reese was 38 and had lost a few steps, and he was playing more at third base because of his diminished range. Furillo was now 35 years old and his knees were hurting; Hodges was 33; Erskine was only 30, but his arm miseries were paining him. The Dodgers' young pitching was its strength. Don Drysdale won 16 games and Sandy Koufax exhibited flashes of his brilliant potential. Koufax, who would later pitch four no-hitters and go on to the Hall of Fame after his success in Los Angeles, was up and down in performance, but everyone recognized the promise.

O'Malley let Ebbets Field deteriorate. He knew of his planned move, but he hadn't received official approval yet. But he didn't want to spend any more money than he had to on Ebbets Field, and the place began to look frayed. It needed paint, and the playing surface needed work. The crowds were off, the Dodgers weren't playing well, and the team finished in third place, trailing the Milwaukee Braves by 11 games.

Joe Pignatano, a Brooklyn native who made it to the Brooklyn Dodgers during their last season in Brooklyn, recalls when the players knew that the

Sandy Koufax — Brooklynite as a young Dodger.

move was definite. "In August, O'Malley was asked to guarantee that the Dodgers would be back in Brooklyn. When he failed to issue a guarantee, we knew. We were going to move to LA."

By late season the move had been all but announced. The Dodgers' last scheduled game at Ebbets Field was on September 24, 1957, against the Pittsburgh Pirates. Only 6,702 depressed Dodger fans attended, and the Dodgers defeated the Pirates by a score of 2–0 in only two hours and three minutes. Dodger organist Gladys Gooding played "Auld Lang Syne" and it was over. The Brooklyn Dodgers were on their way to Los Angeles.

Mark Lazarus was born in Brooklyn in 1949 and has lived there most of his life. As a boy, he lived close to Ebbets Field, and the Dodgers are a vivid recollection of his youth. He was one of the first fans to buy season tickets to the new Brooklyn Cyclones.

Mark Lazarus: "In 1957, we knew that the Dodgers were going to move to Los Angeles to play in the Coliseum. The minute the news came out, we all knew it. It didn't really hit home until on Opening Day the next year when they weren't here. As far as I was concerned, I was still a fan rooting for Snider and Hodges, even though they were out there. The thing that hit me hardest during the off-season between their being here and their not being here was Campanella getting hurt. [Campenella, driving on icy roads, was in an accident in which his car overturned, leaving his lower body paralyzed.] That bothered me more than anything else, that Campanella wouldn't be able to play another game. Maybe it was like destiny. He was the backstop; as a catcher he was the leader of the team. It all began to fall apart after that. He was no longer in baseball; the Dodgers were no longer in Brooklyn."

Some people thought that within a few years Brooklyn would get another major league team. Brooklyn, whose population from 1957 to 2002 was in the range of 2.7 million people, more than most major league cities, never had a baseball team for 44 years, or basically two generations.

Ebbets Field was demolished in 1960 to make way for a housing development. The Polo Grounds was left standing, and it became the home field of the expansion New York Mets when National League baseball returned to New York in 1962.

For over 50 years, the Dodger and Giant fans had the fiercest of baseball rivalries. Then, in one year, both teams were gone. For a few years their games were carried as radio recreations in New York, but soon their fans began to lose interest in the teams, and the games were dropped.

The Dodgers had a poor first season in Los Angeles, but then rebounded to win the World Series in 1959 over the White Sox. The Dodgers were led by the pitching phenoms Drysdale and Koufax, and they still had Hodges, Snider, Furillo, Zimmer, Neal, and Podres. Roseboro now caught in place of Campanella; Roseboro was backed up by Brooklynite Pignatano. But most Dodger fans had lost their allegiance to the Dodgers when they moved. The fans held nothing against the players. But when Los Angeles won the second World Series in Dodger history, only four years after winning their first, few fans in Brooklyn cared.

There was a clamor to bring National League ball back to New York, and once more Branch Rickey was involved. Rickey was involved in the new proposed major league, called the Continental League, which would put a franchise in New York. The prospect of competition from that league forced Major League Baseball to set up an expansion franchise for New York, and the Mets came into existence in 1962.

For all of the century, Dodger and Giant fans had been rivals. Now New York would again have National League baseball, but it would have only one team, not playing in Brooklyn, but temporarily in Manhattan before the move to Queens. Now for the first time, Dodger and Giant fans came together to root for one team. Casey Stengel, who had played for both the Dodgers and Giants, managed the team. The initial Met team obtained a number of former Dodgers. Gil Hodges played first base. Hodges had moved to Brooklyn when he married and had never left. The Mets had Roger Craig on the mound,

Don Zimmer at third base and Charlie Neal at short. Later in the season, the Mets would pick up Joe Pignatano and Clem Labine. The Met uniforms reflected their baseball heritage. Their colors had blue, for the Dodgers — and orange, for the Giants. The Mets had brought National League ball back to New York. The first year they were terrible, winning only 40 games and losing 120, but the fans loved them. In two years, they were in Queens. Under manager Gil Hodges, they won a World Championship in 1969, and they won a second World Championship in 1986 when the Cyclones' pitch-

Gil Hodges at home in Brooklyn.

ing coach, Bobby Ojeda, was their mound ace, and Cyclones hitting coach Howard Johnson was one of their key players. Lots of Brooklynites rooted for the Mets, but some in Brooklyn rooted for the Yankees. Brooklyn didn't have its own team. It would take a new century for that.

Old and New Haunts

In the period of the Dodgers' greatest triumphs, 1947–1957, a Dodger fan could follow the progress of his team from almost anywhere in Brooklyn. One could walk down the street and listen to the game as it came broadcast from the open windows and from the stoops of houses. Go to the beach and it was the same thing. Transistor radios on the beach and boardwalk kept the game within easy listening range, so that a fan didn't need to miss a pitch. Kids would listen to the games in the neighborhood candy stores, and then wait around for the early editions of the newspapers to read about what they had just heard, or if they didn't have a radio, to pick up the running scores of the night games. For kids, the hangout was the candy store. For adults, the hangout was the local tavern.

At the time Jackie Robinson arrived, following the Dodgers while not at the game was done mainly by radio. All the bars had radios, and they were usually tuned to the Dodger games. As Carl Prince recounts in his extensive account of Brooklyn's baseball culture *Brooklyn's Dodgers,* fans would sit in bars such as the Dodgerville Room at Junior's Restaurant, or Jay's Tavern, listen to Red Barber and Connie Desmond's radio broadcasts and engage in friendly (and sometimes not so friendly,) debate. Later, in the early fifties, television became predominate in bars. It was before most homes could afford it. Fans gathered around the tiny ten-inch screens for televised games, but most games weren't televised, and radio remained a big part of bar culture throughout the Dodgers' stay in Brooklyn.

Fights in Brooklyn bars over the Dodgers occurred, but there is little evidence to say that actual physical fights happened at any greater rate than at bars in other cities (or in the case of New York City, boroughs). There were plenty of verbal arguments, and the bartender often settled them. Sometimes, however, things got rough. As recounted in Prince's *Brooklyn's Dodgers,* a patron from New Jersey was thrown out of several Brooklyn bars when he was trying to watch the 1952 World Series between the Dodgers and the Yankees, and he mistakenly made his allegiance to the Yankees known. Another incident from *Brooklyn's Dodgers* bears mention. In the same World Series, another Yankee fan was in a Brooklyn bar and was rooting for the Yankees when he was told, "Why don't you go back where you belong, Yankee lover?"

"I got a right to cheer my team," responded the Yankee fan. "This is a free country."

"This ain't no free country, chum," countered the Dodger fan. "This is Brooklyn."

Baseball legend has it that sometimes Brooklyn fans became so embroiled over arguments about the Dodgers that people died in barroom fights, but the only murder concerning the Dodgers in a Brooklyn bar occurred in 1932. There was a 1955 killing, but it happened in the Borough of Queens and it was done by a Yankee fan who "couldn't stand the thought that the Yankees had lost even once."

Hugh Casey's Tavern was right near Ebbets Field, at 600 Flatbush Avenue. It was very popular with the Dodger players in the 1940s. Casey, while pitching for the Dodgers, even lived in an apartment above the tavern. It was popular with the players as well as Dodger fans who wanted to talk to the players. In this age before widespread television, players were not the visual celebrities that they are today, and the interaction between fan and player was more down to earth. The fact that most of the Dodger players of the team's golden age lived in Brooklyn, in the midst of their fans, made drinking at the same bar a natural thing to do. Also, fans and players of the time were not separated as much by income as they are today. Most players made a good income, but they were not anything close to millionaires, and beginning players and substitutes often had salaries comparable to those of many of their fans. Hugh Casey's Tavern kept Brooklyn fans even after Casey was traded, and even after his suicide in 1951. Red Barber noted that Hugh Casey's was often the place where the Dodger players celebrated many of their victories.

Johnny Podres started his minor league career with Newport News in 1951, and then won 21 games for Hazard, Kentucky, in the Mountain States League. He was with Brooklyn two years later. In the 1955 World Series, this gutsy 23-year-old left-hander beat the Yankees in Game 3, and then shut out the Yankees in Game 7 to give Brooklyn its only World Series championship. He was the 1955 World Series Most Valuable Player. He spent 1956 in the Navy, then led the National League in ERA and shutouts in 1957. He won Game 2 of the 1959 World Series and helped the Dodgers to their first post–Brooklyn World Championship.

Johnny Podres won the greatest game in Brooklyn Dodger history as he shutout the Yankees to win the 1955 World Series. He discusses some Dodger haunts of the 1950s.

Johnny Podres: "You'd have your favorite places where people went. On Montague Street, you had two or three great places for Italian food. There's a little place some players would go after the game, near the Bossert Hotel, called The Fisherman, and there was Armando's Restaurant, and there was a place that had great steaks called Tony's Supper Club. There was a place across the street from Ebbets Field, owned by a guy named Gus, and we'd play a day game on Thursday, and after the game he's make corned beef and cabbage, and we'd play two handed pinochle with him. Boy, it was great."

Carl Prince's book *Brooklyn's Dodgers* shows that Jay's Tavern at 22 Clinton was a middle class milieu and was in Brooklyn Heights, one of Brooklyn's finest neighborhoods. A number of the Dodgers frequented Jay's, including Hank Berhman, George Shuba, and Rocky Bridges. Jay's was dark, quiet and more private than most bars, and the Dodgers could relax there in relative anonymity.

Another favorite hangout for Dodger fans was the Dodgerville Room at Junior's Restaurant. Despite the name, the bar welcomed Giant and Yankee fans. The bar also welcomed women, which many bars in Brooklyn at the time did not.

A partial list of some other watering holes included the Parkside Tavern, the Dodgers' Cafe, the Pineapple Bar, Rattigan's Bar, Pat Diamond's Bar and Grill, the Web Café, and Freddie Fitzsimmons Bowling Alley and Restaurant. Farrell's was a very famous hangout for Dodger fans.

Carl Erskine: "In Bay Ridge, we used to go to the Hamilton House, out near Fort Hamilton. That was a nice restaurant. And we'd go to Casa Bianca, and for people from the Midwest there were a lot of dishes we'd never heard of. Like baked clams and rolletini, and they'd treat us like royalty. They couldn't do enough for us. And on off days, we go on picnics, go to Staten Island to a park. We'd sometimes go to Bear Mountain on off days. We'd play golf at West Point, that was one of our haunts. Before I was with the Dodgers, they'd go to Bear Mountain for spring training."

The Brooklyn Cyclones didn't have a long time to develop their haunt habits, but their favorite place was Peggy O'Neills, in Bay Ridge. This was a long, narrow place, in the Irish bar mode, with a 12-seat bar, some tables and a pool table, a dartboard, and a small bandstand area for rock groups, on weekends. Sometimes the bar was not so crowded, but on weekend nights it was pretty packed. The players mixed easily with fans and friends. The line blurs in minor league ball where the players are so accessible. The team executives would even show up after some games, like when the Cyclones clinched the regular season first place. It is a nice place, a friendly atmosphere, not upscale but not downscale, a middle class, attractive place where the players could relax. It was only a few blocks from where many of the players lived at Xaverian High School. Sometimes the Cyclones hung out at The Salty Dog, another Bay Ridge pub. The Salty Dog is built in the mode of a firehouse and has a replica life-sized antique fire engine right in the bar. It was a hangout for New York City firefighters and policemen, and Brooklyn Cyclone ballplayers.

The Cyclones also spent a few evenings at an old Brooklyn favorite, Lundy's Restaurant, in the Sheepshead Bay part of Brooklyn; these were scheduled evenings where they could mix with the fans. Some of the Spanish speaking players on the team hung out at other Brooklyn restaurants where the predominate language was Spanish.

Another favorite hangout of the new Brooklyn players was the Mermaid Deli. Located only a block from the ballpark, the Mermaid Deli had over fifty items of food in large trays on a huge buffet table. Players could fill up a plate for $3.99 a pound, and they often walked to the Mermaid Deli for lunch before a ball game. Sometimes the deli gave them a break when they weighed the food.

The Dodgers Leave Brooklyn

Walter O'Malley is a name that even today causes consternation when it's mentioned in Brooklyn. O'Malley, the Dodgers' owner, wanted to build a new stadium in downtown Brooklyn to replace aging Ebbets Field. When he couldn't get it, he moved the team to Los Angeles. But according to some players, it wasn't all O'Malley's fault that the Dodgers didn't remain in Brooklyn.

Joe Pignatano: "There was a whole bunch of rumors, and when O'Malley wouldn't commit himself to staying, we knew we were going to move. This was about July, or the beginning of August; then we knew we were going to L.A. All the people here blame O'Malley, but it wasn't O'Malley; it was the politicians. O'Malley wanted downtown Brooklyn. Flatbush Avenue, Atlantic Avenue, Fourth Avenue, and the Long Island Railroad were right there. He wanted to build a ballpark right on top of the Long Island Railroad, and he was going to build it; he didn't want city money. They said 'no' because right behind the Long Island Railroad was a string of wholesale meat houses. It was called the Fort Greene Meat Market. And they sold wholesale meats, and they didn't want to chase these guys out. Two years later, they moved to Hunt's Point. So they didn't give it to him. I believe that if they had given him that, he would have stayed.

"When the Dodgers moved, I had no choice. I had finally made the big leagues, and it's in my hometown, and I got to leave. It all worked out later because I spent 14 years with the Mets when I was home. [Pignatano became a longtime Mets bullpen coach.]

"It all goes back a long time. Time and time again, you always hear that O'Malley killed the Dodgers, and he brought them to LA, and all this stuff, but it's not Walter O'Malley that did it, but it was a man named Moses who did it and there is no doubt whatsoever. Walter O'Malley said, 'I'd love to have the ballpark here. It's going to be domed.'

"And when you think where you want the ballpark, we've got Flatbush and Atlantic Avenue in downtown Brooklyn, the Mecca of downtown Brooklyn, and there is nothing there. The Paramount Theater was about the best thing there, and there would have been growth there. And not only that, he was putting his money where his mouth was, and I think O'Malley had a right to do what he did because the ballpark was not able to accommodate what was coming. There was no doubt that baseball was going to expand. And it's going to go worldwide before it's all over, unless the owners kill baseball."

Mark Lazarus was eight years old in the summer of 1957. Like almost all the boys in his neighborhood on Parkside Avenue near Prospect Park, he loved the Dodgers. He now happily presides over Section 14 — the section in KeySpan Park just in back of the Cyclones' dugout, on the first base side. He is known as "The Mayor of Section 14." He's 5' 8" and 155 pounds, with sandy hair and lively eyes. By day, he works on Wall Street. At night, he's at the ballpark. It's not hard to let his boyish enthusiasm help you imagine him in Ebbets Field, rooting on his Dodgers.

Mark Lazarus: "In 1957, we knew that the Dodgers were going to move to Los Angeles to play in the Coliseum. The minute the news came out, we all knew it. It didn't really hit home until on Opening Day the next year when they weren't here. As far as I was concerned, I was still a fan rooting for Snider and Hodges, even though they were out there [Los Angeles]. When the Dodgers first left Brooklyn, you could still get their games on the radio. They were radio recreations, but at least you could still hear how they were doing. You could still follow the team. But after awhile, after a few years, you couldn't get the Dodger games on the radio anymore and as more and more Dodgers retired or were traded, interest in them tailed off.

"I remained a Dodger fan until the mid-sixties, and by then I had gradually become a Met fan. By the mid-sixties, you couldn't see the Dodgers anymore, you couldn't listen to the Dodgers anymore, and the Dodgers weren't the Dodgers. Koufax had retired. Drysdale was pushing it. Gilliam was getting older. Most of the old Dodgers were gone. Walter Alston, the manager, was still left. Hodges wasn't there anymore. Snider was gone; Furillo was gone; Campanella was gone. None of them were there anymore. So it wasn't the Dodgers that I grew up with, so I lost my attraction to them. Dodgers were no longer in Brooklyn."

"It wasn't until the Dodgers moved out that my father took me to a Yankee game, and he was a Yankee fan. But it was just to see a game; there was no real rooting interest for me. The difference was that at Ebbets Field I felt at home; in Yankee Stadium, I felt [like] a stranger, isolated. Partially, it was the size of Yankee Stadium, but it was also that Ebbets Field was just up the street, and it was filled with people from Brooklyn."

Marty Adler was born and raised in Brooklyn and began attending Dodger games in 1947. He is the president of the Brooklyn Dodgers Hall of Fame and is now a Brooklyn Cyclones fan.

Some Dodger fans felt as Marty Adler did:

"When the Dodgers left we weren't sad — we were angry. You could check the atmosphere. For the last three, four, five or ten games, attendance was down. Nobody would go. You could take the Empire State Building and put it in Ohio; it's like taking the Brooklyn Bridge and putting it in Maryland. You can't do that. This is 'like someone died.' You were angry."

The Decision to Field the Cyclones

Major League Baseball is in a very real sense a monopoly. There is only one Major League Baseball, divided into the National and American leagues. Major League Baseball has a set of affiliations with minor league baseball in which each major league team typically owns or has a working agreement with six minor league clubs in the United States. All of these minor league clubs are part of the National Association, and the National Association of minor league clubs and the major league teams form what is known as Organized Baseball.

The major leagues, in order to protect their franchises from intrusion by other major or minor league teams, had a rule in which the major league team had a protected zone of 75 miles around its home park. No other major or minor league club may establish a team within this zone without permission of the hometown team in the middle of the zone.

This rule worked fine for decades, but in the 1990s a new phenomenon began: the success of "Independent League" baseball. Before Branch Rickey had established his chain of minor league teams with the Cardinals, most minor league teams were not affiliated with major league teams. The teams owned their ball players and would sell them to higher minor league teams or to the major league teams. Independent leagues gradually died out until their recent revival. The independent leagues owe no allegiance to the territorial rule of Major League Baseball. After all, it was still a free country and capitalism allows competition. A Holiday Inn could build right next to a Ramada Inn in the United States, and so could an independent team establish their own territories irrespective of "Organized Baseball."

At first, the independent leagues were sloughed off and not taken too seriously by Major League Baseball, but the recent baseball strikes and the major's ticket prices have made minor league ball attractive for the affiliated leagues. Independent leagues began to want to get in on the game, and they sprang up all over the country. The Atlantic League, established in 1994, features teams in an area surrounding New York City. There is a team in Atlantic City, a team in Somerset County, New Jersey, a team in Bridgeport, Connecticut, and so on. There were rumors that the Atlantic League wanted to bring a team into Brooklyn. The Atlantic League played a schedule of about 120 games from May to mid–September and was eventually considered by most baseball people to play at least Double-A level, often using older players.

Thus, the Yankees and Mets, whose territory had heretofore been sacrosanct, were now open territory for the new leagues. Although never officially acknowledged as a reason for the Mets and Yankees to field farm teams in their own territory, it was speculated by some that one reason the Mets and Yankees wanted to bring minor league ball to their territory was to preclude an independent team from coming into town. In effect, the Mets and Yankees would be providing their own competition.

The Yankees wanted to establish a team on Staten Island, and they needed the Mets' permission to do so, since Staten Island was in the protected territory of both the Mets and the Yankees. The Mets possibly wanted to protect Brooklyn from "invasion" and so they made a deal with the Yankees. Each would agree to let the other establish minor league teams in New York City — the Mets in Brooklyn and the Yankees in Staten Island.

The Yankees bought the Watertown franchise of the New York–Penn League and took their affiliation with Oneonta and switched it to Watertown. Then the Yankees moved the franchise to temporary facilities in Staten Island, at the college of Staten Island. Playing with temporary metal bleachers and with tents set up as concession booths, the atmosphere was very minor league, but the Yankees had their foot in the door. The Mets did not own the Pittsfield franchise, their New York–Penn League affiliate, and negotiations to purchase the franchise fell through, so after the 1999 season, the Mets purchased the St. Catherine's franchise in the New York–Penn League. But the Toronto Blue Jays had a working agreement with the St. Catherine's team through the conclusion of the 2000 season. This meant that the Mets owned the franchise, but Toronto supplied the players, manager, and coaches. Meanwhile, the Mets had one year to go on their contract to supply players to Pittsfield.

In February of 2000, the Staten Island Yankee team, working through New York City's Economic Development Corporation, arranged a deal in which New York City would construct a $71 million stadium near the Staten Island Ferry Terminal. The 6,500-seat stadium was to be financed by tax dollars raised during construction of the stadium.

The Mets wanted to move the St. Catherine's franchise to Brooklyn at a temporary ballpark at the Parade Grounds, next to Brooklyn's Prospect Park in the center of Brooklyn. But neighborhood and other political opposition to the plan became noted as residents objected to the Parade Grounds as a site, citing fears of parking problems, traffic congestion, and a lessening of recreational use of the Parade Grounds for youth sports, noticeably soccer. The Mets were striving to get authorization to have the city build a permanent park at Coney Island, but they needed a field for the 2000 season. The Mets needed a temporary field quickly and arranged a deal to use the baseball field at St. John's University, and to add temporary seating and install lights.

The Mets in 2000 moved the St. Catherine's franchise to the Borough of Queens at St. John's. Meanwhile, the Mets' farm hands played at Pittsfield, while Toronto minor leaguers played at Queens, but the Mets operated the St. John's stadium, sold the tickets, and ran the concessions. The new team was called the Queens Kings. In the 2000 season, attendance at Queens was sparse, with the club averaging 1,200 fans a game. Fans knew that the team was temporary and that the team was just holding the fort until the Mets could play in Brooklyn — hopefully in 2001.

Brooklyn Borough President Howard Golden opposed the Mets' idea to bring their short-season A team to Brooklyn. He had been trying to bring baseball back to Brooklyn for years, and he argued that the borough deserved higher-level baseball, such as a Double-A full-season team. Golden argued that a higher level full-season team would give Brooklyn twice the number of games to provide for twice the entertainment and twice the benefits economically that would ensue. Despite his opposition, the city council approved construction of a $31 million stadium project (the cost including improvements in the area around the stadium itself).

The stadium would have 6,500 seats. It would be constructed on the site of the former Steeplechase Park, with the right field stands virtually on the boardwalk, and the famous Parachute Jump looming near right field. The site provided a view of the Atlantic Ocean, the beach and boardwalk. The famous Steeplechase Pier jutted out into the ocean from beyond right field. In fact, an extension of the wooden boardwalk was built right up to a ticket booth and entrance in right field. The sight was only a block and a half down the street from Nathan's original hot dog stand.

Behind the left-center field fence was The Cyclone roller coaster ride, still operating. The ballpark had a grass field, with one main level of seating, plus luxury boxes.

There was a parking lot built next to the stadium near the Abe Stark Ice Rink. The stadium lights had pastel rings built around them so that at night each light had a colorful ring around it. The outside of the park had sloping lights evoking the Cyclone ride, and on the scoreboard, in left center field, a wooden replica Cyclone was constructed. The outfield fence had advertisements printed on it, including one that said, "Hit this sign, Win a suit," evoking Abe Stark's long-time Ebbets Field sign of the same ilk. Looking from home plate, the boardwalk ran from beyond the outfield fence from center field to beyond right field. Beyond the fence in left field were the amusements of Coney Island that weren't on the boardwalk. From the seats, one could see Nathan's beyond the left field corner.

The stadium was designed to evoke an amusement park and it did. It felt like a baseball amusement park within a larger amusement park.

Construction began and the official groundbreaking was attended by Mayor Rudolph Giuliani, Ralph Branca, Mrs. Gil Hodges, Met co-owner Fred Wilpon, Brooklyn Cyclones president Jeff Wilpon, and the Dodger Sym-Phony, the band of roving musicians that used to play at Dodger games in Ebbets Field. The team was operated by the Brooklyn Baseball Club, but, in effect, was really owned by the Mets. The team conducted a name-the-team contest and many entrants suggested the winning entry — "Cyclones."

When the team was announced as coming to Brooklyn, the announcement created a national stir. There were articles in the *New York Times, New York Post, New York Daily News,* and *Newsday* about the team. There were also articles in newspapers and magazines around the country.

The Dodger Sym-Phony with Dodger players, Carl Furillo, Duke Snider, Don Newcombe, Pee Wee Reese, Jackie Robinson and Gil Hodges.

Dodger dance band – Duke Snider, Pee Wee Reese, Carl Erskine and Carl Furillo.

But despite the initial flurry of announcements about baseball being back in Brooklyn, no one was really sure what the fan response would be. The Queens Kings team averaged only about 1,200 fans a game, and most of the Kings' fans were Queens residents. How many Queens Kings' fans would remain fans when the new Met farm team was in Brooklyn? The last year the Dodgers were in Brooklyn the team drew over a million fans, actually a fairly high total for the 1950s. But, if the Dodgers drew that total as a major league team, what would a minor league team draw in Brooklyn? Nobody knew. The Cyclones' management was concerned.

The Staten Island Yankees had averaged 3,000 fans in their temporary facility in their second season. Brooklyn, a borough whose population was 2.7 million in the 2000 census, far surpassed Staten Island in population. But Staten Island hadn't had a professional baseball team since the original New York Metropolitans, who played there in the 1800s. It was certain that no one on Staten Island remembered that team. So professional baseball was a novelty on Staten Island.

In Brooklyn, minor league baseball was a novelty, but would a borough that formerly had major league baseball embrace the minor league variety? No one really knew. Initially, season ticket sales were for last year's holders of Queens Kings season tickets. Then after the Queens Kings' season ticket holders had their chance, the general public had a chance at season tickets. When on April 28, sales of individual game tickets began at the Kings Plaza Mall, the line of ticket buyers stretched around the block, and a picture of the line appeared in the *New York Times*. Sales were off and running. By now, it was clear that the team would be a hit. The opening home game was sold out, and ticket sales for the franchise were booming. At the ballpark gift shop, Brooklyn Cyclone hats were sold out before Opening Day.

Between Innings

Brooklyn's Neighborhoods

An independent city until 1898, Brooklyn is a city of neighborhoods, hundreds of them. Downtown Brooklyn has a big city feel to it, but walk a few blocks up Montague Street, past 215 Montague, where the Brooklyn Dodgers had their offices, and where they signed Jackie Robinson, and many others, and you're in Brooklyn Heights, which has wonderful small shops, great eateries, and the small feel of the best areas in Greenwich Village.

Prospect Park is in the heart of Brooklyn, and constructed by the same park architects who designed Manhattan's Central Park. Many feel that the immense Prospect Park benefited from the designers' experience in designing Central Park and that Prospects Parks trails, meadows, ball fields and lake are an improvement over the excellent design of Central Park.

Right next to Prospect Park is the neighborhood of Park Slope, with its brownstones, now an upper middle class area that earns its name by sloping from Prospect Park down to the water. Right next to the park is the Brooklyn Museum, one of the most famous art museums in the world. Next to the museum on one side is the Brooklyn Botanic Garden, also world renowned, and on the other side of the Brooklyn Museum is the main branch of the Brooklyn Public Library, with its famous Brooklyn Collection.

Near the East River is the Williamsburg section, now an up-and-coming area of artists, musicians, and writers, that someday will be noted for the prodigy it is nurturing today. Brooklyn has become an in-place for the young, and a family place for the older residents and their children, and still the borough of choice for many veteran Brooklynites.

Areas of Bensonhurst are like a small town, with many families remaining there for generations. Brighton Beach is now the home of thousands of Russian immigrants, and the predominate language on the streets is now Russian. Midwood looks like the suburbs, and Sheepshead Bay is like a seaport on the New Jersey coast, with its many fishing boats tied up at piers and docks, and its numerous seafood restaurants. Bay Ridge has many one and two family homes on tree-lined streets.

When Marty Haber, the field emcee during the Cyclone games, would introduce contestants for the various games like the dizzy bat race or the baseball toss, Haber would say, "Here's Tommy, from Bensonhurst," not "Tommy, from Brooklyn." The Brooklyn residence was understood, so Marty skipped the borough and got right to the neighborhood, the only exception being the occasional contestants from the other boroughs or New Jersey or upstate New York.

Happy Felton.

Carl Erskine: "While I was living in Bay Ridge, there was a respect and a kind of awesomeness about a Dodger living right down the street, and our kids were small, and we had baby sitters, girls that we knew from the neighborhood. And my wife would shop at the stores, and we got acquainted with the people who ran the businesses. And I'd take my kids for haircuts, down at Cosmo's Barbershop, and all the Italian guys in there would all yak about baseball. Oh, the Dodgers this, and the Dodgers that. The guy in the deli, too.

"I came from a small town in Indiana, and when I came to Brooklyn, it was like a foreign country, goodnight! All these people. But in the Bay Ridge neighborhood of Brooklyn, it was like a small town. And we went back to the same neighborhood every year. I lived on Ninety-Fourth Street near Third and Fourth Avenues. The whole place was called Lafayette Walk. They were row houses. The row houses are still there. I went back there last year to look, and it looked *exactly* the same. My son Gary is 50 years old, and he was six years old when we left there, and he went to the back of the house and looked where he used to play stickball with his brother. Gary said, 'Remember when if you hit it over there it was a single, over there was a double, and against the roof of the garage was a home run?' He said, 'Look, over there are still clothes lines hanging across the back,' and then he said, 'And, oh yeah, Dad, if you hit a pair of panties it was two runs.'

"The back yard was behind the houses. The garage was down low. And coming between the houses was a long, narrow driveway, and behind there were the garages. And that's where they played. There was a man in the neighborhood, Mister Keough, and about once a month he'd take a bushel basket and go up on the roof and retrieve all the balls. They used a lot of Spaldeens. And he'd give them back to the kids. And here's how I paid him back. Every year, we had two sponsors — Old Golds and Schaeffer Beer — and each week we'd get a case of the cigarettes and a case of the beer, and I didn't use either one of 'em. So I'd give them to Mister Keough and he would take care of my kids. I still hear from my baby sitters, Grace Monahan and her sister, a few times a year. When I was back and took my family back to Bay Ridge, I met a gentleman and I asked him if Mister Keough still lived here and the gentleman said, 'No, he's dead, but his daughter still lives there.'

"My point is what happened in Brooklyn could still happen today. When I went on a two week road trip and left my wife and children, no one felt threatened. The neighbors were all gentle. The neighbors were all great and took care of my family. I go back and think about the butcher, Joe Rossi; we'd buy our meat at Joe's butcher shop and Joe would say, 'You have a day game, come over and eat with us Tuesday night.' And Pee Wee and Duke and their families would come over and have a big feed, a big Italian meal at his house. Or Morris Steiner was a pediatrician who took care of our kids, at East Nineteenth Street — a beautiful man, and his wife Martha, and he'd invite us over for elegant meals after a ball game. So we were just like a small town. That could happen today; I don't think that's dead."

Mark Lazarus: "In '55, I remember seeing the victory parade down Flatbush Avenue. It was on a school day, and nobody was in school. Everybody was at the parade. I remember the paper and the yelling.

"At Ebbets Field, I remember the front facade when my father and I would go up for our tickets, and I remember going into the stadium and standing by the fence where the players would go into the clubhouse and go by that ramp, and I remember seeing the ballplayers walking to get into the dugout and out on the field. I remember the feeling of the crowd watching the game and being caught up in that.

"Back then, just like every other kid in Brooklyn, I knew the players' backgrounds, their statistics. I remember at night standing on the corner or playing box ball, or box baseball, and talking baseball incessantly. There was a game we would play over milkshakes, at the candy store, where you would have to guess the name of a ballplayer the other guy was thinking of. If you could guess it without any clues, it was a home run. If you guessed it after one clue, it was a triple, two clues a double, three clues a single. First, you stated whether the player was in the American or National League; the first clue was a team, the second clue a position. The third clue was initials. If you didn't get it after three clues, you were out. Naturally, you usually picked the most obscure players possible. This way, we learned about the players on all the teams in the majors.

"We would do this over milkshakes while we were waiting for the newspaper truck to come with the *Daily News* or the *New York Mirror*. We would look at the One Star Edition. That would give us the starting pitchers and maybe one inning. Then later would come the Three-Star Edition. That would give us the line score for maybe three innings. Then later would come the Five-Star Edition. That would give us maybe five innings. So we would wait for the papers while we were at the candy store. This would go on until we got the final paper or until the candy store closed.

"In those days, you would get the scores quicker that way than from the radio. The radio stations didn't have the news services that they have now. Plus, they didn't have transistor radios like they have now. If you were lucky, maybe you had a crystal set. They mostly had the big diode sets at home. So we would hang out there at Max's candy store. That was our hangout. It had the soda fountain. The candy. A few booths. So long as you had a soda in front of you, you could hang out there all night, unlike today where if you don't have ten dollars of food in front of you, it is 'so long.'

"Max knew all the families in the neighborhood. For most of us, it was carte blanche in there. We could order a milkshake and a hamburger, and put it on a tab, and our parents would come in at the end of the week and settle up with him. We never had money; we never needed money; we could just put it on the tab. We could walk in there and get a hamburger, fries, bubble gum, whatever we wanted. He'd even lend us a dime to make a phone call.

"It was a good twenty of us who literally were born there; we went to school there; we went to the candy store there, all the time; we went to the ball games, et cetera. It was always the same group of kids.

"We used to go out to the school yard at eight in the morning and use that big, thick chalk to make perfect foul lines for stickball, punch ball, whatever we were going to play. We were really nuts about making sure we had the proper distances for the bases. Lots of times the parents used to come out and watch us play. That was our life, especially in the summer. We'd play from morning till night. We played softball, touch ball, and stickball."

Duke Snider hit 326 home runs during the 1950s, most of them for Brooklyn. Duke could hit major league fastballs and curves, but he had more difficulty with stickball. "I tried it a few times, but I never played stickball very much because the broomstick was too light for me. I couldn't hit with that broomstick."

Mark Lazarus: "My earliest remembrances of stickball was as a four-year-old watching my older brother play. Before the playground was built, dozens of kids played in the street. As little kids, we would watch, and we'd run and get them the sodas, and they'd let us get the two-cent deposit for the bottles.

"Back at the candy store, we'd have the lime rickies, the Reese's, and our favorite, the egg creams. For an egg cream, you put in two fingers of milk, two fingers of U-Bet syrup, and stir it. Then you'd have a seltzer bottle that gives you the hard arridation (*sic*), gives you the foam. It's not the same now. The seltzer isn't as strong. You squirt in the seltzer. Even today, you can still get the U-Bet's chocolate syrup in just about any supermarket in Brooklyn, but for some odd reason you have to get it in the ethnic section of the store. Maybe because it's kosher, I don't know. The old soda trucks, that used to deliver the seltzer to houses, once a week; well, they also supplied the syrup. So egg creams were a natural part of our growing up. Even now, I'll send some of the egg cream syrup to Florida to my ex-wife so she can make egg creams because you can't get the right kind of syrup in Florida."

Marty Adler: "It was great. It was a great time to grow up. It was safe. It was fun. I mean you look back and you forget some of the problems and everybody, but you play ball on the street, low organization games. We didn't have equipment. No one took lessons. You learn [the] sport, but you could walk [in] all the low organizational games like punch ball, stickball, stoopball, caulk ball, they were all you played — sluigi or running bases. That's what we call a guy in the middle; he had to catch a ball. Sluigi. I haven't played that for 100 years. All these low organization games were to help you develop skills for baseball, punch ball, stickball, everything. [In a] low organizational game, if you had twenty guys who wanted to play, twenty guys played. If two guys played, two guys would play. You had a stick and a ball, or a fist and a ball. The stoop ball or box ball, which is a form of this or that. Everything was geared to honing the skills of baseball."

Duke Snider: "We had a block party every summer, a big barbecue. We lived in the same area for quite a few years. We got to know the people. I got to know the area and baseball-wise, we were at home. Even though I was born and raised in Southern California, Brooklyn was my home during the summer, and Vero Beach was my home during the spring, and we were very comfortable there. And so Brooklyn was a very comfortable place to live at that time. Some of the fellows lived in downtown Brooklyn at the Bossert Hotel, and there were a couple of restaurants down there. We just moved in the same place every year, and it was just like we never left it. We lived in a home attached to another home. The people owned a home, and they had another place out in Breezy Point, and they'd go out there every summer, and we'd rent their house."

Clem Labine was the Dodgers' key relief pitcher in the 1950s, yet two of his most notably victories were as a starter — he shut out the Giants in Game 2 of the 1951 playoffs and blanked the Yankees in a 10-inning triumph in the 1956 World Series. In the 1955 World Series, Labine pitched 4⅓ innings of relief to win Game 4 and also recorded a save in Game 5. He went with the

Clem Labine, Junior Gilliam, Duke Snider and Billy Loes.

Dodgers when they moved to Los Angeles, and later pitched for Detroit and Pittsburgh before finishing his career with the Mets.

He's six-foot and trim. He now lives in Vero Beach, where he attended so many spring trainings as a Dodger, and now is coaching adult baseball campers at Dodgertown.

He won some of the most pressure-packed games in history. He speaks calmly and with an evident fondness for his days in Brooklyn. After his baseball career, he became a successful clothing manufacturer back in his native Rhode Island.

> **Clem Labine:** "In Brooklyn, I lived in Bay Ridge, up near Dyker Beach. And that was wonderful. We had a lot of people up there: Preacher, Duke, Ersk, Russ Meyer. It was a place where we could be together. We could ride into the ballpark together, whether it was Ebbets Field or the Polo Grounds. It was very family orientated.
>
> "We lived in predominately an Italian neighborhood, so pasta was always forthcoming, and baby sitters were easy. My wife would go to the ballpark most any time she wanted to, and we knew we had safe sitters because most of the time the sitters were mother and father, and they'd say, 'Bring the kids over.' And they'd never charge you, either. They'd say, 'Go to the ball game. Go to the ball game.'"

Clyde King, from Goldsboro, North Carolina, first pitched for the Brooklyn Dodgers in 1944 when he was only 19 years old. He was an effective relief pitcher for them for six seasons. Later, he managed the San Francisco Giants, the Atlanta Braves, and the New York Yankees. He was also the Yankees's general manager. He still works for the Yankees as a special assignment scout and still resides in Goldsboro.

> **Clyde King:** "We lived out in Bay Ridge. We lived next door to Duke Snider, in a big house on Marine Avenue and Lafayette Walk, near Ninety-Second Street, and above us lived Rube Walker and his wife, and around the corner lived Pee Wee Reese, Carl Erskine, Andy Pafko, and Preacher Roe. And we'd drive to the ballpark together. It was great. We had a large house, though, and a lot of times the wives would bring a dish over, and we'd talk baseball after the game and have dinner. I didn't

Clyde King — Dodger pitcher.

know what the stock market was in those days. It would be on a Sunday afternoon after the game or after a day game during the week. We did this once a week or every two weeks.

"We had kids coming to our door all the time. They would ask for autographs. Well, I asked this one young boy, who asked for an autograph, if he'd like to go to a game with us that day, and we took him to the game. And about four or five years ago, he wrote an article in the *New York Times Magazine* about how nice we were to him.

"If you were to drop out of an airplane and land on the streets of Brooklyn, you would think you were in your own hometown. They had beautiful, tree lined streets, and we would have dinner a lot at the Hamilton House. There was a drugstore on the corner near where we lived, and the fellow at the drugstore always listened to the game on the radio, and when I stopped in the drugstore after the game, he'd have a quart of ice cream there for me to take home. I loved Brooklyn.

"My years in Brooklyn were just fabulous. The people, the fans were just great the way they treated us. I've never enjoyed any other time in baseball more than I enjoyed my time in Brooklyn."

INNING 4

Opening Days

The Cyclones' First Game

It's not 2001 in Jamestown. Oh, you can find a calendar and prove that it is, and if you look closely, you can find a few computers in the press box that might give a clue, but it's not really 2001.

This is where the Cyclones will open the season, in Diethrick Park — which was built in 1941 and although remodeled since, it still has at least a 1950s look. You can find the park from the center of Jamestown by driving through a neighborhood of wooden homes that are from the earlier part of the 1900s. It's a sleepy neighborhood; there is hardly any traffic, and small children play in the front yards.

When you see the ballpark, it has a settled look. Parking is on a grass lawn next to the stadium. It's free. There are no gates or attendants. You just park where you want and you head for the stadium. In front of the stadium, on a yellow advertising sign, like the ones that sit in front of highway restaurants, black plastic letters announce, *Jammers vs. Brooklyn.* Seeing the word *Brooklyn* on the sign gives a thrill and a strange sense of surreality. Brooklyn? Here? Of course, it's the Brooklyn Cyclones the Jammers are playing, not the Brooklyn Dodgers of old, but "the time seems out of joint." In this settled upstate town, the sign should say, *Jammers vs. Batavia,* or *Jammers vs. Pittsfield* but *Jammers vs. Brooklyn?* Brooklyn should be playing the New York Giants or the New York Yankees, but Jamestown? Jamestown in many ways is as far from Brooklyn as you can get, and the distance is not only figurative. Literally, Jamestown is about as far as you can get from Brooklyn and still be in New York State. It's 407 miles and Jamestown is so far west the people talk with a Midwestern accent — or at least what sounds like a Midwestern accent to one used to the speech of Brooklyn, or anywhere else in New York City. The sign in front of the stadium only presages what is becoming obvious. Brooklyn is not just another addition to the venerable New York–Penn League.

New York City Police man the gates as fans wait at players' gate.

When Brooklyn mixes with Jamestown, something different is happening. Some new combination is occurring. This isn't the return of the Brooklyn Dodgers. But this isn't the same old New York–Penn League, either. Brooklyn is mixing with Jamestown. Something brand new is happening. And it's starting here. Tonight.

It's 4:30 P.M. The gates haven't opened to the public. The Cyclones' bus arrives from their hotel, a Red Roof Inn five minutes out of town. As the bus parks next to the stadium, the Cyclone players get off the bus, to total silence. They quietly enter the stadium gates and go to their "clubhouse," which is a small cement building behind the first base stands. It is the size of a small high school field house where there is just enough room for the players to change. To get to the field from the clubhouse, the players and staff have to walk across a cement concourse that separates the stands from the concession area, and then they walk through a small gate to the field.

After the Cyclones have changed for the game, they come out of the clubhouse in their road uniforms — gray with blue pinstripes, with blue caps with an interlocking B/C on them (for Brooklyn Cyclones) — and head across the concourse to the entrance to their dugout. After 44 years of no Brooklyn baseball, this entrance is eerily quiet. It seems routine.

The Cyclones assemble in the outfield and then take a short jog near the outfield warning track. The Jamestown Jammers, an affiliate of the Atlanta

Braves, take batting practice, and the Cyclones jog loosely, some of them always keeping an eye out in case any long drives are hit their way. The only significant sounds are cracks of the bat on good drives. The Cyclones form a large circle in the outfield and stretch.

Outside the stadium, about twenty people wait in line. The gates haven't opened yet. Most people arrive by car, but some are on foot. Fans greet each other, and the ticket-takers know some of the fans. The line outside the stadium swells to thirty people as inside the stadium the mostly teenaged concession workers scurry about getting the food ready. The gates open, and the fans enter the park. Nobody seems in much of a hurry. The only man in a sports jacket in the stadium is Noah Diethrick, on the Jammers' board of directors. He greets people entering the stadium, some of them by name.

John Blackburn is a young umpire in his second professional season. He was working the plate as part of the two-man umpiring crew for tonight's opening game. He resides in Brick, New Jersey, and like the players, is trying to work through the minors and reach the big leagues.

John Blackburn: "When we first got to the park, all we noticed is that there were camera crews everywhere. It was like 'wow,' it was going to be interesting.

"We figured it would be a few extra crews because there were some camera crews from Brooklyn. We knew New York papers were going to be coming up just to get some shots for the first game, but there were a lot more than we expected.

"Our first concern was to make sure that these guys [photographers] are going to be off in the safe distance so that it didn't disrupt the game and they're in a safe area.

"The first thing we saw, we went straight to the GM [general manager] and asked him where the cameramen are going to be. He told us, and we agreed to that.

Fan with "Dem Bums" sign.

"We did our daily routine. The first time in a town, we get there a little bit earlier, just to get ready. First day in the town we usually arrive an hour and a half before the game. We like to take a walk around the field just to check out the outlay of the whole field, maybe notice that there might be a hole in the outfield fence, or if there are any peculiarities to each field so that if a ball is hit on a certain area we know how to handle it.

"We have to think ahead There might be a hole in right-center field, so that if a ball goes that way we already know … someone will have to go out there and, check that just to make sure that it's legit. So if someone said, 'Hey, the ball got out of the fence,' we're already well aware of the fact that there's a possibility that it could happen. In some games, they had all those different billboards, different heights and all that. We're going to look at all those to see how they connect to the main fence. Is that a recessed fence where the hit is a home run?

"We get through this so we're checking all those things, checking all of the outfield fence. Are there any holes in the dugouts? How do the dugouts play? Is there a lip in the front that the ball can bounce off and still be live?"

The Brooklyn team is now taking their batting practice. As the visiting team, they hit after the home team, a practical consideration allowing a visiting team more time to arrive at a stadium, a time which they may need after long bus rides. Brooklyn is written in blue script across their chests, but somehow it's a surprise not to see the team more Dodger-like, in their uniforms.

Minor league teams don't hire batting practice pitchers. The coaching staff generally does the honors. First on the mound is Edgar Alfonzo, the Cyclones' manager and the 33-year-old older brother of Edgardo Alfonzo, the Mets' second baseman. Edgar Alfonzo, known as Fonzie, was a minor league infielder for 13 years, never making the majors despite having productive minor league seasons in Double-A. Alfonzo throws from behind a protective screen from a distance of 50 feet, closer than the official distance of 60 feet six inches. This saves wear and tear on the pitchers' mound and also enables a batting practice pitcher to throw a reasonably challenging pitch with only moderate speed because of the close distance. Alfonzo quickly throws one pitch after another. To linger in batting practice means to get fewer swings because the Cyclones only have 30 minutes to hit, so after his turn hitting, a player quickly leaves the batting cage as another player jumps in. After Alfonzo throws to a group of five Cyclones, Howard Johnson takes over, pitching workmanlike strike after strike.

Later, Bobby Ojeda takes his turn. Ojeda loves this. Looking as if he could still get batters out in the Bigs, Ojeda sometimes mixes in a curve or his "dead fish" fading change-up, a pitch that acts like a combination change-up and screwball, fading from the batter — like a dead mackerel. Sometimes batters later admitted that they wish Ojeda would just lay the ball in, after all, it's only batting practice, but Ojeda, who goes about life with a zest that's irrepressible, can't help himself. For 15 big league seasons he battled hitters from the mound, battling them right into the 1986 World Series, which his Mets won. Old habits die hard.

As the Jammers take infield practice, the Cyclones rest in their dugout. If they need to change their jersey, grab another bat, or use the clubhouse bathroom, they have to leave the dugout, then walk past the stands and across the concession concourse, which now has a few fans in it. This is no big deal to the fans as the occasional Cyclone passes them near the hotdog stand. This is not Mike Piazza passing, it's Francis Corr, his name on the program, or it's Forrest Lawson, or Noel Devarez, players of whom the Jamestown fans have never heard.

> **Frank Corr:** "The first game out at Jamestown, it was a good feeling. You still had a little bit of butterflies. I said to myself, 'Oh, God, my first minor league ball game.' I said to myself, 'I just want to get one hit, just one hit. That's all I want.' I was kind of nervous. But it was kind of good to start on the road, because when you start in an atmosphere that's much smaller than Brooklyn, it kind of made it feel like a normal game.'"

No one asks for autographs — hardly anyone looks up. Jamestown has had professional baseball off and on since 1939, and these fans are not easily awed or particular interested in the visitors. But they're not in the least antagonistic toward Brooklyn, either. These fans have not been to see the Jammers play since last year, and they are more interested in renewing ballpark acquaintances and in saying hello to people in the ballpark. It may be Brooklyn's first baseball game in 45 years, but for these Jamestown fans, there is a sense of a ritual being renewed. It's Opening Day, not for the first time, but it's Opening Day, once again.

Nearly all of the fans are here to root for Jamestown, a farm team of the Atlanta Braves. But behind first base are three exceptions — loud exceptions — young guys, in Brooklyn Cyclone caps. The Jamestown fans are sitting quietly. These Brooklyn fans are standing, jumping around with nervous energy. They're cheering in batting practice for the Cyclones. It turns out that they drove the eight hours from Brooklyn to Jamestown, leaving this morning for the night game. Too young, in their twenties and thirties, to remember the Brooklyn Dodgers, they are the officers of the newly formed Brooklyn Cyclone fan club. Peter Witt, president, and two friends were there for Brooklyn.

A few fans quietly gather behind the Cyclones' first base dugout. They have recognized Howard Johnson, the Cyclones' batting coach and former star infielder with the Mets' 1986 World Series winner. Jamestown, despite its distance from New York City, still has predominately Met and Yankee fans — cable television makes it easy — and the fans ignore the Cyclones' players, of whom they have never heard, and ask Johnson for autographs. He's serious, obviously more concerned about his young players loosening up in front of him, but he politely signs the autographs, and quickly gets back on the field. Down in the right field bullpen, Bobby Ojeda, the Cyclones' pitching coach, chats with his pitchers, as Ojeda is yet to be undiscovered by autograph seekers.

The Cyclones have taken infield practice. They sit in their dugout as the field is readied for the game. The sellout crowd of 4,003 sits, talking to one another, or waiting in line for food; to most of the fans, Brooklyn seems to be merely an opponent for the night. Any team might do as well. It seems like the night is special because it is Opening Night, not because the opponent is Brooklyn.

However, there is a special guest: former Brooklyn Dodger pitching great Carl Erskine. Some of the older fans have noticed him as he stands near the Jamestown dugout, near the third base line. Wearing a royal blue Brooklyn Dodger satin warmup jacket and gray slacks, the 5' 10" Erskine doesn't appear much above his old playing weight of 165 lbs. He has gray hair now, and wears a Brooklyn Dodger hat with its white letter B on a royal blue cap. For baseball fans, used to pictures of him in his twenties and thirties, it takes a while for it to sink in that the Carl Erskine outside the Jamestown dugout is the Carl Erskine from memory. After all, he is now 74 years old. But the smile is the same; the eyes still twinkle like before; he looks good. And then the realization hits. Brooklyn baseball wasn't just in the previous generation. No, you look at the kids in the Brooklyn dugout now, and you see Carl Erskine,

and you realize it was two generations ago that Brooklyn had baseball. The kids in the Brooklyn dugout have fathers who are about 50 years old. Carl Erskine is the age of their grandfathers.

Gray-haired fans in the third base stands come close to the field boxes and call out to Erskine. They shout, "Hey Carl!" It's a friendly greeting, like at a reunion. Erskine turns toward the fans and waves. Another fan shouts, "Hi, Carl!" and Erskine turns to him and waves. Some of the gray-haired fans send what appear to be their grandchildren down to the edge of the field to ask Carl Erskine for an autograph. One girl of about ten asks a writer, in his fifties, for an autograph. Not knowing who the writer is,

Carl Erskine throws out first pitch at Jamestown, New York.

she has assumed that he is Carl Erskine. She has only underestimated things by about a generation, and the writer asks Erskine to sign for the girl, which he graciously does. While technically a night game, it's still a little before 7 P.M., and on June 19 it's practically the summer equinox, so it is still light out; it seems like afternoon. Nobody in this ballpark is making a fortune for playing, and the fans didn't pay a fortune for seeing the game. It's a warm night, it's the start of baseball season, and summer is two days away, and having a ten-year-old granddaughter get Carl Erskine's autograph for herself— or maybe for her grandfather — seems right. No money changes hands. The autograph, like the evening, is a gift.

Erskine is waiting to come on the field to throw out the first pitch. Standing near the Jamestown on-deck circle, he casually talks to local dignitaries and to a writer. When asked how he felt in seeing a team called Brooklyn play again, Erskine took note of what he coined "hybrid hats," referring to the Cyclone hats with the letter B, reminiscent of the old Brooklyn caps, entwined with the letter C, standing for the new, the Cyclones.

"When I saw the Cyclones run onto the field with Brooklyn on their shirts, then I felt a twinge," says Erskine and he points to his heart. It's 49 years to the day when Erskine pitched his first major league no-hitter.

Erskine gets a signal from a club official, and he strolls out to the mound. When he's there, the public address announcer tells the crowd that this evening marks the return of a baseball team to Brooklyn, and that Carl Erskine, the former Brooklyn Dodger pitching great, will be throwing out the first ball. The brief announcement gets good applause, but not announced was that this man had pitched for six pennant winners, won 122 games, had a winning percentage of .610, had pitched two no-hitters, had once held the single game World Series strikeout record of 14 (against the New York Yankees) and had helped the Brooklyn Dodgers win their only World Series, in 1955. Most of the Brooklyn Cyclone players do not know who Carl Erskine is.

Erskine goes into his windup and throws toward the plate. The pitch is high and inside. After he leaves the mound and is again near the dugout, Erskine jokes, "Not a strike, but nobody would be digging in against me."

While chatting with Erskine, I mention that I heard that he will be playing "Take Me Out to the Ball Game" on his harmonica during the seventh inning stretch. Looking forward to the rendition, I state, "'Take Me Out to the Ball Game,' the greatest song in the world."

Carl Erskine considers the statement for a second and then replies, "Second greatest. The greatest song in the world is "Happy Birthday."

The game is about to begin, and the event seems incongruous. The return of professional baseball to Brooklyn conjures big crowds in an urban environment with the stands packed with Brooklyn supporters. Somehow, the clock would be turned back to the 1950s. The players would be familiar faces, men in their mid-twenties to mid-thirties, with a history we all knew.

Yet here in Jamestown, a city with the gilt off the rose, a place more like a big town than a small city, were the anonymous Brooklyn Cyclones, a team averaging 21 years of age, opening in front of only a handful of fans actually rooting for them.

The first Brooklyn batter in 44 years is scheduled to be David Abreu, a 22-year-old second baseman from the Dominican Republic.

It's minutes before the start of the game. Carl Erskine is asked how he feels about the return of baseball to Brooklyn. "I wonder how many people will remember us," mused the Brooklyn legend. "That's more than a generation. It's really skipped a generation since we played there. Forty-four years is a pretty big gap. How many will remember?"

Many fans in Jamestown did remember. They even remembered the no-hitter that Erskine pitched on exactly this date, June 19, a mere 49 years ago.

The field is ready for the start of the game. Jamestown takes the field and "The Star Spangled Banner" is played. Lead-off man Abreu approaches the plate.

Coaching at first base is Howard Johnson and the other base-line coach is Alfonzo, who, like most minor league managers, coaches third.

The initial Brooklyn Cyclones' lineup had designated hitter David Abreu, who hit .288 last year for Capital City, leading off. Shortstop Robert "Mac" McIntyre, who played part of the year at Pittsfield in 2000, followed him. Hitting third was catcher Mike Jacobs, a left-handed hitter. Hitting clean-up was Noel Devarez, a right fielder up from Kingsport, with the bat held so far behind his head that it's almost wrapped around his neck before the pitch — a strong hitter. Fifth was Jeremy Todd, a big lefty swinger who played last season at Pittsfield and who is still learning his position switch to first base from

Frank Corr — Cyclones outfielder.

catcher. Sixth was left fielder Frank Corr, playing his first pro game, the stocky power hitter from Florida's Stetson University. Batting seventh was Forrest Lawson, in center field, up from Kingsport. Batting eighth was third baseman Edgar Rodriguez, making his United States pro debut, and hitting ninth was Leandro Arias, a second baseman coming back from an injury who last played professionally for the Mets' former franchise in the Gulf Coast League. On the mound was Luz Portobanco, the Nicaraguan who migrated to Miami, had a 94-mile-per-hour fastball, and was learning to speed up his curve and perfect a change-up.

On the mound, Jamestown right-hander Zach Minor, a top prospect, threw the first pitch to a Brooklyn batter since 1957. It's a fastball. Ball one. Then Abreu fouled a pitch off. On the third pitch, Abreu dropped a bunt near the first base foul line. As Abreu was racing to first base, near the foul line, his foot brushed against the ball. The Jamestown pitcher grabbed the ball and threw to first, too late to get Abreu. In the walkway just outside the Jamestown dugout, mild mannered Carl Erskine, instinctively taking the side of the pitcher and his competitive juices flowing, is yelling, "The ball hit him in fair territory. He's out! He's out!"

The Jamestown manager, Jim Saul, races out of the dugout and onto the field, arguing, as did Erskine, that the ball hit Abreu in fair territory so he should be out, rather than safe, as called by the first base umpire. Alfonzo races in to add his opinion that Abreu is safe. The discussion heats up with both umpires and both managers really going at it.

Home plate umpire John Blackburn described what happened next.

"The ball went down, and the second the ball went down, the catcher jumped right up to go after the ball. I got totally blocked out of the view, so all I knew is I saw the ball get hit. Next thing I see is the back of the catcher. I look out, the ball is out in the field. So that's when I went to Jason [the base umpire]. I said, 'Jason, did you see this?' He said 'No.' He told me it hit the batter while he was in the batter's box.

"I believe that's what it was, so we had to bring him back to the plate.

"Honestly, the managers started to yell and I said, 'Give me a second, we'll straighten this out.' So that's when I called both managers. I said, 'This is what happened. I got blocked out. I went to him for help. He told me what he had. Here's how we're going to fix it.'

So, after an absence of 44 years, it took the new Brooklyn team three pitches to start the first brouhaha of the new millennium. Go back to 1955 and ask a Brooklyn fan, "What are the odds that in a mere 46 years Brooklyn will be playing at Jamestown, and an argument breaks out with Carl Erskine taking Jamestown's side," and the Brooklynite's answer would probably be unprintable. But it happened. Brooklyn's would re-enter baseball kicking and screaming. What else?

After running up a full count, Abreu popped up to first, then McIntyre struck out and Jacobs bounced out. Luz Portobanco took the mound as the first Brooklyn pitcher.

> **Luz Portobanco:** "The opening against Atlanta [Jamestown] was pretty exciting. The stands were packed. But I was pretty sick. I had a cold, I couldn't hear, my nose was stopped up, but I didn't go through two months of extended not to pitch. No pain, no gain. I pray to God — 'Just be with me and let me be strong and go out there. The result will come later.'"

Portobanco held Jamestown scoreless in the first.

In the second inning, Noel Devarez singled for Brooklyn's first hit since 1957, but Jeremy Todd flied out to center and Frank Corr, in his first pro at bat, grounded out to third, but Devarez moved to second. Then Forrest Lawson grounded out to short to end the Cyclones' half of the inning. The Jammers took the lead in the bottom of the second on two doubles, and the score stayed 1–0 Jamestown until the top of the fifth when the Cyclones' wiry third baseman, Edgar Rodriguez, tied the game with a 420 foot home run blast to right field, the first Brooklyn home run in 44 years. In the top of the sixth, Brooklyn catcher Mike Jacobs led off with a walk, and after the next two hitters made out, Frank Corr, hitless so far, came up for his third professional at bat and got the hit he had been praying for, as he put Brooklyn in the lead with a double to left. Chad Bowen pitched a scoreless inning in relief of Portobanco in the sixth.

In the bottom of the next inning, the time for baseball's traditional "Seventh Inning Stretch," Carl Erskine came out to the area behind home plate and set up to play "Take Me Out to the Ball Game" on his harmonica. The field microphone wouldn't work however, and Erskine quietly walked off the field.

Brooklyn failed to score in the top of the eighth, and then Carl Erskine came back on the field for another try at "Take Me Out to the Ball Game." The microphone was fixed and Erskine played a fine rendition of the song, thus creating another oddity for Brooklyn's reappearance in baseball with a musical performance of the "Eighth Inning Stretch." Then Bowen held Jamestown scoreless, and Australian Matt Gahan pitched two scoreless innings after Bowen to keep Brooklyn in the lead heading into the bottom of the ninth.

After getting the first two batters, Gahan allowed singles to the next Jamestown batters, bringing up DH Kevin Green with the tying and winning runs on first and second. Manager Alfonzo stuck with the Australian, and Gahan went to 1-2 on Green, and then struck him out swinging to give the Brooklyn Cyclones their initial win.

After the game, Alfonzo looked relieved to have the first game completed. The players shook hands with each other, and the cheering was limited, mainly provided by the three representatives of the new Brooklyn Cyclone fan club.

The Jamestown fans filed out of the park, most heading for the grass parking lot next to the stadium, but some living so close that they began walking down the residential streets toward home. Nobody looked too upset. Baseball had been in Jamestown for a lot of years. People seemed happy to have baseball back.

The Cyclones left their clubhouse and boarded the bus for the five-minute ride back to the Red Roof Inn, their hotel just out of town.

The next morning, the Cyclones went to a breakfast in which Carl Erskine addressed the team, and the next night, Brooklyn took its 1.000 percentage back to Diethrick Park. The lineup had John Toner, the Joe Hardy look-alike from Western Michigan, as the designated hitter. McIntyre moved to lead-off, Lawson batted second and Toner hit sixth; otherwise the position players remained the same. Starting for Brooklyn was Matt Peterson, a second round pick from the 2000 draft who had not signed in time to play in 2000. A tall, thin right-hander, Peterson and the Cyclones were at 0–0 after four and a half innings. Jamestown scored an unearned run, helped by Peterson's throwing error in the fifth. An Arias single and Lawson double tied the score in the sixth. In the bottom of the sixth, Jamestown took the lead on a single, an error on a Peterson pick-off attempt, and a two out triple.

In the eighth inning, David "Big Bird" Byard, the Cyclones' reliever, made his initial appearance and held Jamestown scoreless, but in the Brooklyn top of the ninth, Jacobs, Devarez, and Todd went down 1-2-3 to give Brooklyn baseball its first Cyclone loss, and the first loss for Brooklyn baseball since 1957.

The next day gave Brooklyn baseball another first since 1957 — its first rain-out — so in a doubleheader on June 22, Brooklyn started lefty Ross Peeples in the first game of a scheduled seven-inning game. (Baseball games in minor league doubleheaders are shortened to seven innings).

Peeples looks big and strong, but his speed is considered below average for a potential major leaguer, and Peeples relies on great control. The Cyclones' hitters break out as Jeremy Todd gets three hits (one a double), Frank Corr gets two hits, Rodriguez hits two sacrifice flies and Noel Devarez hits a three run homer.

Peeples pitched Brooklyn's first complete game and first shutout (albeit in a seven inning game). He painted the corners, throwing only 85 pitches, only 19 of them balls.

In the second game, Brooklyn started Wayne Ough, the second of their Australian pitchers. Ough, who can throw 94 miles an hour, gave up no runs in three innings and was removed for Junior Cabrera after three innings because of Ough's pitch count. (Pitchers in the minors and majors often are under pitch counts in which, depending on various factors such as their age, experience, previous pitching, injuries, wear and tear etc., they are limited as to how many pitches they can throw. In the minors, the pitch count is set in consultation with the minor league coordinators. Teams are usually given some flexibility, perhaps seven pitches over the count, but that's the limit).

The teams were tied 1–1 going into the bottom of the seventh, and last, inning. Blake McKinley, a thin lefty from Texas Tech, made his Brooklyn and professional debut. He retired Jamestown in the seventh, allowing only a walk and striking out two.

In the top of the extra inning eighth, Brooklyn's backup catcher, Francisco Sosa, short and stocky, got on after being hit by a pitch. That brought up "Mac" McIntyre, and the leadoff man powered the third pitch over the left field wall. Leandro Arias followed with another homer to left, and McGinley then closed out the game by retiring Jamestown in order, ending the game on a strikeout. It was on to Vermont.

The team left right after the game for the 494 mile trip to Burlington, in upper Vermont. On the way to Vermont, the team got lost and Howard Johnson and the bus driver got out three maps, resulting in a lengthy discussion on the best way to get to Vermont for tomorrow's game. They were scheduled to play a game on Saturday and one on Sunday. The one on Saturday was rained out and another doubleheader was then set for Sunday.

Vermont's stadium, Centennial Park, is on the University of Vermont campus. It was built in 1922. It has a large wooden grandstand and old wooden seats. It's an anachronism that is a part of the New York–Penn League. The Cyclones started Chad Bowen and got only three hits, losing 4–1. Anthony Coyne made his Cyclone debut. An infielder from Yale University, Coyne played last year at Kingsport and Pittsfield; he started this game at DH and went 0 for 2. In the seventh inning, Michael Piercy, a 24-year-old outfielder from Hillside, New Jersey, also made his Cyclone debut — pinch hitting for Coyne. Piercy walked. Cyclone pitchers Chris Sherman and Jason Scobie also made their Brooklyn debuts in relief, combining to hold Vermont scoreless for 3⅔ innings.

In the second game, Portobanco made his second start and pitched well, giving up only 2 runs in 6⅔ innings, but Brooklyn managed only three hits and lost 2–1. Now it was back on the bus for an overnight trip to Brooklyn.

The home opener was the next night.

The Home Opener

The circus was coming to town. And nobody knew it.

Not the players, used to playing before college crowds, or 500 fans at Kingsport, or 1,500 at Pittsfield. Not the Cyclone management, whose large press box, by far the largest in the New York–Penn League, could handle about 35 of the working press and radio people in a league where press boxes were often the size of press boxes at small high school stadiums and could typically accommodate six writers, plus two small booths for radio announcers. About 400 persons were given press credentials for the game, a number roughly 12 times the capacity of the press box. Not all the press credentials were for writers; some were for television, the game being scheduled for the Public Broadcasting System. Photographers who shot from field level covered the game, but the Cyclones' management was scrambling to find room for the press and other media. The staff set up tables behind the last row of stands on the concourse. Surrounding the ballpark, these tables went from first to third base. As the press began arriving four hours before the game, the Cyclones' small staff was finding out they were part of the circus.

Manager Edgar Alfonzo and coaches Bobby Ojeda and Howard Johnson were finding out it was a circus too, as the media descended on the field during the Cyclones' batting practice. Crowds were forming outside the locked gates, the parking lot was filling up, and dignitaries were arriving.

Ken Howard, formerly the star of *The White Shadow* television show, was preparing for his pregame interview for Public Broadcasting System. Outside the stadium, a parade was being formed that would march down Surf Avenue, the street that the stadium is on, one block from the boardwalk, running parallel to it.

Mayor Rudolph Giuliani was there. So was U.S. Senator Charles Schumer. So were the fans of Brooklyn.

Radio announcer Warner Fusselle explains what the Cyclones' Opening Day was like for him. In the minor leagues, radio announcers usually have no engineer present and no producer. Fusselle must set up all his own equipment. He works in the front row of the press box. The press box has two rows of seats outdoors and one row inside a glass booth. In order to see better, Fusselle sets up in the front outside row. But his equipment and papers are subject to the wind and possible rain. When it rains, he relocates under an overhang farther back.

Directly under the radio announcers, over a ledge of the second deck, hangs a sign. that says "The Catbird Seat." The expression was made popular by Red Barber during his Brooklyn announcing days. It was one of Barber's pet Southern expressions, and it meant "sitting pretty" — being in a good spot — like the Dodgers having the bases loaded and a 3–0 count on Duke Snider. That's sitting in "The Catbird Seat."

Warner Fusselle: "I'm not there as an observer. I'm not there as a fan. I'm not there as a politician. I'm not there as a newspaperman to study it, to observe it, to take notes about the reaction. I'm broadcasting my first home game. I'm still worried about setting up the equipment, because even though I've had it on the road for a week, I'm setting it up at home. Each park is different. Everything's got to work. I'm concerned about the weather. I'm concerned about the wind blowing all my stuff away. I'm concerned about who is on the board at the radio station, what time we go on. I'm concerned about getting my pre-game interview. I've got to get it in plenty of time. I've got to get back up here [to the broadcast booth] and just like on the road, in the Home Opener for me there's no leisure moment for anything. I'm always hustling so much and sometimes you're hustling

and have so much to do that you really can't take it in, and it can help you, too —
where you might be so nervous. Here, you're so busy that you're not nervous, so
you just say, 'Let's just do it. Come on, it's got to get done, let's just do it.' So
that's kind of what was going through my mind before the game. I don't even
remember whom I interviewed before the game that night because we've been on
the road. Before the game, I was running around like crazy. I don't remember talking to any specific people. I don't remember anything. The game started, and we
did the game. So that is often the case for all my broadcasts, because you're always
scrambling to try to get everything done.

"I think on the first pitch I may have said, 'Strike one called, and yes folks, baseball is back in Brooklyn.' I think I said something like that. I knew the whole
world would be listening and checking that out on ABC Radio, the network. I
knew they were taping it and everything. I found out just recently they sent it all
over everywhere, all over.

"Yeah, I just thought of another thing. Dom Alagia, the public address
announcer, comes down to me when I'm setting up in 'The Catbird Seat,' and he
says, 'when you introduce these people on the field, are you going to say such and
such?' I say, 'I'm not interviewing people on the field.' He said, 'Well, I have the
format sheet right here, and it says you're introducing the senators and the con-
gressmen. You're introducing the mayor. You're introducing Hillary Clinton. I say,
'Whoa, wait a minute.' I said, 'No, I'm on the radio,' and he said, 'Well, I didn't
know; I just got the format; here's your name as the emcee.' I said, 'Well, it's news
to me.' So here was something else to worry about. It's such a difficult thing to
get the lineups for both teams. It's difficult to find out who the umpires are. There
are a lot of things you have to get. I was concerned about a lot of things, concerned about the pre-game show, concerned about things I didn't know were coming. They got TV announcer Ed Randall to be the emcee.

"So that's what went on with me, and I didn't have to introduce those people. Ed
Randall did a real good job of that, and I kid him about this — that my trivia question — who was the first person ever booed in KeySpan Park. It was Ed Randall, and
he invited it with one of his comments. He said, 'Let's be nice to the players, and let's
cheer for good plays, and let's cheer for Brooklyn. We don't want to get the reputation of a place where everybody boos.' So instantly, everyone booed Ed Randall. So
I thought that was great. Hey, they could have been booing me, but I wouldn't say
that. I was thrilled to death that Ed Randall was down there and that he was getting
booed, and I was happy and safe scrambling for my life up in The Catbird Seat.

February 2002

Three former Brooklyn Dodgers talk about past Opening Days as they
take a break from coaching middle aged baseball campers in Vero Beach.
Duke Snider, Carl Erskine and Clem Labine are all in Dodger uniforms. They
each wear a Brooklyn Dodger cap. Maybe they're two generations removed
from their Brooklyn playing days, but seeing them in Dodger uniforms and
Brooklyn caps still lifts the spirits.

Duke Snider: "Opening Days at Brooklyn were like the first day of school. You're
very anxious to get back to school and see your old friends, and you're very anxious to get back to Ebbets Field and see your old ballpark. It's a very special day.
You always have a little flutter in your stomach on Opening Day. And then the
umpire says 'play ball,' and then you get down to business."

Clem Labine: "The first Opening Day that I pitched was in 1952, and I got bombed. [In spring training] I hurt my arm right out on that field [Labine points to a field right in front of him], with a photographer. They were just coming up with a timed sequence camera, so he wanted me to go out and do some timed sequence. And it was a very cold, blustery day, and there was just no warm-up because what I was going to do was just give him some motion of the ball, going through with my hand and throw the ball over his head; that's all I had to do. So he kept saying, 'I need a little more motion; I need a little more motion. Look like you're throwing hard.'

"And that's exactly what I did do; I threw a little hard and I hurt my arm. It was right in the big tendon."

Carl Erskine: "In a subtle way, there's competition on the team. Now whether it's spoken or unspoken, you would like to be the lead pitcher on the staff and have the best spring and have the manager say, 'You're my Opening Day pitcher.' Now there are a lot of factors in there, there are injuries, but normally, when you come out of spring training, that is a high dividend to be selected to start Opening Day. Now, I think I pitched five opening days in my career. Four in New York, and I pitched the opening in Los Angeles, the first game there, 80,000 people in a makeshift stadium. There is a special, special excitement about Opening Day. It's sort of akin to a World Series, but in a way it's more charged than a World Series. You're starting on this long trek, and if you're the lead horse when you're in the starting lineup of a brand new season, there is something heady about that. And the crowd; there's been a lot of buildup about it, and you want the first pitch to be a strike. You think about all these little things, everything is fresh. Opening Day, you've got to get everything rolling. Those are the little subtleties that go through your mind. I always felt it was a badge of honor to be out of spring training and to be handed the ball for the first game of the season. I think fans had this anticipation.

"Even players are so pumped up. Sometimes rookies are playing. John Roseboro caught the first Opening Day in Los Angeles, and he was so pumped up that he nearly hit me in the face when he was throwing the ball so hard back to me in the opener. There are special things about the home opener. I played in five World Series. The World Series is like the icing on the cake. You won the pennant, you've already been the champions of your league, and now you're playing in this spotlight. But there's still a different charge in Opening Day. Somehow, spring time, there's anticipation of good things; the season's all in front of you. I come down here [Vero Beach] and there's a little bit of that, because I've come down here since I was a kid, since I was 19 years old. The first time I was here was the year it opened in 1948. I go to the same mounds that I worked on then. The same string area. I pitched here 50 years ago this year, Opening Day in Holman Stadium. I've got home movies of it at home. We were on the third base side. Connie Mack was the manager of the opponents, the Philadelphia A's. So this is another Opening Day, so to speak.

"In Brooklyn, a night or two before Opening Day, we would have a big Knothole Club dinner. There were about forty guys on the roster; we didn't have to cut down to 25 guys until about May 15, and [first baseman] Chuck Connors, who later became a television star on *The Rifleman*, would do "Casey at the Bat" and he was an actor *before* he was an actor, and that was always good.

"There was always a lot of buildup to Opening Day. Now remember, the World Series, sometimes you don't know you're in it until the last few days, but from down here you have six weeks to get ready for Opening Day. You have to start for that and build to it. You could often tell, who was having the best spring. It didn't often come as a big surprise. Now, Newcombe, Preacher Roe and I often shared Opening Days."

One Brooklyn fan at the Cyclones' Opening Day was Mark Lazarus, the 53-year-old Brooklyn native who remembered the old Dodgers, and who lived only blocks away from Ebbets Field. Lazarus discusses his days of growing up in Brooklyn.

Mark Lazarus: "I was born approximately April 18, 1949. That's what I was told. I lived at Parkside Avenue, right near Bedford Avenue, about six or seven blocks from Ebbets Field. This was in the Flatbush section. It was two blocks away from Prospect Park. I grew up there, on-and-off, until my college years. Later, I moved to Thirty-Second Street and Avenue H.

"Growing up, I played one year of Little League, and I played a lot of street ball: stoop ball, stickball, punch ball, all the playground kinds of ball. All that good stuff. My first glove came from my father, which I promptly lost, and then he bought me my second glove, which is the one I still have. The first glove was, I think, a Spalding, a black leather glove. I can't recall the model. The model that I have now, that I played all my ball with, is a Roger Maris model. I got that when I was 13. It's been relaced a few dozen times. I used to play third base. I had a good arm. When I was in sleep-away camp one summer, the first game of softball, our regular first baseman wasn't playing. The coach's son was playing first base. The first ball hit to me, I threw to first. My throw hit the first baseman right between the eyes. I knocked him right out — cold. From then on, if the regular first baseman wasn't playing, so I wouldn't knock out the substitute, they moved me to left field. I could hit and throw, but I was always too small for anything beyond Little League. In my thirteenth year, I had a growth spurt from 5' 2" to 5' 6". I was then around 110 pounds. At 14 or 15 I grew to 5' 8" and around 155 pounds, which is what I am now.

"I have a brother who is eight years older than me, so growing up, there was always too much of an age difference for us to play much ball together. But growing up, I was right next door to a public school, P. S. 92, and we had plenty of kids to play ball with — hundreds of kids. And we had a playground built right behind the school in 1955, so we played most of our ball at the playground. Before that was built, we played stickball in the streets. We had the Parade Grounds right up the block, which is where Joe Torre played, and I played Little League there.

"I only got into about three Little League games, so because I wasn't playing, I said to myself, 'Why even bother going down?' Maybe I was too small, or maybe it was because I had a big mouth, a lot of people didn't like me because of that; I never felt I got an opportunity to play, so I'd rather play street ball than sit on the bench and watch everybody else play. I must have been about nine or ten.

"When I was a kid, I would go to Ebbets Field. The first game I ever went to was when I was seven years old. It was a doubleheader against the Phillies, and the Dodgers lost both games. We sat down the third base line, and I remember watching Gino Cimoli in left field. I think Don Zimmer was playing third base.

"My favorite player was Duke Snider. I loved Duke Snider. I loved him primarily because he had a great arm in the outfield, even though Furillo had a better arm. But what I liked about Duke was his styling at the plate. Everything about him was just so fine. His warm-ups. His swing. His elbow up in the air. I just thought he was a classy ball player. It was just so classy and fluid. Growing up then, you had to pick your favorite center fielder in New York: Willie, Mickey, or the Duke. The Duke was my favorite player of all, and he happened to be a center fielder, so I always watched him play.

"I was a natural right-handed hitter, but I learned to also bat lefty, not to imitate the Duke's lefty swing, but because of the configuration of the playgrounds then. Depending on how we set the school yard field up, one field — either left or right — was really short, say thirty feet behind third or first base. So, if we set the field up with a short left field, you would have to hit to right or it would be called an out. So I learned to hit left-handed so I could pull the ball to right.

"Ebbets Field used to have a policy that after the seventh inning, admission was free. So towards the end of the Dodgers' stay in Brooklyn, sometimes my brother would meet me at school when we got out, and we would walk to Ebbets Field and catch the last few innings of a day game and make it home before it was dark.

"I can remember that before I began looking at newspapers, I would look out of my living room window to see if the Ebbets Field lights were on, and then I would know it was a night game. And if I saw the lights, I would flip it on the radio or watch it on TV."

Duke Snider wasn't at the Cyclones' home Opening Day. Carl Erskine was home in Indiana, but he would be there later in the season.

Jackie Robinson had passed away in 1972; in Brooklyn there was now a junior high school named after him, in back of where home plate was in Ebbets Field. Some fans had undoubtedly gone to the city that day from Queens on the Jackie Robinson Parkway. Gil Hodges wasn't there. Hodges had passed away in 1972 in spring training, while he was the Met manager. Still living at her home on Bedford Avenue in Brooklyn, as she did while her husband was with the Dodgers, Mrs. Gil Hodges was at the Cyclones' home opener. Some fans made their way to the game after crossing the Gil Hodges Bridge from Rockaway, Queens to Brooklyn. Roy Campanella had passed away in 1993. He was working with the Los Angeles Dodgers as a coach and consultant until his death. Campanella has a street named after him at Dodgertown in Vero Beach. Carl Furillo, a hard-hat rebel with no streets in his honor, who patrolled right field in Ebbets Field like an emperor and was known for his great arm and clutch hitting, was gone, too. So was the third base acrobat Billy Cox, slick infielder Junior Gilliam, shortstop Pee Wee Reese, left fielder Sandy Amoros — one of the heroes of the 1955 World Series win — catcher Rube Walker and pitcher Karl Spooner. And many more.

But Ralph Branca, who won 21 games for the Dodgers in 1947, was at the Brooklyn Cyclones' home opener, and so was Joe Pignatano, a native Brooklynite who spent nine years, including two for military service, in the Dodger farm system before finally making it to Brooklyn in their last major league season.

Mike Cox, the young left-hander who spent last year in the New York–Penn League with the Mets' affiliate at Pittsfield, started the season at Capital City, a step above Brooklyn. He talks about being sent back down to the New York–Penn League to play for Brooklyn, and his arrival the night before Brooklyn's Opening Night.

Mike Cox: "After the Major League All-Star break, I was sent down to Brooklyn. I was in Macon, Georgia. This was before a game. You know when stuff is going to go down. When we see the rovers [instructors] is when we get the feeling that changes are going to be made. Guy Conti and the manager, Ken Oberkfell, brought Angel [Pagan] and myself into the office, and they told us what their plans were for us, and they did it in a professional manner. Both of us didn't take it too well. It was kind of humbling for us. I was starting to come on, and Angel was hot. When they call you into the manager's office they lay it all out for you. They don't hide anything from you. They let you know everything they think. They don't do it in a shoddy way, like call you, or tell you as you're leaving.

"They brought us in and said that they want us to go down and help the Brooklyn team out. They said Angel was doing great, but at this level there was no room for him. They told me that I wasn't getting enough innings in, and I understood. It was common sense what they did. It wasn't a dumb move. We didn't like it, but it made sense.

"We were both nervous sitting in there because there's no telling what will happen. It could be a release speech; it could be a promotion speech, or a demotion speech. We were a little on edge. But they've done it so much it made it easy on us. We stayed there that night. They wouldn't let us travel at night [for safety reasons]. That's just another professional thing to do. And they woke us up early and sent us on our way. Then we drove up to Columbia and got our stuff. They don't allow you to arrive before a certain time so that you don't drive all night.

"They make you stay in a hotel and bring them a receipt. It's just professional, just good business what they did. We stayed in Richmond, Virginia. It took eight hours to get there, and the next day another seven hours to Brooklyn. We pulled into the Brooklyn stadium, and we were told to look for R.C. Reuteman [the Cyclones' vice president]. The guys at the gate didn't know who we were, and then they finally let us in, and R.C. walked us around the stadium, gave us a tour. We knew Brooklyn was going to be great. I told my parents last year, 'You know, this is just normal for me. I leave college and they build a new stadium. I leave the Penn League and they build a new stadium.' The tour was the day before the first game at Brooklyn. I knew that I wasn't going to play the first game, but Angel was going to play. [Angel Pagan turned out to be the first home batter to bat for Brooklyn since 1957.] I knew I wouldn't pitch, but I was as fired up as anyone else.

"The manager had a list on the bulletin board at KeySpan Stadium saying when to be there for practice the next day. We stayed at the Radisson, right at J.F.K. Airport.

"The next day I was meeting all the new guys. I knew some from spring training. I wanted to meet them all before the game so I knew who I was rooting for. Angel and I got to the ballpark early the next day, around twelve. We ate before we left and then ate the spread of food that was in the clubhouse. Angel and I had to find 'Clubbie' Kelly to get sized up for our uniforms. And Kelly is trying to go zero to ninety trying to please everybody. People were asking for new socks. Everybody wanted to look spiffy for Opening Day.

"We had one home and one away uniform, plus a batting practice shirt. The starting pitcher must announce it after batting practice what jersey the team will wear, the regular shirts or the batting practice shirts. The pitcher will tell Bobby [Ojeda]; Bobby will tell the manager, and then it goes down from there.

"The night before, Angel and I sat and watched Staten Island's Opening Night on TV, and then we couldn't sleep much, and we decided that the next day we would be the first ones at the new stadium. We said, 'Hey, we have to be there early to get our uniform and locker, and also to soak it all in.'

"It was real exciting, but I knew I wasn't pitching, and I almost felt like I was in the stands.

"The Brooklyn fans, when they talked to Bobby Ojeda, that's when you could see it. They just acted like he was an old friend. They'd say, 'Hey, Bobby, great to see ya!' and you know Bobby's probably never seen them before in his life, and he'd say, 'Hey, how you doing?' to anybody who would talk. And that's the difference with Brooklyn. They're not afraid to just yell out what they think.

"The Brooklyn fans would talk to anybody about anything, and they'd be yelling at us from a hundred yards away; it wouldn't matter. That's what stood out for me."

Ralph Branca: "I loved playing at Ebbets Field. The ballpark was great. The fans were great. This new ballpark is beautiful, and it's good for Brooklyn. Good for the community."

Mark Lazarus: "I drove past the new Coney Island stadium a number of times to watch its progress. Then when they finally built the rampways, I remember walking around to the back of the stadium so we could look in. I asked one of the workmen if we could see, so the workman opened the stadium, and I walked up the ramp to the boardwalk to look in; this was in say April, so I had an idea what the ballpark looked like.

"I didn't read anything in the papers about the new team until about two or three days before the season opened at home. I read that on June 25 baseball is coming back to Brooklyn. Maybe there were a few things on WFAN radio about it, but I don't recall reading anything about it. But when Opening Day came, I knew it was a sellout and that the park was going to be jammed. I didn't know what to expect. My friend Mont was going with his kids, so I had someone I would know at the game. Of course, me being me, by the time the night was over I knew the names of about twenty or thirty people in my section.

"What was to expect? I expected someone would throw out the first pitch, the mayor would be there, and Wilpon would be there. I had no idea what the team would be like. I remember at some point reading that the team was going to be based on pitching and speed. How apropos that a team back in Brooklyn should be based on speed and pitching, which is what the Dodgers became in Los Angeles when they left, with Koufax and Drysdale, and Maury Wills and Willie Davis. And that was it. They didn't expect much offense.

"Before Opening Day, I remember people saying, 'Hey, you got two tickets for the game? You got four tickets for the game?' These were people I worked with on Wall Street. They knew that I had tickets. They didn't listen, and they were sorry, and now everybody's got their name on lists for season tickets. My ticket broker was after me all season long for tickets to sell. He could have brokered tickets all season long.

"Opening Day itself, I got there early to make sure I got parking. My curiosity ran to what the concessions would cost, what souvenirs would be like, and their cost. I was gearing myself up for what it would cost when I took my kid to games. The win or lose aspect of the games, I wasn't even thinking about it. I was more curious as to what that experience of the first baseball game in Brooklyn in 44 years would be like. And what would the team do for Brooklyn? I knew about the

Cyclones Brett Kay and Luz Portobanco sign autographs.

promotion that minor league teams do. I expected a mascot, but I didn't expect anything like Party Marty [a Cyclones' ticket account executive, Marty Haber was "Party Marty" during games — the on-field emcee], which really enhanced things because he was a member of the team. There was a connection to the team right there. The attitude of the players, signing autographs, this was unexpected — that it would be so open. I went there with open eyes and open mind to absorb whatever they were going to throw at me.

"After being a season ticket holder for the New York Rangers' games for so many years, I knew it was important to meet the people around me as quickly as possible and forge friendships with them, 'cause these would be the same people that you would see game in and game out, and hopefully, season after season, for years as a season ticket holder. You want a friendly atmosphere around you at all times, so you have to be on your best behavior at all times so that you can forge these friendships. I knew what I had to do to make me and the other people comfortable. I brought my camera to take pictures. You go, 'Click, click, click,' and then the next time you give them a picture. And I would learn their names. You are showing people respect if you know their names.

"The ball players are gonna change. Some of the people in the stands are gonna change. But for the most part, you're going to be seeing the same people — and people who know these people — in the stands. You have to make the entire environment comfortable.

"Immediately after I found my seat, I remember seeing David Hartman there. And that meant that PBS television was involved, and that meant that this game was a big deal. After he was done filming a TV interview, I went to the edge of the field and talked to him for a few minutes. So right away, I felt comfortable.

"Then I went back to my seat, and I checked out the dimensions of the ballpark, checked the sightlines from my seat, so I knew what I could see from my seats. When people came into my section, I introduced myself to them. This was more important than the pregame warmups that were going on down on the field. Because we didn't know any of the players. I recognized David Hartman, and Edgar Alfonzo, and Hojo and Bobby O., but we didn't know any of the players yet. We couldn't converse with the players; we couldn't know the players that easily. Their names were on the program, but their names weren't on their jerseys. So it was hard to converse with the players, but you could converse with the people in the stands who were around you."

Marty Adler rooted for the Brooklyn Dodgers during his boyhood. He grew up in Brooklyn, and he is the president of the Brooklyn Dodger Hall of Fame. He was at the Cyclones' Opening Night and attended games during the season.

"I was born in Borough Park, Bensonhurst, 50th Street between Fort Hamilton and New Utrecht Avenue. First 24–25 years of my life I lived there, and I attended Public School 160. From there I went to Pershing Junior High, that's 220, and from there I went to Fort Hamilton High School. I played [for] Fort Hamilton's baseball and cross-country teams. I was also the captain of the tennis team. From there, I went to Brooklyn College, and from there to the army and a short stay in Texas, and I started my career as a teacher in the New York City Board of Education. As they said, the rest is history.

"I got married. I married Linda, and her parents and my parents went to school together. Our uncles and aunts — both sides know each other. I remember I must have been about ten or eleven. I remember beating the heck out of her one day with snowballs. She attended 160 Pershing, and she went to Fort Hamilton High School, and subsequently to Brooklyn College as well.

Cyclone brain trust — Bobby O., Hojo, and Fonzie.

Then we got married. We had an apartment, at Flatbush, for a couple of years, and then we moved out to the Island in '65.

"And we're still there. Long Island in some areas is just like Brooklyn. Just the way Brooklyn was in the '40s, honestly. Everybody is a transplant out there. We got the same culture.

"We played a lot of basketball. We played roller hockey in 53rd Street Park at Fort Hamilton, and roller hockey and football at Sunset Park. Baseball is big at the Parade Grounds [where he played baseball]. The Gowanus International League is what it was. I still got my tags. Then I played second base for Fort Hamilton High School.

"The first game I went to at Ebbets Field was, I think, '46. I was a kid, and Pete Reiser had just come back from the Army, and he's my favorite. If he didn't get injured so badly I think he's destined for the Hall of Fame. He can do anything; could have done anything. I remember seeing him. I remember Arky Vaughn in '47, Dixie Walker and, of course, Jackie came up, and Pee Wee, and Duke. From '47 on, you could walk anywhere in Brooklyn and meet a stranger and say, 'What's the score?' and immediately you became friends. The connection is made. Everybody knew what you meant.

"You got three million people living there every year. Three million from the '20s on, and nearly everybody is a rabid Dodger fan. It was nice. It was a common thread that united the whole borough, and we were proud to be Dodger fans. They were good and they're colorful, and it was a lovely place to go to. If you went to the beach, every blanket had a radio listening to Red Barber and the Dodger game. On the streets, everybody in Brooklyn is known for sitting on the stoop . I'd walk down 50th Street and I'd walk down to 13th Avenue, every stoop had a radio on if there was a game on. You heard the game."

The Cyclones had added Angel Pagan, a speedy center fielder just learning to switch hit, sent down from Capital City, even though he was playing well and hitting .310 for the higher level club. The Cyclones wanted to have a strong club for Brooklyn's initial season, and the Mets' management felt that Pagan would benefit by playing in the crucible that is Brooklyn. Robert McIntyre was batting second, at shortstop. Hitting in the third slot was lefty hitting catcher Mike Jacobs; the clean-up hitter was big DH John Toner; fifth was Frank Corr, now living with his aunt in Mill Basin, Brooklyn; hitting sixth was Noel Devarez, in right field; seventh was Edgar Rodriguez, the 19 year old at third base; batting eighth was Jeremy Todd, at first base; batting ninth was second baseman Leandro Arias. Starting the first home Brooklyn game in 44 years was Matt Peterson, the tall right-hander.

Outside, on Surf Avenue, the street that runs behind the third base side of the ballpark, people were preparing for the Opening Day parade. The parade featured many Brooklyn Little League teams, like the Bergen Beach Bombers, and the Jackie Robinson United Little League. There were also marching bands, a drum corps and the Dodger Sym-Phony.

Top: First Brooklyn home batter since 1957 — Angel Pagan. *Bottom*: The Dodger Sym-Phony now.

Inside the stadium, the players continued to warmup. After the parade, the Little Leaguers, most born in the 1990s when the Dodgers were long established in Los Angeles, trooped into the stadium.

The 1950s singing group the Tokens, Brooklyn natives, were scheduled to sing, a capella, "The Star Spangled Banner." The flag in center filed waved in the strong wind blowing in from the ocean.

There were a number of first pitches. Mayor Giuliani threw out one ball, and then the threesome of Met owner Fred Wilpon, and former Brooklyn Dodgers Joe Pignatano and Ralph Branca also threw out first pitches.

Fred Wilpon, in Brooklyn, a co-owner of the New York Mets, went to Lafayette High School with Hall of Fame pitcher Sandy Koufax, who pitched for Brooklyn and then went onto fame with Los Angeles. Wilpon actually pitched more for their high school team than did Koufax. "Sandy Koufax and I used to ride on the same school bus," said Wilpon. And sometimes in the morning, we'd get the bus driver to stop at Nathan's, and we'd get hot dogs for breakfast. If I tried that today, I'd die."

The stands were packed with 7,500 people, the stadium's capacity recently increased by 1,000 with the newly added outfield bleachers, which were just in front of the Coney Island boardwalk and connected to the boardwalk by a boardwalk runway. The crowd was a total mix of ages. Gray-haired fans with Brooklyn Dodger hats and Brooklyn Dodger blue satin jackets mixed with fans in their thirties and forties, and there were plenty of teenaged fans, and fans the age of Little Leaguers.

First pitch participants — Jeff Wilpon, Fred Wilpon, Bob Catell (CEO/chairman of Keyspan), Mayor Giuliani, Ralph Branca and Joe Pignatano.

Coney Island parade.

Frank Corr: "Opening night was a real thrill. I had butterflies like you wouldn't believe, like it was the first baseball game I ever played. That was the biggest crowd I ever played for. I was like, 'Oh, man!' Not many colleges are going to get 7500 people to a game. In a regional championship or the College World Series, you'd be lucky to get seven to ten thousand. And I never made it to the College World Series."

The field was cleared. The Cyclones ran out to their positions, each with a Little Leaguer with him. The Tokens sang the national anthem. They were good. The Little Leaguers ran off the field. The Cyclones, closer in age to these Little Leaguers than to the old Brooklyn Dodgers, who were the age of their grandparents, remained. One of those grandparents was the grandfather of the starting pitcher, Matt Peterson.

On radios within a range of a few miles, people listened to Warner Fusselle. But on the Internet, all over the world, people were tuned to the broadcast. Especially interested were the families of Australian pitchers Matt Gahan and Wayne Ough, where it was already the morning of June 26th. In California, Jay Caligiuri's parents were listening on the Internet, as were Brett Kay's. Back in Brooklyn it was still June 25, and the first batter for Mahoning Valley was approaching the plate.

Few of the fans at the ballpark had paid much attention to Mahoning Valley. It was tough enough for the fans to identify the Cyclones. Brooklyn

Brooklyn Cyclones line up for the anthem.

fans were familiar with Bobby Ojeda and Howard Johnson, both members of the Mets' 1986 World Champions. As coaches, they were receiving more attention than were the players. Many Mets fans recognized the name of the manager, Alfonzo, but this manager was Edgar Alfonzo, not Edgardo Alfonzo, Mets second baseman. Edgar looked like his brother. Knowledgeable fans recognized Tim Teufel in the dugout; Teufel was an infielder on those '86 Mets, and was an infield coordinator in the Mets' system.

The last Dodger game at Ebbets Field was against the Pittsburgh Pirates. It was a 2–0 victory for Brooklyn with 6,702 fans attending.

Tonight's game, against the new Brooklyn team, is with Mahoning Valley, a farm team of the Cleveland Indians located in Niles, Ohio, about an hour and a half from Pittsburgh and an hour from Cleveland. Their nickname, the Scrappers, comes from the area's background, as coal and ironworkers were known to fight a bit.

The wind was blowing straight off the ocean in back of center and right fields. The center field flag was flapping. In left-center field, the "Hit sign, Win suit" sign seemed an inviting target. In foul territory beyond left field, subway cars snaked along the curved, elevated tracks. Behind the left field fence the actual Cyclone roller coaster ride was rolling, and on top of the left center field scoreboard was a wooden painted version of the Cyclone ride. On the Cyclone uniform shirts the word "Cyclones" was itself a waving version of the up and down roller coaster. The lights in the merry-go-round beyond left field lit up the sky. From the press box level, one could look behind and see the skyline of Manhattan. Ahead, across the bay, was the Rockaway Peninsula in Queens, with its single family homes, some bungalows, a beach area that even some residents referred to as Brooklyn because it felt like it, and was connected to Brooklyn by the Gil Hodges Bridge. Across the water, one could see Sandy Hook, New Jersey, and even Rumson, New Jersey, home of Bobby Ojeda, the pitching coach. You could see Staten Island, and ships in the lower Bay. You could see the lighted Verrazano-Narrows Bridge, home of that famous scene in *Saturday Night Fever*.

You half expected the old Dodgers to reappear, but they didn't. These were young men on the field that practically no one but their families knew. Everyone needed a program; some of the players had arrived so recently that not even all the team knew every other player's name.

The first Mahoning Valley batter was Maximo Mare, a second baseman. Bobby Ojeda, in the home plate end corner of the dugout, waved to the stands to his daughter; Howard Johnson stood next to Ojeda; and next to Johnson was Edgar Alfonzo. The three most recognizable Cyclones were all unable to play. It was up to the kids in the field.

Peterson took the sign from Jacobs. Peterson went into his windup. The crowd was on its feet roaring. Peterson delivered. A fastball down the middle for a called strike.

Seated in his perch, in the Catbird Seat, Warner Fusselle had the honor of calling the first pitch in professional baseball in Brooklyn since 1957.

Warner Fusselle: "It was called strike one. I may have said, 'Strike one called, and yes folks, baseball is back in Brooklyn.' I think I said something like that. I knew the whole world would be listening and checking that out on ABC radio, the network. I knew they were taping it and everything. I found out just recently they sent it all over everywhere, all over the country. Well, I don't know what they said, but they were very interested because baseball was back in Brooklyn for the first time in 44 years. I think I did on the first pitch say, 'Yes folks, baseball is back in Brooklyn.' I thought about that because I said something special should be said here. You don't want to overdo it or be corny."

The crowd roared its approval. The next pitch was hit to second baseman Leandro Arias, who threw to first baseman Todd. More firsts: The first assist and first putout at Brooklyn for the Cyclones. The crowd yelled once more and sat down.

The next Mahoning Valley batter, Jon Van Every, worked the count to 3 and 2, fouled off a pitch and then grounded out to second. The third hitter flied to left to new temporary Brooklyn resident Frank Corr, and the Cyclones had a 1-2-3 first inning.

After a 44-year pause in the purgatory of no baseball, an angel appeared as Brooklyn's next batter. He might have been heaven sent, but this batter was a flesh and blood angel with the beautifully oxymoronic name of Angel Pagan, in Brooklyn from his native Puerto Rico. Already a pregame hit with the teenaged girls because of his slicked back, black hair and matinee idol looks, Pagan walked to the plate and looked at third base where Alfonzo flashed him the signs. Still learning to bat lefty so that he could better utilize his speed, Pagan stepped into the box against right-hander Luke Field.

The wind off the Atlantic Ocean would make it difficult for Pagan to pull a pitch into the right field stands. The fans were once again on their feet. Field's first pitch was bunted foul. Then Pagan ran the count to 3 and 2, fouled off a couple of pitches, and grounded to the first baseman. Pagan raced for the bag. The play would obviously be close, and first baseman Curtis Gay threw to Field covering. Pagan was called out by first base ump Jason Day. Immediately, the Brooklyn fans began to holler at the umpire, calling him "blind" and saying "Open your eyes!" Forty-four years, and the first Brooklyn batter gets thrown out and creates the first Brooklyn baseball home argument. Even as the fans yelled at the ump, you could see a gleam in their eyes. The fans meant it. They thought Pagan was safe, but you could also see that they loved having the opportunity to yell. Some of the older fans hadn't yelled at a Brooklyn umpire since 1957, and one could sense that beneath the yelling voices was a kind of joyous release. The fans were just getting warmed up.

The next Cyclone hitter was Robert McIntyre. Thin, but with wiry strength, McIntyre was a 5' 10" shortstop from Florida. An Afro-American, he wore number 1, a number immortalized by Dodger shortstop Pee Wee Reese, the Dodger captain. Reese, who was instrumental in helping to pave the way for Jackie Robinson, baseball's first black player of the twentieth century, was a player from Louisville, Kentucky.

McIntyre, in his second professional year, stepped in, but he got behind 1 and 2 in the count, and then struck out swinging. That brought up catcher Mike Jacobs. At 6' 2", he was built more like a basketball player than Brooklyn Dodger catcher Roy Campanella, who was a rotund 5' 9". And Jacobs was a lefty swinger, as opposed to Campanella's taking his cuts righty. Like McIntyre, Jacobs struck out swinging.

In the top of the second, Peterson recorded the Cyclones' first home strikeout when he got Rickie Morton swinging; then Peterson retired the next two Scrappers. In the bottom of the second, Brooklyn's clean-up hitter, the Li'l Abner–appearing John Toner, struck out swinging, and Brooklyn went down 1-2-3 for the second inning in a row.

Peterson allowed the first hit of the ball game in the third, but Mahoning failed to score. In the bottom of the inning, Leandro Arias broke a 44-year drought for Brooklyn home field hits when he singled, but once again the "Brooks" failed to score. Mahoning Valley singled in the fourth, but was scoreless. The Cyclones' McIntyre and Jacobs both struck out, each for the second straight time, and Brooklyn was still scoreless after four innings.

In between innings, "Sandy the Seagull" (Ricky Johnson), the Cyclones' mascot, performed for the crowd, as did Marty Haber, by day a Cyclones' group sales executive, but at night a kind of master of ceremonies as he strolled through the stands and on the field. Known as "Party Marty," he held a portable microphone and conducted events like the "Dizzy Bat Race." The 26-year-old Haber, a tall, blond extrovert, with his engaging personality and energetic mannerisms, lent a party air to the festivities.

In the top of the fifth, with one out, the Scrappers' Eric Thompson singled and was singled to second by Bryce Uegawachi, the 5' 6" shortstop from Japan. After a fly-out, Thompson baptized Brooklyn's new home plate when he scored on an error by second baseman Arias. Despite a double by Edgar Rodriguez, Brooklyn again failed to score in the fifth. Peterson had reached his pitch count, so Matt Gahan was brought in to start the sixth inning. A bespectacled accountant off the field, Gahan was sort of an Australian version of Clark Kent turning into Superman when he came in to pitch. Off went the glasses, and out came a dogged pitcher — and instead of Superman's cape, Gahan had on the red socks, white uniform and blue cap of the new Brooklyn. Gahan punched out the first Scrappers' batter swinging, and retired the next two, the last another strikeout.

In the bottom of the sixth, Brooklyn once more failed to score, going down 1-2-3 when Jacobs struck out swinging for his third time in a row.

In the top of the seventh, with a man on first and one out, Australian Matt Gahan faced Japanese shortstop Uegawachi. The international confrontation ended with Uegawachi flying out to Frankie Corr, the new Mill Basin, Brooklyn, basement resident. (Born Francis, he came into the game as Frank, but by this time the Brooklyn faithful had already put a little Brooklyn twist on things by christening him Frankie.) Then Scrapper Maximo Mare doubled in the run with a fly ball lost in the wind. Both teams failed to score in their next at bats. Brooklyn had Arias on second in the eighth, but he was left there when Mike Jacobs came up and took three swings out of the first four pitches. He missed all three times to achieve the extremely rare "quadfecta"— four strikeouts in a row.

Gahan stopped Mahoning Valley in the ninth. Brooklyn came up for their last at bat. The Cyclones trailed 2–0. The game was only about two hours long at this point, and Brooklyn had no runs on only six hits. John Toner took his muscles to the plate and worked the count to 3 and 1 before drawing a lead-off walk. Corr came up to the plate looking to drive the ball, but he popped out to third. Noel Devarez came up, his bat wrapped behind his neck until he went into hitting position as the pitcher was almost ready to deliver. With the count 1-2, Devarez swung and struck out.

The Brooklyn fans had almost all remained in their seats to this point, but the crowd was growing silent. Brooklyn hadn't shown much offense. They were one out from defeat.

Now up at bat was Edgar Rodriquez. A lithe 185 pounds at 5' 11", about the size of Brooklyn legendary third sacker Billy Cox; Rodriguez was noted for being very quiet, almost as quiet as Cox. Rodriguez was a friendly fellow that everyone liked, but if you didn't speak Spanish, you couldn't get much out of Edgar except a smile. But Edgar showed that batting speaks louder than words as he made himself understood by driving a fastball so deep to left center that the ball went so high over the wall that it just scooted under the wooden Cyclone cutout on top of the scoreboard, and the ball headed out toward the real Cyclone ride. It would be understated to say that the fans cheered. They were on their feet, screaming and yelling, almost unbelieving. One out away from defeat in their opening home game, they had been saved by their 19-year-old third baseman.

Warner Fusselle: "I thought about some special things, like if there were home runs or whatever, what should I say, and I said, 'I'll just let it take care of itself,' but I was thinking. I think I did this on the road for maybe the first couple of home runs on the road that when somebody hits the home run, I don't like to ramble on and on. I'd like to say it, and then let the crowd noise take over. I think I said, 'Home run, Brooklyn.' I thought it sounded pretty good. It wasn't zany or crazy or cute, but it said, 'Home run, Brooklyn.' So I was thinking for that first home run at home I'd say, 'Home run, Brooklyn.' I kind of like that, and I thought it kind of had a sophisticated sound. It would be good without being stupid. So many announcers work on coming out with these crazy home run calls or things just to showcase themselves, to showcase their own voice. Sometimes they don't apply, but I've had things I've said since the '70s when I was in the minor leagues before, and I basically kept the same thing. Since the '70s on special home runs I would often say, 'Sweetheart, goodbye.' I said I don't know if I want to say that or not, but I was thinking 'Home run, Brooklyn.' I think when Edgar Rodriguez hit that home run I think I gave it a "Sweetheart, goodbye!"

Mike Cox: "When he hit the home run, I ran out to home plate to jump around and high five everybody, and I was trying to remember the name of the guy who hit the home run."

When Jeremy Todd flied out into the wind in right, the fans' happiness continued. Brooklyn had, for the moment, been saved.

Mark Lazarus: "Brooklyn hadn't scored a run. But they're losing 2–0 going into the bottom of the ninth, and for all intents and purposes, they were dead. And in my mind I'm going to myself, 'Yep. It's pitching and defense. And I haven't seen any base runners to know about team speed. And it's obvious we haven't got any hitting on this team.' And then, all of a sudden, as everybody is getting ready to go home and saying to themselves, 'Let's see what it's like to get out of the parking lot,' all of a sudden, 'Boom!' Edgar hits the home run, and he's jumping up and down like a wild man, and all of a sudden it became exciting and everybody's screaming and yelling and it's, 'How great a script is this? To tie the ball game with two out in the ninth? How wonderful! How great is this?' Now if they can only find a way to win the game, everybody will go home with a memory that they'll have forever."

The "Big Bird," David Byard, replaced Gahan at the top of the tenth. The heaviest Cyclone, Bird resembled lefty David Wells in size, but Big Bird threw righty. Byard moved with a grace that belied his heft. Off the field, he was already considered the funniest Cyclone, but on the mound he was all serious, a bulldog. Byard got Mare to ground out to short. Van Every singled and went to second on a passed ball. Then Byard walked Ken Quintana on four pitches, bringing up Ricky Morton. After a called strike, Morton grounded to short. McIntyre grabbed the ball, threw to second, forcing Mare, and Arias threw to first for a double play. The Cyclones could win if they scored in the tenth inning.

Nate Fernley came in to pitch for the Scrappers. Leandro Arias led off the tenth for the Cyclones and drew a walk. Pagan bunted for a hit. Robert McIntyre drew a four-pitch walk. That loaded the bases and brought Mike Jacobs to the plate. The potential winning run was on third base. Jacobs had struck out swinging four straight times in the game. Jacobs swung at and missed the first pitch. He was two strikes away from striking out five straight times. Jacobs swung at the next pitch. Up to now he had not hit a fair ball all day, but this time he hit a fly to left field. Arias tagged at third and beat the throw home, and Brooklyn had its first home victory since their last Ebbets Field game on September 24, 1957.

Warner Fusselle: "My visual, recollections were after the game was over, sitting up there in 'The Catbird Seat' and just watching the people down on the field, the players, and over on that dugout seeing all the media and thinking, 'This looks like a World Series celebration.' There were all these people in front of the dugout, and I remember the catcher, Mike Jacobs; I can remember seeing him clearly. He drove in the winning run with a sacrifice fly, and he was standing there and Reggie Armstrong [the other Cyclones' radio announcer] said it on the air. 'He looks likes a senator with his people out there.'

"This is just so remarkable. People all over the world are interested in tonight's game, and what a way to end, and, of course, it just totally shocked me, caught me off guard."

Mark Lazarus: "That just set the stage for everything. You knew one thing right there. Here was a team that couldn't be considered dead until the third out. You have to believe that this team can do something even when it looks grim. To win a game like that at home Opening Day? Now I thought, 'Why did I give my tickets away for the following night?' "

The public address system played "The Brooklyn Bridge." The crowd seemed in no hurry to leave, and while some left, many others lingered to enjoy the moment. Brooklyn, down to its last out in the ninth, had rallied to tie the game, and then won it in the tenth. On the field, reporters, television announcers, and photographers surrounded Mike Jacobs. Later on, he described what it was like being surrounded by the horde of media. "I felt like a senator," he admitted.

Warner Fusselle: "The media was incredible. That's what stands out in my mind, not the winning run scoring or whatever, but the media horde in front of the dugout and Jacobs and these guys down there. You could see him. You know this is early in the year; you still can't recognize all the players and all. You can see it was Jacobs and it was like John Kennedy standing down there. He looked so cool, and he was enjoying it, but he was cool and they were all taking it in like this is a normal thing.

"The players. I mean a lot of these guys, this is the first place they've been. They didn't know this is the minor leagues. They didn't know that there are minor leagues where they play before 36 fans that night and nobody boos or cheers. They don't know this. Some people said, 'Wow, this is what the minor leagues is all about!' Well, no, this is the extraordinary thing that you will have never have again in your life in all probability, but they didn't know that. I was thinking of that all along. This is amazing. I know how special this is. I think some of them think this is routine. Some had played at Kingsport the year before; they played in the Gulf Coast League or the Florida State League. They knew this wasn't routine. So they had different views, but for me to sit up and look down, I'm thinking this is the '68 World Series between the Cardinals and Detroit Tigers. And Denny McLain is out there and Mickey Lolich and Bob Gibson and these guys. It's like [*New York Daily News* writer] Dick Young down there talking to 'Senator' Mike Jacobs and the horde of photographers and writers. This is an electric moment."

On this night, Mike Jacobs drew more attention than the real United States senator in attendance, Charles "Chuck" Schumer. Mike Jacobs had been getting close to a fate most professional players have only in their nightmares. Jacobs had struck out four straight times, and had his count at 0-1 on his fifth at bat. He was close to striking out for a fifth straight time.

Mike Jacobs: "I have three swings to get the job done. If I don't, it's going to make for a pretty lousy night, that's for sure. I went out, and I swung at the first pitch. I missed that, and I stepped out and said to myself, 'Let's go. Now you have two pitches. You got to get this job done. Let's go. Think of your team right here.' And I did."

After the game, Jacobs called his mother on his cell phone. She had grown up at Rockaway within view of KeySpan Stadium, and as Mike was talking to her, while she was in California, she was watching highlights, including his game-winning run batted in, on *Sports Center* television.

The Los Angeles area has had professional baseball even prior to their Hollywood and Los Angeles teams in the Pacific Coast League days, and they have had major league baseball since 1958. To fight the LA traffic, Los Angeles Dodger patrons are often in the parking lot by the seventh inning.

On Coney Island, Brooklyn, on this night, many Brooklyn fans had waited 44 years to attend a professional game in their borough. That Brooklyn tied it up with two outs in the last of the ninth and won in the bottom of the tenth inning was a storybook ending. The field was jammed with reporters and photographers. Cyclone players smiled, and laughed and signed autograph after autograph for the kids in attendance, many of them the grandchildren of the older former Brooklyn Dodger fans in attendance. The Cyclones' parking lot was filled. Only a few people were leaving for their cars. The rest stayed and stayed.

When you've waited for 44 years, who wants to leave?

Between Innings

Mike Cox

"After the first game, nobody wanted to go home to the hotel. We just wanted to be there and soak it in, and as we left, as we were walking out, it was incredible. No one had ever seen that before. In Pittsfield, you'd just walk out after the game with the fans, and they wouldn't bat an eye, they wouldn't turn. In Brooklyn, I couldn't get used to walking out the players' entrance with about two hundred fans out there. I couldn't get used to that for the longest time. And they wanted your autograph; I was in college before, where nobody cared.

"In Pittsfield, a few people asked for your autograph, people who followed the team. I probably signed a hundred all year. In Brooklyn, in one night I might sign close to seventy-five or a hundred."

Minor league teams almost all have mascots. The Cyclones' mascot is Sandy the Seagull. Dressed in the six foot Seagull costume is Rick Johnson. He is about 5' 7"; the costume's head adds to his height. Rick has to keep the Seagull's mouth open — he sees out of the mouth.

Sandy the Seagull has a lot of yellow in his head, making him more colorful than the real seagulls who fly around the park that borders the Coney Island boardwalk.

Sandy, the Seagull — Cyclones' Mascot (a.k.a. Rick Johnson)

"I'm a huge sports fan and I love baseball, and as an actor I think this is the perfect situation. It's an opportunity to combine being a

Sandy the Seagull — with Harold Eckert and Luz Portobanco.

Sandy the Seagull — unmasked.

character and being part of the game, without actually going out there and playing it. Every kid's dream is to play sports, but when you can't get there, this is about as close as it gets. and this is the perfect marriage for me of having both sports and acting together.

"I was born in Queens and I still live in Queens, and I got my start when last year, the Queens Kings, the team that played over at St. John's in the Blue Jays' organization, had an ad in the paper listing a bunch of jobs, including that of mascot. I had been in sports entertainment before, and I was working at St. John's, so I thought, 'Hey, this is a great opportunity.' I live two blocks from St. John's, so I came down and interviewed for the job and I got it. Last year, I was Elvis the Lion. The mascot was a lion because of the show *The Lion King,* and the name was Elvis because Elvis was the King. So it was cute. And I had a blast. I loved it.

"I loved sports, and I got into acting late, at 15. I used to drive my mother nuts by doing voices. In college, at Queens College, I started taking theatre courses. I acted in 16 shows and was president of the theatre guild. I'd love to get into film. Here, with the huge crowds, and the exposure of the media and the huge press, it's a huge stage. It's a big challenge to get the crowd into the game and entertain them.

"When I was first doing Sandy this year, I was trying to do him a lot like Elvis, last year. But as the season wore on, Sandy kind of took on a life of his own. He became a different character. The suit and the head of the costume itself influences the character. I think of Sandy as being a really cool kind of guy. He gets along with everybody, and I can be on the level of little kids as well as be on the level of adults.

"I don't think Sandy has an age. He's like a college guy who is like a kid in a way. I always hope that my personality comes out in the character.

"As far as Party Marty's thing, he provides more of a human interaction, and my character is more like a Disney character, more of a cutesy thing.

"Just the other day I wandered, as Sandy, into the Pittsfield dugout, and one of the guys said, 'Hey, get out of the dugout!' I took it as a kind of half-kidding remark. And the trainer and one of the players tried to yank my head off.

"I said to them, 'Hey, come on guys. If you pull my head off, I'm going to get fired! You're going to traumatize the kids if you pull my head off!' So they backed off.

"So I thought, 'Hey, I'm okay now.' So I wandered off. Then about two minutes later, the trainer and some players grabbed me, and they tied my legs together with an Ace bandage. During the pitching change in the fifth inning, two Pittsfield players carried me out of the dugout and dumped me on the field. So I had to roll myself back into the dugout.... I literally rolled myself back into their dugout, and then I kind of hopped away. They eventually untied me, but they got a good laugh out of it. And I did, too.

"The other day, one of the fans said, 'Sandy, get out to second.' The field was being cleared. I thought that was a good idea. So I went back into the Cyclones' dugout to get a glove, and as Caligiuri was throwing grounders to the infield, the third baseman overthrew Caliguiri at first base and hit me right in the back with a baseball. So I collapsed down the stairs, and I ended up with my head on the dugout steps and my legs on the floor. So one of the photographers started taking pictures of me, and I was yelling, 'Get the trainer!'

"The fans here are terrific. Some of the fans call me 'Salty.' They compare me to Mister Met. I have all the respect in the world for the guys who do Mister Met; I know them and have worked with them. They sweat like crazy under that big head.

"Last year, I sweated a lot more as Elvis. And I lost a lot more weight. I feel it when it gets humid. The way the head is designed when it's humid, I find it hard to breathe. Sometimes I come off the field, and I take my head off to get a breather. I don't mind keeping the head on if it's not too hot or humid.

"Early in the season when I went into the stands, before the fans got used to it, I got smacked around and smacked, and punched and kicked. But then I developed a relationship with the fans, and they're so much nicer now. Especially the kids. Now the kids say, 'Hey, Sandy. You're the man.' Earlier in the year, the kids were looking at it like, 'Here's a man in a costume we can kind of kick around.'

"I'd get punched in the head. Last year, I got punched a few times, too. Usually the kids who do this are around ten, or eleven, or twelve years old.

A little kid takes to it a lot better. When they get around ten or twelve, it becomes a show-off thing, and it's like, 'Hey, watch this. I can punch the mascot in the head.' Usually one of the interns will tell a kid, 'Don't hit Sandy,' and the kid will back off.

"Earlier in the year, Brett Kay would grab me around the chest and Edgar Rodriguez would smack me with a towel. Noel Devarez likes to punch me — in the head. Most of the guys will stop to talk. They're cool. The coaches are the same way. I think the player I talked to the most was Vladimir Hernandez. He was really nice. He was staying at St. John's and he walked into a diner where I was eating and we had a great visit. When he got promoted, I realized I missed him a lot. He was friendly and we used to talk a lot. He always had a smile on his face.

Vladimir Hernandez (left) with Opening Day hero Edgar Rodriquez.

"These guys know me without the head. I became friendly with Glen Johnson, Hojo's son, and Gio, Edgar Alfonzo's son. They are really nice kids.

"A lot of girls are flirty with Sandy, but they don't know what I look like without my head. It's kind of like being an actor in costume who gets a great ovation and then later walks out into the audience, and they don't recognize him. I don't get a lot of recognition, but I do the best I can every night, even if people don't recognize me out of costume.

"My goal is to help to keep up a winning atmosphere because it is a special circumstance this year. I want to keep the fans in the game and help the players stay relaxed. I want the players to know I'm always rooting for them.

"Having fans like Chuck [Monsanto] and Ed [Gruber] come every night is great . They're always respectful fans.

"Right before the season started, my grandfather passed away. So I was feeling down at the start of the baseball season, and around that time I broke up with my girlfriend. But when I came out to the park each day, my spirits rose because I got an emotional lift just being a part of the special feeling that was going on at the ballpark here each night. I'll never forget the fact that this was a huge blessing for me this summer. There's something about all these New Yorkers coming out for minor league baseball. They've all just fallen in love with this team. That's why New York is such a great sports town. 'Cause of the passion that they have for sports."

Marty Haber is a tall young man who looks like he could be a Cyclones player. He's blond and athletic, and he's kind of like the animated host of a party, or the ringmaster of a circus. He carries a toy monkey, dances on the top of the dugout, with the monkey or with fans, runs on-field contests between innings and interacts with fans and players, often talking over his portable microphone.

His job requires someone who is not a wallflower. Marty is not.

Party Marty — Cyclones' Field Emcee
(a.k.a. Marty Haber)

"I was born and raised in Marine Park, right here in Brooklyn, about ten minutes away from the ball park here. My father worked for the Topps Baseball Card Company, obviously very into baseball.

"One day he asked me, 'Marty, do you want to play some ball?'

"And I must have said, 'Yeah!'

"So I started at four years old with the Ty Cobb League on Avenue X. The Torre family is from Marine Park, and Joe Torre's sister still lives there. I lived on Twenty-Ninth Street. I played Little League at Marine Park and high school at Madison High School, and then I played Division I college baseball at Hofstra, out on Long Island, for four years. I was a pitcher. I wanted to play professional baseball. The greatest thing about playing baseball is the camaraderie, meeting the players after class in our little locker room and talking about the day, talking about the girls that we met or whatever, and then going on the field. Playing Division I baseball was probably the greatest thing I ever did. I graduated in May of 1999. Before I was done with college there comes a time when you know you're not going to be drafted or signed. Two months before we graduated, my mother said to me, 'Marty, what are you going to do?'

"I didn't want to go into stocks or sit at a computer all day. So I sent out 230 résumés — to every major and minor league team. I got a phone call

Party Marty — Party Marty 2 Much Fun.

two days later from the Helena Brewers of the Pioneer League. They asked me if I wanted to do an internship that summer. It was a paid position — about a hundred and fifty dollars a month, free room and board. I accepted. I was a ticket and souvenir manager. It was a very small souvenir booth. They drew about two hundred people a game. I drove out to Montana. It was a two-and-a-half-day trip out there. I've never lived anywhere but Brooklyn my entire life.

"I met some great people, but me being from Brooklyn, they thought I was an alien. My personality. My goals that I had in my mind. They were very laid back people.

"A week into the season, our clubhouse manager disappeared. He didn't tell anybody. I told the general manager, 'I'll do the clubhouse.' So now I did the tickets and souvenirs, and now I did the clubhouse work. I wanted to get my feet wet with every aspect of minor league baseball. I did the laundry. I served the players. I knew what the players wanted because they were basically college baseball players, and I knew what college baseball players wanted. I knew about uniforms, caps, food before a game.

"After that short-season team's season ended, I drove to Las Vegas for a baseball job fair, and I got a job with the Rancho Cucamonga Quakes — at that time an affiliate of the Padres in California. I drove back to Brooklyn and worked for the Topps Baseball Card Company so I could save up some money to drive back out there. At Topps, I edited slides of pictures of baseball games. I worked on the statistics that they do for the back of the cards. I called scouts and got information from them.

"I accepted a full time position with Rancho Cucamonga with group sales, and I also worked on stadium operations, fixing seats, whatever needed to be done.

"I went to a job fair in Anaheim and asked about the new Brooklyn Club I had heard about, and I asked who the general manager was, and I was told that he , Steve Cohen, was right there. And I literally freaked out, just staring at this man.

"I spoke to him, and he said to keep in touch and I did. I called him once a month and also wrote letters every few weeks. Finally, I told him that at the end of the season I'm quitting the Quakes, and Steve Cohen said to talk to him when I got home. I was so excited about talking to him that I drove home, nonstop from California. It took me 39 hours. I got home at 2 in the afternoon. I said hello to my mother, and I didn't even unpack my car. Nothing. I went straight to the phone.

"We spoke, and a few weeks later I had a position on September 30, 2000, working for the Brooklyn Baseball Company. I was working in a trailer in Queens, selling season tickets. People who didn't know about us hung up the phone. People who knew about us jumped on it.

"In the team's office, I happen to have a lively personality, so when they needed someone to act as an on-field master of ceremonies during the games, they picked me to emcee.

"I'm also in charge of the Brooklyn Cyclones' Knothole Gang. For the Knothole Gang, I'm in charge of organizing the events. For $10 a child, the child gets a T-shirt, a membership certificate, free clinics, autograph sessions, an end-of-the-year party, discounts on special events. We have about three hundred kids in the Knothole Gang.

"I went to a school to try to arrange a group outing, and a man came up to me. His name is Louie Mannarino, and he introduced himself, and he said that he was an original member of the Knothole Gang. Happy Felton took three kids onto the field, and as a nine year old kid Jackie Robinson taught Lou how to field grounders. Lou Mannarino lives right there on Cropsey Avenue, between Fourteenth and Taft. Lou has the tape of his fielding ground balls with Jackie Robinson. I viewed that tape with him looking at it with a tear in his eye. We're going to try to bring Lou to one of our meetings so the kids can see what the old Knothole Gang was like. It's kind of weird because every minor league club in the country has some form of Knothole Gang or Kids' Club.

"My father, Bill Haber, was the statistician and historian for the Topps Baseball Card Company. He went with them in 1967, compiling the back of the baseball, football, basketball, and hockey cards. Topps was located in Sunset Park, Brooklyn. Once Topps got bigger, he did only baseball, so that they had statisticians for each sport. I was born in 1976. He came home with baseball cards, and I collected baseball cards since I was six or seven years old. He passed away in 1995, and six people filled his position at Topps. He was also one of the five founding members of SABR, the Society for [American] Baseball Research.

"My father did the research and found that there were 550 or so cases of ball players who played only one game in the majors. He had a passion for baseball, because he himself, who could have played professionally, through these other areas of baseball did the next best thing. He lived on Avenue P and East Third Street, and he grew up a big Dodger fan. He went to Ebbets Field all the time, taking the train there with his friends, and he would tell me stories about Ebbets Field all the time.

"I'm a very active person, and I'm always on the go, and when I was a kid I would listen to the stories about the old Dodgers, and I didn't really connect. And now that I'm older, and he's passed on, and I'm heavily involved with this, I would like to sit down with him for years and years, and listen to his Brooklyn Dodger stories forever. Most of his baseball work is in the library in the Baseball Hall of Fame in Cooperstown. We donated his work to them. He corrected hundreds of errors in the *Baseball Encyclopedia* on statistics, middle names, all kinds of things. I'm very proud that he gave me his knowledge and love for baseball.

"Carl Furillo was his favorite player. I was always kidding around with my dad. I'd say, 'Hey Dad, who has a better arm, Carl Furillo or Dave Winfield?'

"And my dad would say, 'Carl Furillo. Carl Furillo by far.'

"And I'd say, 'Dave Winfield has a hose.'

"And Dad would say, 'I know, but nobody has a better arm than Carl Furillo.'

"My father was a master of useless knowledge. He would tell me about people who sat next to him in sixth grade — he would tell me their middle names, their birthdays. I would ask him, 'Dad, why would you want to know that information?' He would just know it. He liked to impress people with his train of thought.

"I'm not as good as my father with memories, and birthdays, and middle names. But I brought my love of baseball with me. When people come to baseball games they are very happy with the on-field activities, getting them involved with the things we do like getting them on top of dugouts, things like that, so I feel my dad has passed on something to me.

"I'm a fourth generation Brooklynite, so I'm very proud when I come to the ball park every day and spend fifteen hours here every day. In fact, I would do this job for free, but I have to pay rent. As I tell people a lot, I take this job very personal. If people say to me, 'I haven't been to a Cyclones game yet," I say, 'What, are you kidding me?' I can't stop thinking about the Cyclones.

"I live in Bay Ridge now. The entire front office had a day off yesterday, and we went to see a ball game in Boston, and fans were stopping me there and saying, 'Hey, that's a Cyclones shirt.'

"We had three days off in the last three months and I went to baseball games on all three of them. I went to Shea, I went to the Long Island Ducks because a buddy of mine that I played college ball with just got signed by the Ducks, and I went to Fenway Park last night. And at all the games I purposely wore my Cyclones hat; I have a lot of pride. People come up to me and say, 'I heard it's hard to get tickets — that it's the best stadium ever.' This is at Shea, at Long Island, Fenway. The buzz is non-stop, and it's going to get better.

"Brooklyn is a very tough market in one way, but actually a very easy market in another. As long as you know how to deal with Brooklynites, you'll make it anywhere. In Brooklyn, there's a saying, 'You gotta do the right thing by people. One hand washes the other.' Dealing with a person correctly. Not like you're talking down to a person, but like you're talking with them. Trying to have personality. Trying to show that this ball park has personality, which it does. A Brooklynite likes flair, they like difference.

"The ticket prices are very affordable [$5–$10], so people like that. So really, we're doing the right thing by people, the way we're dealing with people.

"When I dance on the dugout? Well, I'm a *huge* Cyclone fan, but I just happen to be on the inside. I'm a fan that just happens to be on top of the dugout dancing. I love my job. I want to watch the team grow. I want to watch the ball park grow. I want to be here forever."

R.C. Reuteman

R.C. Reuteman is the Brooklyn Cyclones' vice president. He spent 19 years as a minor league executive in Binghamton, and got his start in baseball as a batboy for the old Milwaukee Braves. He helped form the original Mets' Binghamton franchise.

R.C. Reuteman: "I couldn't be happier with how things went at the Home Opener. The thing couldn't have been scripted better. The fans enjoyed it. The stadium is gorgeous. I'm used to getting started in April, so this short season thing is new for me, and we needed the time, but it's been a long wait.

"My experience in starting up the Binghamton franchise helped to prepare me to start up the Cyclones. There are so many things to do in starting up a new club, from the logos, to the uniforms.

"I probably take fifty or seventy-five calls a day. I was in Binghamton since 1972, and it was tough to leave, but I needed a new challenge.

"The community has embraced this team so greatly that we made an ownership decision to add the new bleachers and those extra thousand seats will help everybody out. Now, with the new bleachers, I think with 7,500 we have the largest Class A facility in the country. And it gives us a chance with the mayor's office to give away a hundred tickets for each game to the community.

"*The Daily News* ran a contest last year to chose a name, and the fans chose the Cyclone name.

"We have to thank the Los Angeles Dodgers for allowing us to use that old Brooklyn B on merchandise. The Los Angeles Dodgers still have the rights to use that B. Their Bob Daly is a Brooklynite, so he understood. Our sale of hats has been unbelievable.

"We had a chance to mix three themes: obviously, baseball; plus the beach — our right field jutes up against the boardwalk; and the other theme is the amusement park, and we've married these themes — our ushers all wear Hawaiian shirts."

Steve Cohen

Steve Cohen was born in Brooklyn. A man in his early thirties, Steve is already an experienced minor league executive, spending a good part of his career as the general manager of St. Petersburg in the Florida State League.

In 2000, Steve Cohen was the general Manager of the Queens Kings, a franchise operated by the New York Mets, but staffed with players from the Toronto Blue Jays. After the 2000 season, he became the general manager of the new Brooklyn Cyclones.

Steve Cohen: "A lot of people said that they came to games at KeySpan and saw people here that they hadn't seen in a long time. It had the feel of a neighborhood coffee shop in a way. It made Brooklyn feel a little smaller.

"People would run into each other on the concourse and catch up on events with each other while they watched a few innings there.

"Our ownership, including Fred Wilpon, being from Bensonhurst, wanted to bring baseball back to Brooklyn, and we originally were trying to build a temporary stadium at the Parade Grounds and then we went to St. John's with the Queens Kings, and in only a year we had this ball park built at Coney Island.

"The architects, Jack Gordon and John Ingram, designed the ball park to fit in with the community. It mixes baseball with an amusement park feel, along with a beach feel. At night, we can walk around, and we still get the feeling that we're in Coney Island. We can walk around and see the neon rings over the lights — which is unlike any other park in the country. You look over the left field wall and see the Cyclone roller coaster going; you see the Wonder Wheel going; you hear the people screaming on the rides; you look over the right field wall and see the boardwalk and the beach. We have the neon lights in different colors on the concourse. You don't feel like you're outside of Coney Island — you feel like you're in it.

"Before the season, we would have hoped to reach a goal of 4,500 or 5,000 a game, but before the season no one really knew what our attendance would be. We did have a concern of the unknown. Minor league baseball was new to the New York City area. We're playing between the New York Mets and the New York Yankees, and the area was perceived as a major league market. The Coney Island area had had some negative publicity over the years. There were a lot of things that gave us reason to work and not take it for granted.

"We were here six or seven days a week. We went right from the ball park at St. John's to here. We knew in August that we would be here at Coney Island by the next season, but it took about three months of advertising to get the word out to the people.

"In the early fall, when we got our team name and established a logo and established our office, that got things rolling, and we were under way. In January, it really started picking up, and then when spring training started and our stadium here was up, things really started steamrolling."

Mike Jacobs

The Cyclones were playing the Mahoning Valley Scrappers at home on June 27, two days after the home opener. Catcher Jacobs had been hit twice by pitches his first two times up and then had base hits his next two times.

He was a home opening night hero two days before by driving in the winning run with a sacrifice fly.

In the top of the fifth inning, the Mahoning Valley Scrappers had a 1–0 lead with one out and the Scrappers had a man on third base with a 3-1 count on the batter, and a fan came out of the stands and started to run around the bases. The fan rounded second, and steamed into third, and everyone in the park was shocked because no Cyclones fan had done anything like this before.

Mike Jacobs: "I looked up and the guy was running around third base, and it didn't look like the security guards were going to stop him. But they had a run on third, and we didn't want him to score, and the man running around the bases was a distraction — one that we didn't need. I didn't really think about it at first when I first saw him coming towards me, but then once he was about

Mayor Rudy Giuliani congratulates Opening Night hero, Mike Jacobs.

halfway towards home I thought it would be fun to take him down. I played defensive end for three years in high school, so I had some experience at this."

Jacobs made the tackle. The fan was the only fan to inappropriately run onto the Cyclones home field all season.

Jay Caligiuri

Jay Caligiuri played at a good college program. He talks about adjusting to professional pitching.

"I thought minor league baseball would be tougher at the plate. Still, every day, it's like facing a number one hurler in college. You have to be more patient and wait for your pitch, every at bat. When I first got here, the fastballs were blowin' by me a little bit, but when I started getting more at-bats I started seeing that pitch longer, and I was able to react to it better. With two strikes, I would foul it off. With two strikes, I'm always looking for a fastball, and I trust my hands that I can handle an off-speed pitch. If you're looking off-speed, and waiting for a seventy-five mile per hour pitch, and he comes with a ninety-two mile per hour pitch, you're done."

Harold Eckert

Harold Eckert started the year at rookie level Kingsport. Coming back from arm surgery, he did well and was quickly promoted to Brooklyn.

"On the first game, they had told me I would make a piggy-back start [come in to the game in relief of the starter], and I just wanted to make a good impression. They told me, 'Okay, he's got fifteen pitches left. You're going in next inning.' When you go out there, you know you have a pitch count.

"Pitching in Brooklyn, I'd pitched in front of more fans than I ever have. My parents were at the game. It was the first time I pitched professionally in front of them. It was exciting to pitch in front of people maybe for the first time ever. Sometimes before I pitched, I would take a little look up and see my parents there. Sometimes between pitches, I'd take a look and see them there and that kept me strong. My dad put the ball in my hand when I was three, four, whatever.

"After the home games, at least ten or fifteen people would be waiting for me after the game outside the clubhouse. When I was a kid, I would talk to my friends and we would say, "Wouldn't it be great if you could come see me pitch in New York some day if I make the majors?" Then it happened. It was in Brooklyn, a step below the majors, but it happened.

"I had a couple of friends who still lived in Edison who went to J.P. Stevens High School with me, and they came to every home game.

"In the first game, Ough pitched and he gave up no hits. I came into the game and going into the eighth inning, we had a no hitter. I came into the game in the fourth inning, and I had waited for this years and years. I was excited nervous, but not afraid nervous. I was charged up."

INNING 5

Cyclone Road Trip

After their game against Lowell, the Cyclones went home and tried to get some sleep before their scheduled departure at 8:00 the next morning for their four game series at Pittsfield, Massachusetts. This is not as easy as it sounds. The Cyclones live all over the map of the New York City metropolitan area. The majority of the Cyclones live at St. John's University in the Borough of Queens. A few hundred feet from home plate at the St. John's ballpark — the field where the Queens Kings played their games last year as a farm team of the Toronto Blue Jays — is a dormitory that was used by the Queens Kings last year to house both home and visiting players. St. John's is located in an almost suburban area of mostly single family homes on residential streets, and since the dorms are vacated by most students before the New York–Penn League season begins, the dorms make a safe and cost-effective place to house ballplayers.

The Cyclone players are charged $200 by the club as a fee for their housing at the dorms or at Brooklyn's Xaverian High School, another venue used by the club to house players. There are some security personnel around the St. John's dorms, the rooms are all together, and there's plenty of parking. The problem is that plenty of parking doesn't matter because most of the players have no cars. Some of the players can't afford to have cars, and some have a car at home but chose not to drive it to New York. A few of the players take cars to the ballpark, but mostly what the players do is all pile into a van supplied by the club. There is no official driver for the van, but "Big Bird" David Byard has assumed the role of van driver. The Cyclone presence has been gradually increasing at St. John's. Sometimes, the players squeeze a lot of Cyclones into a van meant for nine people. One day during the season, with no driver with a car available to drive them to the ballpark, they squeezed, like clowns in a circus, 17 players into one van.

The players get up when the earliest one wakes up and bangs on the others' doors. The players like to "ride shotgun," in the seat next to the driver. They have to leave early. St. John's to Coney Island is a trip that normally takes about 45 minutes, but traffic can make it take an hour and a half, and nobody wants to be late. Being late for the bus could cost players a $20 fine — each. To the players, who make $850 a month before taxes, a $20 fine is enormous. In equivalent terms, it would be like fining Cal Ripken $20,000 for being late for the bus. The players take home about $600 a month, then $200 a month is deducted by the club for housing, which leaves them about four hundred dollars a month. Players can also be fined for being late for the pregame stretch, usually held at about 3:00 P.M. for a home night game. These guys might be about the age of college students, but they take a much more serious approach to punctuality than do many undergraduates. These players, when told to report to the ballpark for a three o'clock pregame stretch, usually get there sometime between one and one-thirty.

While the atmosphere around the team often was that of an amusement park, the atmosphere within the team was often that of the military. The Cyclone players thought no more of being late than a marine private thought of being late for morning roll call. Within the team, then, there was a military-like hierarchy.

With most of the players staying at St. John's all inside his van, "Big Bird" drove through the streets of Queens. After stopping after a few blocks for a few boxes of doughnuts, the players continued toward Brooklyn. Encountering passersby along the way on the sidewalks, Big Bird would beep the horn and wave to them. No angry beep came from this chauffeur; on the contrary, David would catch hard-bitten New Yorkers off guard with a friendly toot and a wave and big smile. He'd keep driving and waving and beeping. When David "Big Bird" Byard was driving the bus (van), you were going enjoy the trip, whether you wanted to or not. A family man with a wife and child in his hometown in Ohio, he was built about the size of a late-career Babe Ruth. Plenty of girth, plenty of mirth and a team extrovert, he drove as he lived — outgoing, funny, witty, but harmless. When players were asked to describe him, they always laughed, not at him, but at some memory of how he made them laugh. Away from the pitcher's mound, Big Bird made people forget their troubles, but on the mound he brought troubles on — to batters as he came in to close out a game.

The van pulled into the KeySpan parking lot early, and the players entered the players' entrance, a door on the first base side under a sign that said, "Brooklyn Baseball Company." Right outside the players' entrance was parked Academy Bus #528, driven by Fred Wood. The players went into the door and walked through another door, then turned right and entered the locker room. They went to their lockers, large stalls five feet wide, four feet deep, and eight feet high. The clubhouse was carpeted and had 35 lockers. It was about 30' by 60', not including the showers and bathroom at the far end. This was not a typical minor league clubhouse. In the middle of the lockers were tables where food spreads, usually hot dogs and french fries, were set after games. There was nothing minor league about this clubhouse.

The players' uniforms were hung in their lockers. Each player had only one away uniform: a pair of pants, one game jersey, one practice jersey, socks and a hat. The players packed two bags, one with their baseball stuff, a long bag five feet long, and a bag with their personal clothes. Bats were usually put in the team bat bag.

The players stored both their baseball equipment bag and their personal equipment bag in the luggage area that was under the seating area of the bus. Players took their cell phones, CD players, books, and newspapers with them on the bus. And they also took food. This was a key element, as the trip to Pittsfield would be a five-hour ride, and there would be only one stop, at a highway rest area along the way.

Some of the players walked the one block to the Mermaid Deli on Coney Island's Mermaid Avenue to get some food for the trip. Singly or in twos, the players gradually boarded the bus. There was no one else around. No fans. No family. No friends. For the players, almost all of whom who become night owls, this was the early morning. Conversations were almost nonexistent. The team began boarding the bus early. The bus was scheduled to depart at 9:00 A.M. While the players had to be aboard at that time, it would be considered unprofessional of them to board the bus just before nine. Boarding at 8:50 could get a player a look from the manager. As Howard Johnson had told Harold Eckert, "Being on time means being fifteen minutes early." The players were all at the clubhouse at least an hour before the nine o'clock departure, and began to board the bus at around eight-thirty.

At a few minutes before nine o'clock, the baggage has been stowed and the bus is seemingly full. The manager, Fonzie, is in his accustomed seat at the front right of the bus. He sits with his nine-year-old son, Giovanni, known as Gio, who is out of school now and is along for the trip. On the front left seat is Howard Johnson, behind him sits Bobby Ojeda, behind him is Warner Fusselle. Behind Fonzie is the trainer, Eric Montague. Most of the players share seats. Most of the pitchers sit in the rear of the bus. The next game's starting pitcher gets the privilege of a seat by himself.

Montague, the trainer, counts the number of players, but does not call a roll. When the count seems accurate, he asks players to see if their roommate is there, as a double check. If a player weren't there, the bus would not wait. Fonzie runs a tight ship. A player missing the bus would be fined, and would have to travel to Pittsfield on his own. It would also be a very serious strike against his reputation in baseball. With the competition so fierce, no player is even close to being late. At exactly 9:00 A.M., Fonzie signals driver Fred Wood, and off the bus goes. It goes a half block onto Surf Avenue and heads for the Belt Parkway. The bus will cross the Verrazano-Narrows Bridge onto Staten Island, go across Staten Island into Jersey, then go into New York State and cross onto Massachusetts near Pittsfield, which is in far western Massachusetts, only about 20 miles from the New York State border.

Between Innings

Mike Cox

"Anything over five hours, we sleep on the floor of the bus. Whoever is brave enough gets to sleep on the floor of the bus. You can't be wide, and you can't be tall. I fit the bill there, I think. You can't take up too much room 'cause they get their feet out in the aisle.

"If you need to use the bathroom in the back, you have to climb over the players on the floor to get to the bathroom. The coaches hate it, but they deal with it because those players asleep on the floor are the ones going to be playing the next day."

Harold Eckert

Harold Eckert comes from Edison, New Jersey — it's only about a 45-minute trip from Edison to Coney Island. He lives at his boyhood home while living his boyhood dream — playing professional baseball, hopefully on the way to the major leagues.

He discusses one of the player's basic activities — the hunt for food. Off the field, players concentrate on the basics like having money, getting sleep and having food — lots of it.

"At home, my mother might make me lunch or ask if I wanted a sandwich to go, and if I did she would make me my favorite sandwich, a salami and provolone on a roll, and then she'd make me another, and I'd take that to the ball park. I always wanted to have food. You always wanted to have food on you. The guys that eat the best always carry around lunchboxes with them. We had guys like Brett Kay who would always take care of me. If we were going on a road trip he'd get an egg sandwich down at the Mermaid Deli, and he'd give me one. You want to have food and juice, and a lot of water with you on the bus. The bus is sometimes like a restaurant. Countless times, guys are giving each other food and bits of sandwiches. Guys ask others for bites of food. Every time you get off the bus, there are bags, water bottles. We got in trouble for leaving the bus a mess once. From then on we had to take a garbage bag and clean up for ourselves."

The players ate and slept their way through New Jersey, stopping at the rest area near Bear Mountain, New York. From there, it was three more hours to Pittsfield, but the team wasn't going to Pittsfield, it was going to North Adams, about a half hour farther north. Because the Mets have certain preferences for their hotels, the team stays in North Adams.

The bus enters the North Adams Holiday Inn parking lot at 2:00 P.M. The players check into the hotel. The players will have about two hours to eat, unwind, and rest before they get back on the bus and go a half hour back in the direction in which they came, to Pittsfield.

North Adams is a town nestled in the midst of the Berkshires. It has one main street. Most of the businesses are within a three-block area. It has an old theatre, in the center of town, that is closed for renovations. The Holiday Inn is at the center of town and is the tallest building in North Adams — at five stories. The hotel isn't fancy, but it's respectable and well maintained, and certainly not a hardship as far as accommodations.

Mike Cox

"On the trip up to Pittsfield, there were a lot of questions being asked about how the ball played in the outfield there, and the hitters asked about the bunting ground, their field right in front of the plate. I told them the ball might make bad hops in the outfield because they play high school football there, and it would be rough. I told them the mound was okay. They asked about the visitors' bullpen mound, and it gave Portobanco some problems there; it was a high mound and it went downhill, and it strained his arm a little.

"They wanted to know where the sun set. I let them know that we were probably going to have a sun delay, but none of them believed me. The sun is supposed to set in the northeast, but here the sun set right behind centerfield. That's the only place I've ever seen a sun delay."

The players are back on the bus and on their way to Pittsfield at 4:00 P.M. Pittsfield is an old town. The Berkshire Mountains are in the distance beyond the outfield wall. Pittsfield's Waconah Park is a block off the main drag. It's set near a tavern and some one-family homes. The field doesn't dominate its surroundings — it blends in. Pittsfield's stadium isn't set outside of town. It's right in it. The downtown area has an old feel to it. Most of the stores and homes seem to be from the 1930s to the 1950s, and with the exception of a few buildings, the town could seem out of the past. The stadium has few modern amenities. Instead of the large souvenir shops in modern minor league stadia, Pittsfield sells most of their souvenirs from a small wooden stand near the entrance to the park. Pittsfield is a city, but it feels like a large small town rather than a small city.

From the ballpark, if you look behind the first base line, you see the back of the tavern, the back of houses, and the back of stores. You get the view that one has when on a train passing through a town; you see the rear of buildings and homes, the parts that aren't fixed up like the fronts — the rear view, somewhat cluttered with boxes, assorted furniture, odds and ends, things put out of view of the important visitors expected at the front entrances.

Pitcher Mike Cox, a Texan, recalls last season when he was on the Mets' farm team with Pittsfield. He lived with a "host" family there.

Mike Cox: "I was sharing a house with [teammate] Chad Elliott. We shared a house with an 86-year-old lady. She was wonderful. She taught us a lot of Northeast history that we never learned about. There was a little bit of culture shock being up there. The lady's name is Rita. Her son was with her, and this year when we were in Pittsfield, her son came to see us both in Pittsfield and at Brooklyn. He followed us around a bit.

"I lived within walking distance of the ballpark. A real nice house upon a hill, and the walk was downhill. We usually rode to the park; on days when I pitched, I would walk to the park so I wouldn't have any problems. We both had our own rooms upstairs.

"That's the nice thing about staying with a host family; you get to meet a lot of nice people. And you go over to other guys' host families, and you go over to the other host families for dinner. One host family might have a pool, and you go over there because most of the host families know each other. They had every-thing set up pretty nice for the players. At the last game of the season, we get to acknowledge the host families by giving them roses or flowers or something to show that we appreciated it. Sometimes it's sad for the families and the kids — and for us.

"Pittsfield was just a normal town. We were welcomed there, but they've seen so many teams come in and out that it really wasn't a big deal to them, unlike Brooklyn. In Brooklyn, if you said you were a Cyclones player, people would go a little crazy.

"In Pittsfield, there was really no place to go out, which was good for young players like us. We went to Applebee's, that was the main place. The other team stayed in North Adams. I didn't have a car, but some guys did, and you could always get a ride to wherever you wanted to go.

"The ballpark was humbling, I guess. After you've been signed, you're thinking major leagues and all this money that's in baseball, and then you wind up at Waconah Park. It's not run down; it's just old. And the fans liked it that way because they were used to it that way, and that's where they're going to go.

"You got a lot of bad bounces in the infield. Some pitchers would try to keep it in the air because of the size of the park.

"There wasn't much to do there except for the theater or a restaurant. The restau-rant was by the Applebee's. There wasn't too much else. They had their other restaurants, but the Applebee's was centrally located, so we often met there. I didn't have a car, but there were always guys around who would give you a ride."

The Pittsfield ballpark, built in 1919, the year the Yankees acquired Babe Ruth from the Red Sox, and the year of the Black Sox World Series, has a front office that is about a third the size of the Brooklyn Cyclones' clubhouse. The Pittsfield front office is located to the right of the men's room, in a sep-arate wooden building. The whole front office is about the size of a main office in a small high school. The door is open. One can just walk in and talk with anyone. Of course, there are a few computers and a fax machine, and mod-ern telephones, but otherwise, the desks, chairs, and ambiance are out of the 1950s. The few front office employees are busy, but they are friendly to visi-tors. It could be the ticket office to a small summer stock theatre, with its informal atmosphere and low-key ambiance.

The field itself has unusual dimensions. The left field line is 375 feet, cen-ter field is 385 feet, then the outfield wall from center goes out so that in right-center the park stretches to 430 feet, before the fence angles back in towards right field, where it's 337 feet. With the power alley in right-center so deep, very few homers are hit there in right-center. Straight away center is a much shorter shot.

Frank Corr: "Pittsfield is a little shaky. Their playing surface might have been a little not up to par, but I'm not real greedy, man. As long as you have a place to play, then go ahead and go after it, you know what I mean? We were spoiled. We had a fantastic facility. It was unbelievable. I liked the change. I liked going into Pittsfield and getting that different atmosphere. That old ball park. That real old field. Kind of real bumpy in the outfield. Kind of sandlot type. I like that kind of place; it's always good. Kind of keeps you realistic. Makes you think we're playing our home games on our field. And these guys are winning all their games playing on a field like this."

Tonight is the opening game of a four game series. The park is filling up. It's the start of summer, and there are a lot of camps in the area, and some campers are here. There are retirees and teenagers and parents. It's a mixed lot.

Pittsfield is on a nine-game winning streak. Up through last year, they were the Mets' farm club for 12 years. The Mets had operated the Queens Kings last year, but the Toronto Blue Jays staffed the team. The Mets maintained their franchise in Pittsfield. Now Pittsfield is a farm team of the Houston Astros.

Pittsfield is located in the geographic center of Berkshire County, in far western Massachusetts. It is, according to Howard Herman, beat writer for the *Berkshire Eagle*, "the great demilitarized zone" as far as fans are concerned, with American League fans being evenly distributed between the Red Sox and the New York Yankees. And since many New Yorkers have summer homes in the area, there are also many New York Mets fans in Berkshire County. Pittsfield is only 20 minutes from the New York State line, 60 minutes to Albany, New York, and a two-hour drive across state to Boston's Fenway Park.

Just south of Pittsfield is Tanglewood, the summer home of the Boston Symphony, and there are theatre festivals in the area, including the Williamstown Theatre Festival. Arlo Guthrie and James Taylor live in the vicinity, and part of the summer culture for visitors in the area is to see Waconah Park, which, like Tanglewood and the Williamstown Theatre Festival, is a tradition. And tonight, there would be another tradition, the July 4th fireworks.

Before the game, a few fans say hello to the former Pittsfield Mets, but for the most part there is a feeling that it's the Fourth of July and it's a holiday and there will be baseball and fireworks — which is the way it's been here for years. There is talk that there won't be New York–Penn League baseball here next season — that the franchise will move to Troy, New York, about an hour away. The realization hits. This town has had professional baseball for about as long as the Dodgers were in Brooklyn, and, in a sense, the Pittsfield team moved to Brooklyn when the Mets switched their affiliation from Pittsfield.

It's time to play ball. Brooklyn starts what is becoming their first-string lineup, with fleet Angel Pagan leading off and in center, followed by Robert McIntyre at shortstop, who played part of last season at Pittsfield. Catching is opening night home hero Mike Jacobs, and the clean-up hitter is Jay Caligiuri playing third. Noel Devarez, with a strong arm and innate power at bat, is batting fifth and in right field. He's followed in the lineup by first baseman Jeremy Todd, who played last year at Pittsfield and drove in 47 runs, excellent for a short season league. Sixth is Frank Corr, normally in left field, but tonight a DH. Forrest Lawson is in left field with newcomer Danny Garcia at second and Luz Portobanco on the mound.

The Pittsfield Astros, after having lost their first five games of the year, have won their next nine straight and enter the game with a better record than the 8–7 Cyclones. After three and a half scoreless innings, Pittsfield loaded the bases in the fourth and wound up scoring three runs without hitting Portobanco really hard.

In the top of the sixth, Danny Garcia singled to center and scored on a two out double by Jacobs to make the score 3–1 Pittsfield. With relief pitchers in for both teams, there was no more scoring going into the ninth. Brooklyn needed two runs to tie the game; the Cyclones' Noel Devarez hit a two out single to right, bringing up Jeremy Todd. The big lefty swinger swung and missed at the first pitch, and then fouled off a pitch before missing the third pitch to strike out and end the game.

The Pittsfield fans were pleased, but not ecstatic. Practically no one left the stadium, and most fans went down to the field where they were allowed to assemble to watch the fireworks. Standing on the infield grass, the fans watched as the fireworks exploded above them. Pieces of fireworks slowly drifted down upon the crowd, some of the fireworks still smoldering, but no one seemed to mind, and seeing the sometimes still hot pieces of fireworks fall on the wooden ballpark didn't seem to alarm anyone either. The Brooklyn players made their way to and from their clubhouse almost unnoticed.

After the game, the team took the bus back to North Adams, over a two-lane highway, and over a tall mountain pass. Back in North Adams at nearly 11:00 P.M., the players were hungry, and North Adams was basically closed. The few downtown blocks of stores were almost all shuttered, but there was a crowd near the Burger King that was a block from the team's hotel, the Holiday Inn. The crowd was at the only apparent activity in the town. They were waiting in the parking lot for the North Adams fireworks, which had been postponed after an earlier rain shower. They waited calmly as players trooped from the hotel to the Burger King. Other players went for a five-block walk to the open Subway sub shop, and a couple of players walked two blocks uptown to the open pizzeria. Some players made phone calls from the hotel lobby while other players went to their rooms and watched late night television, mostly sports recaps. Players had a midnight curfew, which meant that they had to be in their rooms, but could be still up. At a quarter to midnight, a few players came back from a walk. One of them was the team's leading home run hitter, Noel Devarez. What did the team's big hitter do to live it up in North Adams? He had a package in his hand. He opened it as he entered the hotel lobby. He had a cheeseburger and a pint of milk.

As a few hundred people watched the fireworks right before midnight, the rest of North Adams was quiet. Players, not interested in the fireworks, trooped into the hotel lobby and headed upstairs. Some were carrying pizza, or submarine sandwiches. Wound up from the game, the players almost all became night owls, unable to sleep for hours, but the scene on the hotel's fourth floor was like a college dorm almost anywhere in America. Players gathered in rooms and watched television as they ate their just gathered food. One could picture this scene throughout the country as thousands of minor league ballplayers gathered in hotel rooms watching late-night baseball recaps, on *Sports Center*, seeing the major leaguers whose jobs they coveted, and dreaming of the days years from now when other young ball players would watch them.

The next morning, Coach Bobby Ojeda was up early and working out downstairs in the Holiday Inn's small gym. Players were up later and strolled around the town, after they got up around noon. A player and a girlfriend, here to visit him, shopped at the drugstore across from the hotel. Later, Ojeda ate breakfast with Howard Johnson in a small health food restaurant on the main street.

The air smelled as fresh as can be, and it was cool. In all directions, one could see the Berkshire Mountains. Near the hotel was a museum, but nobody visited it. By 3:30, the players had to be back on their Academy Bus for the trip back to Pittsfield and the evening's game.

Harold Eckert: "If you're staying overnight when you go on the bus, it's called a road trip. If you're just going for the day and coming back right after the game, it's called a commuter trip. I don't know which is worse. When you go on a commuter trip, you get back to the ball park in Brooklyn late at night; actually it's usually more like early the next morning, and then you have to go home and almost come right back to the park for a home game that night.

"We had one set of uniforms on a road trip. We had pants, a regular jersey and a batting practice jersey. On the road trip, we had an assignment after the game to drop our laundry off at a certain room number at the team hotel, usually it was at the room of the trainer, Eric Montague, or later, Mike Herbst. And then we are told to pick it up at that room at one P.M. the next day, and it would be all ready for us. The hotel would wash the uniforms or if the hotel didn't do it, then Mike Herbst would do it, and the uniforms would be all clean and ready for us the next afternoon. Sometimes on the road they would tell us to be in uniform at the hotel, and we would ride to the ball park all dressed for the game. Usually, we would take the bus to the ball park in street clothes and change in the locker room. Sometimes guys would want to ride to the ball park half in uniform, maybe the uniform pants on and a regular sweatshirt or something, but the coaches were pretty strict about that, and they wouldn't let us because it would look bad to go to the game with guys dressed in all different ways."

Brooklyn started basically the same lineup as the night before with Brett Kay catching and Jacobs as DH. The batting order was shuffled a bit, and Matt Peterson started.

After four-and-a-half scoreless innings, Pittsfield scored a run in the fifth inning. Australian Matt Gahan came in to relieve Peterson and retired the last batter, Todd Self. In Brooklyn's eighth, Mike Jacobs walked and took second on a wild pitch to Caligiuri. Caligiuri walked and then Jacobs and Caligiuri moved to second and third on another wild pitch. After Devarez struck out, John Toner walked. Frank Corr pinch hit for Jeremy Todd, and then another wild pitch scored Jacobs, and then Corr walked, and a single by Kay brought in two more. Then in the Brooklyn ninth, Pagan, Garcia, Jacobs, and Caligiuri got four straight hits — there was another wild pitch in there — and the Cyclones scored three more runs, and Gahan closed out the game to let Brooklyn snap the Pittsfield winning streak at ten, before a more typical Pittsfield crowd of 1,873.

Back in North Adams, the routine was more of the same: late night snacks before all the stores closed at midnight and the town closed up.

The next night, Ross Peeples, the lefty from Cordele, Georgia, started for the Cyclones, and radio announcer Warner Fusselle, knowing that Ross' family at home in Georgia was listening on the Internet broadcast, had fun making puns about all the Peeples' peoples listening in Cordele. Brooklyn started a familiar lineup, but Leandro Arias was playing third, and Jay Caligiuri was playing first in place of Jeremy Todd.

A crowd of only 947 was on hand as Peeples' excellent control kept him hitting the corners and getting by with his 85 miles per hour fastball. A scoreless game went to the bottom of the second inning. Pittsfield shortstop Ryan Stegall stepped into the batter's box and stared out towards the mound. The sun was just setting over the trees beyond the center field fence. Umpire Brett McCrery took a look towards the mound and waved his arms. Stegall stepped out of the box, then began to head for his dugout. The Brooklyn players looked confused. Then they began to leave the field. To many of the fans, seeing the players leave the field in the middle of an inning was something they had seen before. For others, this was a new experience, one which was soon announced by the public address system as being a "sun delay."

In the radio booth, Warner Fusselle had heard about Pittsfield sun delays, and he scrambled for an on-air discussion. Reggie Armstrong, who announces with Warner for home games, wasn't there to help, and Fusselle grabbed Brooklyn writer Mike Dolan for an on-air discussion. Both teams left the field to go to their clubhouses, located in a small building behind third base. Fusselle couldn't leave, and in a style reminiscent of Red Barber's discussions during Brooklyn Dodger rain delays, Fusselle kept talking with Dolan — for 25 minutes, until the teams resumed play when the sun had gone down enough for the batter to hit safely.

For most players, well accustomed to rain delays, it was the first time they had ever seen a sun delay. For the fans, accustomed or not to sun delays, it seemed to be taken in stride. There was an air of quiet acceptance. No one cared about the delay. No one chanted for the game to resume. In the background, where the glaring sun poked over the center field fence, were the Berkshire Mountains. It was warm out, summer had just started, and the 947 fans virtually had open seating as they could sit practically anywhere in the stands, in a $3–$5 seat that would cost $60 in Boston or New York. Fans chatted or visited the concession stands. This was not a traffic tie-up in Manhattan's Time Square. It was a sun delay in Pittsfield, and no one was in a hurry to go anywhere, because it seemed they were already where they wanted to be.

When the game resumed, Peeples took a long warmup before allowing a double to Stegall, then a walk on four pitches. For Peeples, who hadn't allowed a run in the entire season, 14 innings of pitching, it didn't appear like resuming pitching after sun delays would be his strong suit. The next batter pushed the runners to second and third with a sacrifice bunt, but Peeples regained his form, and a strikeout and groundout got him out of the inning with his scoreless streak now up to 15 innings.

After Cyclone runs in the fourth and fifth innings, Peeples finished the fifth inning and left with a 2–0 lead, which Brett McGinley held as he pitched four scoreless innings, allowing only one hit and striking out seven. Brooklyn kept adding runs and won 5–0.

The next day was the series finale, and Brooklyn had to check out of their rooms by noon. Two rooms were retained as getaway rooms where the players could watch television or just hang out until the team left for the ballpark. This procedure allowed the team to stay at the hotel without paying for rooms they wouldn't use this evening, and it allowed the hotel to begin renting out the rooms to their other incoming guests.

Harold Eckert knew he would be pitching today, but not at the start. Big Brian Braswell, on injury rehab, was scheduled to start, to be followed by Australian Wayne Ough. After Braswell pitched two scoreless innings, Ough was roughed up a bit, giving up a total of four runs in four innings. Brooklyn started a four run rally in the fifth, begun by a bunt from backup catcher Francisco Sosa. Asked all year by fans if he was related to Sammy, fellow Dominican Sosa always told the truth, that he wasn't, and then had to see their lack of interest in him. He was playing all year with an arm recovering from an injury. Ough started the sixth inning by allowing a double, a walk and another double, to give up two runs with a man on second. Now Eckert, who had foregone much time out in North Adams, came into the game. Eckert struck out three batters in a row, and then proceeded to throw three scoreless innings. After nine innings, the game was tied at four. In the top of the tenth, the Cyclones' DH Brett Kay drew a walk. Pagan came in to run for him, and when Toner singled to center, and the center fielder made an error, Pagan went to third. Jeremy Todd, not playing so much recently, came on to pinch hit for Arias and hit a sacrifice fly to score Pagan with the leading run.

In the top of the tenth, Eckert struck out the first two batters. Then Todd Self, whose last name seems to belong in a "Who's on First" Abbott and Costello skit, drew a walk. Then Self was taken out for a pinch runner with the unlikely, but also "Who's on First"–appropriate, name of Likely. Likely, as was likely, stole second. Here was Eckert, pitching his fifth inning, still making his comeback from Tommy John surgery, and Pittsfield had the potential tying run on second, and the winning run coming up. Cyclones manager Edgar Alfonzo stuck with Eckert and Harold went to a full count on Stegall. Stegall fouled off the next two pitches and then Eckert got him to bounce out to second.

The Cyclones had won three in a row over Pittsfield, and with a record of 11–8 had moved over the Astros into first place. After the game, the players sent the starting pitchers out for food from the snack bars, and the team quickly showered, and boarded the bus for the trip back to Brooklyn, with bags of hamburgers, hot dogs and French fries on board; the bus took off right from Waconah Park and headed for Brooklyn, where it would arrive at 4:40 the next morning.

As they departed the bus back in Brooklyn, the players hurried to get home: for most of them, back to the St. John's dormitory, for others to Xaverian High School in Bay Ridge, for Frank Corr to his aunt's house in Brooklyn, and for Harold Eckert to New Jersey. They would get home around 5:00 A.M. and have to be back to KeySpan in about ten hours. They were in first place, but there was no time or inclination to celebrate. Sleep was foremost on everyone's mind.

Between Innings

Denizens of the Coney Island Ballpark

ROBERT MARTIN

Robert Martin is a Brooklyn Cyclones season ticket holder in Section 14 — the area right behind the Cyclones' dugout, on the first base side. He's about 6' 3" and has a shock of gray hair. He has an easygoing manner and is at KeySpan for almost all of the games.

> **Robert Martin:** "When I was a child, I lived in Atlanta, and I got a chance to see Lou Brissie. He was a veteran of World War II and he had, I believe, 26 operations because a Nazi tank had almost amputated his leg. He didn't want them to cut the leg off. He was having this fantastic season for the Savannah Indians, something like 25 and 3, and he made it from the Savannah Indians on up to the Philadelphia A's. I followed him through the year of Bobby Shantz, and Alex Keltner, and Gus Zernial, and all those guys. Of course, they never did that well. But I got used to being involved with underdogs. They moved to Kansas City and then Oakland.

"Then I came to New York, and I always had hated the Yankees, and I wasn't a National League fan, and the Mets and Shea Stadium just didn't appeal to me. But somehow, having been living in Brooklyn these past 28 years, I kind of absorbed and followed the kind of quiet anger and resentment for having the ball team taken from them. If *I* absorbed it, you can imagine what it must be like for people who were actually born here and lived here when they left. I hear it all the time.

"I live in Park Slope Heights, right near Prospect Park. For example, for tomorrow night's game I've given my two tickets to my optometrist. He can remember at six years of age going to Ebbets Field. As he described a story to me, his eyes watered up, and he became very emotional. He's going to take his 15-year-old son to the game. So what that means to me is that he's already passed along this mythology to his son.

"So when you look around this stadium today, what you see is people who have been passed on this sense of loss, this sense of yearning. On the Internet, you see expressions like, 'I don't know why, but when I went to my first game, I couldn't get enough. It's like a drug.'

"I think that's the way it is. I think something was taken from Brooklyn that symbolized Brooklyn as a city. This team is returning. I'm not a Yankee fan. I'm not a Met fan. Frankly, I don't give a hoot about the Mets. But this is a Brooklyn team playing on Brooklyn turf, and I'm intensely loyal to Brooklyn. Because this is a Brooklyn team.

"Almost everyone where I live is talking about the Cyclones, and if you're wearing a hat or a T-shirt people will stop to you and talk about the Cyclones — whether you're in Brooklyn or Manhattan. I've also been kind of proselytizing about the Cyclones and trying to get them to see a game. A young woman I brought here recently said after the game, 'The people are even better than the game.' There's a sense of family, especially in this area right behind the dugout. It's like a small town of 7,000 people.

"I think Angel Pagan has a lot of potential, but I'm just wondering if he has the power that major league clubs want in an outfielder; he has all the other tools. Caligiuri, the first baseman, has hit really, really well and he's a terrific fielder. I think he's the best fielder in the infield. He's very bright, very talented, very take charge. I saw Devarez get six home runs early in the season and then go into a terrific slump and I understand that Howard Johnson has really helped Devarez by getting him not to wrap the bat so far behind his head when he's in his stance. The first time I saw Devarez try that new stance he initially looked very tentative, and then with two strikes he hit a home run over the left field fence. Ever since, he's been hitting to all fields and the other night he hit a ball over the center field fence. So you can see that the coaches are really doing a superb job with the players.

"I think the Mets are kind of startled by the success of Brooklyn. I hope that brings a full-season club to Brooklyn as soon as possible. And I also hope that when the Mets aren't broadcasting or televising, that they have a radio broadcast of the Cyclones' games. The one big problem this year is that there's no radio, in effect, because you can't receive the broadcasts except on the Internet. And I think there's a tremendous commercial potential for the Cyclones, but you don't want the Mets to feel threatened.

"What they ought to do is send the Cyclones to Shea and bring the Mets to Brooklyn, because this is the place to play. This is the mythological center of world entertainment. This is the amusement center of the world, and it's just coming back — and to have the Mets have a lock on that is great. I would like to see the team go up to at least full-season Single-A, or Double-A. They could add at least 500 more seats, and we could all crowd in here. They could do that without losing the intimacy, or losing the breeze from the ocean.

"When I was a case worker in New York, I fell in love with Coney Island, and I used to come to Coney Island on weekends, and I used to party right across the street from where the park is now. And I'm working on a scenario for a film that is set in Coney Island. It's such a unique place."

ED GRUBER

Ed Gruber is another Section 14 regular. He usually attends the Cyclones' games with his teenage son, Steve. Ed has long hair, in a ponytail. When he talks, he's animated and enthusiastic.

"I was a fan last year of the Queens Kings, and I made the players Buffalo chicken wings. These guys are on the road, and we know from last year that the only things these guys have to eat are what's at the ball park or at the same diner that's across the street. They're on a limited budget, so we figure to give 'em a little bit of home cooking. I figure it might do them some good. I know we have somebody making cakes for them, so I'm going to check to see if they like nice juicy food and make 'em up a batch of Buffalo wings.

"I did that last year for the Queens Kings, and when we saw some of their players this year, when we saw Charleston play [many of last year's Queens Kings moved to the Charleston team of the South Atlantic League], especially Derek Nunnerly, he was asking for them.

Gene Berardelli (over section 12/14 sign), Ed Gruber and Chuck Monsanto (in Cyclone jersey) — Brooklyn fans.

"Last year with the Kings, we would talk to the players after every game outside the stadium. This year, when we went down to Lakewood [New Jersey], to see Charleston play, after the game, before they got on the bus, we hung out and talked to them, and my son was able to get a picture of them holding the Queens Kings' jersey. We try to find them now — wherever they are — and say hello.

"What they did last year burned a warm spot in the heart, and now we root for them individually, no matter where they are. Last year, they were just a bunch of guys who made a great effort and showed a lot of heart.

"My son's favorite, Martin Malpica, was back on this year's Auburn team. John Taylor, we saw here. We didn't want to see them here, but we're glad they're still playing. We want to see them all move up to the major leagues. Well, Brandon Lyon [former Queens King pitcher] is pitching already in the Major Leagues. He pitched yesterday. His record is 1–2. He started off this season in Double-A; they bounced him up to Triple-A; and then they brought him up. We were expecting him to hit the majors, but not until the rosters expand in September.

"Usually we talk to the players before a game, especially if they were on a road trip. Boost them up. Let them know that we listen to the games.

"We hear the games, through the computer, as often as we can. The station isn't strong enough for me to pick up on a regular radio. But because of the webcast, we do pick it up.

"We know some players more than others — Harold Eckert, Ross Peeples, and Jay Caligiuri — he's like the ambassador of the team. Jay's tremendous. He says 'Hi' to everybody and gives everybody an autograph. There were so many nice players, and all these guys, deep down inside, they got good hearts. And from nice families, not all well-to-do, but they've been brought up right. And they have handled themselves quite respectfully.

"After the game against Auburn, we stayed outside to talk to some of the Auburn players that we remembered from the Kings. My son and I have taken the ferry to see the Cyclones play at Staten Island, and I've also taken my son just to see a game [not involving the Cyclones] over in Staten Island. I am a diehard Mets fan. My allegiance is to the Cyclones — and anybody who's playing the Yankees.

"I have a guy sitting here in front of me who has a baseball glove, but he can't catch a ball. Every foul ball he tries for, it bounces off his glove, so I call him 'Frankie Fingers.' His real name is Frank. A ball that I could catch, he sticks his glove up and it bounces off, so neither of us gets it. This has happened a good three times this season.

"Last year, my son Steve got a lot of foul balls. Last year, we had about 500 fans at a game. Here there are a lot more fans. We're meeting just good people at the games.

"Against the opposing team, we're ruthless. We'll try to get into the opposing pitcher's head. Nothing vulgar. Nothing that would be insulting in a family way or nothing like that. That language doesn't belong here in this park. Tonight, we have the Yankees in. And Shelly, we're going to get right in his face. I think it was the third Cyclones/Yankees game, the one at Staten Island's Richmond County Stadium, Shelly Duncan ran into Brett Kay at home plate and Brett shoved him back. When the teams came back here, we started on him. He complained to the Staten Island paper that he couldn't understand it, and it was bothering him, so, he sealed his fate. That's the only way to put it — nicely. We're really going to get on him. It's going to be a continuation of Monday. Now, Shelly Duncan is one of the key hitters on their team. And if we can get into his head, then we can take his bat out, then we're doing our job.

"To make the Buffalo wings, I do it fresh. I pick up a 40 pound box, then I've got to split them, then I give it a bath in sauce that I concoct. My sauce has a secret recipe, but the sauce eats the aluminum foil, without a doubt. The basis is Durkee red hot sauce. Then I have about a dozen other ingredients that I put in. Once I find out how to break down some things, I will be putting it on the market. I will be the next 'Famous Amos.'"

NICK CUNNINGHAM

Nick Cunningham isn't a season ticket holder, but he's almost always at the games. He usually sits in the bleachers, but he can be found all over the park. Nick likes to tease the Cyclones, and when he roots for the Staten Island Yankees, he'll make fun of the Cyclones to their faces and then ask the Cyclone players for free tickets. They give him the free tickets, impressed by Nick's nerve. Nick's a blond, animated fan. He is 26.

Nick Cunningham — Brooklyn fan — and Sandy the Seagull.

"I work at Coney Island. I do the games and the rides out there. I work at Kiddyland on Twelfth Street. I do the basketball games, bushel baskets, whatever game. Some of the players came over and were walking around with their friends. I saw John Toner and Lenny DiNardo, and a couple of other guys. After a home game, I'd often see a couple of the Cyclones walking around, having a good time. I've lived in Brooklyn all my life. I live in Bay Ridge. I'm a Yankee fan through and through.

"I heard about that they were building a stadium in Brooklyn, and as a baseball fan I appreciate that they were bringing baseball back to Brooklyn after 44 years. My grandfather was a Brooklyn Dodger fan, and then he became a Met fan.

"Some of the fun of going to the Cyclones' games was just the fans, the players, the new faces. You get to meet a lot of new faces out there at each game. I rooted for the Cyclones during the season. The only time I rooted for another team was when they played my team, the Staten Island Yankees. Later in the season, I went for the Cyclones all the way.

"My favorites on the Cyclones were Jay Caligiuri, John Toner, Brett Kay, to name a few.

"Just hanging out with some friends and watching a young fellow develop were some of my best memories. I had a better time than going to a Yankee or a Met game. It was fun watching and hoping some of these guys make the majors. I hope Mike Jacobs, Jay Caligiuri, and Brett Kay, and so on, make the majors.

"Sometimes the players would ask me who I'm going to root for when the Cyclones play the Staten Island Yankees, and sometimes the players goof on me for being a Yankee fan, and I goof on them, and I say, 'What happens when a Yankee scout sees you play and someday offers you more money than the Mets? You're going to come to the Yankees and play.' A lot of them, like Luz Portobanco, goof on me and say, 'We're going to take the Series.'"

GAIL BLOCK

Gail Block lives close to Coney Island. If this Cyclone season becomes a feature film, Gail could be played by a younger Ethel Merman. Gail has that kind of energy. She is with some of her students.

"I'm with the New York City Board of Education as a drug prevention counselor. I teach drug prevention, but you can't talk to them constantly about drug prevention. I teach them about positive things, like bringing them skating at the Abe Stark Rink over here. I brought my kids to the game here last night because I'm also involved in Mothers Against Drunk Driving. So I called up Gary Perone; he spoke to the big shots and we got a table last night, and I called up a lot of my students, and they came down here last night, and sat in the bleachers.

"They got some baseballs. I wish I had bought season tickets. I didn't know it was going to be so great. My father was a semi-pro umpire in the Queens League, and they would always say, "Throw the umpire out!" And I would say, 'Don't talk to my father that way.'

"There's such a family crowd here. Some people said that it wouldn't be safe here, but it really is. My husband works nights, and I live near Lincoln High School, and I walk home from here alone, walk along Surf Avenue, and then cut down by the precinct, and I feel absolutely safe.

"The guys on the Cyclones are the nicest. They should only stay this way when they get to the major leagues. When they start making the big bucks.... These guys are bubbies. They relate to the kids really well. They sign autographs. They pose for pictures.

"These are students from P.S. 121. This is a fifth grader, and this one's going into fourth. I have pre–K to eight in one school, and pre–K up to 5 in another. So I go around doing my stuff—positive experiences. So I wrote on the blackboard, 'We're having a Brooklyn Cyclones game. It's a nice outing, The food is good. You get to meet other people.' So a lot of my students are here. I run into them at the game. This is the best thing Giuliani did, besides cleaning up Forty-Second street.

"I should have been like Gary Perone, a public relations person. So I want them to feel welcome. So for ethnic night, at Jewish night, I said to the players, 'I'm going to make you matzo balls.' These guys said, 'What's matzo balls?' So I made them and gave it to them.

"So I felt so sad for Vladimir [Hernandez]. He quit the team and now he's back. He didn't have his brother here.

"So I made a little bit of the soup with the matzos. And I brought it in to security, and they took it to the locker room at two-thirty in the afternoon so that the players could eat it before the game. That's it, a little knish. Then, another day, I made sweet noodle pudding, after the ethnic night. Then I made potato latkes; it's like the hash browns at McDonald's. You can dip it either with applesauce or sour cream. It's just a tradition.

"Then security starts, 'What about us? What about us?' So I made them potato latkes.

"Last week, I made a cake for the team, graham cracker with chocolate pudding. It's called an 'ice box cake.' It's graham cracker layered with chocolate pudding, then graham cracker layered with chocolate pudding. And then you crunch up the top with graham crackers. Then you put it in the refrigerator. That's it. It's cheap. But it's cool, good.

"Then I baked them a cake, and I wrote the number sign on top with the number one, 'numero uno.' And I brought it on Monday; but it was missing! They didn't have it until yesterday. It was in the clubhouse refrigerator; nobody knew where it was. So they got it on Tuesday, the rainout day.

"So I saw Vladimir and I said to him, 'How was the cake?' And he said, 'Very good. It was delicious.'

"So, that's my life story."

On July 14 and 15, Tsuyoshi Shinjo, New York Mets outfielder, was sent to the Brooklyn Cyclones for a two-day injury rehabilitation for his injured leg.

Shinjo played his first Cyclones game at Staten Island and had a hit. When he grounded into a double play he almost re-injured his leg trying to leg it out to first as he was caught up in the competitive excitement.

He played the next night at Brooklyn, and finished his Cyclone career at 2 for 7, and led the team in photographers and media drawn, as the Japanese media followed him like a rock star.

Shinjo — New York Mets player "guests" for Cyclones.

Between Innings

Update on games played through July 16

After the first four weeks of the season, the New York — Penn League standings were the following:

McNamara Division	*W*	*L*	*Pct.*	*GB*	*Streak*
Brooklyn	19	8	.704	- -	W11
Staten Island	16	9	.640	2.0	W 1
Hudson Valley	16	10	.615	2.5	L 1
Pittsfield	14	12	.538	4.5	L 2
New Jersey	12	15	.444	7.0	L 1
Vermont	11	16	.407	8.0	L 2
Lowell	9	18	.333	10.0	W 1

Pinckney Division	*W*	*L*	*Pct.*	*GB*	*Streak*
Williamsport	17	9	.654	—	W 4
Batavia	15	10	.600	1.5	L 2
Oneonta	14	11	.560	2.5	L 1
Jamestown	12	14	.462	5.0	W 2
Utica	11	14	.440	5.5	W 1
Auburn	11	16	.407	6.5	W 2
Mahoning Valley	6	21	.222	11.5	L 7

The Cyclones' 11 game winning streak had taken them to the top of the McNamara Division standings. In team batting average, Brooklyn at .257 was second in the league to Williamsport's .260. Brooklyn led the league with 23 home runs.

Individually, Jay Caligiuri was second in the league with a .354 batting average. Brett Kay, joining the team after the first week of the season, did not have enough plate appearances to qualify as a league leader, but his batting average was .408 after 49 official at bats. Angel Pagan was hitting .300, and in limited at-bats, Francisco Sosa was at .450.

Noel Devarez was leading the league with six home runs, while hitting only .157. Surprisingly, shortstop Robert McIntyre, not regarded as a power hitter, was second on the Cyclones with four home runs. Kay and Corr each had three homers.

Brooklyn's pitching was leading the league with a miniscule earned run average of 0.82. Individually, Matt Gahan had the lowest ERA in the league at 0.40, Ross Peeples had the second lowest at 0.75, Luz Portobanco was fifth with a 1.31 and Matt Peterson was tenth at 1.62. David Byard and Mike Cox hadn't pitched enough innings to be included with the league leaders, but Cox's ERA was 1.32 and Byard hadn't given an earned run in 14 innings.

As for won-lost records, the Cyclones' best were: Peeples 3–0, Cox 3–1, Eckert 2–0, Byard 2–0, Gahan 2–0, Peterson 2–2, and Portobanco 2–2.

Leading the division, on an 11 game winning streak, leading the league in pitching ERA and second in batting average was a nice start to the season. Brooklyn was also leading the league in attendance with 98,256 fans — at an average of 7,558 fans a game, higher than their seating capacity of 7,500. In second place was Mahoning Valley with an average attendance of 5,475 per-game. At the other end of the scale, the bottom four in league attendance were Pittsfield at 1,512 a game; Oneonta at 1,390; Utica at 1,275; and Batavia at 1,190.

Survivors

Food. Sleep. Money. Time. Girls. Family. The Brooklyn Cyclones' players weren't worried about multi–million dollar contracts or free agency. They didn't worry about the stock market or about finding a mansion to live in during the season. They didn't worry about their chauffeur crashing their Rolls Royce because they didn't have a chauffeur or a Rolls — most of them didn't even have a car.

Popular during their inaugural season was the television show *Survivor*, in which contestants attempt to become the lone survivor of a treacherous place. Yet these Cyclone players were on a survivor quest on their own, and this one wasn't designed for television. These players were vying to move up to the major leagues, and in order to do so they had to survive off-field conditions that could impact their on-field performance.

Food. The Cyclones are players who are generally from 19 to 22 years of age — in other words, they are the age of college students. In fact, many of the Cyclones were still in college only weeks before they were drafted and signed with the Cyclones. A few of the Cyclones' high draft picks signed for large bonuses worth several hundred thousand dollars, but the majority of the Cyclones received very little money to sign. After the first few rounds of the draft, bonuses tail off rapidly. More on money later. Just be assured that most of the Cyclones didn't have any. What does money have to do with food? Lots. Because good food and the Cyclones seldom met because these young men couldn't afford good food.

Cyclones ate ballpark food. They cooked at home. They ate at a Coney Island deli that sold food by weight ($3.99 a pound) and sometimes gave the players a break. They ate at rest stops on highways. They figured the bills down to each man's share, right to the penny. Getting food on the *Survivor* show was infinitely easier than it was for these guys. While some worry about interest rates, these guys worry about their next meal.

Money. Food and money go together. The Cyclones' battle to eat was handicapped by the lack of money, which handicapped them in other ways as well. The Cyclone players made $850 dollars a month before taxes. That left them with about $600 a month take home. Not so fast. They had to pay $200 a month for the rooms at either St. John's University or at Xaverian High School. This left them with about $400 a month, which translates to about $200 take home per semi-monthly paycheck. They did get $20 a day meal money on the road, but many of their away games were "commuter games," trips of under three hours, so the Cyclones went to these games and back in the same day — no meal money. They were much poorer than most of their fans.

Time. Wouldn't it be easy to have a job where all you have to do is play a ball game on most days? First of all, the Cyclones didn't just play on most days. It was practically all days. They had only three scheduled off days in their entire season. Their home and away games generally started at 7:05. At home, the Cyclones were assigned a reporting time at usually 3:00 P.M. Most of the players were there much earlier, usually by 1 or 1:30. The games generally ended at 9:30 or 10:00. The players generally wouldn't leave until after 10:30. Sometimes they left immediately after a night game for a bus ride to another city. Sometimes they arrived at the stadium at 4:00 in the morning after a road trip and had to be back there that afternoon to prepare for a night game.

Sleep. The lack of time related to their lack of sleep. The Cyclones slept where and when they could. They tried to sleep on the bus rides, but most players found it hard to sleep much on the bus because there were usually two players per double seat, which made sleep difficult, and it was hard to sleep on the bus seats, and with the noise and bumps of the ride. If a player had to use the bus restroom, he had to walk on the seat handles to avoid stepping on the sleeping players on the floor. Sometimes players' hands were stepped on — which was not conducive to sleep — except when the agile coach Howard Johnson vaulted his way to the back of the bus: left foot on one hand rest, right foot across the aisle on another; he was "like a monkey at it," said Warner Fusselle. After a late game, or after arriving home at 4:00 A.M. from a road trip, some of the players would sleep that night in the clubhouse rather than travel home at that hour. Sometimes Brett Kay would stay in the house several players shared in August on Staten Island rather than travel to his apartment in Manhattan. The Cyclones often sleep late because they stay up after late games — they peak for the games emotionally and then have to wind down, so they seldom get to sleep before 1:00 A.M. and often sleep until noon. Sometimes they arrive early at their ball park and sleep on the clubhouse floor. Sometimes players staying at St. John's in Queens would stay with other Cyclones in Brooklyn to avoid the trip back and forth to Queens. That way there was more time for sleep.

Girls. The Cyclones were popular in Brooklyn, but they were on the road half the time and many declined meeting new female friends because the player was attached to a girlfriend back home to whom he talked, or saw if she visited the New York area. The players only had three off days during the entire regular season, so practically every evening they had to be at the ball park. When in a nightclub, some of the unattached guys often avoided mentioning that they were professional ball players because they didn't want to meet a girl only because she heard they were professional baseball players, but some of the unattached players would "drop the bomb," or say that they were Brooklyn Cyclones. For the single, unattached guys, they met their share of young women, but all the travel made it difficult.

Family. Most of the Cyclone players were single. Only one lived at home: Harold Eckert. Most had families far away, many in Florida or California, or in the Dominican Republic, Puerto Rico, Cuba or Australia. The families almost all followed the Cyclone radio broadcasts on the Internet, and often a family would visit Brooklyn or New York during the season. Players kept in touch mainly by phone calls, on cell phones. Sometimes, on the road, a player's grandparents would drive a few hours if the Cyclones were playing near the grandparents' home in Ohio, or in Massachusetts.

Food. Money. Sleep. Time. Girls. Family. Survival needs. They were all related. There was little time to eat, and little money for food when there was time because the players spent a lot of their money on cell phone calls to family, girlfriends, and friends. The players spent time trying to survive. The television show *Survivor* featured contestants who often had better food than what the Cyclone players managed to scrounge. The *Survivor* contestants had their needs provided for and almost all had jobs back home that paid more than $850 a month like the Cyclones. The *Survivor* candidates had time to sleep, time to rest, and more time to meet girls — don't forget the huge production television crews out of camera shot and the relatively stable setting of the show. Both the *Survivor* television candidates and the Cyclones missed their families.

For the fans of the new Brooklyn team, watching their new Cyclones try to survive was infinitely more compelling than watching a contrived contest for television. The Cyclone players had to deal with food, money, sleep, time, girls, family — basically the lack or scarcity of all of them — and then go out in front of 8,000 people at Coney Island and attempt to survive short season Single A ball and get a promotion to full season Single A ball at Capital City (Columbia, South Carolina).

And reaching Capital City was only the next step in a Darwinian process. It would probably continue for years — if the players were lucky. The Mets' farm system was relatively stable, with six teams in the United States and two more teams, in Venezuela, and in the Dominican Republic, feeding those teams. There were players both above and below the players on the Brooklyn Cyclones and more players (about forty for the stateside teams alone) would be signed every year, meaning an equal number of players would have to be sold or released.

These Brooklyn Cyclone players were already survivors of a winnowing out process that began for them, and for millions of others, in tee-ball and Little League. This survival of the fittest process had whittled their age group down more and more each year. The major leagues carry 750 active players on their game rosters. About one in ten minor leaguers ever makes it to a big league roster. Want to watch a real survivor contest? See a minor league baseball game. The players try so hard that a real baseball fan even hopes the opponents do well — just not against his team.

The Ferry Series

The Brooklyn Cyclone and Staten Island Yankee franchises are natural rivals. Not only are they each the farm club of one of New York's major league teams, but there is in many memories the rivalry of Brooklyn with the Yankees — major league variety. The Verrazano-Narrows Bridge connects the two boroughs, but there is another way to travel, and that is by ferry, albeit special ferries arranged to take fans from Brooklyn to Staten Island and vice versa.

For the first game of this "Ferry Series," July 14, the ferry boat left Steeplechase Pier, off the Coney Island boardwalk, behind right field. Not much publicity had been generated about the available ferry ride, but some fans made the trip, along with Sandy the Seagull. Also on board was Brett Herbison's mother.

Brett Herbison is a 24–year old New York Met farmhand who had pitched as high as Double-A and had been a high draft choice. He had seriously injured his arm and was trying to come back after surgery, so he was with the Cyclones on an injury rehabilitation program. He was scheduled to pitch that night on a very limited basis against the Staten Island Yankees. Mrs. Herbison had come in from Illinois to visit her son and see a few of his games.

The mood on the ferryboat was festive, and the passengers, mostly Cyclone fans, spent most of their time on the deck of the ferry, gazing at the New York skyline. Mrs. Herbison sat quietly. She always keeps a scorecard at the games and records each of Brett's pitches. Later, she calls her husband, back home in Illinois, and reports Brett's outing in detail.

Also playing for the Cyclones tonight would be Shinjo, on the first night of a two day rehabilitation stint from the New York Mets. At the ballpark, there was a media frenzy over Shinjo, with numerous Japanese newspaper, radio, and television outlets following his every move.

Shinjo went 1 for 4 and had an RBI, but he found himself running harder than he wanted in trying to beat out a double play grounder. He was so caught up in the excitement of the crowd that his competitive instincts took over, and he forgot to baby his leg injury — but he didn't re-injure himself.

Herbison started the game for the Cyclones and threw 43 pitches. His velocity was subpar, but he managed to get through three innings, allowing only one hit, striking out two, walking none and giving up no runs. The low velocity was a concern. This year would be one for Brett Herbison to try to recover his arm strength.

Vladimir Hernandez

Vladimir Hernandez escaped from Cuba to the United States by way of Mexico. Vladimir played as a back-up infielder for the Cyclones, joining the team in July. He was among the most popular players, friendly to everyone. He has excellent speed, fine hands, and as a hitter he was adjusting to using wooden bats, to which he was not accustomed.

Vladimir Hernandez: "My dad introduced me to baseball, and I started playing at about 14 years of age, and I didn't play any other sports. I went to Ho Chi Minh High School, in Havana, and we played about a three month season. Then, if you have a special talent for a sport, you can be selected for a special school for sport. I was then selected for a special sports high school for excellent athletes. The practice there was very hard — we practiced, practiced, practiced, every day.

"There were a lot of very good players there, and before that my practice had been mostly with players from the neighborhood. I think everything I have is from God, and if I practice hard, God will support me. Later, I went to national competitions. I represented my neighborhood, my school and my state. After five years, I continued to practice baseball, and I had the chance to play minor league in Cuba. In Havana, when the competition is finished, the coach of the Industriales team in Havana, picked me for his team. I was on the bench at first, everyone knows the [tough] competition in Cuba, but then I had the chance to play third base. Finally, I was on the major league team for Industriales I was 20 years old.

"When we got to the championship playoffs, I got into the lineup every time. When we finished the championship, I had a .300 average. We continued to practice, then the commissioner in Cuba said that my team would go to Mexico.

"I was there in the championship tournament in Mexico, and I thought I would like to stay there and not to go back to Cuba. I have a lot of friends in Mexico because many of them came to Cuba before to play in games.

"While I was at the hotel in Mexico, my friend called me on the phone and said [Vladimir whispers, imitating the tone of voice of his friend], 'Hey, Vladi, we are here. You have the opportunity to stay here with us and never go back to Cuba.'

"When they were in Cuba, before this, they called me in Cuba and then later they wrote me letters. And then when I was in the competition in Mexico, and then when I was in Mexico for about ten days they called me again on the phone and said [again imitating his friend's voice], 'Hey, Vladi, come with us today, man.'

"That night, they called me again at the hotel and they said [whispers], 'Vladi, we are downstairs in the hotel.'

"I really think this was an opportunity for me to become a professional baseball player because that is what I trained for in Cuba. When I went downstairs in the hotel, I went through the gate to the swimming pool, because someone may have been watching me, and then I left the hotel and started running. I had to run two blocks to where my friends had parked the car. And they said, 'Quick, jump in,' and they drove me to Veracruz where I lived with a family for about a year, in the mountains, and I didn't tell anyone where I was from, and I had to stay there and not play too much baseball, not be too good at baseball [or his presence would be too obvious] so I did a lot of running to stay in shape.

"I have family in Cuba. I have a mom and dad there, and a sister and a brother, but I couldn't call them from Mexico because I didn't want to get my friend in Mexico in trouble with immigration for having me stay with him. I knew my family, knew they were safe because I think my friend called my family for me, and he told me not to worry because he said my family was fine.

"My family had told me, 'You go ahead, you never know what can happen here.'

"Then my friends said, 'People know you are here. We will go to Yucatan. There are a lot of leagues in baseball there, and you can play there.' I came to play baseball in Yucatan, and the coach told the Mets that there is a good Cuban player here. I lived out of town in a little town from where I played in Yucatan.

"And then I was told, come to Merida, and the scout would see me. So I had a tryout with the scout and the scout said, 'You can play baseball.' And one month later, someone called me again. Finally, I signed with the Mets."

Bobby O.

Bobby Ojeda had been out of baseball for seven years. He returned to baseball with the Brooklyn Cyclones, as a first year pitching coach.

Bobby O.: "When I took the job [pitching coach with the Cyclones], I called Perry [Ron Perranoski, Ojeda's former pitching coach when Bobby played for the Los Angeles Dodgers]. And I just kind of talked to him about little stuff. He approached it as he did when I was pitching. He didn't give me too much information early. He didn't want me thinking. He used to say, 'Go get 'em.' But there's a lot going on in his head. It is really like a chain: Mike Rourke, Mel Stottlemeyre , Ron Perranoski [some of Ojeda's own pitching coaches].

"Johnny Podres, another pitching coach I had, was awesome. He taught me the change-up. He was 'The Pod.' The year before I signed in June, and I went to Elmira and I went 1–6 with a 5 ERA, but I worked hard and I got invited to Instructional ball in October. That's where 'The Pod' taught me the change-up, and the following year I was 15–7. So he taught me a lot more than the change-up.

"If young guys didn't have a lot of ability, they wouldn't be here. So after that, it's a matter of having them believe in themselves and then just be themselves. Sometimes a coach gets too involved in putting thoughts in his head. Johnny worked with me on the change-up, and obviously he got me to believe in myself.

"Years later, someone told me that 'The Pod' said that in the Instructional League that I was going to make it. And he said this *after* I was 1–6, *before* I went 15–7. And he had the reputation for looking at kids and saying, 'He's going to make it. He won't make it.' And he was almost always right. I'm sure that he spent time with me teaching me confidence. For the change-up he used to show me the grip and the leg, and then he used to say, 'Pull down like it's a window shade, you know that little circle thing? Well, pull down. The Pod was awesome. Even as a young kid, I would put it into a thought process that worked for me.

"In 1978, I signed with the Red Sox for five hundred bucks and was supposed to go to Elmira. I had to call 'em two weeks after I was supposed to be there because they didn't even know I wasn't there. When you sign for five hundred bucks, and you're invited to go to Elmira, they're not real concerned where you're at. They were supposed to send me a plane ticket; they said they'd get back to me, but someone forgot. When I called the Red Sox, they said, 'Oh, yeah.' and they sent me the ticket. With my little five hundred dollars, I bought a suit, a pair of shoes, and took my parents out to dinner, and that was the end of my bonus. When I got to Elmira, I had on my $150 suit and my $30 shoes, and everybody thought that dressed like that I was a coach.

"I love teaching the game. I found it a very fulfilling experience to share something with these boys. It's something that physically I can no longer do, but I think I have the satisfaction of what I was able to accomplish with my ability, for me to sit back and teach. I learned it's a wonderful game when you're out on that field in uniform watching these boys and knowing that it's all ahead of them.

"Some guys in the minors think about the major leagues all the time and others just say to themselves that they're going to work as hard as they can and see what happens. There are as many responses as there are players. I just tell the players that I signed for five hundred bucks, and I made it. Just go out and prove yourself every time you pitch, and at every at bat. And the rest will take care of itself."

BOBBY DISCUSSES PRESSURE

Bobby O.: "Sometimes guys can't make the jump to the major leagues. They'll have great Triple-A or Double-A careers, but for some reason, — the crowds, the pressure — they can't make the jump to the majors.

"Some guys get intimidated by guys that are as good as them. Those are guys, if they stay in the game, they usually talk about how tough they are. There's a saying: 'The further they are from the front, the more they hate the enemy.' They crashed and burned. The more successful ones say, 'You know, it ain't really different.'

"The guys who really talk tough are the ones who failed. You have to learn how to handle the pressure, both on and off the field.

"You have to learn how to handle guys who maybe intimidate you. I don't think scared is the word. Gorman Thomas used to intimidate me. He was a tough guy, but my job was to get him out. And to beat that intimidation that I would feel, not only from him, but from other ones, was hard.

"You either can do it or you can't. You have to learn how to step up and teach yourself how to do it, and learn from others how they do it.

"Keith Hernandez would be running [playing] at about 150 percent, but his saying that he was only trying at about 85 percent was his relaxation mode. He's running at 150 percent, but he's thinking he's running at 85 percent. It's all mind games, and some guys have a weaker mind. It's all the mind taking over and getting your to the next level. But Keith Hernandez was never at 85 percent in his life. No way was he ever at 85 percent at anything. I could call him on it right now. Your mind is controlling your adrenalin and making it work for you, instead of against you.

"We're not like actors, or singers. We're being physically challenged. I'm not trying to get someone out for anyone's entertainment. I'm trying to get someone out because I'm trying to get him out. I'm a competitor, not an entertainer. Billy Joel can be singing a song now, and a song 50 years from now, and the people will react entirely differently. When you're a competitor, when your playing days are done, you're done. You're a warrior, and when you're done, that's it. They're nothing alike. They're like poets. They're artists. They're gifted in a different way. It's a performance because we're in an arena — it's a performance, but it's really a competition. It's me, and you. When you're at the highest level in the world, you get in that situation, going in there to beat that guy, knowing that you're one of eight or nine hundred guys in the world. Some guys can do pretty well when they're losing 1–0, 2–0, and when the game is over people say, 'Hey, good game.' Why? 'Cause they can pitch pretty well when the monkey's off their back.

"Hey, that's nonsense. You lost! I'd rather lose 15–1, than 1–0. In 1986, if we had lost that sixth game [World Series], well, the heck with those 117 wins. That would mean nothing to us. That's how we were. That's what made us what we were. That's why people remember us. Why do you think we came from behind, down two strikes, two outs, from defeat? Very few people can do that."

Bobby Ojeda talks about Brooklyn baseball — past and present.

Bobby O.: "For me, my father taught me baseball, and my Uncle Arthur was a Dodger fan, and for me Brooklyn was a hallowed ground for baseball. I was a lucky man to step into that [being pitching coach for the Brooklyn Cyclones]. And it was a history lesson. And a human nature lesson. I really have a hard time putting it into words. When I was growing up in Southern California, I was a Dodger fan. I've had a '55 Dodger poster hanging in my office for years. I was incredibly ignorant about the romance of the Dodgers. The best way I learned about it was when an older guy told me at the beginning of the season, he said, 'When the Dodgers left Brooklyn, we were *hurt.*'

"I never had a chance while competing to know what we meant to the Met fans, but I know what they meant to us. And they were great fans. The New York fans are something. The old Brooklyn Dodgers were part of the fabric of the neighborhood — they were part of the neighborhood — they weren't just coming in and playing and leaving. From what I get, they belonged to Brooklyn, not in a bad way, but in a good way. They were their team, legit, for real. They were a part of their life. And it mattered to them, tremendously. They were playing and they wore Brooklyn on their shirts. There have been people there [at KeySpan Park] who hadn't been to a baseball game in 44 years. They came back. They came back 'cause it was baseball, and because they missed the game for 44 years.

"They may not remember all the names from this year, but they will remember that a part of their life that was taken away, literally, is now back."

Hojo

Howard Johnson was a member for the 1986 World Series winning Mets and loves his job as the Brooklyn Cyclone hitting coach.

Hojo: "I signed with the Detroit organization. My first two years I spent with Lakeland in the Florida State League. I was there for '79 and '80. Basically, I was out of high school. What was different back then was they had a January draft, and that was for players who were drafted in June who didn't sign, so they went back into the draft, kind of like a supplementary draft. They were real honest. They said we want you to sign now and come to spring training, and you'll have a chance to make the club in Lakeland instead of going to rookie league.

"I remember the first day of spring training, and I took live batting practice against a guy who threw 98 miles an hour, and I was using a wooden bat for the first time. I couldn't believe it, but I was able to make contact and put the barrel on the ball. You just don't know if you're going to be good enough because these are the guys who are the best in the country. Especially when you're out of high school, you have no clue as to what the next level is, from college and right on up. I went in there with a mindset to just prove what I could do.

"I was a Yankees' draft choice in the 23rd round the first time. Then I was drafted again in January by the Detroit Tigers. I went to junior college, St. Petersburg Junior College, and played fall ball and then was drafted."

Hojo Discusses Hitting

"There's a sequence there when a guy is hitting, and I'm looking for guys to hit in that sequence. And it happens so quickly that there are things that clue you in to whether they're hitting in sequence.

"Usually I can trace things back to their set up. I don't care how they hold the bat to start. All good hitters get into a certain hitting position. They have to have some form of that.

"After their stride, they have to be in a balanced position. This should be a 60/40 back/front ratio before the stride, and after the stride it should be 50/50. And at that point they can start to rotate, and it can be smooth. If they get top heavy, the whole swing breaks down. It gets real wobbly. I break it into balance from front to back, and up and down, also. From the waist up and the waist down, and from back to front, also. So I've got it down to four ways that you can be out of balance.

"Some guys, they can be balanced in their lower half, but their upper half can be out of balance. Sometimes he gets top heavy, which is what Frank Corr is doing in his top half; he's not getting his top half 60/40 back to front, so that when he strides he's committed. When his front foot comes down he's 60/40 on the front side. See the theory is that you generate your power from the torque that's generated from your hips and your legs. And the other theory of hitting is that you generate your power from the back to front. These theories can conflict. When you go front to back to swing, you are losing your balance, and that's what pitchers are trying to do — get a hitter off balance. So I don't want anything to encourage that.

"Frank's desire is to get the bat head out front. It's just the only way he's known. He's always had a little of that front to back thing, but we've been able to control it. I showed him tape last night during the game, and he saw it. I just had a new video camera, my own video camera. I brought it out into the dugout so he could see it. They learn when they hear from me, but it's better when they see it.

"During the game, one of the pitchers will tape the hitters. I had Bowen do it this game, and then when I get in the dugout from coaching first base, I'll show it . When Corr got off the field, I showed it to him real quick. He's getting his weight 60/40 front, and it's causing a lack of power, and he's not getting any power with his lower half at all. When you shift to the front, it becomes an upper half swing and instead of the hips leading, the hips are following. There's all kind of sensations you get as a hitter, you get a feeling of being locked up, 'I can't get the bat head out there.' Well, you're right. Unless your hips move, you can't get the barrel head out front and hit.

"When guys don't use their hips to swing, then they have to get the barrel head out further in order to get the proper extension that they need.

"If you use your hips, then you don't have to hit it out front. You can see a pitch just a little bit longer. So you don't have to commit to a pitch so early. You can wait longer. Like on a breaking pitch — you can wait just a split second longer to see the break. You can see the ball deeper in your zone. If you have to get out too early, you have to commit much sooner, and you can't stop your swing.

"It's all leverage. You actually break your wrists after contact. We want them to finish off their swings right around the ball.

"One thing I'm working on is with Toner, for example. He's so strong he just needs to relax. He can hit the ball out of the ball park. He tries to muscle it out of the park. Hitting is mental and physical. Angel [Pagan] has a tendency to want to run before he hits the ball. That's why he'll take swings and miss off balance. I'm trying to get him to swing and stride right towards the pitcher.

"Angel has to stay back so he hits it into the hole, and not just volley it over the shortstop. But he's getting better at it.

"For Caligiuri, he needs to keep himself in good shape because he's naturally built a little rounder than most, and if he doesn't keep himself in good shape, that could get in the way of his swing.

"Jiannetti has a tendency to get really out in front, but he keeps his hands back and he can do that as long as when his front foot comes down, his hands are back, then he starts his swing.

"Vladimir [Hernandez] has a real short stroke. I kind of let him go. He clears his hips fine; he wants to stay inside of it. As long as he stays back, he'll get his hits. I think he's a little too far from the plate, but I haven't mentioned it to him yet. I'm letting him adjust for awhile.

"When you work with these guys, I try to keep it very simple, a concept they can understand. Anybody can understand back to front, being top heavy. I know the sensations that they feel when they're struggling. Okay, you can't get the head out, I know exactly that feeling, because you're not getting enough of your legs in the swing, you're not getting enough torque. It's kind of like working backwards almost.

"It's almost like I'm explaining like a scientist how all of this works."

Reggie Armstrong

Reggie Armstrong does the play-by-play of Cyclones games with lead announcer Warner Fusselle. Reggie, always in trim shape, was relatively new to announcing, and he is an animated speaker — on and off air. He became Brooklyn's first black baseball announcer, and he's a Brooklyn resident.

Reggie Armstrong: "I was in the automobile business for nearly 20 years. I also worked on Wall Street, and the military, where I was honorably discharged from the Navy. Sports have always been an interest of mine since I was eight years old. Nineteen ninety-eight was when I began the [announcing] quest. I was fortunate to do a couple of New York Knicks games on tape to the satisfaction of Madison Square Garden, I had a few other play-by-play opportunities in store, and then the Brooklyn Cyclones became the first major league professional gig, so to speak. I wanted the Brooklyn job because of the lush history of Brooklyn and the community. We go all the way back to the Dodgers. When I hear the names Robinson, Furillo, Newcombe, and Hodges, among others, they are fables to me. I wanted to be a part of being on the air knowing we would be the professional announcers doing Brooklyn after Vin Scully — and Jerry Doggett and Red Barber before him.

"I was born in Dallas, but now Brooklyn is my main residence. I live directly across from the Brooklyn Museum, which rings up another dynamic. Ebbets Field was a stone's throw away from here [his home]. So when you recall the history of this borough, it's incredible that I'm this close to where Ebbets Field was.

"I also think about my Uncle Earvin, who was a huge, huge Dodger fan. He lived back here in Brooklyn when the Dodgers were here, and then he moved to Los Angeles around the time when the Dodgers bedazzled out of New York. He's gone now. When we went to games in Los Angeles, when I was in the Navy stationed on the West Coast, we would attend ten or eleven games a year, and he would always wear Brooklyn Dodgers paraphernalia. It would be [a shirt with] 42 for Jackie, 13 for Branca, 6 for Furillo. He would wear that with his beat, and his friends would say, 'Hey, the Dodgers are in Los Angeles now.' And he would say, 'That's right, they're in Los Angeles; for us they're still the Brooklyn Dodgers.' If he were here today, it would really be something for him to know I'm doing professional baseball in Brooklyn.

"My uncle remembered the '51 playoff series. He remembered '55 when the Dodgers won what would be their only World Series, and he remembers that great catch by Sandy Amoros. He said, 'Thank God the guy had the wrong glove on at the time.' [Amoros, left-handed, made the catch with his gloved right hand fully extended, a catch Amoros wouldn't have made if he were right-handed.]

"Uncle Earvin, being a man of color, like many others, was a Dodgers fan, since most of the big leagues were white then, and the Dodgers were the first team to bring up players of color. He loved Newcombe, and Joe Black , and Campanella, and, of course, Jackie.

"Jackie was so special as a human being in that time and place. It was a trying time, particularly for a person of color. Jackie had a special talent, and there were others in the Negro Leagues who had equivalent talent, but Jackie had the temperament to withstand [the difficulties]. From what my uncle and others have told me, Jackie wasn't a milquetoast. He stood tall, and he had a stiff back, and he would challenge guys and say, 'Look, if you really want to duel with me, meet me after the game, around the dugout or behind the bullpen.' But Jackie also understood that the weight of future generations would rest on how he handled that particular moment in history. My uncle was there to behold that, and he imparted so much of that to me, which I will never forget.

"For me, this particular billing to be a play-by-play announcer for the Brooklyn Cyclones is more than just professional baseball. It's the history. As a broadcaster, I'm a historian when it comes to baseball broadcasters. Just five minutes from where I live were Red Barber, and Connie Desmond. Connie with the great baritone and wonderful sketches of the action. I have tapes today of these guys. I listen to them.

"When I broadcast, I try to humanize the elements — the players and manager. I want our audience to understand more about the player than they would know elsewhere.

"For example, I was talking on the air about Luz Portobanco's background. Born in Nicaragua and moved to Miami at age five and lived in a very rough and tumble community called Little Havana. His mother didn't want him out on the streets. He took up boxing and was in the Golden Gloves. His mother didn't want him to play baseball because it would put him into situations where he would have to be on the streets at night, and that really worried his mom. This year, Luz really loved Alfonzo. He thought he was like a father. Bobby Ojeda was also so important to Luz, teaching Luz and the whole Brooklyn staff the change-up, which was so important to the staff.

"Vladimir Hernandez was a wonderful story. He basically went into exile for a year and a half. He was spirited away from Cuba and ended up being in Dallas, Texas [and Mexico]. He kept practicing his trade and Omar Minaya, who is now the Montreal Expos GM, the former assistant general manager of the Mets, went to Dallas and saw him there and said, 'We want to sign him.' Vladimir is one of the most adorable men you would ever want to meet. Look at his smile. He should be in toothpaste commercials, and he has a heart that matches that gleam. He had to come here for freedom. And he has this moral character that he carries. I understand that because he appreciates being here. Whether he plays baseball or not, he can be an ambassador for goodwill, whatever he's done, wherever he goes. I hope I see him one more time.

"Then there's Brett Kay. Brett is a super fellow. He's the son of former Los Angeles Ram player Rick Kay, and Brett was staggered that I knew of his father because his father played in the 70s. He lost his father a number of years ago when his dad was in an accident. Brett is a great kid. Brett's brother works for the Anaheim Angels, and his brother listened to us on the Internet.

"I want to get to the major leagues as quickly as possible. That's the dream. Otherwise, I think this is the best minor league job in the country, and it's classy baseball.

"When I went to California a few times, I don't mind telling you there was just incredible fascination with Brooklyn baseball. Brooklynites are everywhere and they tuned in. I had letters from people, one from Europe, one from Florida, people listened because they're Brooklynites, wherever they live. A lot of hearts were saddened for many years, and the children and the children of those children are now benefiting from the Cyclones.

"I tell you when we went to Jamestown, that was an incredible moment because that was the first game we ever did. As Warner and I were preparing for the game, we're up there recognizing the historical import of it. Then we get the message that the great former Dodger pitcher was there, Carl Erskine. Certainly, I thought about my uncle. I almost got teary eyed over it because I was thinking about all the history and what this means, and there's Carl Erskine on the mound, getting ready to throw out the first pitch. Later, he signed my scorecard, the first Brooklyn Cyclones' scorecard, and we had our picture taken, which I have at home.

"The next day in Jamestown, Carl Erskine spoke at the Lakewood Lodge and Country Club, near Jamestown, and he talked about his son, Jimmy, who has a disability. Carl Erskine compared the struggles that his son had to endure with what Jackie [Robinson] had done, even though it's two different things, but he saw the struggle and he saw those two people make the struggle.

"Then Carl Erskine talked about when he was in the minor leagues at Fort Worth, Texas, and Jackie Robinson was down there and Jackie said to Carl, 'I expect to see you up with the big boys soon, because you have talent.' And Carl said, 'Yeah.' He was real bright eyed and almost goggling at Jackie. And then Carl was called up to the big leagues, and he had to meet the Dodgers in Pittsburgh and the first person to greet him was Jackie, and Jackie said to him, 'See, I told you so.' And then Jackie just left him, and Carl was beaming for five minutes.

"One more thing that Carl Erskine said at Jamestown was, 'These kids have no clue as to what they're going into when they get to Brooklyn. Tell them they're home when the crowd boos them when they make a stupid play.'

"Going home on the bus from Vermont to play our first game at Brooklyn, there was angst all over the bus. We saw the *USA Today* article in Vermont and ESPN did their little piece, and I told many of the players who came to me, 'Look, you guys don't have a clue as to what you're getting into. If Brooklyn were a city by itself, it would be the fourth largest city in the United States.' They looked at me and said, 'Really? How many people are there in Brooklyn? We thought Brooklyn was really just this small town.' I said, 'Oh no, it's no small town. You're talking about almost three million.'

"I was telling them about the history of the Dodgers, and what they would now represent, and that they were the first players to wear a Brooklyn uniform since Furillo, and Reese and Gilliam, and Drysdale and Koufax, and they soaked it all in, but they still didn't know. It was almost as if you were talking to a kid enjoying his first Christmas."

Tom Knight

Tom Knight is the official Brooklyn Dodger historian. He was appointed to this lifetime position by then Brooklyn Borough President Sam Leone in 1976. A life-long Brooklyn resident, Tom writes a baseball column, "Diamond Reflections," for both the new *The Brooklyn Eagle* and *The Record,* of Staten Island. Tom was involved in helping to create the Brooklyn Dodger Hall of Fame, which its president, Marty Adler, is moving into KeySpan Park. Tom knows people throughout baseball, and his Brooklyn Dodger memories precede the World War II years, when as a youngster he would walk to Ebbets Field. He now lives in Bay Ridge.

Tom Knight: "I was born in Brooklyn, and lived here all my life except for time in the army, and the first professional game that I saw was in 1936 at Ebbets Field. The Dodgers were playing the Giants, the Giants won 8–3, and the Giants Mel Ott hit a home run, and from that time on I was a baseball fan. We also had the Bushwicks, a semi-professional team at Dexter Park, and that was good baseball, kind of like the Cyclones. And we had the Jersey City Giants across the river, the Giants' farm team in the International League, and the Newark Bears, the Yankees' farm team, for Triple-A baseball. So there was all kinds of baseball around. The Dodgers, Giants and Yankees were all within a 45 minute subway ride to any of the ballparks.

"And my uncle was a minor league teammate of Clark Griffith, from the family that owned the Washington Senators, and my uncle would get World Series tickets from Clark Griffith, and so in 1936 my uncle got tickets for the World Series, which was in New York, and I also saw my first World Series game. I've been in love with baseball ever since. I used to go to fifty to seventy games a year.

"When I first started getting interested in baseball, there were about ninety minor leagues, so to make the Major Leagues in those days was really quite an accomplishment. In the old days, a player was often through at 33 or 34, 35 years of age, not because he couldn't play anymore, but because some kid from the minors would literally take his job away. Then the displaced player would often continue to play ball by going to the minor leagues, or by playing semi-pro ball. Today, if you can play ball and stay healthy, you can stay in the major leagues until you are forty.

"We used to go to Sunday doubleheaders and leave the house at noon for a one o'clock start, and we'd be home at six for dinner. The games generally ran under two hours in those days. There was no radio or television, so you didn't have long breaks between half-innings for commercials. In those days, the ball players would leave their gloves on the field between innings, and I used to get a kick out of kids who would imitate the major leaguers when the kids played ball at the Parade Grounds. The kids would leave their glove on the field between innings, and when they went back out on the field for the next inning, the glove was gone.

"The Brooklyn fans were a very colorful crowd; it was different from the Polo Grounds or at Yankee Stadium. At Yankee Stadium, it was more of a gentlemanly crowd. If you had a box seat at Yankee Stadium, you were in a suit and tie; you wore your Sunday best. At the Polo Grounds, they weren't as stuffy as Yankee Stadium, but they were still well dressed. I originally started going to games by sitting in the bleacher seats. Bleacher seats cost 45 cents. At the Polo Grounds and Yankee Stadium, the bleacher seats were just benches, no backs. At Ebbets Field, they had the best bleacher seats in the city; even the bleacher seats had backs and arms on them, so you were really comfortable. The boxes at Ebbets Field ran two bucks, so if you had a box seat, you were well off.

"When I started watching baseball, there was no radio or television of the games, so there wasn't a long time between half-innings to get commercials in. The umps would clap their hand and say, 'Let's go!'

"One of the fans, Hilda Chester, she started out in the center field bleachers with her cowbell. There was Shorty Laurice and his Dodger Sym-Phony band. The only survivor of that group is Little Jo-Jo. There was Eddie Battan, who used to wear a pith helmet like Frank Buck and blow whistles, and he was quite a character. There was another guy called Jack Pierce who had a restaurant in Brooklyn Heights called Lottie and Jack's, and he was a real character. He would sit behind the dugout and blow up balloons and shoot them up in the air. He was a great admirer of Cookie Lavagetto, although Cookie didn't appreciate it because this guy would be screaming, 'Cookie! Cookie! Cookie!' He would drive everybody crazy. He was a colorful fan. Everybody knew him and heard him. When they started broadcasting in 1939 when Red Barber came over from Cincinnati, you'd hear him screaming on the air. You wouldn't hear Hilda, but you would hear Jack Pierce all right, plus you'd hear the Dodger Sym-Phony.

"The umpires all liked Brooklyn, although some of them had some rough days out there. They all liked Brooklyn, and they all liked the Brooklyn fans. National League umpire Beans Reardon said, 'You've never seen a major league game until you've seen one in Brooklyn.' When Ralph Edwards did Beans on *This Is Your Life*, he had Hilda Chester representing the Brooklyn fans.

"I used to live in Park Slope; if it was a nice day, I'd just walk through Prospect Park, and I'd be at Ebbets Field in a half hour. It was great. Ebbets Field was a good place to get autographs when you were a kid because a lot of the players rode the subway to get there, especially the visiting players. Ebbets Field was a small ballpark, as everybody knows, so you had a close feeling. If you were sitting in the lower grandstand, you almost felt that you could touch the players; it was that close.

"There was no greater rivalry than the Giants and Dodgers. A lot of people think the big rivalry was the Dodgers and the Yankees, but the big rivalry was the Dodgers and the Giants. They played each other 22 times a year, and regardless of the standings , they'd still get a big crowd.

"When the Dodgers left Brooklyn, there were people who never went to another major league game, but not that many. When the Mets came in, a lot of Brooklyn people started to follow them.

"No one, in the general public, believed it would happen, that the Dodgers would leave Brooklyn. Stoneham announced in August that the Giants would leave after the season for San Francisco, but O'Malley didn't announce it until after the season that the Dodgers were moving. O'Malley wore a button, right up until the end, that said, 'Keep the Dodgers in Brooklyn.' Many people didn't believe, even up until the final game, that they would leave. Attendance fell off, because people had heard that they would move, but people weren't sure.

"The Dodger fans were more rabid than the average fan. They were more informed. But they weren't vicious. I never met a ball player that didn't love playing in Brooklyn. They loved the fans. Stan Musial loved Brooklyn; the Brooklyn fans would applaud Musial, even though he was an opponent.

"When I first started going to Dodger games it was 55 cents for a bleacher seat, a dollar and ten cents for general admission. I think the box seats were two and a quarter. Scorecards were a nickel. The prices stayed pretty much constant until after the war. A hot dog was about ten or fifteen cents. Soda was a dime in the ball park and nickel across the street in the refreshment stand. Carfare was a nickel. Before TV, the only way to see a major league game was to be there. So when you went to a game, you were like a celebrity in the neighborhood, and you would describe the game to others in the neighborhood. They'd say, 'How did this guy look?'

"I was at Erskine's no-hit game when he beat the Giants, and I was only present at two no-hit games, Carl Erskine's and Sal Maglie's, both in the same year.

"When the Dodgers won the World Championship in 1955, everyone was celebrating. There was no turning over of cars, but just a good feeling. Then there was a parade on Fulton Street. There were a lot of Giant fans in Brooklyn and there were a lot of Yankee fans in Brooklyn. Especially a lot of Italian fans in Brooklyn because the Yankees had so many Italian players. Giant and Dodger fans lived in the same apartment house, and they were constantly kidding each other, ragging each other. The majority of Brooklyn residents were Dodger fans, but there were enough Giant fans around to keep things interesting.

"I heard from Marty Haber that there would be a team in Brooklyn again. The people out there enjoy themselves, the first time I was in Coney Island at night in years. It's a beautiful ball park. I saw Ralph Branca and Joe Pignatano. I saw the opening game and three others — and three out of the four were good games. The Opening Day game was a great finish. Brooklyn had been out of the baseball spotlight for years. I told writer Bill Farrell that for the first time in 44 years people were asking, 'How did Brooklyn make out?'

Rudy Riska

Rudy Riska has had a long time affiliation with the Downtown Athletic Club, D.A.C., in Manhattan. He is also the executive director of the Heisman Memorial Award, which is presented by the D.A.C. Rudy has been involved for years in helping the Brooklyn Dodger Hall of Fame host receptions at the D.A.C. A former minor league pitcher in the New York Yankees' chain, Rudy has lived for 41 years in Bay Ridge, Brooklyn.

Rudy Riska: "I grew up in downtown Manhattan, in the Chinatown/ Little Italy area, so I hated the Dodgers. I went to the Polo Grounds or Yankee Stadium, but not Ebbets Field because it was foreign territory to us.

"We lived near the *Journal-American* newspaper and Rabbit Maranville — a former Braves player and a Hall of Fame shortstop, but as kids we didn't know much about him at the time — used to dispense tickets to these sandlot clinics at the Polo Grounds and Yankee Stadium where the players would give the kids a clinic at about 10 A.M., and then we'd stay for the ball game. Rabbit Maranville was in charge of sandlot ball with the *Journal-American*.

"We used to also get P.A.L. tickets too. That's where my friend met Joe DiMaggio. If you read my book [*A Boy and His Dream*], my friend put his hands on his back and he didn't wash his hands for a week (till his mother smacked him) and he would go throughout the neighborhood saying, 'These are the hands that touched DiMaggio.'

"Where I grew up downtown, we didn't have baseball fields, so we played softball, and we played with the Spaldeen, that was our game. I only had pitched a total of ten games in my life, but the Yankee scout Paul Krichell saw me pitch in the championship game with my high school, and they invited me up to Yankee Stadium for a tryout. I pitched there, and they signed me. I was only 16 when I graduated, and after I signed, the Yankees sent me to Kingsport, in the Appalachian League [Kingsport is now a Mets' farm club].

"Later, when I played for the Orioles, I was in the minors with Aberdeen, and Steve Dalkowsky pitched there, and he was a legend. Cal Ripken, Sr., was my catcher.

"Growing up as a Giant fan, the Giants came back from thirteen and a half games out [in 1951] and were in the final playoff game. When I got home from school, I caught that inning when the Dodgers knocked out Maglie, and Newcombe was throwing aspirins. I got so mad I knocked the radio off the table. I went up to my old school for an alumni softball game, and the school was near the Manhattan Bridge, and then cars started coming off the bridge beeping their horns and I thought they were celebrating the Dodger victory. And a man rolled down his window and he said, 'The Giants win!' I shouted to him, 'What happened?' And he said, 'Bobby Thomson hit a home run!' And I started screaming, and the teachers all thought something was wrong, and I raced home, but I couldn't get the wrapup on my radio because when I knocked it off the table; I broke it.

"Marty Adler started putting together the Brooklyn Dodger Hall of Fame, and he asked me if we could have the dinner reception down here at the Downtown Athletic Club, and that brought the Dodgers back. It was about 15 years ago. And over the years I got to know all these guys — especially, Reese, Snider, Erskine, Labine and they're — just great guys like you expect 'em to be.

"In 1994, I brought back all the living Brooklyn Dodgers except for Sandy Koufax and Don Zimmer (who had a game). The Dodgers have such love and respect for each other — they really do. They have a lot of respect for Jackie Robinson and the same for Roy Campanella.

"In my neighborhood where I live now, in Bay Ridge [Brooklyn], there is tremendous enthusiasm for the Cyclones, especially in people who remember the Dodgers. They are reliving things, and they are transferring some of their tremendous love for the Dodgers to the Cyclones. They have their kids wearing the Cyclone hats, and they're telling them the stories, and they're going to put the Brooklyn Dodger Hall of Fame at KeySpan Park. And some of the old Dodgers, including Duke Snider, are coming in for it.

"I saw the Cyclones play, and I was a minor leaguer, and it reminded me of the days of the minor leagues, but this was the fancy minor leagues. The kids all hustling, just like when I was in the minors, everybody was hustling to move up the ladder."

Between Innings

Luz Portobanco

"I can communicate with everyone on the team, and make everyone feel comfortable. If someone on the team, in my language, makes fun of an American guy, then he doesn't have respect for himself 'cause the other guy doesn't understand him. So I just talk to the Latin guy in his language and tell him not to do that. I talk to everyone in their language. Even the street guy, I talk to him in his language. I'm like a chameleon; I can talk in different languages.

"A lot of times the American guys hung out with the American guys, and the Latin guys hung with the Latin guys, because of the language; it was nothing personal. It was just that the Latin guys didn't speak good English; and the American guys didn't speak good Spanish — so when they all had to communicate, it became confused. But when it came to game time, in the clubhouse, everyone was together; everyone was family. That was the good thing about it."

Dodgers in the Minors

In discussing the minor leagues of the 1940s, Clem Labine matter-of-factly states that, like today, life in the minors was not a picnic.

Clem Labine: "During that time they were trying to build as much talent as they could for the minor leagues. I was taken to a Cardinal tryout. You were allowed to pitch one inning, and if you did well or showed any type of ability, then you were allowed to pitch another inning. And if you did well, then you could pitch another one. Well, I had all my teammates there with me, and they had never hit against me because, after all, we were on the same team, and I struck out nine men in nine attempts.

"This was huge. We had three hundred kids there. So the scout said, 'We're going to be in touch with you, don't worry.' I struck out nine in a row. But I never heard from them.

"My high school coach was a scout for the Dodgers, and there was another scout who was a scout for the Braves. So we were going for a tryout. I was scheduled to go to Boston 'cause the Dodgers were coming in. The Dodgers had first call. We got there with my coach, but we couldn't get into the ballpark; it was locked up. We were waiting in front and carrying athletic bags and all, and a man came up to us and said, he's having a tryout and he said to follow him and we went into the Dodger clubhouse and little did I know that was Charlie Dressen [the Dodgers' manager] who brought us in. I probably had a 30-minute tryout. This was at Braves Field, when they still had Braves Field. Well, they liked me so much that the next day they flew me into New York, and this is when I signed with Branch Rickey. I got a bonus of $500; my father got the $500, and I got a salary of $250 a month, which was pretty high — it was generally $150 or $200. This was in 1944, and I was getting ready to go in the service. But the salary was bad enough, especially when you're renting out a place. I was with Duke and Gil Hodges down at Newport News, Virginia.

"That was my first team, but I wasn't there very much, less than a month because I was inducted into the service. That was B-ball. Without elongating the story, I got out of the service and got married, and went back to playing ball at Newport News, and that was a rough time playing in the minors. There was nothing easy about it, no matter what anyone says. Having a wife and the birth of a child take place while I was down there, I went from a 180 pounds to about 150 pounds because of the pregnancy and everything else. So they said I should go play somewhere else, so I sent my wife home. So because of my loss of weight and everything else, they're going to send me down to play in the Interstate League, in the Carolinas; that was a Class-B league, too. The problem was, I had a car, a very old car and I didn't have insurance, and I had to pay for my wife coming out of the hospital, and now I had to pay to send her home with the new child because she had no place to go. I had exactly $16 in my pocket when I went down there. So I won six games in a row down there with a very low earned run average, so I got boosted up to Class-A. I did well in Class-A and, of course, went to Triple-A and when you get to Triple-A, of course, you generally will sign a major league contract. Then they have options on you, three options, and when you wear out your options, then you must be kept by the club or sold. What happened was on my third try is that I made it, and 1951 was my first real year on the Dodgers.

"I was very nervous on my first game in professional ball. In the minors there, we had no pitching coaches, no coaches at all. All we had was a manager and a trainer. For a week, all I did was practice my windup and practice my control and it was a week before he put me in a game. It gave me a chance at least to watch how the players played, because you're playing not necessarily the best players in the world in high school. But now when you get into professional ball, you certainly see that the caliber has risen a great deal. So I was not so successful, just mediocre when I started, but the improvement started because of the education I was getting on how to play the game and on pitching itself. There were no real what you would call 'pitching coaches' in the minor leagues or even the major leagues at that time, so the teaching was rather rustic as far as teaching you how to throw pitches; for that you had to rely on yourself, or ball players who are good enough, and they are truthfully, you could rely on those people; other pitchers would be happy to share what they had, even though you might take their place, or they might take yours.

"This would be pitchers on your club, or even someone else's club. One of my first major league outings was against the Braves in Milwaukee, and I beat them in a night game, and the next day was a day game at County Stadium, and before the game I was shagging flies. Before the game, someone in a white uniform starts running out, and I don't know who it is until he got closer, and it was Warren Spann. He said, 'I want you to do me a favor. I want you to show me how you throw your curve ball.' Now as a rookie, you have to consider it a pretty nice compliment that someone wants to teach him how you throw your curveball. And we did that most certainly. There was a lot of unselfishness from the players themselves because there's always someone at your back that wants to take your place in any business, whether it's sports, or something else.

"The toughest thing in the minor leagues was the mode of living. If you were on the right team sometimes it was easier than others. Sometimes we lived far away from the ballpark, and most of us did not have cars. So there was bus transportation or something, and ball games ended pretty late at night, and getting a bus could be pretty difficult. Sometimes we'd have to walk to get back. And there was the lack of money. We had to economize, most assuredly. And there were pitfalls; I remember when we had our baby, and we had a friend of ours in the restaurant business, and he got a place for us which was good, because remember, this was still under wartime conditions. He got a house for us, and we got the bottom. The manager's name was Fitzpatrick. And he wound up renting the upper floors. Well, Fitzpatrick called me into his office and said to me, 'You know, there's something that just doesn't happen in baseball. You can't have a manager and a player living in the same house.' So I said to him, 'I understand. Are you going to move?'

And he said, 'No, you're going to move.' And I said, 'Sir, I'm not going to move, and I'm going to call up Mister Rickey and tell him the conditions because I have a family too, and I'm paying more rent than you are upstairs.' Well, I didn't move, and the manager never broached the subject again. It was a two family, just an upstairs and downstairs, with just a staircase in between. This was a shipbuilding town, and it was very busy.

"And the fans can be very tough, too. They were shipbuilders, and they bet on the games, and after the games as you're walking down they're trying to give you dollar bills, and five dollar bills if they made some money. It's not as if we did anything wrong. They gave it to us after the game, not before."

He won 148 big league games in the major leagues, but for Brooklyn fans, Johnny Podres will always be remembered and loved for winning the biggest game in their history, the final game of the 1955 World Series. He's still in baseball, serving as a special pitching instructor for the Philadelphia Phillies.

Johnny Podres: "Well, my first minor league season, I ended up pitching in Class-D baseball, which is the lowest level there was. When I signed, the Dodgers had about twenty-five or twenty-six farm teams; they had two or three Triple A teams, all the way down the line, so I was down at the bottom. I was in a league called the Mountain States League. I started out pitching at Class B, I pitched there for a month, didn't win a game, so they sent me down to Class D. That was going to be my last stop. If I hadn't done well there, I'd have probably gotten released.

"I signed a Triple-A Montreal contract when I signed, when I signed right out of high school. I got 'X' amount of money for signing. If I'd gone over $6,000, I'd have been a bonus player at that time, which meant that I'd have to stay at the big league level for two years, like Johnny Antonelli. So I signed at the six thousand level. I won twenty some games down at Class D, for the Hazard, Kentucky Bombers. So the next year, I got invited to spring training with the Brooklyn Dodgers. It was something else for me to walk into that clubhouse with the Brooklyn Dodgers and watch the guys like Robinson, and Reese, and Hodges, and Campanella, and those guys. I'm 19 years old.

"All my life, I was a Brooklyn Dodgers fan. Where I lived, up in New York State, most people were New York Yankee fans, but I always just liked the Dodgers.

"In my first big league camp, I pitched great. Charlie Dressen was the manager at the time. And the Dodgers took me all the way to Brooklyn, and the day before the season opened, they optioned me to Montreal. Charlie Dressen called me in and he said, 'The reason we're optioning you is because if you get drafted into the service, and you stay in the service for a couple of years, then when you get out of the service we'd be obligated to keep you on the big league roster.'

"They couldn't option me out. So they sent me to Triple-A at Montreal, and I hurt my back, and I only pitched about 80 innings that year, and I got invited the next year to spring training with the Dodgers, and I made it. That was in 1953.

"Talent. You can see talent. That was quite a bit of competition with 26 teams. Nowadays, if you're drafted and sign for a big bonus, it seems like it's only a matter of time before you get to the big leagues. You know you're going to get there when the club has all that money invested in you. Some get a million to sign. You make an investment like that, where's the player going to wind up playing? I made it on talent. What else are you going to make it on? Charlie Dressen taught me the change-up. I sort of had a sponsor, because he taught me the change-up, so if I did well in spring training, he was going to take me. And at that time, the only left-hander the Dodgers had was Preacher Roe, so if they took me that would give them two lefties.

"Brooklyn [the Cyclones] had a good team down there all year long, plus they had good coaches down there like Bobby Ojeda, who had been big leaguers. They had big league players as coaches, and that's very important to have guys who were big league players. It can help bring out talent a little sooner.

"When we played, we had a manager and a trainer, and sometimes the manager even drove the bus. The first year I played in Class-D we had station wagons. We had some four or five hour trips; there were a lot of trips of 12 or 13 hours."

Joe Pignatano: "The game of baseball is the same. That doesn't change. The way they play the game doesn't change. But the people who play the game change. We had to bust our tails to maintain what we wanted and to do what we wanted and get to the big leagues. When I signed with the Dodgers, they had 28 farms clubs. We had three Triple-A clubs, we had two Double-A clubs, Mobile Alabama, and Fort Worth, Texas. The rest of the teams were A, B, C, and D. The first two years I played, I played two years of D-ball. When I first signed and went away, in late June or July, I played for two-and-a-half weeks and got released. I went to Sheboygan, Wisconsin, but first I went to Cambridge, Maryland, for a week of spring training because I missed regular spring training because I got out of school in June. So I spent a week in Cambridge, then maybe a little over a week in Sheboygan, then I was sent to Cairo, Illinois. I spent a little over a week there, and the first day I got there I played, and I got a standing ovation because I was the first catcher to catch a pop fly. I went two-for-three that day, played the next day and went one-for-three, played the next day and went one-for-three again, and then we got another catcher in and I didn't get to play any more. We were on the road and when we got back home, I got released.

"I got home and it ticked my mother off. God, it made my mother so mad that she called the Dodger front office. And she reamed their butts out. Oh man, she laced into them. They said, 'Mrs. Pignatano, please. What are you doing? Joe's doing fine.'

"She said, 'He's sitting right next to me.' He said, 'What? Put Joe on the phone.'

"I got on the phone, and I was talking to Fresco Thompson, who at that time was either head of the minor leagues or second in command of the Dodgers' organization. He said to me, 'Sit tight. I'm gonna call you back.'

"So he got on the phone, and I don't know who he talked to, but he called me back, and he said that George Sisler, the old St. Louis Browns' first baseman, who was the Dodgers' chief scout, wants to see me at Ebbets Field in the morning. Would I go? I said, 'sure' and I went back to Ebbets Field, and in the stands were five scouts and Branch Rickey, Jr. And I went through all that stuff again. And after it was all over, George Sisler went up to the stands and asked the scouts, 'Now, will you tell me why that man was released? There was no reason for him to be released.' I found out later that they fired the guy who fired me. He was the manager.

"So I re-signed with the Dodgers and the next year I went to spring training, and then went to Cambridge, Maryland. That was my first year. I did not have a good year. I got hurt; I hurt my knee, and I was out for six to eight weeks. They were the Cambridge Dodgers in Class-D. The next year I went to Valdosta, Georgia, and I had a good year, a real good year. And then I got inducted into the Army — the Korean War. So I spent two years in Double A, Uncle Sam's Army, the American Army. When I got out of the Army, spring training was already over, and they sent me to Haskell, North Carolina, which was B. I had a great year there. The next year I got put on the Triple-A roster. I was on the St. Paul roster in 1954. They didn't even give me a chance to make the Triple-A roster, and when I got put on the A-roster, I went in to see Fresco, and I told him, 'Why don't I even get a chance to make that ball club?'

"They said, 'We don't want to rush you.'

"And I also told them, 'There's a reason I didn't want to go to Pueblo,' Pueblo, where they were going to send me.

"They said, 'Why?' I said, 'My commanding officer in the army lives in Pueblo; he was the coach of the baseball team I was on in the army in Germany. And he was a guy who enjoyed having a drink. And if I go there, he was going to want me to go out with him, and I didn't want to do it.'

"They said, 'Right now, that's where you're going.'

"I said, 'No, I'm not going. I'm already mad that you didn't give me a chance to make the Triple-A ball club.'

"So I just packed up my clothes and went home. When I got home, my mother asked, 'What happened?'

"And I told her, and I said, 'I think I'm gonna give it up.'

"Then they called me and asked if I might reconsider. I said, 'I might.'

"So they said, 'Come back to spring training.'

"I said, 'I'm not coming back to spring training. I'll only go one place now. If you want to send me, send me. If you don't want to send me, forget about it. I said I'll go to Elmira, which was A-ball.'

"So when I got to Elmira, the manager, Tommy Holmes told me, 'I got all the catchers I need.'

"As things worked out, I became the first string catcher there. He had two other catchers. Later, he sent one of them out, and the other catcher and I became the best of friends, and we split the duties there. Neither one of us had a great year there, but near the end I came on strong and after that year, I was put on the big league roster. The next year I played at Fort Worth and did not have a good year. And the next year I went to St. Paul and had a great year, and the next year I stayed with the Dodgers."

Some Roster Changes

Early in the season, Michael Piercy was given his release, in order to make room for a younger player. Anthony Coyne wasn't playing and asked for his release, which was granted, and he left the team. Edgar Rodriguez had his wrist fractured by a pitch and was placed on the disabled list. Mike Jacobs, an Opening Day hero, was promoted to Capital City; so was Matt Peterson. Vladimir Hernandez, a shortstop who had escaped Cuba and hidden in Mexico for over a year, joined the Cyclones. He had attended Ho Chi Minh High School in Havana. He was popular with everyone for his engaging personality.

INNING 6

The Media

Dave Campanero is the Brooklyn Cyclones' director of media relations. He grew up in Brooklyn and comes from a long line of Brooklyn Dodger rooters.

Dave Campanero: "That's kind of how I grew up, listening to the stories of how Dad used to go to Dodger games all the time. He was a Duke Snider fan. We saw things all over his house. He's got pictures and ticket stubs from when he was a kid, but he's also got big blowups of a couple of times we went to baseball card shows and met Duke Snider. He was just wonderfully nice to me and to my Dad. My Dad leaves there with a big smile on his face and says, 'You know, he's a good guy; he's a regular guy.'

"I think that probably the most moving story I have is that we used to go to the Hall of Fame every summer, induction day weekend. We'd go so often that I practically grew up there. They have luncheons that are open to the public and things like that. Every once in a while, we would bump into a Hall of Famer. One time I met Ted Williams. A lot of times, it's big groups of people that are kind of clamoring for autographs. We have this kind of tap and dance, just bumping into people, but the most emotional thing was at one of these luncheons we happened to be seated at a table right next to Roy Campanella. My Dad was talking up a storm, 'This is what Campanella used to do, and he used to do this. He could throw people out from his knees, he could hit and he could,' on and on, just couldn't stop talking. Finally, my Mom said, 'Why don't you go over and just say hello to him, introduce yourself to him?'

"We sat down first, and the next thing you know a group of people start walking in, sitting at the table. Then Roy Campanella's wife — he was in the wheelchair — she was making her way, pushing him through the crowd, and we saw he's coming right up to us. He wound up making a turn and sitting right at the table next to us. So my Dad went over to talk to him and literally just couldn't speak. This was for our family, a first, to hear my Dad speechless. He literally could not talk, and finally, after about thirty seconds of kind of standing there, shaking his hands and just couldn't say a word, he just said, "Mr. Campanella, it's such an honor to meet you. You were really an idol of mine."

"I couldn't believe it. I said, 'Wow!' I was probably about 15 years old, maybe even younger. Maybe 13, 14, something like that. I'm 26 now.

"For Christmas this year, my wife and I were trying to think what we could get for my dad. He doesn't buy much. He's not into things. So what we decided to do was look up on e-bay as many Brooklyn Dodger fans that we could and put together kind of like a memory box for him. It's basically a wooden box, goes about maybe three to four inches deep, and it's got a glass facing to it. We wound up buying a 1956 Dodger schedule, an original, and three little pins. One was Duke Snider, one was Roy Campanella and one was Gil Hodges. Snider and Campanella, obviously because they were his favorites, and then Gil Hodges, which is the only other one we could find. We got some baseball cards, a small, little mini three- or four-inch pennant, a small wooden bat. They're all original Dodger memorabilia. Then we just got an older model, actually a Billy Herman model baseball glove and kind of put it inside, made a collage, a memorabilia type of box.

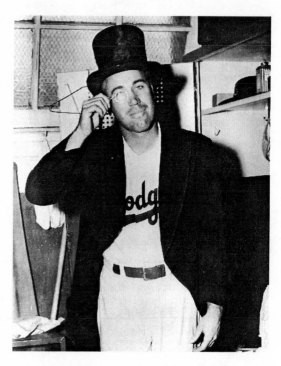

Duke Snider — as a Brooklyn Dodger.

"He opened it up and he couldn't believe it. He said, 'Where did you get this stuff? I remember this.'

"This is going back 30 or 40 years to his childhood, and he just remembers it so vividly. Each one of these little items, he can tell you a story for five or ten minutes on it. It just kind of struck me that this is what baseball does to people. I'm the same way about the Mets. A lot of people are saying, 'What about the Cyclones?' It's kind of the way you remember moments and years in your life. I know from my dad, it is. I know for me, it is, and I think for a lot of baseball fans, that's the way it is. We tell about him and the Dodgers, and how I have this connection to Brooklyn Dodgers. That's where it all started. I grew up listening to him tell stories. He was at Jackie Robinson's last game. He was at the World Series game before the perfect game. He's got all these stories. This is how I kind of grew up becoming a baseball fan.

"My dad actually grew up in Long Island. Then he wound up coming to college; he went to St. Francis, moved to Brooklyn. That's where he met my Mom. She lived in Bay Ridge, which is where I grew up. My dad didn't live in Brooklyn at the time when he was such a die-hard Brooklyn Dodger fan.

"His dad was a baseball fan in Brooklyn. Dad's father was from Brooklyn originally, and then moved to Long Island. So he had a lot of ties with his father, who actually died when my dad was younger. He was twelve or thirteen when his dad died. I have gone to countless Met games with my Dad, from the time I was really, really young. Some of my first memories are really at Shea Stadium and watching baseball and things like that.

"My senior year of high school, I think it really kind of hit me that I wasn't going to be a professional baseball player. I was a good player throughout college, but I knew all along when college was over, things were going to be over.

"When I heard about the Cyclones, I knew this was the thing for me, so I spoke to the general manager, Steve Cohen, and I spoke to Jeff Wilpon, and finally I got the job.

"To me it was mind-blowing, because from my experience I had never been to anything like it before. When I started here, I knew there was going to be a lot of attention. I knew it was going to be bigger than your standard minor league Single-A team. Looking back at this point, I had no idea at how big it was going to be. From the very first day I was here, before I was here actually, Steve Cohen had a stack of requests for media credentials. It turned out that we had around 400 media on Opening Day.

"That day we had tables set up around the stadium. We had really crammed people in that day. Again, we're a facility that seats 8,000. We have a press box that seats in the neighborhood of twenty-five to thirty, and for a Single-A team, that's more than enough. That's bigger and nicer than any other facility in the league. A lot of times other teams won't get 35 different media members to cover all 30 of their games total. We have one press box that sits 35.

"For us it's just a different, different situation, because we're in Brooklyn where you have, 2.5 to 3 million people. It's different. That's no denying that it's different than Jamestown, and that's not to say it's better or it's worse; it's just different. We have, just off the top of my head, I could name 5–10 different media outlets between TV stations, radio stations, newspapers, local magazines. Most small towns have one paper; they probably have one local radio station and one local TV station. If they can get one or two or three people from each one of those, that's great. They're getting full coverage in their area. For us to get full coverage on our area, we probably have 50 people here. Every person, if there was a representative, every media outlet between New York 1, Channel 2, Channel 4, Channel 5, all the locals.

"For example, this year we were covered pretty much on a daily basis by *The Daily News, The NY Post* and *The New York Times,* the three biggest newspapers. Obviously, they're huge here in New York, but what's nice is that they're national papers. So people across the country can read about us. We were covered by *The Village Voice, Newsday,* and *The Staten Island Advance.*

"*The Advance* wasn't here for every game but they were here for quite a few games actually when we weren't playing the Staten Yankees. They do a really good job. It's a different situation again in Staten Island, but the Staten Island Yankees are big in *The Staten Island Advance.* Therefore, the New York–Penn League is big and therefore, we were big. At Opening Day, all the people that I mentioned were here as well as Japanese media, the *San Francisco Chronicle,* the *Los Angeles Times.* There were some media outlets in Germany. Literally, across the world.

"We had TV for Japan, and I believe radio for Germany. It just took off. It had a lot to do with us, but it had much, much more to do with the Dodgers. It had much to do with the fact that Brooklyn was getting a baseball team back. It just made it a big story. The Brooklyn Dodgers are a legend throughout the world. Anyone that has ever watched baseball has heard stories about the Brooklyn Dodgers and has heard a story about how they were such a part of New York; they were such a part of Brooklyn. There was heartbreak when they left. When they left, part of the city died. Everybody has heard that. After seeing something come back, I think it made it a big, big story because New York and New Yorkers are popular all over the world. They are all over the world. I heard somebody saying —

you probably heard this throughout the media, and it's always a different number — that one in six people can say that they lived in Brooklyn or they had a family member that lived in Brooklyn.

"Whomever you talked to, it was different. It probably is true. I heard there's
also six degrees of separation between every single person on the planet. It's probably not that far fetched to say that. Let's say the top of the number, one in ten
people, can trace some type of relationship to Brooklyn. They're going to be interested in this. People in Brooklyn are usually loyal; they're very passionate. Anything that is Brooklyn or from Brooklyn, they take pride in it, and they want to
be a part of it. Baseball especially, the borough has always been kind of tied to
baseball.

"So when they heard that baseball is coming back to Brooklyn, that Brooklyn
is going to have its own team, there was just so much interest that the media people almost had to cover it in order to appease their fans. I know that initially that
there were a couple of days where we had a story in *The Daily News*, a couple of
days when we wouldn't. It depended on what was a big story that day in the sports
world.

"There were also some issues on our end, getting them the information and in
the time that they wanted or the fashion that they wanted. It wasn't tremendously
consistent for, let's say, the first week or the first five days of the season, something
like that. They actually got flooded with letters and e-mails of people saying,
'Please cover the Cyclones on a consistent basis. I'd like to open up the paper every
day to know what happened, even just a box score, even if it's just a final score.'

"They did. Our fans loved it. I don't know for sure if that's the same case with
The Post. People didn't treat this team really much differently than they treat their
favorite team, whether it's the Mets, or the Yankees, or whoever. They knew all
the players; they knew all the stats. Sometimes they know more than you think
anyone would know about the team. When you have that many people that are
that interested, the media almost have an obligation to cover it, to keep their fans
informed and to keep people happy with the information they are giving. So I
think that there are so many factors, but I think that those are some of the big
ones that went into the tremendous crush that we had on Opening Day.

"Now covering the team, you had the Brooklyn media. You had the *Brooklyn
Papers*, *The Brooklyn Eagle*, *The Brooklyn Skyline*, and *The Courier Life*. Yeah, the
Brooklyn Papers cover quite a bit. I think that the Brooklyn newspapers went into
more in-depth in 99 percent of the articles than the major papers did, which is
understandable. I mean, the *Brooklyn Papers* have a very specific target audience,
the people in Brooklyn.

"It was the everyday coverage. I was going through a lot of the clips. The stuff
that Mark Healy wrote, stuff that Jesse Spector wrote, the stuff that Gersh Kuntzman wrote. They got kind of those in-depth looks at these players and of the
team. They wanted to get a little bit of off-the-field flavor, whereas a lot of the
bigger papers — *The Times*, *The Post*, *The Daily News* — their major thing is the
game, but there were some color pieces by the major papers.

"The Brooklyn media are getting a little bit more than the facts. They're getting a little bit more of the personality of the team, and it's not going to as many
people, but it's going to the people — it's going to a lot of people who really cared
about it the most. I think that we developed a nice relationship with the Brooklyn media. I think that they were happy with the fact that they were treated as one
of our priorities. And we were thrilled with the amount of coverage the major newspapers gave us."

Carl Erskine: "The beat writers, Jack Lang and Leonard Koppett, traveled with us, and in those days we traveled on a train, so you kind of got to know the writers. We would have half a dozen writers, at least. Tommy Holmes was from *The Brooklyn Eagle*— he had one arm; *The New York Times* had Roscoe McGowan; and *The Daily News* had Dick Young; and Jack Lang with *The Long Island Press*; and Bill Roeder, and there were six or so beat writers. And in a big series, they would often add writers. Television was new, and we were getting coverage on that.

"On radio, there was Red Barber. We had Connie Desmond and Al Helfer. And Scully came in '50 or '51. But the media wasn't quite as intrusive as it is now. It's now commonplace for press conferences after every game, as in basketball and football, for the coaches to come and the players. We didn't do all that. The guys would come in the clubhouse after every game and interview guys, just comments, but it was kind of one-on-one rather than as it is today, more of a public press conference atmosphere. We didn't do that very often."

Dick Young covered the team for *The New York Daily News,* and his paper was read all over Brooklyn. Young was one of the early writers not to just write the game, but write more about an instance in the game or a particular personality in the game, giving his game story more the feel of a col-

Red Barber — Dodger radio announcer.

umn. Young went to the Dodger offices at 215 Montague Street on a near daily basis and had inside information. Roger Kahn, taking over from Harold Rosenthal, who had given up his Dodger beat with *The New York Herald Tribune*, covered the Dodgers for two years and became close to many of the players, who were often his age. He later turned this experience into the best selling book *The Boys of Summer*, which many fans regard as one of the better books, in any category, of all time.

Carl Erskine: "Red Barber didn't approach his job in the same way that a conventional broadcaster would. He was kind of a Romanticist, kind of poetic. He saw things and described things in a more literary way. And he had this Southern accent. And he had these kind of special comments. If somebody hit one he'd say, 'Oh, Doctor!' Where did that come from? Who knows? And 'The Catbird Seat' that was another one and 'rhubarb', he's been given credit at least for coining the term 'rhubarb' for an argument, like in the old rhubarb patch.

"Red did a lot of one on one with players before the game, so he took a lot of personal things up to the booth with him. There was one of the things he did that causes me to threaten to give an award to broadcasters today. Red had an egg timer with him, and he would give the score and turn over the egg timer so that he would remember to give the score at least once every three minutes. Sometimes I'll tune into a game now and say, 'Please, please give the score!,' and sometimes they won't give the score till the darned commercial, and sometimes in a long inning that's 15 minutes, so I'm thinking, 'Please give the score!' So I think about giving an egg timer award to those announcers today.

"Red made a lot of personal contact and would then have some tidbit about a player to take up to the booth with him, and as I said, he romanticized the game. One of the things Barber did was to use crowd noises for emphasis instead of trying to describe everything. Sometimes when somebody hit a big home run, you would hear nothing except the crowd for maybe two or three minutes, he wouldn't say a word, and you would be drawn right into that, you felt like you were there. So he had some unique techniques.

"Vin Scully [still a Dodger announcer in Los Angeles] was a perfect pup, out of Red Barber. He's not only redheaded, like Red Barber, but he learned so much about the direction of things outside the norm. And Scully himself has become a Hall of Fame caliber broadcaster because he has a poetic way about describing things that's different than just the conventional sports announcers."

Warner Fusselle: "I think I've hosted ten or twelve weekly television shows, some only went to foreign countries, but the Brooklyn thing I'll put up there with anything I've ever done in my life. I wouldn't swap this year for anything. None of these other places in the league had the history of the Brooklyn Dodgers, and all those tough losses year after year to the Yankees. None of these other places had a Red Barber, and none of them had a 'Catbird Seat.' I said to [Cyclones' Vice President] R.C. Reuteman, "I don't like to ask for a lot of things, but one of the reasons I'm here is because of Red Barber, and he always talked about 'The Catbird Seat' and I know it's a different thing, but I'd like to blend together the old and the new, and if I could have a sign up in the press box where I'll sit. If you could make a sign to hang there, with an old fashioned microphone and the words 'The Catbird Seat' I think that would be a nice thing; and he got that for me. And my intro on the radio was the song "I Saw It on the Radio"- and then I would come in, 'In The Catbird Seat, this is Warner Fusselle and welcome to beautiful KeySpan Park.' Underneath would be the bluegrass version of "Take Me Out to the Ball Game," which was also my album, and I came in each game like that. It was a key of blending the old and the new. I was trying to get the old Dodger history because that was one of the reasons I wanted to be there.

"My philosophy was to inform and to entertain. But I had to do a lot of teaching and inform people of how many games you play, and whom they are affiliated with, and bring in the old Brooklyn stuff and bring in the new Mets' stuff and let them know the names of the divisions, the standings, everything about how the league works.

"I am very emotional, and I did get emotionally involved, but I try not to let it sway anything I say. I'm not a 'we' guy. I've studied this philosophy very carefully. I say if you don't say it, you can't go wrong. Nobody can criticize you for not saying it. But, I think if you listen to me it would have to be more than one game. You can know which team that I worked for because there are certain sayings I would use for certain things that happened to the Brooklyn Cyclones, not the opposition, like the 'Sweetheart, goodbye' I would not say on the air that 'Our guys are the Brooklyn Cyclones.' Obviously, on the pre-game show I interviewed more Brooklyn guys than opposing players. So those are the only ways I think you could tell which team I like the most, which team I worked for and whom I was pulling for. I really try to play it straight, and I try to give the other team credit. When they do something great, I say it's great. When Brooklyn does something poorly, I try to state that. So I'm pretty much down the middle, but I think you could tell from voice inflection. That would be the main thing."

Warner Fusselle discusses the new phenomenon of baseball games on the Internet.

Warner Fusselle: "So these guys knew all this stuff. I didn't know all this stuff, maybe a tiny bit. So the guys picked up on the Internet really quickly, and the word spread that you can get the games wherever you are, on the Internet. Ross Peeples' family, they were some of the first ones because he was an early friend of mine, and because of the Georgia background and everything. I told about the people at the Peeples that were there each time he pitched. We drew quite a crowd there, people listening to the Ross Peeples' game. Yeah, Joe Jiannetti, his people listened in Tampa all the time. I received a phone call from John Toner's father in St. Joseph, Michigan. They were out there, the Caligiuri family, listening in California. Brett Kay's people came to the park later in the year, his friends and his brother who works for the Anaheim Angels. And when they played at Yankee Stadium, they had a day game, and he came out to our game at night and I think he was there the night the 19-game home-winning streak ended. Eric, he was very nice and his friends told me they listen every night; so do the Caligiuris. They say they go out on the patio at 4:30 every night, at 4:15 and listen. They say, 'We don't pick up the pre-game show, but we get all the games,' and they say, 'It's a major part of our life. It's just the greatest thing to be able to listen to these games. A lot of people didn't know who I was. They say, 'Who is this guy?' This is remarkable. The big pitcher from Edison, New Jersey, "Edison Eck" Eckert, his people listen. All these guys who come up to me the next day and tell me what all their parents said and everything, which is a real great thing when you're on a tiny radio station.

"You never know who's out there, and I would never solicit opinions or any-thing from these guys, but they would just voluntarily come up to me and tell me. Jason Scobie would come up to me every day. He would usually tell me that the Internet broke down, and his father got upset. His father would call the team. There were some problems early in the year because this was new — how you set it up. It had to be done from the ballpark, even if we're on the road, and they had to get a receiver and all this stuff. It finally worked out, but you had to get peo-ple and all this was done the last second. This was a great thing. These people, 3,000 miles away, could listen to their son playing professional baseball every night, and hear all these things."

Warner Fusselle was informed that Matt Gahan's father, in Australia, lis-tened to his son's games.

Warner Fusselle: "You see, that's a cool thing. I didn't know that. I didn't even mention it to him and I would do my Australian impression sometimes on the radio and act silly sometimes when he would come in. I had great interviews with him. Yeah, I never did get a report of that. I got it now, so I'm glad, but that's a pretty cool thing. So Red Barber never had that [the Internet].

"So that worked out better than I ever dreamed, and there was also a simulcast on TV in Brooklyn. I think many more people got the broadcast from the com-bination of the Internet and the TV than probably from the radio, because the radio went only to the bottom third of Brooklyn, but there's so many people that wanted to listen and couldn't, but they could with the Internet. I thought it was a great thing. I was very proud of how that worked out.

"My sister in South Carolina listens. She heard opening night and thought it was the greatest thing ever. And she listens to all the games, but I didn't even tell her about this Brooklyn thing because I didn't want her to feel obligated to listen to baseball, which she probably didn't care much about, every night. I found out she listened the whole year, and you start it with the greatest thing ever. So I thought that was a tremendous thing. I thought, 'I'm not going to let having a small radio station hurt me.'

"Those people were the nicest people [at the radio station] I've ever dealt with in radio. They were great. I said when Jason Scobie's father complains about the Internet going away in Austin, Texas. I'll say, 'Well, they're working on it, they're going to get it better, hang in there and hopefully it will work out.' And it seem-ingly did. You know, sometimes we'd have a great game or I would feel like I was really on top of everything, and I'd just sit back saying, 'I got to hear from these guys on this game.' Then you wouldn't hear anything, and I'd say, 'Oh, no. I may not have sounded as good as I thought I did.' I hear a couple of days later that they missed that game, or that game wasn't on, or something like that. You know it was on my mind at all times. I would say hello to these people in a funny way or talk about things [on the radio] like the people at the Peeples.

"Yeah, I did it as a joke, the people at the Peeples in Cordele, Georgia, and then I made up characters who were there. I never heard this show, but you know the show from Minneapolis that is on Public Radio? Garrison Keillor. I'm trying to do a little something [during the broadcasts] like he did, although I never heard him, but it's what I assumed he did.

"That you create characters, and I had them coming to the Peeples' house on the People at the Peeples night when Ross Peeples would pitch, and they would all gather around and listen to the game. Oh man, I thought I was going to run out.

I might have Aunt Lucy who drove down from Macon where she was in the waffle cooking school or something like that. One night, I had Uncle Billy, or whatever, who attended the hardware convention in Atlanta, and he was on his way. It was funny. When Coach Peeples [Ross Peeples' father] came up, he said Uncle Billy hadn't shown up yet. He must have gotten lost. I had Aunt Bertha who was driving up from Jacksonville, and then Ross started telling me about *real* people who were there, like Britt and Brett. So I was talking about Britt and Brett. I think one went to Auburn; one went somewhere else. One was a brother; one was a friend — Britt and Brett. I think Brett was the brother, I'm not sure, but I later met him. He came to a game. But Britt and Brett — then he tells me that his cousins in St. Louis are listening. I said, 'What are their names?' So I'm talking about them, and then all these new characters. Then I would throw in my own, and I had some good ones. I made up some really good names.

"Well, I'm just trying to think. I can't recall them right now other than the ones I just did. I think I had Aunt Bertha or one lady at the end of the year. I said that it's a big event in Cordele because she's been a recluse, and had not been out of her trailer in three years. She's coming over to the game tonight. She'll be at the Peeples' house, and she'll be listening. So apparently, they love all this stuff. I told Ross, I said, 'You know what, I hope you make it to the New York Mets and your parents will see you on TV or listen to you on the Internet from the big leagues. I guarantee they'll never have as much fun as they're having right now, and they'll never have characters, people at the Peeples, and they'll never have stuff like what I'm giving them right now.'

"I thought I created a monster because I'm running out of people, but then he started giving me real people, which was just as funny as the ones I made up. I had new characters every game. I had Aunt Alicia who was driving down from Cowpens, South Carolina. I was using towns I knew. My sister's name is Alicia, so I threw in Aunt Alicia. This is a message to my sister listening. I mentioned her name, and she knows that Cowpens is ten miles from Spartanburg, so I'm getting two of them there. I did come up with some really good stuff there. From Al*bany*, so and so is coming up from Al*bany*, Georgia, because he was born there, I think, and people there call it Al*bany* instead of *Al*bany, like in New York.

"I had some great characters, and one night I was sitting there with [announcer] Reggie Armstrong, and we were delayed. There was a rain delay or something like that and so [on the air] I talked about Coach Peeples and Ma Peeples, Connie is her name, but it's Ma Peeples the way I did it. I tried to make it really fit in right and I'd say, 'Ma Peeples is late.'

"I was coming up with what they're serving. I said, 'Ma Peeples was late because she had to go to the church picnic today. And her job was to provide the deviled eggs and the coleslaw, and so at the Peeples tonight, we got lots of deviled eggs, we got coleslaw, we got pork chops, and we got pink lemonade.'

"And I just did all this stuff. Fortunately, Peeples was a great pitcher, and he wasn't getting knocked out and all that. He fit in perfectly, and I was real proud of that. I thought that was pretty cool. Yeah, I had the hardware convention maybe in Smyrna, Georgia. I had somebody coming down from Snellville, Georgia, which is a real place. So is Cowpens, South Carolina.

"I played against some baseball players growing up in Georgia from Snellville, and I thought that was the funniest place. Some people probably thought I was making up towns, but these are real towns. I know I had Smyrna, Georgia. I had Snellville, Georgia. I had Atlanta. I had Al*bany* because I wanted to pronounce it that way. I thought that sounded funny. I mentioned Cowpens, South Carolina, and I talked about the real people. I'm talking about Britt and Brett and I said, 'Nobody is believing this, but Britt and Brett were real people.' Then I'm talking about all these things like that. Yeah, I thought it was pretty funny.

"I remember one day we were somewhere on the road, and we went by a street sign that said something like Oakland Place, and Joe Jiannetti, who often sat across from me, said, 'That's where I live, Oakland Place.' So I would use that on the air. 'I know they're listening on Oakland Place in Tampa tonight to see how Joe Jiannetti does.' Then there was the thing about when his grandmother caught me when she said he was hitting higher than I had him hitting, and she was all upset, and I went back and checked — and she was right.

"I got a card in November from Lakeview Way, Cordele, Georgia. The card said, 'This is from Deirdre and Connie Peeples. We really miss the people at the Peeples listening to the Cyclones' baseball games on the radio through the Internet. Thank you so much for broadcasting the games and giving special attention to Ross. You always had some positive comments about him. It really made us real proud. Junior really enjoyed having the interview with you on the radio. We're still waiting for our Uncle to get here from the hardware convention.'

"That's pretty funny. They're still waiting — he's just lost. He hooked up with Fast Food Freddie and who knows when they arrived in Cordele."

Between Innings

"The Mayor of Section 14"

ALIAS: THE SEEDMAN (A.K.A. MARK LAZARUS)

Mark Lazarus: "I got the nickname 'The Mayor of Section 14' from this woman, Barbara. She was doing an interview with somebody, and as I understand it, the person interviewing her was asking her about me. And Barbara said something about my running the section like I was the Mayor. And I think part of the reason behind the name is that I settle disputes in the section.

"There was an incident. Some people don't like what I do, all the yelling and cheering and loud remarks. But my attitude is that I paid my money, and I'm entitled to do whatever I want as long as I don't curse or become abusive. I do stand up a lot, but I try not to consistently block anyone's view. Someone shouted at me and said, 'Get him to shut-up.' I didn't tell him to go sit somewhere else. I wasn't looking for a fight. So I said to him, 'I paid my money so I can scream and enjoy myself. This is why I'm here.' A beer man was coming down the aisle, and I bought the guy a beer, to show there were no hard feelings. People saw this, and it became a noticed thing, and ultimately Gersh Kuntzman wrote about it in the *Brooklyn Papers* and that's how I became known as the Mayor. That and the seeds.

"The seed thing started on a Thursday night. The fans during the weeknight games were not as lunatic or fanatic as the fans during the weekend games. They had a winning streak going at home, and they were in first place, but the game and the crowd were both dull. Then somebody, I think it was Party Marty, grabbed five bags of peanuts from a concessionaire, and Marty started throwing the bags into the stands, and it made kind of a hit with the fans.

"The peanut throwing must have been on my mind, the reaction that the fans had, when a little later in the game I went up to the concession stand. I said to the guy in the stand, 'I want a box and I want you to fill it.'

Mark Lazarus — Cyclones fan.

"He said to me, 'What do you want?'

"And I said, 'Whatever you got. Cracker Jacks. Peanuts. Whatever you got, fill it up!'

"He looked at me like I was crazy. I took out two hundred dollar bills. He saw the money, then he filled it up and added it up and it came to $147. So I've got this big box of stuff, and I carried it down to my section, and just as I got down to the bottom, Party Marty was there, and I said to him, 'Marty, do me a favor and help me throw this to the fans.' We started throwing it, and the fans are screaming, 'Throw it here! Throw it here!'

"This must have lasted five minutes. And I remember as I was throwing the food into the stands, I looked down at the field and to a man, every one of the Cyclones in the dugout was turned towards the stands and was watching what was going on. They're telling me I'm on the Vision Screen and everyone in the ballpark was seeing Marty and myself throwing this stuff all over the place. Then the fans start screaming, and this continues, and the Cyclones have a big rally and they win the ball game. And at the end of the game, everybody is patting me on the back going, 'You got them going!'

"This was the first night that I recognized the power of what I can do as a fan. This was around the middle of the season. People started saying to me, 'Are you going to do this tomorrow night?' Well, I can't spend $147 every night on food; that would be crazy. But from that moment on, people began to look for me to get the fans going at games. It became like a job almost. It was expected of me.

"Before that, I had done a few things to get my section going. But from this point on, I would start to affect the whole ballpark. Not that they could hear me all over from Section 14, but when I got Section 14 cheering, 'Let's go, Cyclones!' the yelling would spread to Section 12, and 10, and then soon it would filter to the third base side of the field, and pretty soon the whole stadium is shouting, 'Let's go, Cyclones!' It became more of a thing where I became more conscious of myself as a focal point of getting the fans going.

"Soon, I'd be coming back from the bathroom or the concession stand, and people were coming up to me and saying, 'You're doing a great job over there.'

"People weren't offended by what I was doing. They were enjoying it. I was enjoying it. So I said to myself, 'Fine. I'll continue to do it.' I know my ball players are getting a bit of juice from it, and if it's affecting my team, I can only imagine how it might affect the other team's players who aren't accustomed to hearing such raucous cheers. You see it in the 19-game [home] winning streak. You see it in the way teams come in here and fall apart. We'd turn our caps around, wearing them backwards as good lucky rally caps — more times than not when we started screaming, 'Rally caps!' the team would score a run. So we really enjoyed helping to get the team motivated.

"Now, for the seeds. When I went home the night after I gave all the food to the fans, it suddenly dawned on me that I had given nothing to the players. I said to myself, 'I want to do something for the ball players, 'cause they're young guys — they don't have a lot of money.' And it came to me that ball players do two things that they do on TV. They're scratching and they're spitting. They are spitting because they are constantly chewing on sunflower seeds. Half the season had gone by, and I never saw any of them chewing on seeds.

"So I said to myself, 'For a kick, let's see what happens when I get them seeds.' So I went out and got them a whole bunch of seeds. And I got to the ballpark early, and I got hold of Edgar Alfonzo, and I asked him, 'Edgar, would it bother you if I gave the players sunflower seeds before the ball game?'

"He said, 'Of course not; that would be wonderful.'

"So I tossed the bags of sunflower seeds down to him, and he put them on the bench. Now, not the first night, but the second night, the guys started asking, 'Where are these coming from?'

"And the guys, to a man, are chewing on them. And they find out it's me that's been bringing them, and they all start saying, 'Thanks a lot. Thanks a lot.'

"Then one of the bullpen guys, David Byard, he says, 'What about the guys in the bullpen?'

"So I told him, 'If you want them, come down to the dugout and get them.' And the bullpen guys did. So now everybody has seeds. And now, every night when I get to the game, the fans around me are saying, 'Did you bring seeds for the boys? Did you bring seeds for the boys?' So it became a thing where every night I had to bring seeds. It cost between twelve and sixteen dollars a game. Four of the large bags and twenty-four of the small bags. Normally, I would give the four large bags to the team, and the others I would throw out to my section. The fact is, they were appreciated and because it was appreciated, I was glad to do it. It was a small enough thing.

"I didn't start out to do get anything in return for doing it, but ultimately, what happened, it was not anticipated or meant to happen, was that I had an increased relationship with the ball players, and the management, with Hojo, and all of them, because of the seeds. If I went to any of the coaches or players from that time on, any time, any game, and I said, 'If you've got one, give me a baseball' — and they knew it wasn't for me, but for a child in the stands or a special guest of mine — I could get a baseball any time I wanted, so that a child could take one home as a special remembrance. One time I asked Brett Kay if I could have a baseball signed by Johnny Podres, who was at the ballpark that night. Brett got a ball in the dugout and asked Podres to sign it. That was for me. Another time, I had a ball signed for my son. Many times, I got three or four balls in one night, and I gave them to kids. Any of the boys would get me a ball: Brett Kay, Jay Caligiuri, Jonn Toner. They would then take it down the dugout and get it signed by the team. When I gave that baseball to a four-year-old kid, he will keep that baseball forever. It's a memory that will stay with him forever. When all is said and done in life, what do we have? Memories. This is a memory that will stay with the kid forever.

"And in a very un-altruistic way, if that child becomes a fan for life because of that ball, and he buys just four tickets in his life, baseball would have made its money back twenty times over. It gives me joy to give a baseball to a child, and to see the smile on his face when I point to a player and say, 'He gave it to you.' To see a kid with his eyes bright. It's something that I never had as a kid. Even today, I would love to have a ball signed by Snider or Campanella. I don't have that.

"Now it's not signed by a major leaguer, but so what. To a five or ten year old kid, these are still his heroes. You see what's going on at the ball park where these kids adulate these players. It's a major thing to a child. In a sense, I'm providing a service to the fans and to the ballplayers. It's just a club — Brooklyn Cyclones' fans. I've been dubbed 'The Mayor.' I never asked to be called this. It's not a ludicrous nickname; it's not the 'Philly Phanatic' or 'The Chief.' A mayor is a title of respect. I'm very content with that.

"When baseball came back to Brooklyn, what it did was fill a big hole in your heart. When you're a child, and you have something that you love, you adore — this isn't like a toy that was taken away that you can get back in a year. Baseball was taken away from me and thousands of other people. It was an integral part of their life; it was a part of their routine, their existence. It's something that you couldn't get back. They say time heals all wounds, but it was still something that was missing that you should have had. When this thing came back, it's not like you wanted to recapture your youth, but, in a sense, you did.

"It wasn't that baseball was needed to make us fulfill our lives. This minor league team was a gift. Something unexpected. A perk. A bonus. It wasn't like the Mets, who belonged not just to a city, but more like to a state. This minor league team belonged to us. You were lucky if you could read about them in a newspaper. You're lucky if you have a radio with strong enough reception to hear them. And yet, here it is, right in our own backyard.

"It was, in a sense, poetic. As a child growing up in Brooklyn, you had a few things that belonged just to us. You had the Brooklyn Dodgers; you had Coney Island. At Coney Island, you had the beach, the amusements, and a place that was a common meeting ground for all kinds of people.

"When I go to see the Cyclones, I'm not saying that as soon as I walk into the ballpark that I'm transformed into an eight-year-old again. But you can lose yourself in it. You can say to yourself that what I wasn't able to give as a child, that was inside me to give, but never had an outlet for, now I'm able to give it."

JOE JIANNETTI

Joe Jiannetti talks about his Cyclone debut, at Lowell, and then his first game at Brooklyn.

Joe Jiannetti:"Coming from Kingsport where there was only a couple of people at the games and going to Lowell , where it was five or six thousand people there, it kind of felt like being called up to the big leagues. I told somebody that, and he said to me, 'This is nothing. Wait till you get back to Brooklyn.'

"I said, 'Are you serious?'

"I wasn't really nervous before the game [at Lowell]. I walked into the stadium before the game and wondered if they'd fill the place up, but once I saw familiar faces on the team, I relaxed. My first time up I walked. Then I made out. And then I hit the inside the park home run. Coming into home, I was running out of gas. I lost the ball so I didn't know if I had to slide or not, so I slid, in case I had to knock the catcher over. I didn't realize that it counted as a home run until later. I never had an inside the park home run before.

"My first game at Brooklyn was awesome. It was against Auburn. It was amazing. All the people yelling. When I got there and saw the stadium, my jaw dropped. When the lights were on, I saw the rings around the lights. That was so cool.

"I remember walking up to the plate and looking up at the Jumbotron, the TV up there [on the scoreboard]. I remember striking out because I was watching myself on TV. I was trying to watch the pitcher, but my eye kept going up there towards the Jumbotron to see myself, and how cool it was, but I couldn't concentrate on the ball. On my second at bat, I was all right because I was used to the Jumbotron by then. I hit a single between short and third."

More Denizens of the Coney Island Ballpark

JOHN DAVENPORT

John Davenport and his wife try to attend every Cyclone game. They sit in Section 10, in between the Cyclones' dugout and home plate. John is a big man who usually wears a Brooklyn Dodgers cap, or a Brooklyn Cyclones hat. He and his wife are always early arrivals — just when the park opens to fans.

John Davenport: "I was born and raised in Brooklyn, and I've lived in the Windsor Terrace section of Brooklyn for all but three years of my life, and I'm 68 years old, so I've been there for 65 years. I moved to Brooklyn at three years old, from the Bronx. I live two blocks from where I originally moved with my parents. I was very into Ebbets Field and the Dodgers, and we lived around the corner from Tex Rickart, who used to be the Dodgers' public address announcer. And I can remember fondly meeting a lot of Dodgers because back in those days they didn't have night games, so they used to come to Tex Rickart's house and play cards. They used to call up this grocery store on the corner, and the owner of the store used to call me up to deliver the food. There were many nights when I went over and I met Pee Wee Reese and Duke Snider, Gil Hodges, a lot of them. Almost all of them, not all on any given night, but over time. Usually, I'd deliver sandwiches and beer and soda, whatever they wanted. It was from Saverese's delicatessen. I was just a kid in the neighborhood, but Mr. Saverese used to call me up to deliver to the Dodgers, and the Dodgers always gave me a nice tip. I would never ask for a ball or a bat. I was just happy to meet them. I had a couple of things signed by them, but I gave them away because I didn't realize they'd be valuable some day. And unfortunately, I never knew baseball and cards [baseball cards] were going to be such a big thing as they are because I never had them sign anything. Tex Rickart was a promoter of fights, and he used to get us all in the Knothole Gang. That was many, many moons ago. It was a good time. We really had a ball, and it was great.

"In those days, we used to climb the fence on Bedford Avenue. It was a high fence, and the guards never chased you because you'd be in the bleachers, so if you could navigate the fence you could get in, and then once you were in the ball park, the other fans would hide you. They would say, 'Come here, son.' If you knew where to go on the brick wall, there was stucco, and then when you got to the screen, it was hand over hand to get up into the bleachers. You wouldn't do it before the game. You'd wait until the game started, and then the guards would be occupied. A lot of kids used to do it. Some kids used to stand out there beyond the fence because if you caught a ball that was a home run , they'd let you in for nothing. So some guys used to stand across the street in the parking lot, and they used to wait until a ball came across the street; they would grab it and the ball said 'National League' on it and then they'd let them in. So there were a lot of good times.

"I can remember Jackie Robinson used to live on Eastern Parkway, catty-corner to the [Brooklyn] Museum. He used to come right down Bedford Avenue, and if he stopped at a light, you could run up to him and ask him how was everything, and he was very amiable.

"At that time you had Freddie Fitzsimmons' Bowling Alley, which was across the street from Ebbets Field, and the ball players used to grab a few there after the game. And as kids, we used to run over there to get signatures. They'd go in there for a cool one after the game, and the kids would all run across the street and get autographs. Ebbets Field was very family oriented, like here. Everyone looked out for one another.

"To get to Ebbets Field, I used to walk across the Park [Prospect Park]. And then later on, I went to Boys' High, and the trolley used to end right at Ebbets Field, and if you got out early enough — we'd jump off the trolley, and they ended the gate sometimes around the fourth inning, and if there was no guard at the gate we'd just jump in. Sometimes we paid fifty cents for the Knothole Gang. We were just a bunch of kids, a lot of kids from the neighborhood. We knew each other. In those days we'd go to the Parade Grounds; some of the high school teams played there, and in those days, Saint Frances College played there. I can remember Sandy Koufax pitching at the Parade Grounds. He was on one of the local teams from Flatbush. And he pitched there in high school, too. There were a lot of scouts who used to sit in the stands and watch the kids play.

"I was in the service from '52 to '56, and just when I came home is when they were winding down. I was in the Air Force, and I was stationed in Denver, which was the Yankee farm team, and a whole bunch of us went to the games. Moose Skowron was the first baseman, and the reason we went was to wish them evil, to rag them because they were the Yankee farm team. A lot of guys from Brooklyn were stationed there, and we'd rag 'em every chance we got. They took it good-naturedly, but they knew that every chance we got we were going to rag them.

"This carried on when we went to Shea Stadium with my kids. I never forgave O'Malley for taking the team away. Never.

"So when later the Mets were in New York, we used to go to games against the Dodgers, and we'd root *against* the Dodgers, and I'd get people to say to Lasorda, 'You're fat! You're fat!' We'd all be chanting this at Lasorda because I thought he was part of the establishment. I used to really rag on them. So when the Dodgers weren't here, my family all became Met fans.

"Then when we heard about the new Cyclone team; we bought tickets back in January. My wife and I are avid ball fans, so I decided then that no matter what we would buy season tickets, and that's what we did. I already bought my playoff tickets, and at the end of September we'll buy our season tickets for next year. We come to every game. I haven't missed one game, and I don't intend to if I can help it. In fact, the youth division in my church, Holy Name, on the dividing line between Windsor Terrace and Park Slope, bought six sets of 250 tickets. And they come — I know they are coming Sunday night to John Franco Night.

"I have a ball in my pocket that I'm getting signed for a kid who couldn't make it tonight, and I said, 'Fine.' Because somewhere along the line that kid is going to wind up being a baseball fan. When I come down here, I get the players to sign books and balls because sometimes the kids get swallowed up by the crowd, so I take balls down to the edge of the field for the players to autograph for the kids. There are a lot of guys in the neighborhood here. This guy, Eddie Krist, he's a big guy in the electrical union, I just saw him today and he said to me, 'I can't wait until tonight.' He sits a couple of rows down. I have a neighbor about ten houses down who sits behind home plate, and I see him all the time. People talk about it in the neighborhood all the time. They can't wait. Their biggest complaint is that the news doesn't follow them enough. They put the score in, but they want more coverage from the national media. There are people who can't get to the games because they're so popular. The only thing you can get now is general admission. You see, eight thousand people come.

"Jay Caligiuri and Angel Pagan are two of the best with the kids. They sign autographs and pay attention to them. They take care of the kids, that's what I like because if they take care of the kids, then I feel they're doing justice to the team. I don't know if any of them will go up, but they're great with the kids. I think that the catcher that they took up, Mike Jacobs, I feel he's going to go a long way because he was really good, and he was a fan favorite.

"Some of the players I feel sorry for because they're away from home and they don't get much pay. So I try not to rag on them too much. Like sometimes I would rag on Beurelein [catcher Todd Beurelein], and I say to him, 'Why don't you roll the ball back to the pitcher?' And then sometimes when I have something to autograph, he'd look at me as if to say, 'Why should I sign for you?' But my feeling is, these kids have to get better. And if you're going to rag on them, then that will make them mad and make them want to do better. That's my feelings on it, so if you're no good and I rag on you, then you're going to get better. That's my whole outlook on that.

"I used to be in chain stores — Sears and Roebuck — and I'm on a fixed income, and I can't afford Shea Stadium. We used to buy two or three six packs of tickets a year, but with the food and the parking, it got too expensive. We're here. For four bucks I can park. Or I can take the train, as senior citizens it costs us a buck and a half and I can be here in twenty minutes. So I feel that this is conducive to my neighborhood and all of Brooklyn."

Bob Berardelli

"I grew up a few blocks from where the Dodgers used to hold their practices, both before and during the season. The practices were held at a field on McDonald Avenue, near the cemetery, near Bay Parkway and Avenue M. Their practice field was surrounded on all sides by a cemetery except for the avenue going through, which was McDonald Avenue. The field is still there now on the borderline of Kensingston and Bensonhurst. We used to watch the practices all the time. We used to ride there on our bikes. This was in the 1950s. They wore plain uniforms, not Dodger uniforms. There were no numbers on their backs.

"I remember one time I was standing next to Koufax near the fence. My older brother said to me, "Do you know who that was?"

"I said, 'No.'

"He said, 'That's Sandy Koufax.'

"I used to live on East Fourth Street in Kensington. Now I live in Sheepshead Bay. We used to have season tickets for the Mets, but it got too costly. Now I have season tickets to the Cyclones.

"One of the nicest things about the Cyclones is that they're not untouchable. I have a daughter who's 15 and impressionable, and they're very good to her. Her favorite Cyclone is Angel Pagan.

"These fans are unbelievable. Lots of people remember the Dodgers here. Without a doubt.

"The opening night ceremonies were great. We weren't disappointed with Single-A ball. There are a lot of well-to-do corporate people in my section, and they have season tickets to both the Mets and the Cyclones.

"Jay Caligiuri and Frank Corr are great guys. We had dinner with them at Lundy's the other night. They came around and introduced themselves and everything."

SAM COSOLA (AN USHER AT KEYSPAN PARK)
"I grew up in Brooklyn on Baltic Street, and then we moved to Sheepshead Bay. As far as being a Brooklyn Dodger fan, I go back to 1939. That was when I was about 13 or 14 years old. And Larry MacPhail was just beginning to come into the organization, and I started to become a Brooklyn Dodger fan. And MacPhail was revising the farm system, and he made trades. He got a first baseman by the name of Dolph Camilli, he got Whitlow Wyatt, Kirby Higbe, Larry French, Fat Freddie Fitzsimmons. Pee Wee Reese was just coming into the organization. This was around 1940, 1941, and then they played the New York Yankees in the World Series and that was the beginning of their franchise getting bigger and bigger, but Branch Rickey was the one who organized the whole thing. Then the War came and then the new Brooklyn Dodgers came in like Gil Hodges, who started as a catcher, and then they put him on first. Campanella came in, then there was Bruce Edwards and back in 1946 Jackie Robinson came into the organization. Then Duke Snider and Cookie Lavagetto.

"In going from Sheepshead Bay, I would take the Brighton Beach train and walk to Ebbets Field. It was a twenty minute ride and you were there. I was in my twenties coming out of the service, so I always paid to get in. What some of the kids used to do when they were younger was to buy a ticket and get in, then throw the ticket stub down inside a red ball to the next kid, and he would throw the ball down again to the next kid so that you could get three kids inside on one ticket.

"When Jackie Robinson came into the organization, that changed all of baseball. Pee Wee Reese and Gil Hodges and Jackie Robinson all were favorites and so was Campanella, so smart behind the plate.

"When the Dodgers moved to Los Angeles, I was devastated, truly devastated. It was a kind of crisis. And all the other fans were doing the same thing. That's what you have over here now. All the old-time Ebbets Fields fans coming out. They have Ebbets Field on the shirts and Brooklyn Dodger hats on — trying to relive the past. This is really a blessing for all the old Dodger fans. "They may be 75 years old like I am, but they're bringing fond memories back. They're feeling their youth again.

"I've worked as an usher for 35 years. In October, out in Long Island, we're going to have a reunion of all the guys I grew up with. But little by little, we're whittling down 'cause all the guys are in our seventies, but we still get together.

"I like Angel Pagan. I think he's going to make it to the majors, and for power, I like Joe Jiannetti.

WALTER BENTSON
(A DODGER FAN AND A BASEBALL PLAYER HIMSELF FOR OVER 60 YEARS)
Walter Bentson is a regular participant of the Los Angeles Dodgers' Adult Baseball Camp. Here, campers range in age from their 20s to the oldest camper, who is 86 years old. They practice and play a real baseball game every day during their week at Dodgertown. Walter Bentson is 72.

Walter Bentson — Dodger fan, still playing — and Carl Erskine (at Dodgertown).

Walter Bentson: "I grew up in the Hudson Valley in a small town called Staatsburg, near Poughkeepsie, New York. I graduated from a high school with a class of nine. My high school principal got me into New York University — I was an orphan. Ralph Branca also went to N.Y.U., and he was also a good basketball player. I went to school at New York University where I was a catcher on the varsity in the late forties. I played for the same baseball coach there that Ralph Branca did, but Ralph was there in the mid-forties, and I went to N.Y.U. from 1949 until 1952. When I was a boy, I lived with my aunt with my parents from 1939 until 1941 in the summers, and I went to Ebbets Field, and I saw the Dodgers in those years, and in 1941, Dolph Camilli was the first baseman when the Dodgers won the pennant. And he was the Most Valuable Player in the National League that year. We lived in the Bay Ridge section of Brooklyn, on Fifty-Seventh and Fourth Avenue. I would take the subway to Ebbets Field. I played at the Parade Grounds in Brooklyn. I went to Ebbets Field then with my father, and later, in the 1940s, I went on my own. I really loved it. He [Dolph Camilli] became my favorite, and so I wear his number four, and when Duke Snider sees me, we kid around about it because I tell him I'm not wearing it for him, but because there was a Dodgers' number four before Duke wore it, and that was Dolph Camilli. I've been a Dodger fan all my life, even when they moved to the West Coast because I spent time out there as well, and the Dodgers were still my team.

"I have seven children and 17 grandchildren, and a few years ago my son was here playing as well. I have been in 31 camps, twice a year since 1987. I've played a total of over a hundred and eighty games here at Dodgertown. I'll be 72 and meeting the Boys of Summer here — Branca, Snider, Erskine and Labine — has been wonderful for me.

"When I was 15 or 16, in 1947, I pitched a game at Cooperstown, and then a few years ago I pitched there again, so I had gone exactly 50 years between starts there.

"I did play against Satchel Paige. He was barnstorming with the Indianapolis Clowns, and I flied out against him. This was a year or so after he left the major leagues.

"Ebbets Field was a great place to watch a game; you felt like you were right on the sidelines. The Ebbets Field memories are really vivid.

"The Dodgers had Campanella at catcher and then Hodges, Robinson, Reese and Cox in the infield — and Snider and Furillo in the outfield; they always were looking for a left fielder. They had great continuity in those years. Their only lament was that they couldn't beat the Yankees. They had Erskine, Branca, Labine and others pitching. So four of them are right here at this camp.

"If I get down to Brooklyn, I'd like to see the Cyclones play."

CHUCK MONSANTO

Chuck Monsanto is a season ticket holder in Section 14 of KeySpan Stadium. Chuck is an avid Cyclone fan. He grew up hearing stories of the Brooklyn Dodgers from his father, a Brooklyn Dodger fan and a longtime Brooklyn resident. Before and after games, Chuck is a soft-spoken man, but during the Cyclone games his strong voice carries all over the field. He sits near Ed and Steve Gruber and near Mark Lazarus, making the Section 14 area behind the Cyclones' first base dugout the heart of the Cyclone enthusiasm.

Chuck Monsanto: "I'm from Williamsburg, Brooklyn, and I'm a Medicaid fraud investigator for the City of New York. When I first heard about minor league baseball coming to New York, I was thinking about getting season tickets, but then when I found out that the minor league team would be an affiliate of the Toronto Blue Jays, I decided not to get season tickets. I went out to St. John's in Queens to watch the Queens Kings' Opening Day, and I had a blast. I didn't go for the next couple of games, but then I started to find myself driving out there for every home game. They were a great bunch of guys on the team. What was unique about that team was that they lived in the dorms on campus, and they would go down to the clubs on Union Turnpike, and hang out, and we would hang out with them.

"Then, before this season, I was really excited about a team coming to Brooklyn because of the whole history of the Brooklyn Dodgers. My dad told me a lot about the old Dodgers. I bought season tickets, and I had an even better time this year with these guys. There's a huge difference in watching games at a sold out ball park in Brooklyn than in watching games before a couple of hundred people in a college stadium in Queens.

"I've seen a bunch of minor league fans. I've seen the fans in New Jersey and the fans in Hudson Valley, but the Brooklyn fans are the most unique minor league fans I've ever seen. We're more into the game. We're paying attention to the games. In a lot of these minor league parks it's a laid back, relaxed, family experience, which is perfectly fine. In Brooklyn, we're more passionate about the games, we're more into it. I would hear that the opposing players would hate it because you've got eight thousand hysterical fans right on top of you. Then you hear the conversations in the stands and throughout the course of the season we get to know each other, and it becomes like a family. People who know me know that whenever I'm with my daughter, she's glued to me wherever I go, but at the ball park I was comfortable asking the people around me to watch Victoria if I had to get a hot dog, and because it was like I was with family, I knew everyone so that I could briefly leave her with them while I made a food run.

"I know a couple of guys who work in the Brooklyn D.A.'s office; I saw a friend from college there; I would run into a lot of people I knew at the ball park.

"You start by liking these guys, and then you become protective of them, so you want to help them in any way you can. So I would get on the umps. I would try to get the crowd going for them. The first thing is: it's fun! I get a kick out of it. This started back in Queens. I'm doing it to give my team an edge.

"The biggest thing I would do is ride the ump. Sometimes I could see I was getting to an ump. I wouldn't usually get on the opposing team except when the Yankees came to town, and then I was riding everybody. I would ride the third base coach, the players.

"One thing you have to understand is that it was always clean, never vulgar. We police ourselves when it came to that. Once someone said stuff out of line, and we all told him to knock it off. We have children there, it's a family place, so we always were above board and clean. We never got personal.

"We used to ride Shelly Duncan. One time he hit a home run and we said, 'That doesn't impress me. It's just a long out at Yankee Stadium.' Shelly was a good player. He got into some static with Brett Kay, so after that we rode him really hard. Brett was one of my favorites.

"I brought my daughter to a game, and she asked me to get her a ball. And I said I'd see what I can do. I asked Brett Kay for a ball, and he gave me one, and she said thank you to Brett, and then five minutes after the fireworks started, she looked up at me and said, 'Thank you, Dad.' I had tears in my eyes. It was my best moment of the year. My Aunt Bunny lives only two blocks from where Ebbets Field used to be. When I visit my aunt, I go by the place where Ebbets Field was all the time.

"A friend of mine gave me a book about Ebbets Field, and I read through it and see the pictures of Ebbets Field, and I wish I could have seen the Dodgers play there. One of the tragedies of New York is that we tear down cathedrals and put up projects. Ebbets Field is the cathedral of baseball. I went down to Ebbets Field.

"I was down at the Ebbets Field apartments, and where Ebbets Field was was a small place. Being a Yankee hater, I would have loved to have been there. Even though I was born in 1967, ten years after they left, if I had been around when the Dodgers were here I would definitely have fit right in as a fan of the Dodgers, because those Dodger fans really loved their team. Brooklyn Dodger fans were really passionate fans, and they weren't ones you pushed around. My dad eventually switched to the Mets, but for some fans, when the Dodgers left, that was it for them. They never rooted for any other team.

"This year it isn't minor league baseball, it's Brooklyn baseball. It's loud, it's fun, it's colorful. It's the most fun I've had in any ball park, major or minor. We love our team, we love Brooklyn, they represent it. I used to tell the players, 'You wear Brooklyn on your chest, act like it. You wear that with pride.' The Brooklyn fans appreciate effort.

"I was the one who started calling Luz Portobanco 'Yankee Killer,' and he enjoys doing it. He enjoys beating them.

"When Harold [Eckert] pitches, I encourage him. I would pump him up, and they try not to look up, but sometimes Harold would look up and give me a nod.

"Those guys on the field hear everything. One time near the end of the year I was down on the field, and Brett Kay came up to me and squirted shaving cream in my face. Before I got the shaving cream, when Yankee players would ground out, and they were on the field I would yell at them, 'Get off my field.' I would tell the Cyclones, 'You know how I feel about Yankees on my field.'

"After that second game, I felt so drained. I felt wore out. I felt like crying and I tried to watch the game on TV because I taped it, but I fell asleep because I was so tired.

"I would love nothing more than seeing Ross Peeples mowing down Yankees in the major leagues in two or three years to show that the Brooklyn factory is pumping out players who won't be intimidated."

More Between Innings

Vladimir Hernandez

Vladimir Hernandez was born in Cuba, growing up in Havana and playing baseball at an early age.

While playing in a tournament in Mexico two years ago, he defected and hid in Mexico for a year and a half. In July, the infielder signed with the New York Mets' organization and began playing for Brooklyn. Hernandez heard many stories from his father about the old Brooklyn Dodgers. In fact, Vladimir's father used to play baseball in Cuba with Sandy Amoros, one of Brooklyn's first black players and a hero of the 1955 World Series when Amoros made a game-saving catch to help Johnny Podres shut out the Yankees and give the Brooklyn Dodgers their only World Series Championship.

Vladimir was in Brooklyn only for about eight weeks, but he was very popular with fans, staff, and players because of his friendly nature and optimistic outlook.

Vladimir Hernandez: "Playing in Brooklyn was wonderful. The fans were great. Everyone in the stands were saying, 'Come on. Come on.' They were cheering us on all the time. I would love to play in New York again. Brooklyn was like Havana, as a city with hard working people. In Brooklyn, the people seem happy, just like people in Havana.

"The hardest thing for me was learning to speak English. I still take English classes three times a week. Another hard part for me was learning to hit with a wooden bat. In Cuba, we only had metal bats, so when I left Cuba I had to work to learn to swing with a wooden bat.

"My father told me about the Brooklyn Dodgers and about Jackie Robinson, and about Roy Campanella. My father was a catcher and first baseman and my father tried out for the Havana Sugar Kings [a Triple-A team in the International League].

"In my first game for Brooklyn, I [was] excited because it was so new for me.

Mike Cox

"Bobby Ojeda really helped me on the mental side of the game. He always knew the right thing to say. One game, I accidentally went out there to throw

Mike Cox and the author.

with gum in my mouth and I threw really well, so Bobby said, 'You're always chewing gum when you pitch in the bullpen, and you do well, and you threw well this time in the game while you were chewing gum, so here, I got you some gum to chew on for the next game.' He gave me about ten packs.

"So from then on, I chewed gum any time I was throwing. And he told me to get a routine, so after that I always turned to my right when I caught the ball back from the catcher. So any time I turned to my left, I would have to start back over.

"He also talked to me about release points, like to look out into the glove. We would listen to any coach, but we would listen to him because he had actually done it so well himself. He knows what it takes to get there."

Joe Jiannetti

Joe Jiannetti describes his stay at Xaverian High School. Located in the heart of Bay Ridge, Xaverian conducted summer school classes on the first two floors. Some Cyclones lived on the third floor.

Joe Jianetti: "Xaverian is a school with a bed and a dresser and a TV that doesn't really work — in a classroom. We live in an actual classroom. They moved all the desks out; they're in a storage classroom. Right now there are two of us in the room. There are four beds; soon the guys from St. John's will move over, so we'll have four in there. You can watch *Letterman* on the TV at night, barely, if you look through the fuzz. We don't have cable. There's a refrigerator in there, but it's one of those tiny ones that will only hold a few bottles of soda; no room for food. There was a rope stretched across the room where we could hang our clothes. We can't cook there, so we have to eat all of our meals out. Two days in a row I woke up when the bell rang because they were changing classes for summer school. Another day, the bells rang to change classes every three minutes for an hour because they were fixing the bells. This was all in the morning when we were trying to sleep; it was ten or ten-thirty in the morning. We are on the third floor, and there are classes on the second floor, but I don't think the students even know we're there.

"One night, some of the guys were exploring on the hall where we live, and they turned on the light to a classroom, and there was a brother asleep in one of the other classrooms. We didn't even know they were there. He was right down the hall.

"When I first got to Xaverian, Devarez, Sosa, Arias and Pagan were staying there. We would pile in Pagan's P.T. Cruiser he would drive the other four of us to the ballpark. We would leave for the ballpark as soon as we woke up, around noon. Then when we got to the ballpark, we'd walk down to the Mermaid Deli and eat lunch there or at the Spanish place around the corner. I asked if I could live in the locker room, but they weren't having that. After three weeks at Xaverian, I moved to an apartment over Fonzie's house at Avenue P and East 3rd. It was only about ten minutes from the ballpark by subway."

The Streaks

On July 1, the Cyclones defeated the New Jersey Cardinals 8–2 at KeySpan Park. This began a home winning streak that continued for the entire month of July and then into August as the Cyclones won 19 home games in a row. The Cyclones defeated Pittsfield 6–3 on August 3 to run their home streak to 19 games. On August 4, at home against Lowell, the Cyclones trailed 6–1 going into the bottom of the ninth inning. Then, Brooklyn scored four runs to trail by only a run. They had the potential tying run on first base with none out, but their comeback fell short as they failed to score any more and lost 6–5 for their first loss after 19 straight home victories.

In the midst of this streak, the Cyclones also had an 11-game winning streak (home and away) lasting from July 5 through July 18, losing when Harold Eckert lost a game on his birthday, at Lowell.

Hojo and Bobby Wax Big League

Howard Johnson, known even to his mother as "Hojo," and Bobby Ojeda, known in baseball as "Bobby O.," are standing in the empty visitor's dugout in Lowell, Massachusetts. It's about 1:30 P.M., roughly five and a half hours before tonight's game.

They have already been running on their own, near the ballpark, for 30 minutes, in 95 degree heat. These coaches don't just preach fitness, they live it. But they're not perfect; they smoke cigars — giant, expensive ones. They always arrive early at the ball park, and today they stand in the dugout. There's a writer around, but no players.

> **Hojo:** "Trying to make players think is broader than just making them think in a particular game. It's making them think that they must be the best in everything they do."

Hojo played until he was 35. At 41 years of age, he looks as if he could still play in the majors. He was asked if he missed playing.

> **Hojo:** I miss playing, but only as a young player. I don't miss playing as an old player because it took too much for me to get my body ready to play against that level of competition."

Bobby Ojeda helped to pitch the Mets to their 1986 World Series win over the Boston Red Sox. He was asked was it was like to pitch in a World Series.

> **Bobby Ojeda:** "There is something to be said for getting booed by 50,000 people. A World Series is entirely different. You really can't prepare for it unless you've experienced it. Our lives [his and Hojo's] would be entirely different if we had lost the World Series. Sure, who wants to go through life known as a loser? But we won, and we've been riding that tsunami for 15 years."

Bobby Ojeda was in his first year as a minor league pitching coach. He was asked about coaching in the minor leagues.

> **Bobby Ojeda:** "Coaches miss their family for thirty-five thousand a year. When we were in the minors, Hojo and I both had some really good coaches. The first pro coach I had pitched me and pitched me, and I stunk. But he kept throwing me out there, and he stuck with me. I'll never forget that.

They act big league with the clubhouse boy. They nicely send him out for Diet Cokes and for sunflower seeds. They always get sunflower seeds before every game.

In talking about the pitching staff, Bobby becomes very animated.

Bobby Ojeda: "The main thing that is off about Peeples is his rhythm. He's got it partially back, but not totally. We're gonna reel him in. Luz [Portobanco] is one who will make it. A lot of making it is just being tough enough to stick to it. When I first get these new pitchers, I don't like to try to change them. As long as they're not doing anything that might hurt themselves, I let them pitch for a while and get their confidence. Gradually, I start to work with them on some things. The mental aspect is just as important as the physical aspect."

Hojo: "I don't try to change the hitters too much when I first get them here. I let them relax and not press. Then I gradually begin to work with them on their swings and on their pitch selection."

Both coaches discussed how much scrutiny is involved in major league ball.

Bobby Ojeda: "In the majors, if you put one finger just a little bit different on a slider they're going to look at video tapes and find it to get a pitch tipped off."

Hojo: "You have to notice everything. When I coach first base here, I pick up signs from the first base coaching box, but now mainly I try to get the signs for pitchouts."

Bobby Ojeda: "It's a great life playing in the majors, but the minors is hard with all the travel. We do it because we love it; it's not the only thing we can do.

"I don't tell the players that they have to do it my way. I show them a way and then it's up to them. Some coaches let it go to their heads. We're coaches and it's a players' game. You have to see yourself for what you are." [Hojo nods in agreement.]

Hojo and Bobby O. were asked to honestly rate their natural athletic ability, compared to other high school athletes in their schools when they were there.

When asked his natural ability as compared to any high school athlete, Bobby O. placed his in the top 10 percent. Hojo placed his ability in a level higher than that. They weren't being conceited; they were thoughtfully considering the question and then answering honestly.

The clubhouse boy returned with the Diet Cokes and the sunflower seeds. Bobby and Hojo gave him a nice tip. After all, they may be in a deserted dugout in Lowell, Massachusetts, but they're Big Leaguers.

Harold Eckert

Baseball teams generally use five regular starting pitchers who pitch in a five-day rotation. Harold Eckert describes what the regular starters do on the days when they *don't* pitch. One is in the dugout and the other three starters sit behind the home plate screen. They are dressed in civilian clothes, and most fans don't even realize that these players are sitting in the stands.

Harold Eckert: "The day after you pitch, you're in the dugout and it's a day off. That's the day you do most of your off-field stuff, and it's a lot of running, and a lot of lifting so you can even shower up sometimes, put on a uniform and enjoy the game. You've worked hard in pitching yesterday, and this is day your day off.

"The other three starting pitchers sit in the stands in civilian clothes behind home plate. So the first day off after you pitch you get to stay in the dugout; the second day off you have a video camera, and you take about five to six pitches of our pitcher in each of the first three innings, then you're pretty much off with the camera. The camera is a pretty easy job, 'cause if our starter goes six innings, you're pretty much done after the third inning. Till a new guy comes in, and then you have to do the same with him. Sometimes, and we didn't do this too often, wherever their open side was, if it's a righty, you have to go by third base, and a lefty, you have to go by first base. Mostly you get about six or eight pitches on each inning. You want to get a sample, and then you see if later he's getting a bad habit, like dropping his arm or opening up.

"And I think it's also mainly for us. We sit down every week or two with the pitching coach. Your best thing to ever do is have yourself on videotape. I think Tony Gwynn said that, and I think he had every at bat in his career on videotape. And he used to study those. You can look at yourself in the mirror. That's called dry mechanics, but you're not throwing the ball, you're just working on mechanics. Videotape is the best. If you're actually in the game, and then you watch yourself on tape, then you can actually see what you're doing wrong. Someone can say that you're opening up your front foot, and you can try to fix it, but when you see it for yourself on tape, that really helps. Video camera is probably the easiest one, 'cause you don't have to do every pitch.

"On your third day off it's called 'doing the radar gun.' Sometimes you do the other team, for certain pitchers if we want to know what he's throwing, and you do five or six pitches of an opponent. And sometimes we do it for the big-shots in the stands, the Met executives like Guy Conti and those guys. They'll say bring the chart up, and we want to see what the pitcher's doing. Sometimes the video camera wouldn't work, so then you would just help out the guy on the gun or get food for the guys. To do the radar gun, you have to have an open space, and you hold it up so nothing is interfering. You want to be straight on because an angle would probably make it seem slower. If a tall guy sits in front of you, then you have to move. We used to do a little set up where the guy doing the gun sat at the end of the aisle so he would have a better angle for the gun. There's a way to put the gun on a suitcase box. We usually didn't have assigned seats. We'd look for empty seats behind home plate, and then sometimes the people with tickets for those seats would come, and we'd have to move someplace else. Sometimes we'd have to move two, three, four or five times in a game. With the gun, you're taking the speed of every pitch: fastball, curve, change-up, whatever. And at the end of the game, you put down an average of each type of pitch. You put a high, average, and low. You don't have to figure it out exactly. You just look at the chart and put down the high, low, and an estimate of the average speed for each kind of pitch. Most of the time you give the guy the benefit of the doubt. If he's between an 88 and 89 average on his fastball, you put down 89. So most of the time you don't have to clock the opposing pitcher, so you're only busy about half the time. The job isn't too bad because you mostly only have to do your own pitchers.

"The next job is what you do the day before you pitch, and you're very busy with that one. It's called doing 'the game chart.' You keep track of the team that's hitting against you, and you're keeping track of our offense, so you're busy the top and bottom of each inning. You have to keep a pitch count. There's a lot of averages, a lot of writing. So you're always busy. You write down a 1 if it's a fastball, 2 for a curve , 3 if they have a slider, 4 for a change-up, and 5 for other, and then you explain what that other pitch is, like a knuckleball, or a screwball. There's a section for balls and a section for strikes. If the first pitch is a fastball strike, you put it in the strike box and put down a 1. If he swung at it, you circle it. If it's a ball, you put it in that box. This is the busiest job because you have to write stuff for every pitch. When we're hitting, we do an offensive chart for our guys. It helps the manager. After a guy is done pitching, you have to add up all his stuff. How many pitches, how many balls, how many strikes, etc.

"Mainly the game chart is important because most of the time you're facing that same team the next day, and keeping the game chart keeps you studying the hitters. You look for weaknesses. Okay, the three hitter, number 31, slow bat — can't get his bat around on an inside fastball. You make a mental note of that. You pick up certain things. There are so many guys now, you can't learn all their names, but we remember them by what they look like, what their number is, and what spot they hit in the order. It's not like the major leagues where you would see the same guys year after year and learn all their names. When I'm keeping the chart, by the third time a guy is up in the order, I have been studying him, and I know pretty much how I'm going to pitch to him the next day. You learn what their tendencies are. It is harder if I'm following a lefty in the pitching rotation because the situation is different. This year I mostly followed Cox, who's a lefty, so it was harder. But when I follow a right-hander like me, then it's easier for me to see how to pitch these guys as I'm doing the chart. It's easier if I follow a righty because he might have a curve and a slider like me, and I can see how the batters react to his pitches and figure out that will probably be how they react to my pitches.

"Most of the time, especially at this level, you just go right at a guy's weaknesses. You have a certain pitch count, so you don't want to fool around. Once in a while, with a really good hitter, you might save a pitch where you think you can get him out with for a key spot, so he doesn't see it too often and adjust.

"You might be pitching that day, maybe you'll be pitching the fourth day against this team or maybe next month, but you're still watching to see what you can learn about each hitter. Even the day you're in the dugout, I'm already watching, to see if I can spot his tendencies so that when I do face him, I'll know what to do. I keep my eyes open all the time. I'll even try to help the offense. If I pick up a sign, I'll tell Hojo. If I pick up a tendency, if the other team's pitcher rattles the ball round in his glove, and every time he does that he throws a fastball, I'll watch a couple of innings and if I'm on it nine out of ten times, I'll tell Hojo, and then if he sees it he'll tell the players. If I'm going to be an all-around baseball player, then I want my team to score runs and I'm going to help out if I can. The coaches are always watching for tendencies. Baseball is such a thinking sport. I don't throw 98 miles an hour. I have to be always thinking.

"Baseball, you have to think so much. Maybe on a curveball he'll be slowing up his arm. You're always trying to help your team out and trying to learn by watching. The main thing is to help your team. Every day, you are probably going to learn something.

"For a seven o'clock game, when we're behind the plate 'charting' sometimes we get a little sandwich in the dugout, but by game time you're usually pretty hungry, so we try to get out there behind the plate a little early. Then we get food — cheeseburgers, fries, Cokes. We wait in line like anybody else. The girl in Hudson Valley — she knew we were players, she could tell, and she gave us a discount.

The last time we went up there we said goodbye and thanked her for the discount because at the other places we didn't get a break on the prices.

"After the game, since we're in street clothes, the other guys had to hurry and shower, and change, and get on the bus, and we were already in our street clothes, so we had more time, and the players, and coaches would always give us money and ask us to get them food, hamburgers, sodas, whatever, for the bus ride home. Bobby Ojeda and Hojo had cell phones, and countless times in the games, we'd get a phone call on our walkie-talkie and Bobby O. would say, 'How fast was that [last pitch]?; what was that [last pitch]?; and get us three Diet Cokes,' and we'd bring the Diet Cokes down to the dugout in the fifth inning.

"This is the way it was. We'd get a call from Bobby O., 'Send Eckert out for three Diet Cokes.'

"I'd say on the walkie-talkie, 'I'm busy, send someone else.' See, we'd mess around back with him. Then you'd go get it, and you'd say to him, 'You going to give me any money?' and sometimes he'd give us a little extra.

"After the games, on the bus on the way home, when we'd stop at a Burger King, Bobby O. would give us money, and he'd order food and tell us to get whatever we wanted. He'd stay on the bus. He's a great guy. I respect him so much.

"Where he's coming from is where I'm coming from. I think he signed for five hundred dollars and a bus trip. His first season at Elmira, I don't think he won a game. He did something most players have never done — he won a World Series. He was 18–5 that year. He didn't only go there, he helped them win it. To have Bobby Ojeda as my pitching coach was a great experience. He wasn't trying to look down on us. He was always there with us. If you have a guy who tells you what to do and he's done it, you really respect it. That's a big thing with Bobby and Hojo. You respect everybody. [Lyle] Yates was another guy who helped me; he would work extra after practice with me; Yates made a heck of a difference in my first year."

Jay Caligiuri

"The first day off I was in Manhattan with Dave Campanero and Gary Perone. They took a bunch of guys to the Carnegie Deli, and we judged a sandwich making contest there. Five of us were counted as one judge. They had some big people from New York there. The sandwiches were really big and all good. They put our picture, with the owner, up on the wall with a bunch of celebrities. Next time I'm in New York, I'll have to sign the picture.

"The second day off, I went to the Empire State Building with my parents. We were coming back, and we went to Times Square and were on MTV and after that we went out to lunch at Brooklyn Breweries. Then we went over to Rockefeller Center and had dinner at the skating rink. People were looking down at us saying, 'Who are these people eating dinner down there?' After that, we went to the ESPN Endzone Opening and watched the All-Star Game.

"It was really our first experience as a team together. That was the first time a lot of the guys got to spend time together and got to know each other well. After that, we went on a pretty good roll."

Joe Jiannetti

Joe Jiannetti describes how he handles his diabetes.

Joe Jianetti: "I take an insulin shot when I wake up and then again after infield practice is over, usually around 6:30, just a half hour before the game. I try to do it as soon as possible before the game because I don't want the insulin to kick in too early before the game because I could be low, and then I'd have to go and get a candy bar, and I don't want to do that during the game. I have the insulin with me all the time, and I keep an extra needle. Every day I make sure I have a candy bar with me in case I need it."

Bobby Ojeda

Bobby Ojeda discusses how he teaches his young pitchers — in stages.

Bobby Ojeda: "The other night we got two new guys. They don't know me, and I don't know them. I don't know their personalities, and they don't know mine. I don't really know how much they've been throwing, and how much they haven't. So, the philosophy of the Mets, and I totally agree, is that you can't start monkeying with them when they first get here. First of all, they're all shook up. They're unsettled. They want to show you how hard they can throw and how good their curve is. They're trying so hard to impress you so badly, just like I did, which I totally understand because I was the same way. You put on a uniform for the first time, and you know it's a Mets uniform, even though it is a minor league uniform. At this time, I won't even approach trying to change them. It's more, 'Show me what you've got.' I won't touch them with a change-up; I won't touch a curve ball; I won't even mess with two seam or four seam fastballs. You just let 'em go, and then read 'em as they go along, and then what happens is that they see another guy be effective with something, and then they ask him, 'What are you doing there?' And then they come to you and say, 'What's up with that?' And they gravitate. I handle an older player, Braswell, differently than I do a younger player. It just comes down to my experience as a player at all levels. What's comforting for me is that it's not a guessing game. This is what I believe works. These things helped me, these things didn't, so this is what I'm going to tell you.

"The bottom line is that they've got a short season, so I'm really limited as I go over the stages [of instruction] with them. That's another reason for the stages, because I know from me as a player, too much is too much, and I don't want to confuse 'em. I know as a player, if I was getting 45 pieces of advice, even if it's the greatest advice in the world, it's too much. So, I just try to state the advice that I give 'em, and I believe in it. Whether it's correct, it's my opinion. Am I in agreement with everything that Rip [Rippelmeyer, the Mets' minor league pitching coordinator] tells them? Unequivocally, which is great.

"I know from being on that mound that if I don't believe in a pitch, it's not going to be good. If I believe in it, and I gradually get confident in that pitch, it's going to be bigger. And I want our team to get outs in key situations, and we've done that a lot. Because our pitching has had people on base. But these kids have come through with big pitches at big times. Big punch-outs at big times. You can strike out fifteen, or you can get three strikeouts at critical times, then those three strikeouts could be better than 15. Give me the three that we need at the right time. Now you're picking everybody up. Say your shortstop boots a ball. You now have second and third with a one run lead. What is a better time to punch somebody out and pick your shortstop up? Guess what your shortstop's gonna do. Inside, your shortstop is going to go, 'Yeah. All right!' Because if you give up a gapper right then, nobody is going to feel worse than him. He's not trying to miss. Those are the little tiny things that affect the mentality of your teammates. I don't want a kid hanging a slider at the wrong time. I don't want him doing that. I want him to want to get that guy out.

"I tell my pitchers that it's like two dogs fighting over a piece of meat. Who's going to get it? The dog that wants it the most. There are men on second and third, and the batter is in the box. Well, there he is. Who's going to win, you or him? And if you want it more than him, you're going to beat him. If you don't, then he's going to beat you.

"Here's an example. The other night David Byard had the hitter 0–2. Now this is a simple thing that as they get older, they've got to see it. He threw a fastball right by him. Then a fastball that the guy hits into the dugout. Next pitch slider. A ball. Okay, 'cause we were working on the slider. Next pitch slider. Two-two. Next pitch another slider, a ball. He hit the next one into the dugout. Three-two. David jams him on the next pitch, and the batter hits a fly ball to short left. Game over. Now a few weeks ago, I would have said to David, 'Nice game.' And I would have left him alone. Now he's progressed to the point where I tell him, 'You had the guy 0–2. I've told you, the way a guy takes a pitch, the way a guy swings at a pitch, the way a guy fouls off a pitch — those are all going to tell you what he's looking for or what he can hit and what he can't.' We don't have the benefit of seeing a guy's tendencies and all that with seeing a game report. So he's going to tell you. I said, 'Here's what happened. At this level you were able to get away with it.' See, I'm already talking to David about the future. We were always in the 'now.' But now it's time to talk to David about down the line a little bit. I said, 'You get behind a guy — slider, slider, slider, and this is the ninth hitter in the lineup, too. Suppose you walk him? You're in a one run game, you've got two outs, and you have the top of the order coming up. Suppose the next hitter hits a single, then you have the second hitter in the lineup coming up. Suppose the next guy comes up and hits it out? You had the guy on the ropes, and you let him off. David, there's nothing worse than walking off that mound knowing that you had what it takes to get him out.' Now, it made sense to him, and it dawned on him. He realized, 'You know you're right. When you have a guy, don't fool around and just go and get him out right then.' That's at the higher level, that's future, and he's ready for it. Some of the other guys aren't ready for that now.

"For me, it's fun because it's a challenge, because I get to groom these kids, and it's a challenge to keep them focused and keep teaching them without teaching them too much. So for me, it's a lot of fun in that sense. For me, it's just instinct. Having been in the game and having had to pitch, never having tremendous natural ability, I've had to do it for a long time, so I feel confident in it being a pretty good way to do it.

"At this level, I tell the guys, 'I got my starters and I got the rest of you guys. And you are all going to get the ball. If I could finish this season with all of you guys pitching within ten innings of each other, then I have done my job.' There's no set up man, there's no closer, none of that. I know we have a miniature big league atmosphere here, but the bottom line is we are one hundred percent development. If I lost sight of that, then I'm not worth two cents."

Howard Johnson

Howard Johnson was just the 16th player in baseball history to reach 200 home runs and 200 stolen bases.

"At the level of the Cyclones, it is so difficult to judge who will advance because many of the players are just out of college, and they are basically learning how to play the game all over again. You can see their physical tools, but you don't know how much more is there. Some guys come out of college and perform well, but you don't really know how well they will eventually progress.

"The Florida State League was mainly a pitchers' league. In '79, I had a decent year, I drove in 46 runs and had three or four home runs. The next year I hit 12 home runs and drove in 80 runs, which was pretty good in that league, and I made the all-star team.

"Each year in the minors you hopefully move up. Now in the minors, Double-A is kind of the separating point. From Single-A to Double-A is the most difficult jump. If you can make Double-A, you have some ability. The travel in Double-A makes it tough on you. If you could survive the Southern League, it was like getting over the hump, and it was all downhill from there. In the Southern Association, we had a lot of ten, eleven, twelve hour bus rides.

"We were excited to get Brett Kay, and he struck out a few times and he was a little nervous, and he made the adjustment real quick, and I enjoyed having him around with his enthusiasm. I think he has a shot at the big leagues if he keeps improving and stays healthy. He uses the whole field to hit; he has some power, which is still developing; and he can run; he's not afraid to drop a bunt down. He plays upbeat, and that's good. When he gets in trouble is when he forgets to use the whole field.

"Jay Caligiuri started off well, and he has had a real consistent year. With Jay, we just try to keep him locked in. We just keep him fresh. We just kept his swing short and compact. He has to hit to all fields, and if he uses all fields he has a chance to move up. If his power develops down the road, I think he has a real chance at the major leagues.

"Joe Jiannetti we saw a little of in Florida, and then he was sent to Kingsport, and when he joined us I think he really likes hitting in that stadium.

"Frank Corr came to us down in Florida, and I was pitching BP to him, and I could tell how the ball jumped off his bat right away. He's a guy who has a tendency to want to pull the ball, and hit the ball out of the ball park, and he needs to become a better hitter first. When he's not jumping out there trying to hook the ball over the fence, then he's a better hitter. With Frank, we've worked all year on trying to stay back, and trying to use his power the other way, because if he's going to get to the big leagues, then he has to learn how to sit back and wait and use his power to right field. Eventually, he'll be pitched a lot of breaking balls and be pitched on the outside half of the plate, and he's going to have to learn to not try to pull everything. I like Frank a lot, and he worked hard all year, and he reaped the benefits of that."

Tryouts

In August, the Cyclones had a tryout at KeySpan Park. Ever since the Brooklyn Cyclones had been announced as coming to Brooklyn, individuals had been writing to the team and to the parent team, the New York Mets, to request a tryout.

Most of the individuals requesting a tryout sent a letter, along with a resume or description of their playing experience and their previous baseball honors. The tryouts were conducted at 9:00 A.M. at KeySpan Park, and it appeared that the arriving players, most dressed in the uniforms of their sand-lot teams, were somewhat surprised to learn of the number of players — several hundred — who had been invited to the tryout. They appeared to be like actors who believed that they were to attend a rather exclusive audition and arrived to see that they were part of a cattle call.

To be fair to the Mets, the organization did not exclude or include the potential players based on their letter requesting a tryout. Anyone who wrote was given a chance. The tryouts were conducted under the supervision of Joe Nigro, a Mets New York area scout. Many of the players had family, friends or a girlfriend sitting in the stands watching the tryout, but the mood in the ball park was somber as the reality of the amount of competition set in.

At first, all of the players sat in the stands and attendance was taken. Each player filled out a small card. This was a long process in itself. The players jogged, stretched and loosened up their arms. After more jogging and throwing, the pitchers were sent to the bullpen, where they threw under the eyes of more Met representatives or birddog scouts. The other players were sent to the left-field corner where they were lined up to run a forty-yard dash. Reporters like Gersh Kuntzman and Mark Healey were also trying out, not to make the team, to write about the tryout from an insider's point of view.

An average big league catcher's time in the forty-yard dash is 5.0 seconds, and catchers are usually considered to be slow runners. The times of the runners trying out were often around 5.6 seconds, and some were over 6.0 seconds. The Met representatives running the tryout dutifully recorded everyone's time, even the reporters'. While I was observing a segment of this part of the tryout, only one runner broke 5.0 seconds. The runner ran a 4.8 and was someone who had actually been giving a special invitation to the tryouts.

In addition, the throwing in the bullpen didn't seem to be too spectacular to one used to seeing professionals throw.

Then, the players trying out were assembled in right field, and a ball was hit to them, and they were given a few throws to home. Most of the throws hardly got there and were far off line. Many of the throws were like hump-backed line drives, with an arc to them.

After the tryouts were over, Noel Devarez and John Toner, the Cyclones' right fielders, were making throws from the same area to home plate during the Cyclones' infield practice. The throws by Devarez and Toner seemed like rockets compared to the throws of the candidates of the morning. Devarez and Toner threw straight, hard throws that bounced once and were right at home plate. It became apparent that the gulf between the Brooklyn Cyclones and the major leagues was very small compared to the gulf of ability between most amateurs and the Cyclones.

Not one of the players trying out was ever offered a contract.

The Yankee Killer
(a.k.a. Luz Portobanco)

Luz Portobanco: "The people in Brooklyn were really nice to me. Sometimes when you are going good, people are behind you, but when you have a bad game, people turn away from you, but the people in Brooklyn stayed with me.

"There were two ladies from my country who didn't even like baseball, but they heard there was a Nicaraguan prospect playing for Brooklyn, and they went and saw me, and they used to cook for me. They were really nice. They used to support me. They would make rice, beans, and meat, chicken. They lived five minutes from the park. They heard about me on the computer. I beat the Yankees three times, so they had to hear about me.

"I had fun pitching against the Yankees. I had fun kicking their butts, man. The first game against the Yankees I threw seven innings, and half of my pitches were change-ups. I had eight or nine strikeouts. I shut 'em down. They only scored one run off me.

"Then the second game against the Yankees, I came from a little rehab, to rest my arm. I threw five innings, seven strikeouts, and they didn't score any runs, and I beat 'em at home.

"Then we went to their house and beat 'em. And when I beat them three times, they started calling me the 'Yankee Killer,' and a couple of the Yankees told me I was really uncomfortable to hit against, and that I was one of the best pitchers they'd seen this year. And that made me feel pretty good, and I respect them too, because they have a pretty good team. Their pitching and their hitting were great, and I guess I was just better than them at some point."

The New York–Penn League

The New York–Penn League

The New York–Penn League is schizophrenic. Oh, everybody involved in it seems sane enough, and the people in the stands all appear sane, other than thousands of partisans at key moments in Brooklyn, but the league definitely carries a split personality. To understand the split personality of 2001, it's necessary to trace the league's history.

This league is no "Johnny-come-lately"; it's the longest continuously operating Class-A league in minor league baseball, having started play in 1939 when the league was formed with the following teams: Bradford, Pennsylvania; Hamilton, Ontario; and Batavia, Olean, Jamestown and Niagara Falls of New York. Because the league had clubs from Pennsylvania, Ontario, and New York, the six-team league was named the PONY league.

The league attendance was 267,212 that year, which meant that the clubs were averaging about five hundred fans per game. The league went to eight teams. Attendance increased during World War II and continued to rise after the war as a new league attendance record was set in 1946 as 500,599 attended PONY League contests.

In 1951, a baseball youth organization called Protect Our Nation's Youth was formed in Pennsylvania. The acronym for this group was PONY; so to escape confusion, professional baseball's PONY League changed its name to the New York–Pennsylvania League.

Usually more informally referred to as the New York–Penn League, the league continued to flourish until the advent of the mass telecasting of baseball games in the 1960s. When television of major league baseball games started as a regular feature in the late 1940s, most homes in the United States didn't even have television. Fans would often have to go to taverns to see a major league game on TV. In the 1950s, radio still predominated, and when a local major league team's games were televised, the viewers were usually in the team's area. There were nationally televised games, but there weren't many, and fans in minor league cities, if they wanted to see baseball, would need to go to the local minor league team's ballpark.

Soon almost every home had a television set. As television began more national broadcasts in the 1960s, and as particular teams' games were carried on ever expanding networks, fans in minor league cities could go out to the local ballpark and watch minor leaguers, or stay home and watch major leaguers. Increasingly, the fans stayed home, and minor league baseball suffered throughout the country. Watching major leaguers at home was a novelty.

In 1965, the New York–Penn League was down to only New York teams, six of them in upstate: Auburn, Batavia, Geneva, Jamestown, Binghamton, and Wellsville. Attendance was down, and the league was struggling to survive. Major league teams were losing interest in working with the league. The league's club owners realized that changes had to be made. Because cold weather and schooldays kept attendance down in April and May, the owners proposed having the league not begin play until mid–June. The New York–Penn League interested Major League farm directors in a revised schedule of 80 games that would provide a league for players just signed from the June amateur draft.

The league survived. It expanded to eight teams in 1968, and then later to ten teams. In the mid–1980s, the New York–Penn League began the process that led to the present day schizophrenia. Because of the increasing costs to operate a minor league franchise, and because of the higher standards that Major League Baseball was imposing on minor league ballparks, the New York–Penn League began attempting to operate in larger markets.

By the end of the twentieth century, small cities like Geneva and Elmira were no longer in the league, and teams in more metropolitan areas were added: New Jersey; Lowell, Massachusetts; Mahoning Valley (near Youngstown, Ohio); and Hudson Valley, New York. While these towns were not necessarily in large cities themselves, they were within driving range of some of the nation's largest cities. The New Jersey Cardinal franchise is located in a rural/suburban area, yet it is within commuting distance from New York City and is even closer to many New Jersey cities. Hudson Valley is located in the countryside in Wappingers Falls, New York, yet is only just about an hour's drive north of New York City and also within commuting range. Lowell is close to Boston. Mahoning Valley is located in Niles, Ohio, which is just outside of Youngstown, Ohio, and less than a two hours' drive from Pittsburgh and Cleveland.

Then, the New York–Penn League actually did more than continue moving toward New York City; it moved into it. In 1999, the New York Yankees placed a team in Staten Island, one of the city's five boroughs. Then in 2000 the league added a team in another borough, Queens, as a temporary home for its Toronto Blue Jays affiliate. Then, in 2001, the Queens franchise was eliminated, and Brooklyn became a league member.

Staten Island Yankees' Richmond County Bank Ballpark at St. George.

These new franchises also provided stadia that were new and generally larger than the stadia of the league's older franchises. For example, Vermont's Centennial Field was constructed in 1906 and seats 4,000. Pittsfield's Waconah Park was built in 1919 and seats 4,500. Williamsport's Bowman Field was constructed in 1926 and holds 4,200. Some of the older franchises have new stadia, but their capacity is small. Auburn's Falcon Park, opened in 1995, has a capacity of 2,500, and Batavia's Dwyer Stadium, opened in 1996, seats 2,600. The newer franchises have stadia such as Lowell's LeLacheur Park, which seats 5,000, and Hudson Valley's Dutchess Stadium, which seats 4,344.

As the smaller franchises, mostly in upstate New York, died out, some remained. Jamestown has been with the league, on and off, since 1939. Batavia, Auburn, Oneonta, Utica, Jamestown in New York State — and Vermont, and Williamsport, Pennsylvania, and Pittsfield, Massachusetts, are more of the old guard in the league. Brooklyn, Staten Island, Lowell, New Jersey, Hudson Valley, and Mahoning Valley are part of the new guard. And even here there is a split. Staten Island and Brooklyn are actually *in* New York City and seem to somewhat stand apart from Lowell, Mahoning Valley, New Jersey, and Hudson Valley, who are more suburban teams, on the outskirts of major markets.

So the league is essentially a mix of the old and the new. The new ballparks are full of modern amenities and have fine seating, but the older stadia have a charm of another era. If you see two teams from either side of this divide play each other home and home, it seems like two different events. Seeing Brooklyn play at Pittsfield is a totally different experience than seeing Pittsfield play at Brooklyn.

At Pittsfield, it's as if you're in the country, sitting on an old rocking chair on the porch of an ancient hotel, and at Brooklyn, it's like you're right in the middle of Coney Island — which you are.

To say the league is schizophrenic does not mean that this split personality is unpleasant. It's not. But the abrupt change in venue from Brooklyn to Jamestown, or Batavia to Staten Island, can often be surreal. Not only do the stadia change, but so does the environment. Most surreal can be the change in time. Teams in the New York–Penn League all are within the Eastern Time Zone, but that's not the change in time that occurs. It's a change of a more profound way. In Jamestown, in Pittsfield, in Vermont, the time could almost be the 1950s and it's easy to imagine the Dodgers still in Brooklyn. When you're sitting in ballparks built in 1906, 1919 and 1926, watching a game that (DH rule excluded) has essentially the same rules as it did when Pee Wee, Campy, the Duke, Gil, Oisk, and Jackie were in Ebbets Field, it feels like time travel to go to the older franchises. Seeing the home ballparks of the different franchises in the league is very different from going on a tour of Applebee's franchises in the same cities. Applebee's is a pleasant enough place in any city, but it's always the same, whereas the baseball franchises in every city, whether part of the new or old guard, are always different, each with its own quirks.

There's something else about the New York–Penn League. Going to a game means you will be surrounded by cheerful people. There are plenty of grouchy people in this country, but you'd be hard pressed to find any of them at New York–Penn League games.

The club employees are usually young people, in their twenties or thirties, and while often working 14-hour days, a certain enthusiasm shows through, even when they're harried and tired. The part-time help is usually younger or older, a mix of high school students and retirees, maybe some teachers off for the summer and a few people who come to the park after their day jobs are over. It's hard to find a grouch in that lot, too.

The ballplayers are usually in their first or second year of minor league baseball. They all would like to move up to the next level as soon as possible, but while they want to leave whatever city they're in, they seem to have the Zen-like ability to simultaneously enjoy the moments in the place they are. To a man, they all love being on a ball field, even if they wish it were one on a higher minor league level.

The managers enjoy being there, too. Cyclones manager Edgar Alfonzo spent 13 years as a player in the minors, and then two years as a minor league coach before he became a manager in 2000 for Kingsport in the Appalachian League. Someday Alfonzo, who never made the majors despite some impressive minor league statistics, would like to be in the major leagues for more than the brief time he helped out in September of 2000 on the Mets' bench. He's a serious man on a ball field, but you'll still catch him making a little joke with the players as he pitches batting practice, or takes infield practice with the players, sometimes playfully flipping the ball behind his back on a phantom double play.

The two Cyclones coaches are happy to be there, too. Both the batting coach, Howard Johnson, and the pitching coach, Bobby Ojeda, are used to big league travel and big league hotels, but they rarely complain about the New York–Penn League's travel, or its sometimes-modest hotels.

Warner Fusselle, the radio announcer, has done television for years, narrating the *This Week in Baseball* show and others. He wanted to announce the Brooklyn games, and he's happy about it.

The travel is hard on everyone and practically everyone gripes about that. If one didn't, he'd probably be inhuman, but any griping vanishes when the teams are at the ballpark.

Even the umpires are glad to be there. Their travel is even harder than everyone else's because they get no home games, but while they are the most serious men on the field, you can tell they are doing what they want, and the ballpark is certainly the best place to be, far better than their hotel room or on the highway.

Minor League Baseball

Looking ahead, on September 5, 2001, the Cyclones were scheduled to complete their first regular season schedule with an away game against the Batavia Muckdogs. That game would be played 100 years ago to the day when the presidents of seven minor leagues met in Chicago and established the National Association of Professional Baseball Leagues, now known as Minor League Baseball. The "National Association," as it was called, established rules of franchise exclusivity and mutual respect of player contracts.

The National Association began play in 1902 with 14 leagues and 96 teams. The NAPBL grew to 41 leagues in 1914, but player raids from the then Major League Federal League and the approach of World War I, with the loss of players and wartime travel restrictions, allowed only nine leagues to operate in 1918.

Branch Rickey greatly benefited from a 1921 agreement that the NAPBL signed with the major leagues that allowed major league teams to own minor league teams. Rickey then established the "farm system," where his Cardinals owned or had working agreements with minor league teams, controlling hundreds of players in a pipeline feeding the major league Cardinals.

In 1930, the first night game under permanent lights was played in Des Moines, Iowa. The game attracted 12,000 fans for a home team that averaged only 600 fans. Night baseball spread quickly through the minors and was then adopted by the major leagues.

In 1944, with World War II restrictions on travel and with thousands of minor league players in the military, only ten minor leagues continued to operate. After World War II, the minor leagues went through a boom period from 1947 to 1949. At its zenith, there were almost 450 teams in 59 leagues. The all-time regular season attendance record of 39.7 million was set in 1949.

The spread of televised games began to affect minor league attendance in the 1950s. From its record high attendance in 1949, minor league attendance dwindled to 21.1 million in 1953. By 1957, the last year of the Brooklyn Dodgers, minor league attendance had fallen to 14.8 million. Major league expansion and televised major league games continued to affect minor league attendance, and from 1960 through 1970 attendance fluctuated between a low of 9.7 million in 1961–1963 and a high of 10.7 million in 1970.

Then attendance started to rise. It was no longer a novelty to see a major league game on television. Now, the novelty was to see a game, perhaps in the minor leagues, live. In the 1980s, attendance generally grew, and by 1990 minor league attendance was up to 25.2 million fans.

New stadia were being built and player strikes in the majors gave the minor leagues more exposure. Fans who had never seen a minor league game became enamored with the live entertainment, the fun nature and stunts at the ballparks, the low ticket prices (usually from $3 to $10 a ticket), and the family nature of the evening's entertainment. The baseball movie of the minor leagues, *Bull Durham*, exposed more fans to the minors as well, and attendance continued to rise.

The major league teams pay the salaries of the manager, coaches, and players and provide some of the equipment. The minor league teams make most of their money from ticket sales, advertising, and concession and souvenir sales. The rising attendance had made minor league baseball a profitable enterprise.

By 1993, minor league attendance was up to 30.3 million. In the 2001 season, minor league attendance were up to 38.8 million, almost back to the record level of 1949, when there was more teams and leagues.

With their attendance rising and with their inroads into major cities, the minors weren't so minor anymore.

New York–Penn League Divisions

McNamara Division	*Pinckney Division*
Brooklyn Cyclones (NY Mets)	Auburn Doubledays (Toronto Blue Jays)
Hudson Valley Renegades (Tampa Bay D-Rays)	Batavia Muckdogs (Philadelphia Phillies)
Lowell Spinners (Boston Red Sox)	Jamestown Jammers (Atlanta Braves)
New Jersey Cardinals (St. Louis Cardinals)	Mahoning Valley Scrappers (Clev. Indians)
Pittsfield Astros (Houston Astros)	Oneonta Tigers (Detroit Tigers)
Staten Island Yankees (NY Yankees)	Utica Blue Sox (Florida Marlins)
Vermont Expos (Montreal Expos)	Williamsport Crosscutters (Pitts. Pirates)

Playoff Format: Three game division series between regular season division champions and the second place team in its division. The winners of the three game division series will play a three game series to determine the league championship.

Between Innings

Jackie

Carl Erskine: "You know Mister Rickey was given lots of credit, and rightfully so, for conceiving the idea for breaking the 'Color Line.' No one ever probed him, as far as I heard, whether the ethnic mix in Brooklyn influenced him. I think Mister Rickey was a wise man, and so Brooklyn was the ideal stage, the ideal place. The fans accepted Jackie quickly, very quickly. And he was accepted by the players as well. You hear some racist stories, but that was minor compared to the whole picture. But the hotels and the restaurants did not accept Jackie for a long time. When he went out in his civvies, on the streets, he was a black man in America. He didn't have the accommodations offered to him. So he would stay in private homes. We'd go back to the hotel in Chicago, somewhere, and he wouldn't be with us. He'll be in a cab or a private car, going to stay in a private home somewhere. It's kind of unbelievable. It took until 1954 for the Chase Hotel in St. Louis to permit black players to stay at their hotel, and we had six black players by that time. The hotel let the bars down. They could stay there, but they had a prohibition in the dining room; they couldn't eat in the dining room; they had to take room service. Isn't that amazing? That lasted for about a year and that went by the boards. By the time that happened that was 1954 and Jackie had been in the league since 1947.

"Well, Don Newcombe came back from the service and he said, 'Why, when I just came out of the United States Army, for my country, and I can't even stay in the same hotel as my team?' Newcombe and Robinson went down to talk to the hotel manager and the hotel manager said, 'You can stay here, but you can't use the pool and you can't eat in the dining room.' Now, you can say that was a slap in the face when he saw so much discrimination, but it was a move. Now the next year, that came down.

"Jackie was a very intense person. He was not satisfied that there was so much discrimination out there. He would not be satisfied with his acceptance as a major league star. He brought new excitement to the game. He was controversial because he was outspoken.

"Dick Young [the writer for *The New York Daily News*] had a hard time with Jackie. Young said, 'How come when I talk to Campanella, he talks to me about baseball? When I talk to you, it's always about civil rights.'

"Jackie was civil rights orientated. He said, 'Hey, America is America. It's not for half the people and for the other half to stand on the side.'

"And Campy would say, 'Don't rock the boat. We've got it nice up here. It was a hard time to get up here, and I don't want to mess it up.'

"Well, those were two philosophies, but that never bothered our team. It never came up as a problem on the team, but philosophically Jackie and Campy were in two different camps and neither one wanted to apologize for how he felt. It was genuine.

"Jackie's experience was historic. How he did all that: he was competitive and hard-nosed, and he did a lot for civil rights, and he was kind of a martyr, really. Jackie's first son, Jackie Junior, came back from Vietnam with a drug habit and later was killed in an auto accident, and it devastated Jackie. He felt that he was responsible for giving so much of his time to civil rights causes that he hadn't spent enough time with his son. He said, 'Maybe I gave all my time to civil rights rather than to my son.' I never met a man that was more intense about what he was doing than Jackie. Anything, an issue, no holds barred. Jackie was intelligent, respected.

"There is a story in my little book [*Tales from the Dodger Dugout*] about the LA writer Jim Murray. There was a very poignant experience. Jackie and Jim Murray went at each other like tooth and nail. They were fighting in the newspaper; it was intense and insulting to each other. Yet, years passed and Jackie was losing his eyesight. It was in Cincinnati in the early 1970s and they met and Jackie apologized to Jim Murray in this way. He said, 'I'm sorry, Jim. I can't see you any more.'

"He was going blind. He died not long after that. And Jim Murray wrote this magnificent column, and in the final part of the column he described their differences, but he said what respect he had for everything that Jackie did and what he meant to his race, and Jim Murray ended his column by saying, 'I'm sorry, Jackie. I can't see you any more.'

"It hit me like a ton of bricks that these two men, at opposite ends of the pole on issues, can still have such marvelous respect for each other as individuals, and I just admired Jim Murray so much for that."

Clem Labine: "I'll be at the new Brooklyn ballpark when they dedicate the new statue of Jackie and Pee Wee. My wife and I were on the committee to choose the statue, and all the sculptors' model statues looked great. No matter what one is chosen, it will be fitting. We're looking forward to see it."

In a game at KeySpan against Lowell, the Cyclones were short of pitching help, as a few pitchers were injured, and the Cyclones have strict limits on pitch counts for all pitchers.

With the Cyclones leading 1–0, Frank Corr, normally an outfielder, came into the game as a pitcher and held Lowell to only a run with three hits and a walk over two innings.

The Cyclones brought in David Byard to pitch the final three innings, and the Cyclones scored a run in the 7th inning to take a 2–1 win.

Frank Corr had held the fort.

Mike Cox

Mike Cox enjoys practical jokes. While visiting Lowell, he discovered a shop that sold practical joke items. Cox purchased soap that made it look as if the user of the soap were bleeding. Mike also bought a powder that turned liquids into jell, and he bought some stink bombs.

> **Mike Cox:** "The Doubletree Hotel was about the nicest hotel outside of the Radisson, and I bought all that stuff. I bought chewing gum and the red soap. I gave it to Zaragoza, but it was getting all over him and he came out of the shower and it didn't work so well — but it worked well enough because Zaragoza came out of the shower and said to me, 'I knew you did this.' So it worked well enough. For Brett [Kay], I put stuff in his Gatorade, and it jelled his Gatorade over and he tried to drink it, and it was turned into jell. He couldn't drink it, and, of course, he came straight to me. I got to get someone else doing it so they won't come straight to me. I had one of those sulfur bombs, and we have a couple of rooms where we stay called getaway rooms, and I set them off, and the smell was so bad they couldn't stay in the rooms, and they blamed me again. They had to air out each room. That's the life of a starting pitcher. We don't have much to do. We have to break the monotony somehow."

Update of Games Played Through August 11

The New York–Penn League season had reached the two-thirds mark. In the McNamara Division, Brooklyn was leading the Staten Island Yankees by three games, and third place Pittsfield by seven. In the Pinckney Division, Williamsport had a seven game lead over Batavia. The regular season would end on September 5, two days after Labor Day. Only the first two teams in each seven game division make the playoffs.

Division Standings

McNamara Division	W	L	Pct.	GB	Streak
Brooklyn	38	14	.731	- -	W 6
Staten Island	35	17	.673	3.0	W 1
Pittsfield	31	21	.596	7.0	L 1
Hudson Valley	28	24	.538	10.0	L 3
New Jersey	22	30	.423	16.0	L 5
Lowell	19	33	.365	19.0	L 2
Vermont	18	34	.346	20.0	W 1

Pinckney Division	W	L	Pct.	GB	Streak
Williamsport	34	16	.680	- -	L 1
Batavia	27	23	.540	7.0	L 1
Oneonta	25	23	.521	8.0	W 2
Jamestown	25	26	.490	9.5	W 1
Auburn	23	29	.442	12.0	W 1
Utica	18	32	.360	16.0	L 1
Mahoning Valley	15	36	.294	19.5	W 1

Brooklyn was in first place in team batting average with .278, and the Cyclones also led the league with 38 home runs.

Jay Caligiuri was fourth in league batting average with .338. Caligiuri trailed Juan Francia of Oneonta, the league leader at .349. Brett Kay was hitting .339, but was a few plate appearances short of qualifying as a leader. Joe Jiannetti was hitting .359, but with only 90 official at bats because he played the first part of the season at Kingsport, he too lacked enough at bats, to qualify as a league leader. Pagan was hitting .303. Outfielders Toner and Lawson and Corr were all raising their averages with Toner and Lawson both up to .267. Frank Corr was up to .280. Shortstop Robert McIntyre was hitting only .194, but was tied for second on the team in home runs with six.

Team leaders in RBI were Devarez and Caligiuri with 27, McIntyre with 26, and Corr with 25. Jiannetti had 18 RBI in only 23 games.

Angel Pagan was leading the league in stolen bases with 22.

As for pitching, Brooklyn was still leading the New York–Penn League in earned run average with 2.18. Williamsport was second at 2.42, and Staten Island was third at 2.93.

Ross Peeples was leading the league in wins with eight, ahead of the Staten Island Yankees' Jason Arnold, who had seven. Harold Eckert, continuing his comeback from arm surgery, was tied for third with six victories.

In earned run averages, Peeples was fourth in the league at 1.38; Luz Portobanco was fifth at 1.38; Matt Gahan was tenth at 1.49.

While not having enough innings to qualify as official league leaders, Lenny DiNardo's ERA was at 0.51, David Byard's was at 0.59, Jason Scobie's was 1.19, Brian Walker was at 1.46, and Blake McGinley was 2.01. As far as pitching records, Peeples was 8–1, Eckert was 6–1, Cox was 5–1; and Portobanco was 4–2.

Harold Eckert

"In the rainout game, I pitched against the Yankees for the first time, and I felt really good. I was 6 and 1, and they were in second place right behind us, and I really wanted to get them. After that game, we did the cha-cha slide. Me and Peeps went out there. He did it one time before. I was in street clothes the time before, but I said that next time, I'll help you out. We went out there and started doing it, it wasn't cold per se, but it was pouring out and we were dancing, and we were giving the fans a show. That's what they're there for anyway. I had so much energy inside of me. On the days I pitch, I have so much energy, for two hours after the game I'm still wound up. The fans gave us a couple of dollars in tips. A couple of ladies were behind the dugout. They threw the money at us. We picked it up and kept it. We had a good time with the fans. It was a big game; we were just having fun. After that, when Guy Conti was there, he said when you come to spring training, get ready to teach the whole Met farm system how to do the cha-cha slide. You just listen to the music. It says take a left step, then a right step, then a slide; it's like a merengue almost.

"The next game I pitched, it was against Staten Island over there. It was a chance to get even. I liked it over there. There was a big crowd. A lot of people against you. I like adversity. A lot of Yankee fans and a lot of Brooklyn fans. This game we won, but I didn't get the win. It was me against this Anderson kid. Last year, he was the New York–Penn League Pitcher of the Year, so I was excited pitching against him.

"When I'm pitching, it's like *For Love of the Game.* It's my favorite baseball movie. I just shut the crowd all out, just like he does in that movie. I still watch it today and get kind of teary eyed."

Mike Cox

Mike Cox: "A lot of the team went to a game last night at Shea Stadium. We got to sit in the Diamond Club Suite. Fonzie set it up for us to sit in the Diamond Club Suite, but we also spent part of the time sitting right behind home plate. We were really close. It was great. There were so many of us; some of the guys were Lydon, Portobanco, Pittman, Bacani, Byard, Peeples, Olson and Kay. Brett Kay knows the third base coach on the Mets, John Stearns, and he kind of got us in the clubhouse after the game. Brett's dad played college football with Stearns at Colorado.

"We talked to Franco and Leiter in the clubhouse, and Piazza talked to us for a little bit. It was funny; they knew our record. They knew not just that we were in first place, but they knew our actual record of 49 and 21. One of their coaches John Stearns, came up and said, 'So this is what a team with a winning percentage of .700 looks like.'

"Mike Piazza wished us good luck, and he said, 'Wait till all you guys move up, it will feel like a step down facility-wise when you don't have eight thousand screaming people when you get to the next level.'

"Al Leiter [Mets star left-hander] came over and pointed out that Olson is a left-hander because when he stands, he slumps to the left. Actually, Ross [Peeples] got a glove from John Franco. And Byard got a glove from Todd Zeile. Eight or nine guys got a new pair of shoes, two or three cleats and about five or six pairs of running shoes. They just started passing out stuff. Zeile and a bunch of guys gave us batting gloves. You'll see a whole lot of us wearing new batting gloves tonight that we were given. They were really taking care of us.

"When you talk to the major leaguers in the clubhouse, you don't ask for autographs, and you don't ask about baseball. They have enough baseball talk from the media; they don't need it from us. We just talked to them about other things and got to meet them.

"Their clubhouse was actually smaller than ours at KeySpan. They have bigger individual lockers, but the actual clubhouse is smaller. They have two giant, flat screen TVs there, and they have all kinds of stuff set out for them like shaving cream, razors, deodorant. We have to supply our own. And I saw players walking out of there with steak, a real meal, not like our hotdogs. As soon as we got out of Shea, the cell phones started coming out, and everyone was on a cell phone calling people to tell them that we were just in the major league clubhouse. It took us about

KeySpan Park — right field side with the Parachute Jump.

ten minutes to walk to our cars because everyone kept stopping to make calls to say what just happened.

"We went to Lundy's Restaurant the other night. All the fans that sit behind the dugout, the real fanatics, were there. They paid to come to the dinner and talk to us, and they want to know everything that's going on, on and off the field. It was really nice.

"Trevor and Samantha were there. Trevor is in about the fifth grade and his sister Samantha, she's about ten, rides the bus to the game every day. She is upset because she's going to go on vacation now because she has to miss the games. She gets up early in the morning to ride the bus. Her dad is a New York City bus driver in Brooklyn; his name is Don Vito. And she rides the bus all day with her dad and then he lets her off the bus at six o'clock at night, and she comes to every game. She made sure that she'll be here for the playoffs."

Frank Corr

"On the previous off days, one time I went golfin' with David Byard. That was an experience in itself. We went in Flatbush at the Flatbush Golf and Country Club [*sic*], I guess. We just went out there to swing the shillelaghs, not worrying about what our scores were. Just to go out and have fun, and we ended up not doing that bad. This was the first off day.

"The second off day I did nothin'. I laid around.

"The third off day, I went into Manhattan and just walked around. They went into the wax museum. I didn't go in there because it was too expensive. It was like twenty bucks a head. I said to the guys, 'I mean it's an experience, but you guys take a lot of pictures. I'd rather look at the pictures.' A couple of guys that day had the opportunity to go to *TRL*, *Total Request Live*, for MTV, and I guess they went, and they were on live TV. Brett Kay was one of them, Ross Peeples. Somebody set it up, and they were wearing their jerseys on TV, so that was pretty cool.

"As far as living on a budget, there's always going to be times where you see something at the store, and you want to get it and that would dig into your finances a little bit. What I did was I sent my check home, and I would have my mom deposit it for me, and then I would just use my A.T.M. card, 'cause if I had the cash on me, then I would spend it. I spend less with the card. If I wanted something, I got it. It's only money, man. And as long as you're having fun, then it shouldn't matter. If I wanted to go out to Outback three nights in a row, then I would go.

"I went to Peggy O'Neills a couple of times; I went to The Salty Dog a few times, and that was about it. The Salty Dog was close to Peggy O'Neills. They were the easiest and closest to go to from where we lived. Sometimes when we went, there they were empty. Other times we went there, they were crowded. It's nice to hang out with people that you don't ever see. We would go with five or six guys — play some darts, play some pool, sing karaoke, just have a good time.

"In some ways, it's hard for the players to meet girls with all the traveling around; in other ways, it's easy. But I don't want a girl to know me because I'm a Mets baseball player. I don't 'drop the bomb' on them and say, 'I'm a Cyclone, I'm a Cyclone.' It's tough on me because I'm not real good at talking to them. There's a certain moment, place and time for that stuff. I met a few girls up there, but I was afraid of those girls from New York, man."

Jay Caligiuri

In the Ebbets Field days only a few players ever hit the Abe Stark sign (in the outfield) that promised a free suit for hitting it. The sign was near ground level behind the right fielder. In KeySpan Stadium, the sign was deep in left-center field.

Jay Caligiuri: "I hit the 'Hit Sign/Win Suit'" sign about a month ago. We were aware that you would win a suit if you hit the sign, but it's not like you're aiming for it or anything. It's on the Garage Clothing sign, right under the scoreboard. When I hit the sign, I really wasn't that aware of it because when you hit the wall there the ball bounces hard off it and is in play and all I was really thinking about was to keep running so I had a double. I didn't think about it until after the game when Gary Perone [Cyclones executive] told me that I hit the sign and I won the suit. And I said, 'Oh yeah? Sure did.'

"This was about a month, or a month and a half ago. It took awhile to get the ball rolling. But we had the day off yesterday, so they got us an appointment and I went to the Garage Clothing store to pick out the suit, and they had a whole wall of suits, and they said, 'Pick out any one you want.' And I picked one out, plus I was given a real nice shirt and tie. It was a dark gray suit, the tie was a lighter gray than the suit, and the shirt was a real light gray. I wore it last night. Before I went out I had to do a little alteration with the suit — I pinned up the pants because they were a little long.

"I took a friend to see *The Lion King*. It was my first Broadway show ever. I was ear to ear smiles the whole night; it was so entertaining. I've never seen anything like that. I think I'm the only one on the team who was able to see a Broadway show this year. I had a real nice date, and I was all dressed up. I had a good time.

"The night before we had a little celebration at Peggy O'Neills because we had a day off the next day. We've been to The Salty Dog a few times. We don't get out that often because we don't have time or don't have cars.

"We're looking forward to the playoffs, and we want to get the home field advantage. We don't lose at home."

Luz Portobanco

"I've never been to Brooklyn before. They said a lot of bad things were going to happen, and this and that. But, you know, it's bad everywhere you go. I grew up in Miami, in Overton. It's really bad there. Every place is gonna be bad in some place, man. So just go out there and be yourself. I really felt at home. Just be yourself. You act different, then you got problems.

"I took the subway home after games and nobody bothered me. In the beginning of the year I lived at St. John's University, and then when we had to move out, I lived with Jiannetti in the apartment over Fonzie's house. Sometimes, Fonzie would give us a ride home, but most of the time we took the subway home. It was five stops on the 'F' train.

"We would always get to the games early. We would get there and do early work. If we had to be at the park at three, we would get there around noon."

Harold Eckert

"If you were late for pregame stretch, you would maybe get a fine. One time I didn't feel well, and I was in the locker room, and Edgar was mad that I was late, and Bobby O. told me to explain it to him, and when I did he finally said, "All right." If they said report at three o'clock for stretch, they didn't mean 2:59 or something. You wanted to be there maybe fifteen minutes early. They had a saying coming out of the coach's mouth that on time means being fifteen minutes early. You had to be ready to go. I was out on the field early every time. When stretch was at three, I used to get there maybe around twelve so I wouldn't have to rush to get my work in. Every day you have things to work on, running or whatever. If I got there at one o'clock, then I might be rushed.

"A few of the pitchers used to run on the [Coney Island] boardwalk and so did Bobby Ojeda. When I'm on the baseball field, I feel different. A lot of people don't understand when they watch baseball how much it is a mental game. Greg Maddux used to say that he knew two or three pitches ahead what he was going to throw. So even when I'm running around the field, I'm thinking about my last game. I was bouncing the curveball. So I'm thinking what I have to do to fix it. Sometimes when I'm running around the field I think about a good game I had, and it keeps you fired up, and that keeps you going, and you kind of give yourself the chills sometimes. And sometimes you think about a bad game, and how a guy hit a double off me, and I have to work harder. I have the headset on with my music on, and I'm thinking about my game. There's a lot of things that happen inside the mind of a baseball player. I have a special stopwatch, so I can check my time on the laps I take around the field.

"You're always working on your legs, or your arm, the rotator cuff. You usually do most of your running the day after the game. You stay on the edge of the warning track all the way around because the grass is easier on your legs."

Brett Kay

"Before the game, I'd usually go down to the Mermaid Deli, which was just a block from the ballpark. Sometimes before the game, some of us would go out on Steeplechase Pier and watch the people fishing. Just think. Sometimes we'd just go out on the boardwalk and people watch. I lot of times people would recognize me — of course, I had a Cyclone bag with me, which made it easier. Some people would say, 'You're my hero.'" That was awesome. You're not going to get that anywhere else but here in Brooklyn.

"For me, living on a budget wasn't tough. My buddy owned the place where I stayed [in Manhattan], so rent was free. So the money I saved I used for food, 'cause I bought food all the time. And we'd go shopping on the road. I bought breakfast, lunch and dinner every day. I bought orange juice, bread and peanut butter just to keep me going, but when you eat out the money goes by fast in New York. When I was eager to go shopping once I ended up calling back home, my girlfriend's dad, for money.

"I called home a lot. My first phone bill was eight hundred dollars for two months. I called home, to my girlfriend, to as many people as I could."

INNING 8

The Playoffs

How the Cyclones Sought the Playoffs

The Cyclones went through August with a small lead over the second place Staten Island Yankees. This lead fluctuated back and forth. Most of the fans' focus was on the team hopefully defeating their rival Yankees and finishing in first place, but the league champion is the team that wins the playoffs, and the first object of business is to make the playoffs. The first and second place teams in each division make the postseason. The first and second place finisher of each division then play a best of three series to advance to the League Championship Series, also the best of three games.

On August 20, the Cyclones' lead was four games over the Yankees and nine games over third place Pittsfield. Cyclones fans who had been former Brooklyn Dodger fans remembered when the Dodgers lost a 13½-game lead over the Giants in 1951 and lost the pennant on Bobby Thomson's famous playoff home run, but this was different. The season in the New York–Penn League ends two days after Labor Day, and the fans were more focused on the Cyclones holding off the second place Yankees so that the Cyclones would win the division and have the home field advantage in the playoffs. But Brooklyn fans have learned, through bitter experience, to take nothing for granted, and so while they kept an eye on the Staten Island Yankees, they also noticed the Pittsfield Astros, and lurking behind them, the Hudson Valley Renegades. Tonight, the Cyclones played New Jersey, and it was John Franco Night. The popular Franco helped to draw a Cyclone record crowd of 8,168, all squeezed into a 7,500 capacity stadium, reminding many of when the Dodgers used to squeeze over 34,000 fans into a 32,000 capacity Ebbets Field. Franco, the Mets' longtime relief pitcher, grew up in Brooklyn in a housing project not too far from Coney Island. His father worked as a member of the New York City Department of Sanitation. Later, John lived in Bensonhurst, Brooklyn, only about ten minutes from Coney Island, and the fictional home of Ralph Kramden, of the hit 1950s television show *The Honeymooners* and later as the

John Franco addresses crowd at John Franco Night.

home of the John Travolta character in the movie *Saturday Night Fever*. Tonight, John Franco has many friends and relatives in the stands, and there is a large contingent of current and former New York City sanitation workers, some in faux orange work shirts, in the stands near the left field line. Franco, who now lives the short distance across the Verrazano-Narrows Bridge in Staten Island, has brought the team members and coaches of his son's Little League team. The Little Leaguers are lined up in front of the Cyclones' dugout, and before the National Anthem, they will run out on the field, and stand with a Cyclones player in their respective positions for "The National Anthem." Franco, in honor of his deceased father, always wears a New York City Department of Sanitation shirt under his uniform shirt when he pitches, emphasizing his love for his father. When he speaks to the crowd before the game, Franco says "that no matter what anyone else thought, my father always believed in me." Franco also says how much he enjoys his son's baseball team. Franco, who is 5' 10", on the small side, mentions that when he was a young player, some people said he was too small, and he says his father always believed in him. Franco adds that because his dad believed in him, then he believed in himself. Listening to all these words in the Brooklyn dugout are the Cyclones:

> **Mike Cox:** "When I heard John Franco speak, that encouraged me, because I'm not big, and I'm a lefty like he is, and he talked about never giving up and that inspired me."

> **Brett Kay:** "Some players may think they should be in a higher level than Class A, or they get down on themselves because they're not playing well. But look at Frank Corr and Jay Caliguiri. If you look at them, you'd think they're not the

greatest baseball players in the world. But Frank is one of the best players I've ever played with — he's so talented and mentally focused, and Jay's the same. And Bacani, too. Their physical stature isn't the greatest in the world and neither is mine, but somehow they've found a way to play."

Mike Cox started for Brooklyn and took his inspiration to the mound where he struck out the New Jersey Cardinals' leadoff man on four pitches. He continued to pitch well and held the Cardinals scoreless through five innings, striking out six and allowing only two hits. The Cyclones were also held scoreless through their first four at bats, but in the fifth, speedster Wayne Lydon, the fastest Cyclone, hit a triple and then scored on an infield error.

Because Cox had reached his pitch count, Australian Wayne Ough took over in the top of the sixth and had a rough inning, giving up three earned runs on two hits, a walk, two wild pitches and a hit batter. In the bottom of the sixth, power hitter Frank Corr hit a shattering blast. Unlike many of his power pokes, this one was a foul ball that broke the shatterproof glass in the press box high behind home plate, causing quite a commotion, no injuries, and laughs and cheers from the fans.

Another foul ball had Cyclone fan Mark Lazarus razing the sanitation department: "The foul ball went into the stands down the left field line," he said. "A sanitation worker tried to catch the ball, but dropped it. I yelled, 'No wonder my garbage is all over the street.'"

John Podres throws out a ball.

Blake McGinley, the stylish, thin lefty from Texas, came on to pitch the last three innings for the Cyclones and started off by working quickly, throwing strikes and retiring the Cardinals in order in both the seventh and eighth innings, and striking out three.

The game went into the bottom of the eighth with the Cyclones trailing by two runs. Jay Caligiuri, the Brooklyn first baseman, led off the inning, knowing that if he got on base it would bring up the potential tying run. Caligiuri, playing it smart, worked the count to three and two before drawing a walk and bringing up Frank Corr, the outfielder who tonight was the DH. Corr didn't break any glass this time as he hit the ball over the left field wall to tie up the game.

Hard-nosed third baseman Joe Jiannetti and catcher Brett Kay followed with singles, and after a fielder's choice, Forrest Lawson, coming on strong in August, also played it smart as he was looking to drive the ball out of the infield and he did just that, driving in the go ahead run with a sacrifice fly. Shortstop Robert "Mac" McIntyre drove in an insurance run with a triple.

Then McGinley went back on the mound. The Cyclones were leaving after the game for their longest road trip of the season — 425 miles to Mahoning Valley, Ohio — and perhaps McGinley heard the Academy bus in the parking lot, because he wasted no time striking out the first two Cardinals and getting the last to fly out to left, all on nine pitches to send the Cyclones to the showers, and the record crowd of Brooklyn fans home happy. With the sparkling efforts of smallish lefty Mike Cox and tall lefty Blake McGinley, and Brooklynite lefty Johnny Franco watching with lots of sanitation workers, it was the Cyclones who cleaned up and headed for Mahoning Valley.

The Cyclones boarded their bus and were gone before midnight for the eight-hour trip through New Jersey and Pennsylvania to Niles, Ohio, in the Youngstown area, where they were scheduled for a four game series with the Mahoning Valley Scrappers.

Mahoning Valley

The Cyclones were staying at the Days Inn, a modest motel on Youngstown-Warren Road, a highway in Niles. The motel was like something at which a Brooklyn Dodgers farm club in the 1950s might have stayed. It had a small wooden office in front and a two storied wooden motel with an outdoor swimming pool. It was a place where the frayed carpeting fit the decor, but the motel wasn't seedy or unsafe, just an economy place that was a reminder that this was still a short-season A League.

The highway area where the Cyclones stayed was suburban. What was most distinguishable about the area was its lack of place. In 2001 America, this could be anyplace. A few local restaurants and gas stations stood among chain stores like Staples and K-Marts. To writers who had experienced the singular features of Coney Island, the view of the New York skyline from the ballpark at Staten Island, the Berkshire Mountains behind Pittsfield's Waconah Park, the cornfield behind the outfield in New Jersey, the canals and brick of Lowell, Massachusetts, Mahoning Valley felt generic, almost frightening in its homogenous conformity. But the players liked it. The very preponderance of chain restaurants and chain stores reminded them of some aspects of their hometowns. And they were here for four days, not just one night as on some of their road trips. They could unpack and settle in.

As usual in the New York–Penn League, there was no off day for travel, so the players, who arrived at 7:00 A.M., had to play a game at 7:00 that night. Some had slept on the bus a bit, but most found sleep on the bus an elusive goal, only managing to nod off for brief minutes before being awakened. They slept at the hotel and then around noon began to stir. There was a China Buffet restaurant about 200 yards up the highway, and some of the players ate there for $6.95 for all you can eat, always an attraction for the budget minded players. About a ten minute walk in the other direction is the E-Mall, a huge mall, and behind that was Cafone Field, the home of the Mahoning Valley Scrappers. There was only one way in and out of Cafone Field and that was through the mall itself. The field was completed in 1999 and seats 6,000. The dimensions of the field, like the area, are generic and conforming, with 335 in both left and right fields and 405 in center — a uniform, average sized field. A unique feature was the pedestrian toll. Since the only way to enter the stadium is to first drive through the mall, there is a parking charge when one enters the stadium parking lot from the mall parking lot. But some baseball fans prefer parking in the mall and then walking in to the ballpark to save the parking fee. To prevent this, pedestrians are charged a $2 fee to enter the parking lot, the only such charge in the New York–Penn League, if not in professional baseball.

In the first game, the Cyclones started Lenny DiNardo, the 6' 4" left-hander out of Stetson University. DiNardo, who pitched for Team USA and was a third round draft pick, started the game by giving up three straight hits and two runs, then he retired 15 out of the next 16 batters, allowing only a walk in the third inning. Meanwhile, the Cyclones were possibly showing the effects of the all-night ride as they were shut out inning after inning. After the Scrappers scored two more runs in the sixth off reliever Rylie Ogle, the Cyclones continued to flail away without much success and ended the game with a 4–0 defeat, with only Joe Jiannetti getting more than one hit as he singled twice, and the Cyclones' other three hits weren't enough. The Cyclones made three errors, and after a mere 2:09 of playing time, they headed back to the clubhouse.

On the mound the next night was Ross Peeples. Peeples, who had been painting the corners all year and had been developing a slider and change-up with help from Bobby Ojeda, came into the game with a 9–1 record. Brooklyn had Francisco Sosa catching. Peeples continued to do well, holding the Scrappers to one unearned run in five innings and allowing only two hits. First baseman Jay Caligiuri hit one over the wall in left to tie the game in the fourth, but Mahoning Valley scored four runs in the eighth off Cyclone relievers to take the lead.

In a nightmare defensive inning, the Scrappers made six errors, including three by their catcher, and this gave the Cyclones three unearned runs in the sixth. This was the most errors many fans had ever seen in a half inning of professional play, and it was all the more shocking since most of the New York Penn–League games contained more mistakes than would occur at the major league level, but the games were not abnormally full of errors, and many were very well played defensively by both teams. There were more base running gaffs than on higher levels, but actual fielding errors in the season were not particularly high, with the Cyclones making 97 errors in the entire regular season.

The Scrappers scored four runs in the bottom of the eighth against relievers Orlando Roman and David Byard. Mahoning Valley held a 5–4 lead as the Cyclones came up in the ninth. Forrest Lawson, playing in about half the games each week, continued his good August as he doubled to lead off the inning. After Sosa lined out to first, McIntyre, in a late season battle to finish over .200, flied out to right. With two out, Kay pinchhit for Lydon, now starting and leading off in center field, with Pagan having a leg injury. Kay flew to left, and the Cyclones had lost two straight.

On August 23, the Cyclones were out to break a possible losing slide as they again faced the Scrappers. With Harold Eckert going for his seventh victory against one loss, the Cyclones must have caught up on their sleep. Eckert allowed only an unearned run in sixth innings as the Brooklyns pounded out 15 hits. Frank Corr hit his 12th home run, Noel Devarez also homered, and the hot Lawson had three hits, as did Joe Jiannetti. Brooklyn won 7–2.

Between Innings

Joe Jiannetti

"My best game was the third or fourth game that I was there, when I hit two home runs. I had a real good series at Mahoning Valley. Most of my family lives near Cleveland and I had about eighteen people at the game and I couldn't go up there and not perform. My grandparents were there, and my aunts and uncles and cousins.

"My other grandparents, Maw-Maw and Paw-Paw, are from West Virginia, but they moved down to St. Pete. Maw-Maw keeps all the stats on me, and she listens to all type games on the radio. So one time she called me up after a game and said, 'Warner says you're hitting this, but you're really hitting ten points higher. You go and tell him.' So the next day I went up to Warner, and I told him that Maw-Maw says she has me hitting ten points higher than he said I was. So Warner said, 'I don't think so. I keep pretty careful records.' So he pulled out his book and he checked my average. And he said, 'You know, she's right.'

"And after that , that night on the Internet, he said, 'I have to be real careful about my stats, Maw-Maw and Paw-Paw are keeping me on my toes,' and he mentioned what Maw-Maw told me. He got a real kick out of that."

The next night was Jimmy Buffet Night at Cafone Field. Before 5,089, about the Scrappers' usual crowd, Luz Portobanco was looking for his sixth win. Perhaps the crowd was its usual size because Jimmy Buffet was not there for Jimmy Buffet Night, nor was he scheduled. Jimmy Buffet Night means that a lot of the fans (well, some of the fans) wear Hawaiian shirts and drink in the Tiki Bar area near right field. The "Margaritaville" song also was played over the public address system and by a local band in the right field picnic area.

Perhaps Luz wasn't a Jimmy Buffet fan, and his control was off and he pitched four innings and gave up two runs on three hits and five walks. During the early innings of the game, something strange was going on in the Scrappers' bullpen. From the press box, Warner Fusselle lifted his binoculars and observed that the whole bullpen contingent was lined up, shoulder-to-shoulder, wearing giant sombreros. Then in the next inning, the sombreros disappeared. A few innings later, the sombreros were back.

A messenger traveled from the near empty press box (it was the start of the high school football season) to the bullpen. One of the relief pitchers explained the sombreros. "We wear them to cause a rally, but if we wear them too much, we can cause the sombrero power to be lost."

The sombreros might have been helping. There were worn when Mike Guglielbyski homered for the Scrappers in the fifth. Left-hander Brian Walker, the Mets' fourth round draft choice out of Miami University and a member of their national championship team, took over in the sixth for Portobanco. But maybe the sombreros weren't helping too much, as the game was tied at four going into the ninth. The Cyclones then scored six runs highlighted by a homer by Edgar Rodriguez, one of the heroes of the Brooklyn home opener. Jason Scobie closed the door with his third inning of scoreless relief, and the Cyclones had beaten the Scrappers and their giant sombreros.

After the game, the Cyclones didn't spend much time showering. They had another all night drive ahead as they drove the 425 miles back to Brooklyn so that they could get there for breakfast and then be back at the park later that afternoon for a game against Hudson Valley. Tomorrow's starter, Mike Cox, slept on the floor of the bus, which is actually the best place to sleep on the bus. Oh, those spoiled minor leaguers.

The next day not much happened. Only a combined 18 hits, a combined

Brawls and Bliss — the marriage proposal.

15 runs, two hit batters, five home runs, 23 strikeouts, a marriage proposal (accepted), and a bench clearing brawl with seven ejections. All of this non-activity occurred in two hours and 51 minutes. Radio announcer Warner Fusselle had written on the page of the game in his scorebook, in red ink, "Brawls and Bliss." Tonight was a night that reminded everyone that they were essentially performing in the midst of an amusement park. Lest they forget.

Perhaps if Mike Cox gets to the big leagues he'll buy his own bus so that he can sleep on its floor before big games, because eight hours on the floor of the Academy Bus did wonders for his pitching. Cox struck out the first Renegade batter, allowed a home run to Edgar Gonzalez, and then struck out the next two hitters. Cox struck out three more batters in the second, but he did walk a batter in that inning, and then, now driving the bus, shut the door, as he did not allow another base runner until a mere single in the sixth. Mike Cox reached his prearranged pitch count and left after six innings with 14 strikeouts. While Cox was striking out the Renegade world, the Cyclones had scored two runs in the third and another pair in the fourth, and with Blake McGinley taking over for Cox in the seventh, the Cyclones added two more runs in the seventh to take a 6–1 lead.

Normally, Friday night is Fireworks Night at KeySpan Park, but on this Saturday, the fireworks would all be on the field. Luis Candelario hit a homer over the left field fence for the second Renegade run in the top of the eighth.

And now for the bottom of the eighth. Leandro Arias, playing second base tonight, hit a homer to (where else) left. Then after a run, the bases were loaded with two out. Frank Corr, temporary Mill Basin, Brooklyn resident living in his aunt's cellar, came up with the bases loaded. Proving that Frank is a cellar dweller in residence only, he promptly hit the next pitch high into the night, over the left field wall and headed for Auntie's home for a grand slam and his league leading 13th homer. Rounding the bases, Frank was serenaded with calls from the stands of "Frankie, Frankie" as the Brooklyn crowd celebrated. Forrest Lawson was up next and hit another homer, also over the left field wall. (Because of the prevailing winds from the ocean.)

The Hudson Valley reliever, Pequendo, had now given up three home runs and six earned runs in the inning, and his earned run average was getting higher every minute. Francisco Sosa, the catcher, was now in the batter's box. The first pitch was a ball, and then the second pitch headed behind Sosa's head. This is the most dangerous pitch in baseball, as the natural inclination for a batter is to back away from a pitch near his head, and batters have been seriously injured backing into a pitch behind their head. The pitch hit the bat behind Sosa's head, and the ball rolled into the infield. The pitcher, Pequendo, fielded the roller and Sosa raced to first. The throw beat Sosa and Sosa crashed into the first baseman. Sosa and the Renegade first sacker were fighting, and both dugouts emptied.

And then there was literally a Coney Island brawl as a Renegade player fired a helmet at Sosa, but the helmet sailed into the stands. Both benches emptied. Luz Portobanco had run out of the dugout to defend his good friend and regular battery mate, Sosa. Joe Jiannetti, the former high school football star, raced into the middle of the brawl. Noel Devarez came out of the dugout too, along with all the other Cyclones. Even Mike Cox came out, but he didn't feel like fighting.

Mike Cox

"I think the main factor in my pitching that night was that my curve ball was under control so I could throw it even behind in the count. It was my best game anywhere. The biggest compliment I've gotten from anybody was when Howard Johnson said it looked like, 'You're just playing catch with your catcher. 'Cause he never looked up to see the hitter.'

"That was the night of the fight when I struck out fourteen in six. When I was in Pittsfield last year, we also got in a fight with that team. The pitch was behind Sosa's head, and then it hit his bat, and he ran down to first and ran into their first baseman. Then the fight broke out, and I wasn't in a mood for a fight after having a career day, so I tried to grab Portobanco to keep him from running onto the field, and then a big guy charged at Portobanco and they went at it. And then I told Ross and Eckert to get back in the stands, they were in civies, 'cause they could get in real trouble if they were on the field, but I guess the tapes of the game didn't show them out there. I didn't want them to get in trouble because we would be losing two starting pitchers."

After the wild melee, more of a real fight than most baseball brawls, which often involve a lot of wrestling, the umpires threw out four Cyclones: Sosa, Portobanco, Jiannetti, and Devarez, along with three Renegades.

Brawls and Bliss — the fight.

Joe Jiannetti: "I saw their third baseman running around, and I thought he might go after someone from the side, so I was trying to stop him from doing that. At first after the game, we didn't hear anything, but then a couple of days later I was told that I was suspended for four games. Plus, I got a hundred dollar fine. They took the hundred dollar fine right out of my paycheck, but actually, Maw-Maw paid for it."

After order was restored, McGinley allowed a leadoff home run in the top of the ninth and then closed out Hudson Valley for a 21–3 Brooklyn victory.

The next day, DiNardo and the Cyclones dropped a well-played, peaceful 3–2 game at Hudson Valley.

The Cyclones went into the game against Pittsfield on August 27 with a chance to clinch a playoff spot if they beat their closest pursuer, the visiting Astros. The Cyclones started the game with a 47–20 record and the Astros trailed the Cyclones by seven games at 39 and 28. If the Cyclones won, they would clinch a playoff spot because third place Pittsfield mathematically couldn't catch them, although Pittsfield or fourth place Hudson Valley could catch the Staten Island Yankees to finish second and earn the remaining playoff slot.

Ross Peeples started the game looking for his tenth win, a great total for a short season team, roughly equivalent to winning 21 games over a major league 162 game season. There were 8,025 fans at KeySpan but not all of them were aware that the Cyclones would clinch a playoff spot if they won. Peeples was hit more than usual, and he walked four batters, and Pittsfield advanced their own playoff hopes with a 9–2 win. Brooklyn would have another chance to clinch a playoff spot in the second game of the series.

The starter in the next game of the home series against Pittsfield was New Jersey native Harold Eckert, born in Perth Amboy, which can be seen across the water from Steeplechase Pier, the Coney Island pier that is just beyond the right field fence. As usual, Harold had a group of about thirty family and friends at the game. "Eck" was hit around a bit and gave up four earned runs in six innings. Jay Caligiuri drove in Arias and Jiannetti with a double in the first, and in the second Noel Devarez, after over two months of play, hit the first-ever home run to center field at KeySpan Park. In the fourth, newcomer at shortstop Sean Pittman, recently called up from Kingsport, singled Sosa to third, and Pagan drove the catcher in with a sacrifice fly. In the sixth, Sosa hit his first home run of the season. Pittsfield scored in the seventh, but the Cyclones took a 7–5 lead into the ninth. Relief pitcher Roman held Pittsfield scoreless, and Brooklyn had clinched the playoffs.

It wasn't the majors and it wasn't the Dodgers, and it wasn't even a clinching of first place, but for the first time since 1956, a Brooklyn baseball team would be in the postseason. Older Brooklyn fans couldn't turn back the clock, but after all those years of the past, there now was a present tense and baseball. And there was a future tense, too. Brooklyn was going to the playoffs, and it wasn't the World Series, it was 2001, and the ex–Ebbets Field faithful were going to see the New York–Penn League playoffs, and they were plenty happy about it.

Pittsfield wasn't happy about it. Rumored to be in their last year in the league, Pittsfield might not have baseball next year at Waconah Park, and the team and their fans were making possibly their last run at the playoffs. Brooklyn had lost their team to Los Angeles after 1957, and the Mets' New York–Penn League affiliation had switched from Pittsfield to Brooklyn for 2001. In a way, Brooklyn had replaced Pittsfield, who had now an affiliation with the Astros, but an affiliation that might wind up in the Troy area for 2002. So Brooklyn was just beginning again, and Pittsfield was probably ending.

With second place clinched, the Cyclones set about trying to clinch first place over their arch rivals, the Staten Island Yankees. Going into the last day of August, Brooklyn held a four game lead over the Yankees, who were trying to catch Brooklyn and yet hold off Pittsfield and Hudson Valley, who had outside chances of overtaking them.

The Cyclones' regular season was down to seven games, all against the Batavia Muckdogs. Batavia is located midway between Buffalo and Rochester and is a good spot for growing onions. A muckdog is a dog that goes into the soft ground, the muck, and digs up the onions. Most Brooklyn fans had no idea where Batavia was, and none of them knew what a muckdog was, but 8,088 of these fans came out to see the game. Brooklyn was playing some-body — and that was enough.

The Batavia club is a Phillies farm team and their uniforms were Philadel-phia hand-me-downs. Brooklyn might not know anything about Batavia, but the fans were familiar with Philadelphia teams. Brett Kay homered in the first, then lightning fast Wayne Lydon created a run all by himself. Wayne reached on a walk in the fifth, and then stole second and third, and scored on the Batavia catcher's wild throw toward third. Lawson, playing right field, stayed hot as his second hit of the game drove in the winning Brooklyn run. McGinley took his record to 5–0 with three perfect innings of relief.

After a 2–1 loss to Batavia the next night, in which Caligiuri went 3 for 4 with a home run, the Cyclones entered the month of September with a chance to clinch first place in the McNamara Division with a win over Batavia. Clinching first place would mean a home field advantage in the first round of the playoffs, a two games out of three event in which the team with the higher seed gets the second and, if necessary, third games at home. It would also be a chance for Brooklyn to take it to the Staten Island Yankees. For some Brooklyn fans, this rivalry was Brooklyn versus the Yankees, a rivalry in which the Yankees, except for 1955, always won. For other fans, the rivalry meant Mets versus Yankees, a rivalry sparked by the just completed Subway World Series. And for other Brooklyn fans, it was Brooklyn against Staten Island, a rival borough just minutes away across the Verrazano-Narrows Bridge. No matter how you looked at it, Brooklyn fans wanted to win. Other fans around the league all wanted their teams to win, but in Brooklyn it felt different. Here, Brooklyn fans *really* wanted to win. To most Brooklyn Cyclone fans, there was a matter of borough pride in this. And maybe a little defensiveness. Brooklyn for years has been the subject of jokes. Look at some old World War II movies where the guy from Brooklyn always speaks exaggerated Brook-lynese and is the butt of all the jokes. Brooklyn residents like making jokes, but they resent being the objects of condescending humor. Brooklyn fans remember all the years of Brooklyn Dodger frustration, losing year after year to the Yankees in the World Series and always saying, "Wait till next year." Their next year finally came in 1955, and then two years later their team was gone to Los Angeles.

Many of the Cyclone fans weren't even born in 1957, but even the younger Brooklyn fans had picked up the underdog mentality from their parents and grandparents. Brooklyn has traditionally been looked down upon by some in Manhattan, despite Brooklyn having many great residential neighborhoods, Prospect Park, renowned cultural centers such as the Brooklyn Museum and the Brooklyn Academy of Music, and the Brooklyn Botanic Garden. Actu-ally, Brooklyn was now in many ways a trendy place with a burgeoning colony of artists and writers in Williamsburg and many "hot" restaurants and night spots in the borough.

In baseball, Brooklyn had been robbed too many times. This was Class A baseball, but the fans didn't have the Dodgers, they had the Cyclones, and after 44 years they had a chance for a division championship — in effect, a pennant.

Mike Cox started for Brooklyn. Some of the Cyclones like Jiannetti, Devarez, and Sosa had been suspended for a few days because of the fight, but the New York–Penn League kept this very quiet and never actually released a suspension list. Portobanco was also suspended, but his suspension hardly affected him, as he only had to push back his starting assignment two days.

Cox's control was off. He struck out seven batters in 2⅔ innings, but he was often pitching with full counts on batters and was issuing walks. An error and some hits led to six runs, only one of them earned. But Cox had thrown 94 pitches and was removed for DiNardo in the third inning. In the Brooklyn half of the third, red-hot Forrest Lawson hit a home run, Edgar Rodriguez doubled, and John Toner singled in Rodriguez. The Cyclones kept rolling on with single runs in the sixth and seventh. DiNardo held Batavia scoreless for four and two-thirds innings, and Jason Scobie pitched the eighth and continued the string.

In the bottom of the eighth, Brooklyn's Brett Kay drew a walk, and after Caligiuri popped out, Frank Corr was hit with a pitch. Lydon ran for Corr. Then Lawson was on with a fielder's choice and an error, and Kay scored on the play. Then Rodriguez hit a double, pushing Lawson to third. Then in a play reminiscent of the Bill Buckner error on a soft Mookie Wilson grounder that gave the Mets life in the 1986 World Series, John Toner's soft grounder to first was missed by Batavia first baseman Margalski, allowing Lawson to score the tying run. In the top of the ninth, Scobie once again stopped Batavia and the Cyclones came up in the bottom of the ninth with a chance to clinch the McNamara Championship.

With one out, second baseman David Bacani bunted for a hit and moved to second on third place hitter Brett Kay's single to left. Jay Caligiuri flew out to right and the runners held. Then Wayne Lydon was up. Lydon had come in to run for DH Frank Corr in the eighth inning and remained in the game as the DH. Lydon hit a grounder to short that was muffed for an error and Bacani came around to score the winning run. It was the run that gave Brooklyn its first baseball championship in 45 years.

Pandemonium broke out on the field as the Brooklyn players celebrated. The players pounded on each other and then lined up on the infield to dance to the Cha-Cha Slide, this year's version of the Macarena as far as baseball songs went in Brooklyn. Almost all the fans stayed to celebrate, and the player's celebration moved on to Peggy O'Neills for a victory celebration that went on with fans, club officials, and friends.

The next game was anticlimactic as Brooklyn dropped a 1–0 game, played in two hours and six minutes, to Batavia. Ross Peeples pitched well, but the

Cyclones clinch first place — the "Cha-Cha" slide.

Cyclones managed only six hits and his record fell to 9–3.

Now the Cyclones were off to Batavia to continue playing the Muck-dogs for three more games, all of them meaningless in the standings. After those three games, the Cyclones would have to play the very next night after driving 366 miles, at Staten Island in the opening round of the best of three semifinal playoff series, going against the second place Yankees.

To the uninitiated, Batavia sounds like the name of a country that would declare a non-violent war against the United States just to receive aid from the United States after it lost (see the film *The Mouse That Roared*). Batavia is part of the old guard of smaller cities in the league, those teams like Oneonta, Utica, Auburn, and Jamestown from New York State that still remain in the league after similar cities like Elmira and Geneva are gone.

Batavia's field is in a residential area of older wooden houses. Once again, it seems to be the 1950s and the intensity is way down. Batavia is a small city — the way the entire New York–Penn League used to be.

The Cyclones pitched Eckert, with a record of 8–1. The Cyclones recovered their hitting as they pounded out 19 hits and won 14–6 with Eckert getting his ninth victory. After 8,000 fans a night in Brooklyn, Batavia's crowd of 1,309 felt miniscule. Brooklyn lost the next night, 2–1 in 13 innings. And in the regular season final, Brooklyn won 8–1 before a Batavia crowd of only 983 as Tommy Mattox, up from Kingsport, got the win as the regular pitchers were rested for the playoffs.

Between Innings

Brett Kay Reflects

"My year of baseball in Brooklyn is unbelievable. It is the most fun I ever had. This is the best year I ever had in terms of being consistent and of getting fun out of the game. In college, we would draw anywhere from between a few hundred to between three or four thousand a night. In the College World Series, I played in front of 27,000 people, but the 8,000 I play in front of in Brooklyn is better than the 27,000 that I played in front of in the College World Series. The fans are so — you just can' t explain. They are just so loyal. Teams are scared to come into Brooklyn because our fans were just so hostile. I lost a bat and a glove to a fan once. We were in an hour and a half rain delay, and I asked him the trivia question: Name four players who started their careers on one team in a city and ended their careers on another team in the same city. There are 16 people, but I just asked him to name four. The answer is: Mays, Aaron, Berra, and Babe Ruth. My trivia questions are almost impossible to answer, but I had heard this question, but the fan got it, and won a glove and a bat from me.

"I know some of the fans in section 14. I hang out with Mark [Lazarus]. I'll keep in touch with him and send out a Christmas card. I'll keep in touch with Christine and her daughter [other fans from Section 14]. I became real close to a lot of fans.

"Usually, after games I don't go out as much as the other players. I live in Manhattan and I usually just go home after the game, watch TV, eat and go to bed. I'm not too much of a social person as much as the other players are. I don't have time to go to too many places in Manhattan. I live in the Chelsea section, and sometimes I go out to dinner. One time I went to the Empire State Building, but I usually just went home. After games, I take the subway home from Brooklyn."

The regular season had ended. Ahead was a playoff game tomorrow against the Staten Island Yankees.

The Playoffs Begin

The Cyclones were originally planning to leave right after the series finals against Batavia and then travel all night, an eight hour trip, arriving at around

Cyclones at Staten Island Yankees — Scoreboard announces Battle of Boroughs.

7:00 A.M. in Brooklyn, then start their best of three game series against the Staten Island Yankees, twelve and a half hours later in Staten Island. Realizing that the Cyclones would have had to travel all night in the bus and then go to their homes after the bus arrived in Brooklyn and then be back at the Brooklyn ballpark less than eight hours later, Cyclone executives consulted with manager Edgar Alfonzo and decided that it would be better for the team to stay for the night in Batavia, and then get up early the next morning for the trip home — except they wouldn't actually be going home to KeySpan Park; instead, they'd go directly to Staten Island; otherwise, the players would basically have to leave Brooklyn just a little while after they got there. The team planned to leave Batavia around 8:00 A.M. and arrive at the Staten Island Yankees ballpark around 4:00 P.M., in time for batting and infield practice.

The night after the series finale in Batavia, radio announcer Warner Fusselle and a writer entered a Denny's restaurant, one of the few places open at 11:00 P.M. in Batavia. As their car pulled into the parking lot, they saw the Cyclones' team bus next to the restaurant. These things happen on the road in cities like Batavia. The players are night owls and most of the townspeople aren't, so late at night, at 11:00 o'clock in a restaurant, or at a Subway shop at 11:30 in Lowell, Massachusetts, or in the only open restaurant/pub on the main drag in Auburn, New York, running into the Cyclone players isn't a coincidence — it's almost inevitable. Like a traveling circus, or an acting troupe on the road, the Cyclones are a traveling community that goes into a town for a few nights, hardly sees the town in the daylight except for a small area near the team hotel, and then leaves for the ballpark in mid-afternoon, only com-

Playoff Game 1 — Luz Portobanco.

ing back to the town at around 11:00 P.M. after most of the town is closed. Usually an evening walk will find the Cyclones in small bunches: two or three at a pizzeria, two in a submarine sandwich shop, five in a tavern, some having beer, a few soda, all eating; a few heading to a convenience store.

Tonight, practically the whole team is in Denny's, players at six large booths, four or five at a booth. Fusselle makes the rounds of the tables, briefly chatting with each group. The Cyclones sit seemingly at random, but there are patterns. Many of the pitchers sit together. Guys just out of college often sit together. The Spanish-speaking players sit together. The Cyclones mix well racially; the few black players who are non–Hispanic usually sit together with the white non–Hispanics. The Spanish-speaking players often sit together just as a matter of ease. They find it easier to talk Spanish with each other, just as the English-speaking players find it easier to talk to other English speakers. Players like Joel Zaragoza, Angel Pagan, and Luz Portobanco, who are all bilingual, help to bridge the gap between English and Spanish speakers and help to bring the team together. Spanish-speaking players usually room together. Again, it's really a matter of language, not race.

On the Dodgers of the Jackie Robinson era, usually the only Spanish speaker was Sandy Amoros. Roy Campanella had picked up some Spanish when he played winter ball and was able to converse with Amoros, and Joe Black knew some Spanish, but the Cuban Amoros must have been lonely.

Today, nearly every team in organized baseball has numerous Spanish-speaking players. Almost all coaches in the minors know some Spanish now.

But tonight, the conversations, in any language, are subdued. They players all seem quiet, thoughtful. There is no raucous laughter, no yelling, and no horseplay. Though these players are college age, this is no college atmosphere. It's a professional atmosphere.

Anyone entering the room could probably figure out that these muscular and trim young men were athletes — the cream of the crop. But if a visitor were told that these fellows were a baseball team from a local seminary, and that they were all preparing for the priesthood, one could believe it. In truth, many of the players on the team are quite religious, but this was not the frivolity of the bar scenes in the movie *Bull Durham*, but the reality of professional ball players at a Denny's restaurant, no one drinking anything stronger than a soda; players eating Caesar salads and others cheeseburgers and fries; no beautiful young waitresses; no girls in the whole place; a team that has just finished a championship regular season and is awaiting the playoffs in about twenty hours at the other end of the state in Staten Island.

Tonight, they had played before a crowd of only 937 fans in a game that found Batavia playing out the string. The Cyclones in the season's finale were playing for a last chance to add to their averages. And they were playing not to get hurt. Tomorrow, they would be playing before what had been announced as a sellout crowd at Staten Island — in what for most would be their first professional playoff appearance. The players seemed reflective, or about as reflective as the relentless New York–Penn League schedule allows.

The Cyclone ride that is the season roars along at breakneck speed. Tomorrow morning, the bus that is the roller coaster car along the highway will take the Cyclones right into the home park of their biggest rivals. The players won't even go home. The Cyclone ride lets you off when the ride is over, not before.

Tonight's game had been truly minor league — running out the string minor league. There would be little minor league about tomorrow's game. It would be televised. A full stadium. The New York City skyline over right-center field. Press coverage from the New York City papers. The game sent all over the world on the Internet. It would be Brooklyn versus Staten Island. Brooklyn versus the Yankees, bringing out mostly frustrating remembrances for the old time Dodger fans, and for Met fans, bringing out the recent pain of the 2000 World Series when the Yankees beat the Mets four games to one.

In the stands would be Mark Lazarus, with 17 friends. And there would be regular Brooklyn fans such as Chuck Monsanto, Ed Gruber and his son Steve, and, of course, there would be Nick Cunningham, who had managed to get a ticket, somehow — he always did.

Lose the first game and the Cyclones would be one game away from ending their season — a season in which they defeated the Yankees in six out of eight games and finished four games ahead of them in the regular season. None of that mattered now. And the game wouldn't be at KeySpan Park, an amusement park within an amusement park. It would be at Staten Island, with a stadium that was nice, and dignified, and with the greatest view in the world: New York at night. To these players, seeing the New York City skyline staring at them just across the harbor must have seemed a little like the green light across the bay that Gatsby starred at in F. Scott Fitzgerald's *The Great Gatsby*— that faint, twinkling green light that was his dream, his dream of Daisy Buchanan, the love of his life. And here were the Cyclones, as well as their counterparts, the Staten Island Yankees, both of them five steps below the majors leagues — their *green* light. And just across that bay was what they wanted most of all, to play in New York City. So many years and so many miles to travel, just to get across that harbor to play in Shea Stadium or Yankee Stadium.

In a Darwinian process that started before they were born, these players were made for this moment, and then developed for this moment. All with athletic ability far superior to most, usually, the best of the players all around them from Little League on up, they fought through layers and layers of players to get to this point of playing for a professional team. They are the most competitive of people, and the more competitive ones among them will have the edge to move up. Just to sign a professional contract, they are already one out of a thousand. Sure they play for statistics and for recognition from the team's executives so that they can move up, but they are by nature and conditioning highly competitive. They are, most of them, far from their families. Many are far from their home country. They miss their families, their girlfriends, their friends. They play, the first year players, for about $20 a day. They spend a lot of that on phone bills and food.

Some of them have been to the College World Series. Some have played for their countries' national teams. They have had three days off in 79 days. They know that next year, if they "move up," they may be playing before lots of crowds of 500 on either of the next two rungs in the system. Many have been playing nonstop baseball since the winter before their last college season. But this isn't the Super Bowl. It's not like the National Football League where players wait a week or two before the big game. Here, you play at Batavia one night, and 21 hours later you start the playoffs, a 400-mile bus ride away.

September 6, 2001 4:00 P.M.

The Cyclone bus pulls up to the Richmond County Savings Bank Stadium. Constructed with buff color bricks to match the bricks on the Staten Island Ferry Terminal next door, the ballpark's home plate faces New York City Harbor and the Manhattan skyline. Bobby Ojeda has ordered a spread of food from a Staten Island caterer for the Cyclones' locker room, and the team departs the bus and heads for the locker room, large and carpeted, much

like their own and more major league than the locker rooms in Batavia,
Auburn, and Pittsfield.

> **Mark Lazarus:** "The first playoff game was in Staten Island. Surprisingly, the
> game is not sold out after all. A foul-up in communications resulted in newspa-
> pers printing that the game was sold out, and there are areas of empty seats along
> each foul line. One of the girls in the section, Christine, calls me up and says, 'Do
> you want to go to the game?'
> "I said, 'Of course, but you can't get tickets.'
> "But Christine found you could get tickets, and I ordered 18 tickets and one of
> the guys from our section who wanted to go to the game was Frankie 'Legend,'
> who runs the Legends Limousine Service — they advertise on one of the billboards
> at the KeySpan Stadium. Frankie decides to take our group, most of the 18, in two
> of his limousines, for free. And he drove."

Mark Lazarus, Ed and Steve Gruber, Chuck Monsanto and Nick Cunningham are on the first base side of the field, behind the Cyclones' dugout.

Once after the game at Staten Island that the Cyclones lost, Nick made
fun of the Cyclones saying, 'Hah, you guys lost!' Then he went up to Mike
Cox and asked for tickets for Friday's night game and Mike Cox laughed and
got him the tickets.

> **Mike Cox:** "Nick was a changed man at the end of the year. He was a Yankee fan
> through and through; he was strictly a Yankee fan, but then by the end of the year
> he rooted for us."

The Brooklyn fans are louder than their Staten Island counterparts, and
the Brooklyn fans make up about a third of the crowd, highly unusual in the
New York–Penn League where the visiting team usually has only a few fans,
mostly some friends or relatives of the visitors.

The Staten Island press box is overflowing, and the writers are arrayed
in a special press area set up outside the actual press box. Numerous newspapers, two radio stations and several television outlets are covering the game.

The Cyclones start a lineup of Pagan in center field, Bacani at second,
Jiannetti at third, Caligiuri at first, Corr in left, Kay at DH, Devarez in right,
Sosa catching, and McIntyre at shortstop, with Portobanco pitching. On the
mound for the Yankees is Blankenship, recently sent down from Greensboro of
the higher South Atlantic League. Their lineup featured John-Ford Griffin, a
top batting prospect, and Shelly Duncan, the man Brooklyn fans liked to antag-
onize ever since he had had a run-in with catcher Brett Kay on a tag play at the
plate in an earlier game in Staten Island. Brooklyn fans would repeatedly call,
"Shelly, Shelly!" when he came up to bat. Another key Yankee was Aaron Rifkin,
a teammate of Brett Kay and David Bacani at Cal State–Fullerton.

As the game was about to start, the Brooklyn fans were shouting even
before the first pitch. Pagan flied out, and then David Bacani drew a walk,
and after a Jiannetti fly out, Bacani stole second and then went to third on a
Blankenship wild pitch. Behind first base, the Cyclone fans were jumping up

Playoff Game 3 — Brett Kay and Howard Johnson.

and down, but Caligiuri flied out to end the threat.

After a scoreless round by each team, the Yankees scored in the bottom of the second when Juan Camacho doubled and later scored on a Jason Turner single. Blankenship was shutting down the Cyclones, who threatened in the fourth on a Caligiuri double and Corr single, but failed to score.

After a Yankee run in the fifth, Blankenship continued to hold the Cyclones at bay with his pinpoint control. The Cyclone at-bats seemed to be quickly over, almost before they started.

Portobanco was removed after seven innings, having allowed two runs, both earned, on six hits. McGinley came on to pitch. Then in the Yankees' seventh, Bernie Castro singled and after two outs, the Yankees put together two hits and a walk, to take a 4–2 lead, and Jason Turner followed with a two run triple. The four run Yankee lead seemed huge.

Meanwhile, the Cyclones looked tentative in the field, making four errors, none of which resulted in runs. Blankenship held the Cyclones in the eighth, and after a scoreless Yankee eighth, the Cyclones had their last chance.

Ryan Clark came in to pitch the ninth for Staten Island. Frank Corr hit an 0-2 pitch for a single, and then Kay, with his good batting eye, drew the count to three and two before drawing a walk to put the potential Cyclones' tying run on the on-deck circle. But Devarez struck out, Sosa hit a grounder to second that forced Kay, and then Edgar Rodriguez pinch hit for McIntyre, and on an 0-2 count, he struck out swinging.

Luz Portobanco: "In the playoffs, I pitched the opening game and we came straight from a nine hour road trip and everybody was dead. On the bus trip from Batavia, I had to sleep on the floor of the bus, but like I said, I go out there like a soldier. Ain't nothin' stoppin' me, I go out there and I left the game down 2–1 in the sixth inning, but then the Yankees scored four runs and we lost that game."

It had taken only two hours and 29 minutes to put the Cyclones in a back-to-the-wall position. If they didn't win their next two games, both at Brooklyn, the season would be over. And despite all of the success on and off the field, losing to the Staten Island Yankees would cast a pall on their initial season. If they didn't win the two games back in Brooklyn, it would be that plaintive Brooklyn wail of yesteryear — "Wait till next year!" Brooklyn fans used to say, "Wait till next year" when Yankee or Giant fans taunted them about the end of Brooklyn seasons, most of which ended in the golden years with a close pennant defeat or a defeat in the World Series to the Yankees.

Mark Lazarus: "My impression of the ball game? I had no impression of the ball-game because they played so lousy. They were exhausted. We all knew they were exhausted from the eight-hour bus ride from Buffalo or whatever. And they made four errors and they looked flat. Portobanco pitched his heart out, and their offense was nonexistent that night.

"And the one thing all the fans were saying when we left the park was, 'Wait till they come to our ballpark. We'll take care of them.' We made a commitment as fans to make sure the Yankees weren't going to play their best ball when they came to Brooklyn. We were going to get on them from the first pitch."

In Brooklyn's glory years, the players weren't as distant from the fans as major league players are now. The fans knew the Dodgers from their neighborhoods. The Dodgers often shopped in the same stores, went to the same churches, sometimes lived not only in the same neighborhood, but also sometimes in an apartment in the same house. And the Dodgers weren't almost a brand new team every year as sometimes happens in the major leagues today. The core of the Dodgers team stayed nearly the same for the entire 1947–1957 period. For the Dodgers fans then living in Brooklyn, they almost all knew some of the Dodgers, or at least saw them around.

Although the Cyclones were brand new in Brooklyn, their fans knew them about as well as a 12-week period would allow. The serious Cyclone rooters spoke to the Cyclones at almost every home game and at some of the road stops. Their fans would go to one of the team dinners at Lundy's Restaurant, or meet up with the Cyclones at Peggy O'Neill's or The Salty Dog. The Cyclones had signed autographs for their fans' children or grandchildren. The fans had given the players home cooked food. The players talked to the fans after games outside the players' entrance. Younger fans had never had a Brooklyn team to root for — nor had the fifty year old and over Brooklynite, since

1957 — so the fans were happy to be fans. And the players, who had played before 500 fans a game at Kingsport, or relatively small crowds in college, loved the attention. Some of the players had played before large college crowds, but the enthusiastic Brooklyn fans were something they didn't expect.

Nobody wanted it to end. The Cyclones hadn't played well and refused to use the long trip before the first playoff game as an excuse for their play, but the long bus trip had to take something out of them. The team appeared confident, but a little stunned. One day they were in Batavia playing a meaningless game, then the next day they are one defeat away from elimination. There was no time to rest up or catch one's bearings. The second game of the series would start across the harbor in Coney Island tomorrow night. The Coney Island Cyclone ride takes one minute and 51 seconds, and then it's over. No one knew how this ride would end.

Between Innings

Frank Corr

Frank Corr: "The Staten Island Yankees played a real good ball game against us, but we weren't up to par. Something didn't click the first night. That was the night we got beat. Then we came home, and that was the one thing everybody was talking about in the locker room and on the bus on the way home was that "Hey, guys. We're going back home now." We're going to our house. It's time to step it up a notch.

"We came to the field the next day, and Fonzie said to us, "We would have had to win two games to win it anyway, so why not win these two?" And he's right. It was a totally different team from the night we were in Staten Island to the night we were in Brooklyn. You could just tell it. The excitement, the enthusiasms, the desire, the heart, the hunger to want to get out there and get after it man, and almost go for blood, to tell you the truth."

Harold Eckert

Harold Eckert: "We weren't down, but we felt more pressure because if we lost one more, we're done. The way the rotation worked out, I told Bobby O. I would pitch in relief if I was needed. Bobby O. told me before the game to be ready if I was needed. So I knew I'd probably be pitching in the second playoff game.

"It felt like back to college where I would be out in the game when I was most needed. To me, when an athlete steps it up in the postseason, that's what he's most remembered for.

"I felt before, that driving in from Edison, I knew that if there was a problem, I would be in there. I was in the dugout right from the start. Cox was pitching. He was hit a bit in the beginning. It was close. It was 4–3, and I had a feeling that I was going in. So I went down to the bullpen, and I started stretching and tossing.

"I came in in the sixth inning. I felt it was my job to get us to the next day. To close out the game. I knew it was up to me. It was total concentration. There's playoff fever. The game was on TV. I was fired up. I have the tape at home."

That night there was no relaxing at any of the Cyclones' haunts. Every-

Playoff Game 3 — Angel Pagan steals second base.

body went home and rested.

September 7, 2001

The next night brought another capacity crowd to Brooklyn. There were comparatively few Staten Island rooters in the crowd — they couldn't get a ticket. Mike Cox was scheduled to start for the Cyclones, and Harold Eckert was ready to come in for relief. The Yankees' starting pitcher was Jason Anderson, an outstanding prospect .

> **Jay Caligiuri:** "On the next game, back in Brooklyn, I went out early to sign autographs because I thought 'If this is our last game, I want to take all this in one last time,' and while I was signing autographs, the people were saying to me, 'Come on. There's no way you guys are going to lose. You can do it. You guys were great to all our kids.'
>
> "It was time for a little payback, and the fans knew that. The fans said, 'Either way, win or lose, you guys were great to all our kids, and you've made our summer unbelievable!' It was something I'll never forget, and I go to the locker room and I said, 'We can't lose in front of these people. They're so amazing; they're so behind us!' And we got out on that field, and it was like something special is going to happen."

Brooklyn's lineup would have Pagan in center, Bacani at second, Jiannetti at third, Caligiuri at first, Kay catching, Corr at DH, Lawson in right, Toner in left, and Pittman in place of McIntyre at shortstop. Pitching was Mike Cox.

Mike Cox

"The first playoff game, we can't blame it on the trip from Batavia, but when we lost, the pressure landed on me because I had the start the next night.

"That night, nobody was packing. Nobody was doing anything. Nobody wanted to leave. It was kind of a confidence booster when no one packed, saying, 'If we lose, we're ready to go.' But they didn't.

"I slept fairly well, but that morning I just couldn't keep still. I wanted to actually walk to the park, but I knew it was too far. David Byard would drive one of the team vans to the park.

"There was lasagna there before the game that I tried to eat at the Mermaid Deli, if they had it that day. They told us in spring training to get in a ritual before the game. Just keep it a good routine throughout the day. We got to the park around two that day. I went down to the Mermaid and got food and brought it back, and then I had to wait. That's the toughest part of being a starting pitcher. You don't go out early and stretch and work out. I go out fifteen minutes before game time. When I'm at home, I probably stretch for five minutes, and then I throw for twelve. Bobby has a set time he wants you to leave the bullpen before the game. Bobby would signal the announcer that the starting pitcher was ready, and then the Cyclone announcer would say, 'And now, here's your Brooklyn Cyclones!'

"It was amazing, the atmosphere. Even throwing my bullpen pitches. I was so nervous; I was talking to Forrest [Lawson] and I'm looking down at my feet and trying to wiggle my toes, and I can't feel my toes."

The screaming was out of sight as Cox toed the rubber. Up for the Yankees was leadoff man Bernie Castro. Cox threw three straight balls and the crowd grew a little apprehensive. Cox got a called strike and then walked Castro.

> **Mike Cox:** "I walked the first guy. My first two pitches were one hoppers to the catcher because I was gripping onto the ball so tight. I was just trying to throw it right over the middle, but I was so worked up and so nervous. I finally looked up at Bobby, and he's making a hand motion 'down,' meaning calm down."

Cox then got Andy Cannizaro to fly out and then John-Ford Griffin, whose name sounded Hollywood, struck out, and Castro was doubled up as Kay threw him out trying to steal second. In the Cyclones' second, Pagan was called out on strikes. Then so was Bacani . Then so was Jiannetti.

In the top of the second, shouts of "Shelly, Shelly!" rang out from behind the Brooklyn dugout in Section 14, the key section of Brooklyn rooters presided over by its unelected mayor, Mark Lazarus. Chuck Monsanto, Ed Gruber and Steve Gruber, and Nick Cunningham were yelling "Shelly! Shelly!" It was reminiscent of when the New York Ranger fans at the Madison Square Garden used to chant "Carol! Carol!" at Carol Vadnais when he played for the Boston Bruins.

Cox's first pitch was a ball. Then he came in with a strike, and Duncan swung and missed. The chants of "Shelly" got louder. Cox then got Duncan to swing and miss at his next pitch. "Shelly! Shelly!" said the Brooklyn partisans from Section 14. Cox's next offering was hit by Shelly Duncan over the left field wall.

> **Mike Cox:** "Shelly Duncan just got a good pitch, a fastball away, and he just turned around on it. That's when I heard the roar of the crowd saying, 'Get him out of there. Go to the bullpen.' It wasn't personal, but it was saying get him out so the team can win, which is fine."

After two outs, the Yankees put together singles by Turner and Chris Martin, followed by a two-run double by Omir Santos. It was now 3–0 Staten Island, and Brooklyn saw their season evaporating before their eyes. Cox got the next man, Castro, but the damage was done. Three runs scored and Anderson was still pitching for the Yankees.

After a Caligiuri fly out, Brett Kay worked the count to three and two and kept fouling off pitches. With Brooklyn down three runs, his job was to get on base and he did, finally walking on Anderson's ninth pitch to him. Corr walked. Forrest Lawson flied out to center, the runners holding, and that brought up the eighth hitter, big John Toner. Toner is strong and looks like he can hit a ball out of any park, but this year he has been over trying, trying to hit a ball 500 feet when 400 would be just fine. Batting coach Howard Johnson has been trying to get him to relax at the plate. Easier said than done. Relaxed or not, Toner hit the first pitch on a line to right field for a double, sending Kay home and Corr to third base. Shortstop Pittman drew a walk and then Angel Pagan hit a line drive double to left to score Frank Corr and Toner. Anderson got Bacani to bounce back to him for the third out, but the game had been tied at three.

Now Cox had rhythm, and he retired the Yankees in order. In the Cyclones' third, Kay came up with two out and once again got on base, this time being hit with a pitch. Then Frank Corr doubled to left to give the Cyclones a one run lead. Cox continued to roll and held the Yankees scoreless in the fourth. Then Brooklyn scored three more runs on singles by Pittman, Pagan and Bacani, and some Yankee misplays. Cox stopped the Yankees in the fifth, but Brooklyn was held scoreless in the bottom of the fifth, and the game moved to the sixth.

> **Mike Cox:** "When I left the game, I felt good after I pitched after the home run, and I was telling myself, 'This is going to be the last time you come off this mound.' It was a little bit emotional for me."

Harold Eckert came in to start the sixth for Brooklyn, and after giving up a double to John-Ford Griffin on the first pitch, Eckert got out of the inning without the Yanks scoring. In the sixth, Brooklyn added its sixth run as Toner singled and later scored.

The seventh inning was scoreless, and in the eighth the Yankees scored a run as Andy Cannizaro led off with a single and eventually scored on a groundout. The Cyclones went one, two, three in the eighth, and in the ninth Eckert allowed a leadoff single and then retired the side, ending the game on a called strikeout of Castro.

Brooklyn had come back from a 3–0 deficit to tie the series. The finale would be played tomorrow night at KeySpan.

Mark Lazarus: "And as it turned out, the first game back in Brooklyn, what'd the Yankees make, four errors plus two more bad plays? They played like a sandlot team. They couldn't make a throw. They couldn't catch the ball. We were on them from the first pitch. From the 'Shelly! Shelly!' to 'Strike the Bum out!' and just booing them when they were up at bat. Cox and Eckert shut them down with their pitching, and we won big. From beginning to end we were screaming, and rooting, and hollering. We were just making it loud. Every time they booted a ball, we got louder. Every time we did something good offensively, we just got louder, and straight through the game. And the game in the middle innings was a foregone conclusion.

September 8, 2002

For the series finale, Brooklyn started the same batting order that it went with in Game 2: Pagan, center field; Bacani, second base; Jiannetti, third base; Caligiuri, first base; Kay, catcher; Corr, DH; Lawson, right field; Toner, left field; Pittman, shortstop. The Brooklyn starter would be Ross Peeples. Ortiz started for Staten Island.

The first Yankee batter, Bernie Castro, put down a bunt and Jiannetti threw him out. Peeples walked the second Yankee batter, Kevin Thompson, and then got the next two Yankees. After a scoreless Brooklyn first, Peeples allowed a second inning leadoff double to Jason Turner, but Turner was stranded. Both pitchers were excellent, and the game was scoreless after five innings, the tension growing. After Peeples got the Yanks in order in the sixth, Frank Corr and Forrest Lawson started the Brooklyn sixth with singles, putting them on first and second. Toner moved them up with a sacrifice bunt, and after an out, Pagan drove in Corr with an infield single.

There was a scoreless sixth inning, and then the Yankees came up in the seventh. The first batter was cleanup hitter Shelly Duncan. Once more, Section 14 serenaded him with the chant of "Shelly! Shelly!" Duncan took a ball and then singled to left to put the tying run on base. Then Jason Turner singled to center, moving Duncan to second. With no outs, everyone in the stadium expected a bunt, and the Yankees' Todd Faulkner dropped a bunt a few yards in front of the plate. Kay pounced out of the catcher's box like a cat and grabbed the bouncing bunt with his bare hand when the ball was about five feet in the air. Kay then threw to third and just nabbed Duncan. It was an electrifying play, leaving the Yankees with one out and men still on first and second. That brought up third baseman Robinson Cano. The count moved to 2 and 2, and then Cano hit a shot to left field. John Toner charged the ball and caught it after it fell safe for a hit. Turner was churning around third, heading for the plate. Toner got his full body into the throw, and it was heading toward Kay at the plate. Kay appeared to be oblivious to the throw as he looked out toward the infield. The line drive throw got closer. Turner saw Kay standing casually ahead of him, and Turner slightly slowed. The throw kept coming toward the plate. Kay stood like a relaxed statue, looking away from the throw. The ball was only about twenty feet from Kay when, with only a fraction of a second to react, he suddenly came to life, grabbed the ball and tagged out the standing Turner. Kay had decoyed the runner into thinking the throw wasn't coming in.

Jay Caligiuri: "Some of the plays that were made — well, I think a lot of it has to do with the extra focus we have because we want to give the fans a good show. Brett Kay was unbelievable in that game — the bunt and the play on that throw. You could tell he was locked in defensively."

Brett Kay: "I learned that play in Little League. I call it the 'dead man' play."

Mark Lazarus: "The next night came and Ross Peeples started. It was a tight game. But there was never a sense of any of us that we would lose it. That night I was standing in front of the ballpark, and I ran into Mr. Vincent Viola, who is a boss at the New York Stock Exchange. We talked, and he invited me up to the skybox that they had in the stadium. The early part of the game not much was happening. Around the fourth inning, I went upstairs to the box. I ran downstairs to get a ball from one of the players for Vinnie's son. I brought the ball back for him, and it's now in the sixth inning. So I was leaning out over the railing, scream-ing and yelling, trying to get cheers up. People saw that I was up in the box and they started calling out to me. Now, from what I was told, Giuliani was in the box directly above me, and I'm told Giuliani, who was rooting for the Yankees, was making faces at me. So while I was doing all this screaming and yelling, they put the video camera on me.

"I went down to the concourse and I was talking to people I knew that if we win the game to chant, 'Hey, Na-Na, Goodbye.' These were other fans that I knew, and I told them to spread the word. Now this was when there was the turn-ing point of the game. I was standing just behind the screen behind home plate when the Yankee guy got the base hit to left field and Toner made the throw home and Brett Kay made the phantom tag play, or decoyed the runner and then tagged him out. That play just blew everything open. We were winning [1–0] at the time and that play kept the tying run from scoring. Everybody was in a frenzy. All I remember is jumping off the backstop and slapping five with everybody, and peo-ple were hugging and everybody was yelling. I remember I made a beeline for the left side of the dugout, and the first person I saw was Fonzie, and I slapped him five and he slapped me back. And then Toner came in from left field and we slapped five. And then Brett Kay came into the dugout and I told him, 'Great play!' and we hugged. Then I said to him, 'Now finish it!'"

Peeples got the next batter to ground out. Brooklyn had given up three hits, including a double, in the inning, and yet, thanks to Kay and Toner, the Yankees had no runs.

In the Cyclones' seventh, Toner got a one out walk. Lydon ran for him and advanced to second base on a groundout by Pittman. Pagan's single to left scored Lydon with Brooklyn's second run.

In the top of the eighth, Blake McGinley came in to pitch. He allowed a two-out double off the wall in left by Kevin Thompson, and then John-Ford Griffin drove in Thompson with a single. "Shelly! Shelly!" came the chants from Section 14. McGinley fanned Shelly Duncan to end the inning.

In the Cyclones' eighth, with one out Caligiuri singled. That brought up Kay. After taking a ball, Kay drove the next pitch over the left field wall to put Brooklyn up 4–1.

Jay Caligiuri: "That made the series for me. Running around the bases I felt like I was on Cloud Nine. I floated around the bases."

Pandemonium broke out once again. Brooklyn held a 4–1 lead, but that was the lead that the Dodgers once had in the 1951 playoff game against the New York Giants. This wasn't the majors and the Staten Island Yankees weren't the Giants, but Brooklyn fans have very long memories. It looked good for them, but no one was taking it for granted. Bad karma.

McGinley had been hit in the first game of the series and had given up a run in the last inning. He had been stellar in almost every outing all year.

In the ninth, Jason Turner came up trying to make amends for being

Cyclones celebrating series win over Yankees.

deked by Kay. The count went to 1-2 and then Turner fanned. The next hitter, Todd Faulkner, let two called strikes go by and then fanned on the third pitch. One out to go. Cano, who earlier had hit the double to left, was up. Then count went to 1-2 and then he was struck out, looking.

The Cyclones raced out of the dugout and bullpen, and all met in the infield, jumping up and down, and then they danced the cha-cha slide as the crowd yelled and yelled. The fans stayed and screamed and clapped. Some danced in the aisles. Not one fan did anything untoward. It was mass jubilation, on and off the field.

Frank Corr

"We played a real good game, and I'm not taking anything away from them — they battled us real tough all three games — but it's a little overwhelming for another team to come into a park with eight thousand people every game just yelling at ya the whole game. That's gotta be tough for a player. Some players can block that out, but a lot of others can't. We did what we had to do, and the fans did what they had to do, and it turned out that we turned out on top in the first series."

Mike Cox

"The final game in Brooklyn I was so impressed with Ross, the way he pitched. And then after the game we tried to dance the cha-cha slide, Ross and Eckert did. I can't stand the dance, but I did it. Afterwards, we didn't hope the Yankees thought we were trying to show them up by dancing on the field."

The next day would be a rare off day, but the Cyclones weren't in a party mood tonight. They would stay at home tomorrow and then drive out to Williamsport on the morning of September 10 and play the game in Williamsport, and then return right after the game to Brooklyn in the first game of a best-of-three game in the League Championship Series.

September 10, 2001

The team arrived in Williamsport just in time to loosen up and take batting practice. The Cyclones were in another best-of-three series, this time for the championship of the New York–Penn League. The Cyclones went with a similar lineup, but made a few changes. Robert McIntyre was back in at shortstop. Noel Devarez was in right field in place of Lawson. On the mound would be Lenny DiNardo, the left-hander. The Williamsport Crosscutters were starting pitcher Jose Silva, a major league hurler from the parent club, the Pittsburgh Pirates, who was pitching on a rehab assignment.

The Cyclones failed to score in the first inning. In the bottom of the first, DiNardo's control was off. After he gave up a single, he walked the bases loaded before giving up another single to give Williamsport a 1-0 lead. In the bottom of the second, the Cyclones' Kay started things with a single, and then doubles by Corr and Toner, and singles by McIntyre and Bacani gave Brooklyn four runs. In the Brooklyn third, a Caligiuri double and a Kay single produced another run. After giving up another run in the third, DiNardo was replaced by Tommy Mattox. Williamsport's Chris Shelton homered in the sixth. Three more hits in the sixth gave Williamsport another run. In the eighth, a Corr double, a Devarez single, and a Toner double gave Brooklyn a 7–4 lead. Ryan Olson pitched the last three innings for Brooklyn, and in the eighth and ninth he stopped Williamsport. In the ninth, Olson struck out the side for a 7–4 Cyclones victory.

Now it was back to Brooklyn for another rare off day. The bus left after the game for the trip home. It was a long ride across Pennsylvania, through New Jersey and into New York. The Cyclones had to win only one of the remaining two playoff games, both at home, in order to be the New York–Penn League champions.

Harold Eckert

"On the way home, Fonzie stood up and said he was proud and that we have a day off tomorrow. We don't normally get many days off.

"Portobanco was scheduled to start. And I was told that if it's close, I would probably be in there. So it was an opportunity for me to close out the championship. So I had a good chance to be on the mound in the fifth, six, seventh, eight and ninth innings. There is no better feeling than to be able to close out a championship. I remember Jesse Orosco jumping around on the mound after the Mets won the 1986 World Series. Before my Cyclone career is over I was probably going to have thirty or forty people of my family and friends going to the game. My girlfriend was in town. The next morning, I was going to get up and relax a little bit."

The team bus arrived at the Brooklyn ballpark at 5:00 A.M. The players left the bus and headed home. Today would be an offday, with the playoffs resuming tomorrow, in Brooklyn, on September 12.

September 11

Luz Portobanco and Joe Jiannetti were asleep in their Brooklyn apartment. It was around 9:00 A.M., about four hours after the team arrived back in Brooklyn from Williamsport.

> **Luz Portobanco:** "I was sleeping, actually knocked out, and then Jiannetti woke me up, and he was really crazed, and he was like saying, 'Look, this is happening and wake up!'
>
> "And I said, 'Shut up! Look what time it is! Go back to sleep. It's around nine.'
>
> "Everybody was calling him, his parents and all, and then I said, 'Are you seri-

ous?'

"And he said, 'Yes!'

"We went outside and saw the smoke, and then some lady took us to the top of the roof next door to see the World Trade Center and I thought, 'Wow! I can't believe this is happening!' Then after we went inside, Jiannetti got another call telling him that a second plane had hit. We didn't have a television set, so we found out by phone. So I knew the game was going to get suspended. I said to Jiannetti, 'We can't do anything about it but pray.'

"I said, 'New York's crazy!' We wanted to get out of there as soon as possible. Where we were living was not that far from Manhattan. The smoke was coming toward us. We could smell it on the street as we walked.

"The next day we had a club meeting, and they told us to leave New York. And the next day I left with Pagan and we drove to Miami. We got home safe, thank God. The next day was my birthday, and I spent it with my son and hanging around with my family, and we discussed what happened in Brooklyn."

Jay Caligiuri: "On the morning that it all happened, Ray Goffio [who was a host to several Cyclones who stayed in one of his homes on Staten Island], the guy who owns Brooklyn Egg Cream, was running around the house, and he says, 'Jay, you got to turn on the TV, we're getting bombed or something.'"

"We saw a hole in the World Trade Center, and then we saw another plane hit. So then we went to the shore, across from the skyline, right in front of the [Staten Island] Yankee ballpark. There were at least a thousand people near the fence there, and there was a big cloud of smoke covering everything, and there was no noise, just the sound of jets flying over. We were just standing there quietly — I guess in shock. It wasn't fun being there, I'll tell you that."

Brett Kay: "On the night before the tragedy, we got back from Williamsport at night, and I decided to go back to Staten Island and stay there instead of going to my apartment in Manhattan. I remember the next morning. The guy that we were staying with [Ray] woke us all up and said,

'Watch TV.' We turned on the TV, and we saw the second plane hit, and we didn't know what was going on. We were in awe. It's affected everybody. It's affected me because you still don't know what's going to happen. Are the terrorists going to retaliate? Where? It's a gut check for everyone. We're at war. I called my family. A lot of us have been freaked out. I've been glued to the TV ever since.

"After the attack, we went to where Staten Island's field was, and we looked out and saw where the buildings fell, and you just don't understand how there are people in the world who would do this kind of stuff. It's just a freaky thing. It's going to affect all of us for the rest of our lives. I'm lucky I didn't stay in Manhattan that night before. I could have said, 'I've got a day off— I'll go visit the World Trade Center.' I could have been there. Luckily, I didn't. That's one thing I always wanted to do was go on top of the World Trade Center and the Empire State Building."

Mike Cox: "I was staying on Staten Island, and our host dad, Ray, came upstairs and he said 'Hey, guys get up and look at the television,' And Ross and myself went outside to look. And then some of us went there to look near the Staten Island ballpark, and we took pictures, and then we were asking each other if should we be taking pictures. And then somebody said, 'Are we gonna play?' And then someone said, 'No.' And then we didn't even want to go to the ballpark. We just wanted to be safe with our families.

"Ray was even involved with the fire department as a sort of volunteer, and he even transported some firemen down there [Ground Zero] in his Montero. Then in Staten Island, where they take all the debris, he said it was only a half-mile from his house. Then the night it happened, we tried to get to Manhattan, but they [the police and National Guard] wouldn't let us get there because Brett Kay had an apartment there, and he wanted to get his stuff, but we couldn't get to Manhattan. We went by van actually. Then, a day or two after, we went through the Bronx and went to his apartment, and then we couldn't believe the stuff we were seeing. Seeing busloads of National Guards and then talking to the Coast Guardsmen. We went on the beach near our house on Staten Island and talked to the Coast Guardsmen, and then they said they would be bringing in a big ship to patrol the harbor.

"We had a little farewell dinner, but a few didn't make it because they wanted to get out of there as soon as possible. The dinner wasn't sad. Out thoughts weren't on baseball. Our thoughts were really on what had just happened. We wanted to get together and talk about what would happen next. We weren't too worried about the season.

"I took one of the first flights out. I believe a lot of the guys left Sunday."

Harold Eckert: "The next morning, around 8:50 or 9:00 o'clock, my father calls and wakes me up, and he tells me to turn on the TV, and I saw what had happened and I was devastated. My father works at P.S.E. and G., in Clifton and he looked up and saw the first tower on fire. My uncle works in the Hudson River on a boat, and he was helping to take people away from Manhattan. When this happened, this takes over and when something in the world like this happens, baseball seems a little small.

"The team had a meeting, but I couldn't make it because all the bridges were closed, and I couldn't get to Brooklyn. I didn't pick up my stuff until two weeks later. Bobby O. couldn't make it in either because he also lives in Jersey. I really wish I could have said good-bye to everyone.

"Your whole life is baseball, baseball, baseball, and then all of a sudden it's over.

"I threw out my 2001 calendar book the other day, and I saw in it for September, baseball, baseball, baseball up to Sept. 11, then two days later I saw "class" in it. I was going back to school."

Warner Fusselle: "I live in mid-town New York, near Times Square. After the attack on the World Trade Center, I was walking in Times Square, and it was so quiet — it was eerie. There were hardly any cars — in *Times Square*. And the people — and there weren't many of them — were very quiet. Times Square was like a ghost town."

Frank Corr

"Right away my aunt woke me up when it happened. It was [almost] nine o'clock when it happened. Some of the guys were going to go into the city on our off day.

"The very last day that we had off I stayed at my aunt's house, and I was glued to the TV. I couldn't get away from the TV. I'd get something to drink, and then I'd be right back in front of the TV. There were ashes from the World Trade Center in my aunt's yard. And you could smell the smoke and see it. But you couldn't actually see the Twin Towers from her yard, but you could see the smoke. There were pieces of paper from the World Trade Center blowing down the street. It was pretty crazy, man."

A Pitcher's Call

Bobby Ojeda: "I'm at home, in Rumson, in Jersey. My wife and I are getting the youngest kids off to school at 7:30, and at the same time my oldest daughter is taking the 7:30 Path train from North Jersey into Manhattan.

"Then I was driving on my way into Shea at 9:00 A.M. Hojo and I had a charity softball game scheduled there.

"The train lets my daughter off at the World Trade Center, and she gets off and walks a couple of blocks into work. I'm in the car at 9:00 A.M., and I turn on the radio, and I put on 1010 WINS 'cause I want to see how the traffic is; and I hear that a plane hits the World Trade Center. So I'm thinking, like everybody else, it's a Cessna. So I pick up the car phone and I call my daughter — and I get her on the phone, which is pretty remarkable because unbeknown to me at the time was that the phone lines were a disaster. So I get her on the phone — her train has just gotten there at 9:00 o'clock — and she says, 'Dad, there's stuff falling all around.'

"Her train had just arrived, and she comes up the escalator and goes out on the street, and there's stuff falling — people are jumping out the windows. And I say, 'Go to your office and I'll pick you up and we'll go to Shea.' There's this horrible thing happened, see, and I'm still thinking Cessna. I said, 'Don't hang up the phone.'

"I'm seeing smoke and I'm thinking, 'What the hell is going on?'

"So I'm talking to her on the phone, and I'm listening to the radio, and I've been driving maybe twenty minutes, and I'm near the Outerbridge Crossing to Staten Island, and I hear that all the bridge crossings into New York City have been closed down. I was a minute away from being on that bridge when it was shut down. Then I would have been stuck. I turn around, and I start driving home and I tell my daughter on the phone, 'Stay on the phone!'

"By now I hear on the radio that a second plane had hit the Towers. I think, 'Oh, my God, a second plane hit.' Now I'm only about ten minutes from home and there's a metal bridge where I can see the Trade Towers from where I'm driving, and I'm looking at both Trade Towers burning 'cause as the crow flies I'm only about fifteen miles away. I've got my daughter on the phone, and the radio on, and the lady on the radio says, 'The building has fallen!' and my daughter says, 'Dad, I just heard a loud crash. What was that?'

"I don't want her to panic, so I tell her, 'I'm not sure. Sit tight. Do not hang up the phone!' "

"Now I call my friend, Lenny. He's got a boat, and he lives right down the street from me. I get home and Lenny's there within three minutes. So I lose contact with my daughter. I dial back. I had lost her once before on her cell phone, so I push redial on the phone she called back on. The lady who answers the phone on the seventeenth floor of the building where my daughter works is so calm, she's like a rock. I get my daughter back on the phone, and I say to her, 'Here's the deal. If I lose contact with you, get down to the ferry. Get on the top deck of the ferry. If you see a little boat with a white canopy, you start waving two pieces of paper at the boat, and I'll know you're on that boat, and I'll come pick you up.'

"I took my father's flag — my father was a veteran, and I got the flag when he died. I told my daughter, 'I'll have the flag hanging off the side of the boat.'

"So I've got this plan going, and my buddy Lenny, 'cause he's like that, said, 'I'm going with you.' Now we're on the boat headed for the Verrazano Bridge and I'm thinking that 'cause they have the Coast Guard cutters there that they have the Narrows all blocked off to the city.

"I said to my daughter, 'You get on the ferry!' I lost my daughter on her cell phone, but then I get her on the land line. I keep losing her and then getting her back.

"So now we're under the Verrazano, and there's stuff in the air and there's people fishing! Fishing! And the city looks like a scene out of *Ghostbusters*. The city is in smoke, and ten guys are fishing!

"We get to Manhattan and we head for Pier 17 at South Street Seaport. So we go around an island near the Statue of Liberty, and there's the Coast Guard, so I'm on the phone to my daughter, and we're close to Pier 17, so I tell my daughter, 'Hang up the phone, leave, and meet me at Pier 17.'

"There's a Coast Guard boat there, and the Coast Guard guy says, 'Go ahead.' We go in closer toward the pier, and Lenny's engine dies. There are all these huge tugs there, and there's the incoming current and the wash from all the tugs and Lenny's engine dies. So I'm holding onto the piling on the pier with my hands, and I'm thinking 'I'm gonna fall in the water and your boat is going to drift out to sea, and the Coast Guard is really going to get angry.' So we finally get the engine started and I climb up on the pier, and I see a Rumson cop on the pier. He knows me, and I tell him I'm looking for my daughter. People on the pier are covered in all this dust and grime from the building collapse, and I'm on the pier looking for my daughter.

"Meanwhile, all these people are coming up to me and saying, 'Hey, Bobby, nice job in Brooklyn!' I can't believe it! But here they are — just away from the collapsed Twin Towers, covered in soot, and they're talking baseball. Ten different people. And then I realized — they were in shock.

"Then this guy, he's about thirty, and an old lady, looks like his grandmother, they come over, covered with dust and grime from the World Trade Center, and she says to me, 'Are you a baseball player?'

"I said, 'No maam, I used to be.' And she said, 'I told my son that you were an author,' but he said, 'No, Mom, he's a baseball player.'

"And then the guy said, 'I loved your career,' and he kept talking baseball, and I told him I was looking for my daughter. It was completely understandable. They were in shock. Then fifteen minutes later, I found my daughter; she jumped down from the pilings into the boat and we took off.

"And as we were riding off in Lenny's boat, I looked back at the city and all the destruction, and I remembered the feeling that I had, and I hope I never get it again, and it was when I was looking for my daughter on the pier I was saying to myself, 'Please God, let her be here. Let her be okay.' And now that I found her, and we were in the boat going back towards Rumson, I thought as I saw all that destruction, that there were other people back there who hadn't found their loved ones. And to this day, they never have.

"She was in the building, in the train station, when the building was hit. She was in shock, and she had worked in the city for years, and she couldn't remember how to get to Wall Street, and a lady helped her find her way to her office. She had said on the phone, 'I'm watching people jump!' She had said to me on the phone, 'Dad, I'm watching people jump out of the windows.'

"I said to her, 'How high are they up?'

"And she said, 'Ninety floors.'

"The World Trade Center. (pause) Everybody knows somebody who was there."

Carl Erskine: "After September 11, I think people around the country got to see what real New Yorkers were like. Some people outside of New York had an untrue image of New Yorkers, that they were cold or uncaring, and after September 11, the whole country saw what those of us who had lived in Brooklyn and New York already knew about what New York City people were really like."

After the playoff game at Williamsport on September 10, Mark Lazarus needed a ride back to Brooklyn from Williamsport. He had come to the game, with filmmaker Dan Carey. Mark had to be at work on Wall Street, in 11 hours.

Mark Lazarus: "I caught a ride back to New York with three girls I knew from the Cyclones' games. Who knows that it was fate that I didn't go back with Dan [Dan Carey, a filmmaker doing a documentary on the Cyclone season. Carey arrived home safely in New York the next morning, but if Mark Lazarus had gone with him, there's no telling when Mark would have arrived at work]. On the way back, as we're leaving Williamsport, we stopped at a mini-mart, and who's in the mini-mart but the Cyclones, six or seven of them. So we're hungry. We go across the street to the Burger King, and here are the rest of the Cyclones in there. Warner Fusselle is in there. I was sitting with Joey Jiannetti. He felt bad because he had made two errors. So I said, 'What's the difference? Next game, maybe you'll hit three home runs.' I said goodnight to all the boys, and we got in the van and headed for New York. We travel for a while, got lost, then hours later, the driver says we're getting close to the city.

"Four o'clock in the morning, and we get in the Lincoln Tunnel and she says, 'Am I going the right way?'

"I say to her, 'Look there. There's the World Trade Center. Just head for that and you can't go wrong.'

"We go down the West Side Highway and past the Vista Hotel, and she says, 'Is that the Vista Hotel?'

"And I said, 'That's where it's always been, right at the bottom of 1 World Trade Center.' The Vista Hotel is considered 3 World Trade Center. So we went through the Battery Tunnel, and they left me off to get a cab. And I got home at 5:15 A.M., the morning of September 11th.

"The Exchange where I work is a block and a half away from the World Trade Center. I worked at #4 World Trade Center until around 1999 when my exchange moved to where it is now. In order for me to get to work, I have to walk through the World Trade Center complex. I do that every morning. Because I got home so late, I went to work a little later than I normally do. Normally, I don't have to be at work until a quarter to ten. But usually I get there around 8:30, and I read the paper, shoot the breeze, until the market opens up. That morning, I got off the train within a minute or two of a quarter to nine. Now as most people know, the first plane hit at 8:46. I got off the subway at Broadway and Fulton, a block from the World Trade Center. I crossed the street; I took two steps into the concourse when we heard the explosion up above. I take a look, and I see the building on fire. So needless to say, I, like hundreds of thousands of people, didn't know what happened. All we see is debris falling from the top of the building, and the building on fire.

"And you like to think you're smart, but in all honesty, I think human nature is very, very dumb. Because it takes a while to face reality. You don't think that this is really happening. And I'm watching the flames, and you have to know what the World Trade Center looked like up close and personal to understand how big a hole there was in that building. Put it this way. The hole was as big as the wingspan of the plane that hit into that building. And that area was on fire. We didn't know what had happened. Then, all of a sudden, you start hearing. Then you start to hear that a plane hit into the building. The last thing on your mind is terrorism.

You remember when a plane hit into the Empire State Building, too. Then we're watching debris fall; and then all of a sudden I see this object falling. And the sun was shining from the east, so that any object falling, you're seeing not only the object, but it also has its shadow against the building, so you're seeing two for one. We didn't know what it was until about halfway down; we start to see arms and legs. And then you see it's a body. And then another one. And then another one. And then you see two bodies coming together, holding hands. And it doesn't take long. The bodies that you're looking at falling are landing in front of you. And all you hear is 'Blatt! Blatt!' You don't even realize that it's the sound of the bodies hitting the ground and exploding. (pause) I don't know what else to call it.

"And it was at that point that I said, 'What the hell am I doing here? This stinks!' And I turned around. I'm standing on the other side of Broadway. I turned to cross back over the street to go back to the subway. And all of a sudden you hear, 'Boom!' and I turned around, and I saw the other building get hit. I saw the plane just as it was coming into the building. And you saw sparks and flame shooting everywhere. And I just took off.

"By the time I got out of the crowd and into the subway, the whole foundation of Manhattan seemed to shake. And I could only assume that's when the first building went down. And I might have been on the last train, or the next to last train, that got out of Manhattan. It got me into Brooklyn to the Fulton Street station. But at the station in Manhattan, as soon as everything shook, people started falling. People started diving over the turnstiles, through the doorways — screaming. Most people were trying to get off the street, into the subway, to the north end where they could get to a further tunnel to go north. People were hesitant to get into the subway because 'who knows?' The subway might fall on you. People were thinking they're safer underground.

"So I got to Brooklyn and got off at Flatbush Avenue, and looked up the street which is straight in the direction of where the World Trade Center is. I took a look, and I saw that black smoke, and by that point the black smoke was already open to that fire. And I saw I had a call from my ex-wife, from Florida. And when I got upstairs, I could see the destruction. That was my day.

"People on the Cyclones' website knew I was in that area, which is why they are concerned. People are calling me; I was worried about my brother and my nephew who worked there. My thoughts weren't about the Brooklyn Cyclones at that time. Later, a couple of people started calling me. Actually, I saw the website a week later and I saw that Stephanie [Cyclones' fan] wrote a letter on the website that I was okay. Ultimately, I knew over twenty people who got killed. In one company, five brokers from my exchange were having a meeting at 8:30 that morning on the 102nd floor. They all were lost. A guy I used to come in with every day to work was killed. Other people, I knew them from the Street. In our exchange, we have a whole bulletin board of people killed who used to work for us who were in the building at that time. After 30 years at my business, you get to know a lot of people who work at Wall Street. I'm a commodities clerk. I work for independent commodities brokers at the New York Commodities Exchange. I used to work as a broker for the cotton exchange. That was at building #4, which was demolished by Buildings 1 and 2 falling on it.

"In a baseball sense, it was disappointing because you like to see the season end. There was every indication that we were going to win one of two games to win the championship. But what does that mean on the scale of what was going on at that time? So a baseball game didn't get played. Do you think anyone could have gotten excited watching a baseball game after this happened? Do you think the ball players could have played their best after what happened? Do you think they really cared? Nobody in the ballpark would have enjoyed it because the conversation in the ballpark wouldn't have been baseball.

"I saw a bunch of the guys Thursday at the ballpark. I was zombie-like. I took a drive, and wound up in the team's offices, and half the team was cleaning out their locker. So I got a chance to say goodbye to some of the guys. These guys wanted to get home more than anything else. Everybody wanted to be with their family, where they felt safe, where they felt loved. They didn't want to be at the ballpark. Nobody involved really gave a damn about baseball.

"This was a time to think about the dead. To think about the injured. To think about saving a life. To think about some kind of unity. The worst disaster since World War II. Nobody wanted to play the games. We weren't shortchanged. We had a great season. It was everything, and more, than we could have possibly dreamed for.

"When the fans walk into the ballpark next year on Opening Day the first thing that will hit us is that we haven't seen each other since September 9, or September 7 of last year, and the first thing that's going to come into our minds is September 11th. And it's going to be a matter of, 'Is everybody been okay with you? I know I haven't been in touch with you since last winter.'

"And slowly, we're going to shed the feeling of that and get into the magic of a new season."

The New York–Penn League president, Ben J. Hayes, canceled the remainder of the playoffs. The Brooklyn Cyclones and the Williamsport Crosscutters were declared as league co-champions.

Between Innings

Brett Kay

"We were upset that we weren't going to be allowed to play for the championship. It was kind of not real because we had won over Staten Island and we had a one game lead over Williamsport. We wanted to give ourselves, the fans and the Mets a victory, but compared to the tragedy, those games were so unimportant. We were mad we didn't play the games. It's disappointing, but there's nothing you can do. We just wish we could have been sent off on a better note. It's upsetting because we owe the fans a lot."

Frank Corr

"It's sad, man. Even though it would have been great to win the Penn League Championship in front of a home crowd, that place would have been nuts; it would have been crazy; it would have been great. It's sad to know that there are people in the world who can do something like that. They did what they had to do by canceling the minor league playoffs. It's really nothing you can do about that. It was the tragedy of the country. I think it's right

INNING 9

The Big Dance

For the Brooklyn fans, rooting for Brooklyn was the point of their participation. For the Brooklyn players, as much as they loved their Brooklyn experience, the point of their participation was to move up to the big leagues.

And so, in a way, the point of even having a Brooklyn team was to provide a laboratory in which the whole 76-game schedule within 79 days, and then the playoffs, was a way of evaluating the players as major league prospects.

So after a whole short season and playoffs, clear prospects should emerge. After all, the team won the league co-championship and needed to win one of two home games for the championship. They led the league in both batting average and earned run average.

Ross Peeples led the league in earned run average with a 1.34 ERA, and Luz Portobanco finished seventh in ERA with 2.04. Peeples and Harold Eckert tied for the league lead in wins with nine, which would prorate to 19 wins each with a major league length schedule. Eckert finished fifth in strikeouts with 75.

Frank Corr tied Walter Young of Williamsport for the league's home run lead with 13, Jay Caligiuri finished third in the batting race with a .328 mark, and Angel Pagan was eighth with a .315 average. Pagan tied for the league lead in stolen bases with 30. Caligiuri finished fifth in hits with 78. Frank Corr led in slugging percentage with .594, extra-base hits with 35, and was second in doubles with 21.

After the season, clear prospects should emerge, right? Not so fast.

"Nobody knows nothin'," said noted screenwriter William Goldman when asked about predicting which scripts will make successful Hollywood movies. And it seems that when judging which players from short season A ball will make the major leagues, nobody knows nothin', or if they think they know, they're not telling.

It takes an average of four and a half years of minor league ball for a player to make the majors. That is, it's four and a half years of minor league ball for the players who actually make the majors. Most minor league players do not make the majors, not even for one game.

After various estimates were bandied about concerning the percentage of players from the minor leagues who eventually reach the majors, in 1991 Allan Simpson, the editor and founder of *Baseball America Magazine,* took a survey. He examined all the professional players who signed contracts from 1982 through 1984. His survey included drafted players, nondrafted free agents and foreign players who were not subject to the draft. Those years were chosen because extremely few players make the majors after seven minor league seasons.

It turns out that of the 3,809 players examined, 405 played in the majors. That comes out to 10.6 percent, which was higher than many persons expected. Simpson also calculated the odds on players reaching the majors from different levels. From short season leagues the odds were 9 percent, 244 out of 2,700. From Class-A it was 15 percent, 500 out of 3,260. From Double-A it was 33 percent, 556 out of 1,706, and from Triple-A it was 73 percent, 1,293 out of 1,770. For nondrafted free agents, it was 4 percent, 36 out of 995, and for foreign players, 7 percent, 44 out of 605.

The reason most persons were actually surprised at 10.6 percent is that people forget how many players make the majors for just a few games. It is a generally accepted baseball truism that it is easier to make the majors than it is to stay there.

Broadcaster Warner Fusselle said, "You never know who'll make it. I've seen talented players who seemed sure to make the majors never get out of Class-A, and I've seen guys that nobody thought would make it reach the big leagues."

Injuries play a part, especially with pitchers. Politics also play a part. First round draft choices usually sign for over a $1 million bonus. Early round picks usually sign bonuses in the hundreds of thousands of dollars. Clubs that have invested so much in a player are reluctant to release the player. There are many reputations at stake in an early round selection, and the club executives and scouts who advocated a player's signing want to make sure that the player they championed has every opportunity to make it.

Who might make the majors from the Cyclones? Let's look at the possibilities while bearing in mind that they all have a chance, some chances apparently better than others. We'll start with some of the players who were promoted during the season.

- **Danny Garcia:** A 21-year-old second baseman, Garcia is a fifth round draft choice from Pepperdine University. He hit .321 for Brooklyn, and then batted .301 after he was moved up to Capital City. He's a smooth fielder who can also play the outfield. He bunts , can hit and run, can steal a base, and breaks up double plays.
- **Michael Jacobs:** A 21-year-old catcher, Jacobs was the Mets' 36th round selection in the 1999 draft. He went to Grossmount Junior College.

Cyclones in front of their dugout.

He hit .288 at Brooklyn and then .323 at Capital City. He has good power, and his left-handed bat gives him an advantage, as left-handed-hitting catchers are always in demand.

- **Matt Peterson:** A right-handed pitcher, Peterson, 20 years old, was the second round selection by the Mets in the 2000 draft but signed too late to begin play that year. In 2001, he was at Brooklyn where he was 2–2 with a 1.62 ERA. At Capital City, he was 0–2 with a 4.50 ERA. He pitched 1.2 innings at St Lucie. His fastball reached 94 miles per hour and could get even faster as he matures.

- **Matt Gahan:** A right-handed pitcher, Gahan is a twenty-six year Australian who was working as an accountant when he pitched in a tourney in Australia and was discovered by the Mets. He has a plus 90 mph fastball that did hit 94 mph, but his pitch is slower when he concentrates on throwing an effective two-seam fastball. At Brooklyn, Gahan was 3-0, had an miniscule earned run average of 0.61, and he allowed only fifteen hits over thirty innings.

Of the players that stayed at Brooklyn:

- **Angel Pagan:** A center fielder, Pagan was drafted in the fourth round of the 1999 draft, but he did not sign with the Mets at that time, so he attended junior college while the Mets retained his signing rights for a one-year period until just before the 2000 draft. Pagan did not play baseball for his high school team and was signed after a tryout camp. A switch-hitter, Pagan is further advanced as a right-handed batter. He is working on using his speed from the left side. Only 20 years old, his left-handed swing should improve. He has excellent speed, but needs to improve as a base stealer. He stole 30 bases for Brooklyn. He hit .361 for Kingsport in 2000, and .298 for Capitol City before he was sent to Brooklyn where he could play regularly. At Brooklyn he hit .315.

- **Joe Jiannetti:** A 21-year-old third baseman, Jiannetti was a draft and follow 40th round draftee in the 2000, which meant that the Mets retained the rights to him until just before the next draft. Jiannetti attended Daytona Beach Community College and signed with the Mets in 2001. A hard-nosed player with excellent speed, Jiannetti was shifted to second base in the Instructional League in 2001. He's a good hitter and a hardnosed player.

- **Brett Kay:** A catcher, Kay was the Mets' eighth round selection in the 2001 draft. He attended Cal State–Fullerton where his teammate was Cyclones second baseman David Bacani. Kay, 22 years old, plays the game hard at all times. He is an extremely smart baseball player. He hit .311 with five home runs for Brooklyn. Excellent at calling a game and blocking pitches, Kay runs well enough to have played some outfield for Cal State–Fullerton. Kays shines in big games.

Brett Kay: "I hope my chances of making the majors are good, but it's really not up to me. All I can do is play hard every day. Hopefully, my chances are good — barring injury. But you never really know. Something could happen. You could be traded for some prospect and sit in the minors for ten years. Or I could get released. It runs through your mind sometimes about what it would be like to play at Shea Stadium, but I try to concentrate on each day and do my best. If I make it, it will be exciting to have everybody there to see me, but if it doesn't happen, then I'll say I gave it my best. So far so good. I had a good first season, and I hope it goes well.

"If it doesn't work out, I'll probably be a coach and go back to school for criminal justice. If I make the majors, I'll probably coach after it's over — on some level. Professional, college, Little League, whatever.

Guy Conti, the Mets' minor league instructional field coordinator, discusses the prospects of some of the Brooklyn Cyclones reaching the major leagues.

Guy Conti: "It's hard for me to say to a kid in 2002 that, 'You're not going to make the major leagues,' because I have seen so many kids that I didn't think were going to make it then go and get some time in the major leagues. So right now ,it's very hard for me to give up on anybody. Ten or twelve years ago, it wasn't as diluted as it is now, especially the pitching. There's thirty teams now. So that takes away from the quality of pitching. I've seen so many kids that I thought didn't stack up make it to the major leagues. There's a lot of kids that I never thought would get there who did."

Conti mentions some of the Brooklyn Cyclones' pitchers.

Guy Conti: "Portobanco has to mature and learn. He's a kid that throws 94, 95 miles an hour with movement on his ball. He has to continue to learn, get his innings, and continue to stay healthy. If he doesn't stay healthy, he has no chance. And that goes for all the kids. They have to stay healthy so that their full potential can be realized.

Luz Portobanco: "If players on this team don't reach the majors, they'll probably become coaches, if they really like the game. They'll want to be around the game. Maybe they'll train their kids.

"I can't say what my chances are of making the majors, only God knows that. If I stay healthy and I continue doing what I'm doing, the chances are pretty good."

Guy Conti: "Peeples is a soft-throwing left-hander. He has to prove himself at every level. Peeples is going to tell us whether he's going to pitch in the major leagues. We're going to put him in A-ball, we're going to put him in Double-A ball, and if he's successful there, we're going to put him in Triple-A ball, and if he's successful there he's liable to get a shot at the major leagues. But what he does is going to tell the Mets what he can do at each level because he throws at 84 or 85, so he'll get a chance at each level in turn, and he'll top out, where he tops out and it could be in the major leagues.

"Mike Cox is a small pitcher. Sinks the ball and depends on movement of the ball. He breaks 90, he moves the ball, but he has to prove himself at each level.

"Harold Eckert is another that has to prove himself. His age [25] isn't as important as innings pitched. After 600 innings for a high school kid, or 300 innings for a college kid, I'll pretty much be able to tell you how far he'll go."

Harold Eckert: "If I could make forty grand a year playing minor league ball, I could play forever if I didn't make the majors. I think about making the majors every day when I go to the gym."

Guy Conti: "David Byard overachieved last year, and we're starting to see some movement on his fastball. He has a tremendous sinker, and he controlled the movement on it. He needs to be challenged, and we'll see where he goes.

"Blake McGinley is a very developed left-hander who's been at a top college program. We're looking for him to be a specialty left-hander. He's been at a top college program, so they're a little more polished than a Portobanco, let's say. We're going to check on McGinley and see what we've got there.

"Matt Peterson, the sky's the limit on him. He's 6' 5", 6' 6". He's a high school kid, all arms and legs. He's one of those kids where we need to give him those 600 innings."

Bobby Ojeda: "All these Cyclone pitchers have a chance to make the majors. They all have just as much talent as I did. It's all here [he points to his head,] here [he points to his heart], and here, [he points to his gut]."

Conti then evaluates some of Brooklyn's position players.

Guy Conti: "Danny Garcia was a very experienced kid. He's another like Bacani, we're going to run him out there and see how they can do.

"Mike Jacobs is a highly talented kid, and we think highly of his glove and bat. He did well in the Arizona Instructional League this year.

"Forrest Lawson is a young kid who came up through extended and then played well, and he'll be challenged as well.

"Noel Devarez has some trouble running the bases and had some problems with the curveball and off speed stuff, but he's got some talent, too.

"Jay Caligiuri has to develop more than gap power. Caligiuri is very similar to [Paul] LoDuca when I saw him. LoDuca in college was a hitter for average and gap power; now he hits thirty home runs in the major leagues. He has to hit the better pitching and develop more power.

"Bacani is a small second baseman. He's going to be challenged to see where he tops out. McIntyre, we're not sure that shortstop is his best position, maybe second base is his best shot to move up.

"Jiannetti could wind up at second, third, the outfield or even as a catcher.

"I kid Lydon, and I said that, 'Speedsters that hit fly balls wind up working at Kmart.' They laugh, but think about that. Lydon has to hit the ball on the ground, learn to take walks, get a high on-base percentage, and if he gets on base he is going to steal bases, I don't care who it's against because he has 6.4, 6.3 speed. He has to cut down on his strikeouts, get on base and he can do all these things. Who knows? We time a 60-yard dash. Wayne Lydon, from the left side, has 3.8 speed to first base. Average major league speed to first base is 4.1. He's 3.8 and in a 60-yard dash he'll run 6.4 and average major league speed in the 60 is 6.6, 6.7 seconds. On any given day, when Lydon, Pagan, and Reyes [a top Mets shortstop prospect in the Mets' minor leagues] race, any of them could win.

"Angel Pagan has a tremendous ceiling. He has all the tools in the world. He has the moxie, the flair, got the swagger; you saw that at Brooklyn, they loved him there. He loved to pull off his hat and show his black hair, but think about it. He struck fear into the opposing team; they didn't know what he was going to do. 'This guy's stealing, he's running.'

"We evaluate the flair and moxie that a player has. Absolutely. Portobanco took the mound like, 'Here I come fellas, the game is over!' We watch for body language, absolutely. There's no place in this game for fear. There's no place for lack of confidence. You have that, the opposing team feeds off it. When Portobanco goes out on the mound, he acts like he owns you.... I mean Randy Johnson takes the mound, other players see that, and they don't want to play. They know what's he's got, and they know he's going to come after them. Same way Iverson plays basketball, like he's saying, 'I'll beat you. There's no way you're going to beat me.'

"Maury Wills just talked up there at the stadium [in Vero Beach] and he was saying he fights against what the mothers say to kids. When they're little, the mothers are saying to them, 'Be careful now when you go out to play . Be careful now.' I get them now and they have this 'be careful' in their minds, and I don't want them to be careful. I want them to be aggressive, to be daring, to take chances.

"That's what you have to do in baseball. That's what you have to do in athletics. If you don't believe in yourself, your opponent senses it immediately and takes advantage of it, and uses that against you. If you're the pitcher, one of us is the cat and one is the mouse, and you have to determine which one you're going to be. That's what I see in Lydon. The infield was drawn in and there was a ground ball, and he scored on a routine ground ball to the infield. Even if he were thrown out by a hair on the play, I'd still rather see that because a timid guy isn't going to go to the big leagues.

"Just like Pedro Martinez [Red Sox star pitcher who came up through the Dodgers' farm system]. He's five foot ten, and when you stand in there against him, he's going to knock you down or hit you. He's not going to let you stand in there against him. That's the game.

"I saw Pedro Martinez in relief against the Cleveland Indians in a playoff. Usually in a close game in the playoffs, the whole team is up against the dugout rail, watching. This time, they were all sitting back, watching. They knew it was over. Pedro wasn't going to let them do it.

"There was an aura about the Dodgers of Wills, and Koufax, and Drysdale. There was a swagger about them. Like the New York Yankees of today. You have to beat the organization. Players individually can develop that self-confident attitude. And managers want their teams to develop that self-confidence.

"Like I feel confident right now that I can talk about developing pitching with anyone, anytime, anywhere. But over the years I've developed Pedo Martinez, I can give you a list of pitchers that I have worked with like Pedro Martinez; John Smiley, Pedro Astacio, Guzman; I can give you a list of major league pitchers that I have worked with; and the stuff has worked. They've gone to the major leagues and have been successful. If you would talk with Dickie Gonzalez, or Jarrod Riggan, who's with Cleveland now.

"Look at Bobby Ojeda. He has helped kids in Brooklyn. He may have turned several careers around. He helped Peeples, Eckert; he's going to help DiNardo and Walker in time.

"Now Bobby Ojeda not only has the knowledge, he's able to communicate with those kids. When I was in Brooklyn, Bobby was a little down one night, and I talked to him and I said, 'Look, you've got a passion for the game and the kids believe in you. All you got to do is go into that locker room and say, 'Listen, I want all my pitchers to take their uniforms off. We're going to go out in right field and jump into the ocean.' And they would have done it! Because he said to do it, they would do it. Now, if he tells them to jump in the ocean and they're going to do it, if he says throw your change-up, they're going to do it. Throw your curve ball. They're going to do it. They liked Bobby Ojeda the person, and they believed in Bobby Ojeda the coach.

"The Rule Five Draft enables a player after several years in the minors to be taken by a major league team, and if the team keeps him in the majors, okay. It costs them $50,000 to take him and if they don't stay in the majors for one year then he goes back to the team he was selected from.

"The six year free agency is figured from the point he signs. They are basically saying if someone hasn't progressed to the majors in six years, if he's not on the 40-man roster, he can become a six year free agent.

"Brooklyn was a unique situation for the players this year, with eight thousand fans a game and two or three hundred people for them waiting outside after the game. It was like the major leagues. I'm worried about a letdown after that as they move up the ladder, where they may run into the lack of fans."

Who's going to make "The Big Dance"? Even scouts and executives admit that it's difficult predicting which players from Short-Season A teams will make the major leagues. Politics can play a role; big bonuses always guarantee that such an investment in a player ensure a chance to pay back the investors. But basically, baseball is a meritocracy. The players will have their chance to prove their abilities on the field.

Mike Piazza, star Mets catcher and the acknowledged best hitting major league catcher of all-time, was drafted by the Los Angeles Dodgers in the June

Cyclone outfield sluggers, from left: Forrest Lawson, Wayne Lydon, John Toner, Frank Corr, Angel Pagan, and Noel Davarez.

1988 free agent draft. The Dodgers drafted him primarily as a favor to Tommy Lasorda, who is a friend of the Piazza family. This favor was done when the Dodgers waited until their 61st Selection, in the 62nd round, to select Piazza. Piazza was picked as the 1,390th overall pick in that draft, out of a total of 1,433 draftees. He's a surefire future Hall of Fame player.

Nobody knows nothin'.

Expectation Results

1. I had thought Brooklyn would play at a new temporary field at the Parade Grounds. They instead played at Coney Island.

2. I had expected about 3,000 fans per game at the Parade Grounds, a facility that was supposed to have around 3,500 seats. KeySpan Park drew 8,000 fans per game, more than capacity.

3. I thought there would be many appearances by former Brooklyn Dodger players. Ralph Branca and Joe Pignatano were there on Opening Night. Joe Pignatano went back a number of times on his own, unannounced, just to enjoy the games with his family. Johnny Podres was there to make an appearance one evening, as was Carl Erskine one time. This expectation was partially fulfilled.

4. I had figured that the new Brooklyn players would know more of the history of the Brooklyn Dodgers. I had forgotten how young they would be, and that most of them were born about 23 years after the Dodgers had already left Brooklyn. Asking them about the Brooklyn Dodgers was like asking a 55-year-old fan about the 1922 Philadelphia Athletics. Also, most of the Cyclones hadn't grown up in Brooklyn, or even the New York area, where there is such a collective, residual memory of the Brooklyn Dodgers. Yet, because the Brooklyn Dodgers were so famous, and because of the success and heartbreaking losses and their great players, including Jackie Robinson breaking the so-called color line, many of the players knew something of the Dodgers, just not as much as originally thought.

5. I had thought the fan base would be a mix of all ages and backgrounds. Expectation fulfilled.

6. My expectation was that there would be a Brooklyn Cyclones' rivalry with the Staten Island Yankees. This was fulfilled, as the rivalry grew throughout the season. The rivalry culminated in an exciting best of three playoff series won by Brooklyn in what turned out to be their last home game of the season.

7. I had expected that the new Cyclones would become a part of the Brooklyn community. Many of the players lived in Brooklyn, but they were there for only a 12-week season. They were usually at the ballpark, but they did make public appearances, and they did hang out in the Bay Ridge section of Brooklyn. This was a partially fulfilled expectation.

8. I had thought there would be a new young radio announcer for the team. Instead, there was a veteran announcer, Warner Fusselle, who had done national television work on *This Week in Baseball* and many other shows. He was already a fan of Red Barber and knew all about the old Dodgers. This expectation was partially fulfilled. The announcer was experienced with a full career already established.

9. I thought there would be more coverage in the New York papers on a daily basis. The Brooklyn newspapers' coverage was extensive. The coverage for Opening Night was incredible. Mixed.

10. I thought the crowds would be more sedate, like those for the Pittsfield team I had seen, and that the fans would be nostalgic. The fans were nostalgic, but were much more vociferous. The fanaticism that Brooklyn fans were noted for hadn't disappeared with the Brooklyn Dodgers. It had just lain dormant for a mere 44 years.

11. I thought it would be good to compare the old Brooklyn Dodgers to their new positional counterparts on the Brooklyn Cyclones. This was not so workable. Fans had years to get to know the core of Dodger regulars. The Cyclones were there for two and a half months. Also, the starting catcher, Mike Jacobs, was only there for three weeks before he was moved up; Campanella was there from 1948 until the Dodgers left Brooklyn. Take second

base. The team started with Arias, then went to Danny Garcia; when he was moved up, they used David Bacani. Brooklyn had Jackie Robinson at second from 1948 until around 1953 when he started playing left field and third base. The Cyclones' changes came much faster.

Extra Innings

Baseball came back to Brooklyn in 2001, and the season was memorable in so many ways. The first thing that comes to mind is what fun the ballpark was. I have never seen so many people in such consistently good humor. People were happy at the ballpark. There were families and single fans, fans of all ages and races, men and women, and almost nobody seemed to be in a bad mood.

All around the league was a feeling of happiness. Sure, the crowds in Auburn, Jamestown, and Pittsfield — some of the league's older franchises — were quieter than the crowds in Brooklyn. That was okay. Those towns, all put together, would fit in a little section of Brooklyn, an immense place of 2.7 million people. And the crowds in Auburn, Pittsfield, and Jamestown had had baseball for years. It was no longer a novelty, but it was still appreciated as part of their regular summer.

New York–Penn League baseball was baseball at a lower level of the minor leagues, but played by outstanding athletes, far better athletes than most people realized, athletes so good they were all the cream of the crop in high school or college.

The games had more mistakes and errors than a typical major league game, but this was not to any extreme. There were many games that were superbly played.

Brooklyn drew 289,381 fans in 37 home games, leading the league in attendance.

The whole season raced by like the Cyclone ride itself. After 44 years, baseball's return to Brooklyn lasted only 12 weeks. There were only three days off in the entire regular season.

When the Dodgers were in their glory years at Brooklyn, racial integration was new and prominent in the news. In 2001, integration was an accepted fact and didn't seem to be even a topic of conversation. The game's vistas had expanded, and the Cyclones featured black, white and Hispanic players — players from the United States, the Dominican Republic, Cuba, Australia,

Brooklyn fans — older ones.

and, for a two-game rehab, the New York Mets' Shinjo, from Japan. Edgar Alfonzo, from Venezuela, managed them, and nobody thought too much one way or the other that he was Brooklyn's first minority manager since the Negro Leagues. It had happened without comment.

The Brooklyn Cyclones were an easy team to root for; they were genuinely nice young men who enjoyed talking with the fans. Some had received large bonuses, but many had received very small bonuses or no bonus at all. Living at $850 a month before taxes was not making them rich.

In some ways, the season made me less cynical. I had read about how major league players don't like to play baseball. I think for the most part now that isn't true, not from what I saw in the minors. These kids really do love to play. Who else do you know who gets about $4 an hour in pay and gets to their job two hours before they have to? These young men do.

When you sit in the stands and shout out to the players, you may think they don't notice. They do. Like actors peeking out from a pinhole in the curtain at the audience, the players were well aware of the crowd and just human enough and young enough to be affected by it.

Brooklyn fans — children.

The Cyclones never got to finish the playoffs. It would have been a storybook ending to their first season if they had beaten Williamsport, and Brooklyn had to win only one of two games at home to do it, a place where they had won 31 of 38 regular season games, and no opponent ever won in its first appearance at KeySpan Park. Would they have won the outright championship? Probably. Highly likely. But no one knows for sure. More than the championship, what they and their fans were deprived of was a chance to say goodbye. They probably had at least an 80 percent chance to win one of the two final games and the championship. But what if they hadn't won. I can feel what would have happened. The Brooklyn fans would still have given them a standing ovation for a marvelous season of fun, and for the joy of having baseball back. Brooklyn was no stranger to winning. In the Dodgers' last 11 years in Brooklyn, the golden years, they won pennants six times and won the 1955 World Series. They were no strangers to losing either — recall 1950, 1951 and all those lost World Series. The fans could have handled it either way, but they never got that chance to give the team the standing ovation and for many, the hugs, and handshakes of goodbye. The fans never got the chance to say goodbye to each other.

Reality intruded, some say. But the season was not unreal. It was not some fantasy. It was real baseball, played at its hardest by young men and

Carl Erskine plays the harmonica at Dodgertown.

enjoyed by fans of all ages. How does one reconcile this with the events of
September 11? We're on thin ice here. Fans like Mark Lazarus and Marty Adler
lost multiple friends in the disaster. One firehouse in Brooklyn lost 12
firefighters in the tragedy. Every fan who would have been in the ballpark for
that championship series either lost someone in the disaster — often many in
the disaster — or knows people who did lose friends and relatives. New York
and Brooklyn are big places, but for those who lived there, everyone was not
only affected as human beings were anywhere, but they were personally
affected by the loss of life. How does one reconcile this with baseball? In one
sense, one doesn't.

    Edgar Rodriguez and Michael Jacobs were the new Brooklyn team's first
heroes. Both are nice young men and deserving of all the plaudits they heard.
How does their hitting a baseball compare with firemen and policemen rush-
ing into a burning building, and up the stairs of a burning World Trade Center? Edgar and Michael would be the first ones to say that it doesn't. How
does the loss of a season compare to the loss of a single life? Not in any way
comparable.

    In fact, the two events — the return of baseball to Brooklyn and the Sep-
tember 11 — attack were so opposite, so at jibes with human nature, that

comparison is impossible — but contrast isn't. They were so at odds as to be the polar opposites of human behavior.

Can one have an oasis in the middle of Coney Island? In Brooklyn? In New York City? If so, then the ballpark there was not an escape from reality, but an oasis, a resting place. It often reminded me of the song from the musical *A Chorus Line* called "At the Ballet" where the character sings about how everything was all right in her life whenever she got to the ballet. Well, for a lot of people that summer, everything was all right when they got to that Coney Island ballpark.

For the ball players, when they were living in classrooms at Xaverian High School, or in rented houses or at St. John's, they were basically anonymous

Duke Snider at Dodgertown.

young men; other people didn't even know they were there. At the ballpark, they were stars. The ballpark was where they were most at home, and they loved it there. For the fans, after a hard day at work, they could gather their family, sometimes three generations of family, and go out to the Brooklyn ball game. They could sit back and relax and root for Brooklyn — and if Brooklyn won, that was great. But if they didn't win, having baseball back was winning every night. One couldn't lose, really. There was baseball. A new game every night. What more could one want than to be at the ball game with family and friends?

The Mayor of Section 14 describes the transformation effected by the Brooklyn ballpark.

Mark Lazarus: "When I'm in the parking lot I'm 53 years old. When I come in here, I'm twelve again."

The ballpark also reminded me of the part of an Athol Fugard play, *Master Harold and the Boys*, in which Fugard describes the beauty of ballroom dancing in which each couple dances in their own orbit, yet observes every other dancing couple, and all the couples never interfere with each other, just give the other dancers space and room to maneuver to the music, each in their own way. The ballpark was like that in Brooklyn. Everyone was free to do as one wanted as long as it didn't interfere with anyone else. There were policemen there, but they were seldom needed. When you get a set of grandparents there who remember going to Ebbets Field, with their son and daughter, who may or may not remember it, with their children, who don't, but now have their own memories of Brooklyn baseball, who needs a policeman? Everyone was in too good a mood, even the policemen who were at a ball game with 8,000 happy people.

Clem Labine at Dodgertown.

"The next year there would be a statue showing Jackie Robinson and Pee Wee Reese together, representing Brooklyn Dodger baseball, but more important, representing people of different races being on the same team, on the same side of the larger issues in life. The statue would be near the entrance to the ballpark. The new manager would be Howard Johnson. The pitching coach, Bobby Ojeda, would return. Most of the players would be new. Most of the inaugural team would be playing at Capital City or St. Lucie. There were rumors that sometime, a year or more down the line, Brooklyn would become a full-season team. Perhaps many members of this past season's team would return then, with Brooklyn in a full-season A or Double A league.

> **Frank Corr:** "Hopefully, Double-A will come to Brooklyn, so that if I move up I'll get back to Brooklyn. Then I'll get to see a lot of the people that I met in Brooklyn my first year. Hopefully, they'll remember me. I'm excited about that. I hope they do switch it from short season to the Double-A team. Because one of these days I'd like to go back and play in front of the Brooklyn crowd again."

If Brooklyn does become a Double-A team within a few years, many of the initial Cyclones team would return to reprise their roles as Brooklyn players.

For years, after Brooklyn lost a pennant on the last day of the season, or lost a World Series to the Yankees, the response of the Dodger fans to the Giant or Yankee fan tormentors was, "Wait till next year." The Cyclones were the Co-Champions of the New York–Penn League, and the fans would like to see them win another championship, or many championships.

But the main reason to attend games will be just to be at the ballpark. Fans will pass by the new statue and then see the young hopeful players of the future. And if the fans are lucky, maybe Duke Snider or Johnny Podres, or Clem Labine, or Clyde King, or Ralph Branca will be there. Joe Pignatano will be there a bunch, making the ten-minute trip from Bay Ridge with his grandson. And if you're really lucky, Carl

Ralph Branca at Dodgertown.

Erskine will be there, and perhaps in the seventh inning stretch he'll play "Take Me Out to the Ball Game" on his harmonica.

The Brooklyn baseball fans could now again say, "Wait till next year." And every year, from now on, they could say it again.

Epilogue

Back in New York, the Brooklyn Cyclones were about to start their second season. The Cyclones took a bus from the Coney Island ballpark to Staten Island, a 25 minute trip. As the team approached Richmond County Savings Bank Stadium, the bus drove by the spot on Richmond Terrace where on September 11 Mike Cox, Brett Kay, Jay Caligiuri and other Cyclones had watched the burning World Trade Towers across the bay in Manhattan. Upon entering the ballpark, Bobby Ojeda noticed that the skyline view beyond centerfield was a constant reminder of past events. Ojeda noted, " I live here [the New York area] and I drive around New York all the time. But seeing this view of the skyline as I entered the ballpark today reminded me of when we were here the last time — just before September 11. It puts a ball game in perspective."

When the fans entered the stadium, each was given a small American flag.

The game was a sellout, with 6,500 attending. In ceremonies before the ball game, singing the national anthem was New York City police officer Daniel Rodriguez, the man who sang the Anthem at many public events in the wake of September 11. Throwing out the first pitch was the new Mayor of New York City, Michael Bloomberg. The Mayor was wearing a Staten Island Yankee cap. Last year, Mike Cox, when assigned to the stands to use the radar gun to time hurlers, also timed the tosses of unsuspecting ceremonial pitchers. But Mike on this evening was in Columbia, South Carolina, so that the new Mayor's soft pitch escaped radar detection. Up in "The Catbird Seat" were broadcasters Warner Fusselle and Reggie Armstrong. They would still be broadcasting on the local Kingsborough Community College station, but now the broadcasts would also be on powerful WSNR 620 AM radio. As in the inaugural season, the radio broadcasts would be carried worldwide on the Internet.

Some of regular Cyclone fans were there, seated on the Brooklyn side, behind first base. Mark Lazarus was there, leading cheers. So were fellow fans

Chuck Monsanto, Nick Cunningham, Ed Gruber and his son Steve. Basically, the first base stands looked like Brooklyn's home stands with over an estimated thousand Brooklyn fans in the stadium. The Brooklyn lineup included two of last year's Cyclones in Edgar Rodriguez at third base and Noel Devarez in right field.

Kevin Deaton, a big pitcher up from last year's Kingsport team, was Brooklyn's starter. Before the game, Deaton sat in the Brooklyn dugout and was engrossed in a discussion with writer Gersh Kuntzman about the upcoming famous hot dog eating contest at the Coney Island Nathan's. Deaton seemed more concerned about the hot dogs than his approaching debut, and with nerves like that he was destined to love Brooklyn. And vice versa. The game began, and Brooklyn failed to score. Then Brooklyn pitcher Deaton allowed a leadoff hit to Gabe Lopez and after two outs walked clean-up hitter John Ramistella, but he got out of the inning on a strikeout.

Brooklyn scored a run in the second to take a 1–0 lead. Deaton worked a 1-2-3 frame. In the third inning, Brooklyn scored a run and had a runner on first base with two out. Up to bat stepped Noel Devarez. Just before the pitch to Devarez, the crowd was quiet, and fan Mark Lazarus stood up and shouted, "Hit a homer and I'll buy you a lobster!" Just then the pitcher threw, and Devarez hit the ball over the leftfield wall. The Brooklyn fans erupted.

Later in the game, the Brooklyn fans were quieter than usual. Chuck Monsanto, who usually stands up and can be heard all over the ballpark, was losing his voice. Mark Lazarus was also more subdued as the game wore on. He, too, had almost lost his voice. Perhaps these key Cyclone fans had needed a vocal spring training.

Deaton pitched five scoreless innings and Brooklyn eventually won 8–5, Brooklyn vet Rylie Ogle getting the victory. Arrangements were begun to get Devarez his lobster.

The home opener had been sold out for months. There weren't the nearly 400 media credentials that were issued last year, but the press box was full and the game was on radio stations and cable television. A sign of the changed times was that around and about the stadium, security was heavy. A bomb-sniffing dog made the rounds. There were brightly painted additions around the stadium, colored in Cyclone colors of blue, red, and yellow. The festively painted additions ringing the sidewalks were cement barricades.

National talk show host Larry King, a Brooklyn native, was a special guest, and before the game he noted, "It's nice to be home, smell the fresh ocean breezes and go to Nathan's for a hotdog. Anyone born in Brooklyn knows that they never leave it. You can leave Brooklyn, but Brooklyn never leaves. I want to report to you that there's currently a rain storm in Manhattan, but the sun shines on Gowanus."

Mayor Bloomberg, this time wearing a Brooklyn Cyclones cap, again threw out the first pitch. Marty Haber, "Party Marty," was back this year, again entertaining the crowd as the roving master of ceremonies. Sandy the Seagull had returned, still charming kids of all ages.

Brooklyn started almost the same lineup that it started in the away opener. On the mound for Brooklyn was Yunior Cabrera, a left-hander who pitched a few innings for Brooklyn last season. After the Yankees failed to score in the first, Brooklyn struck for three runs. Angel Santos homered for the Yankees in the second, and Brooklyn picked up three more in the fourth inning thanks to two Yankee errors. A Brooklyn error led to a Yankee run in the fifth, and three walks helped Staten Island to a pair of runs in the eighth.

Brooklyn took a 6–4 lead into the ninth inning. The first batter up in the Yankees' ninth was John Ramistella, who to the inventive Brooklyn fans had already earned the nickname " Stella," as in Marlon Brando's plaintive call in the movie *On the Waterfront*. Over and over the Brooklyn faithful shouted their Brando like "Stellas" and Ramistella finally struck. After a hit batter and a single, the Yankees Scott McClanahan hit a ground shot to second baseman Chase Lambin, and Brooklyn turned it into a 4-6-3 double play. Game to Brooklyn, 6–4.

The first home game of the Cyclones' second season was over. Was the feeling in the stands like that of the inaugural season? The fans were mostly the same. The team had nine players who had played at least part of last season in Brooklyn — this was an inordinately high number of returnees for a team in the New York–Penn League. In considering whether things felt different at the ballpark, fan Robert Martin thought for a long while and then said, "Whether September 11 has influenced things? It's such an easy answer that you tend to discount it. But underneath the surface, it's changed everyone. It's harder to put aside the real world and concentrate on a ball game." And yet the Brooklyn ballpark, located in the middle of Coney Island within the confines of New York City, still retained that quality that former Brooklynite writer Michael Quinn described as "an amusement park within an amusement park within an amusement park."

What had happened between the end of the inaugural season and the start of the Cyclones' second campaign? After the playoffs were cancelled, within days the Brooklyn Cyclones left for home. Sixteen players who played for the Cyclones during their inaugural season were selected by the Mets to attend the fall Florida Instructional League.

Edgar Alfonzo accepted the position of hitting coach for his hometown St. Lucie Mets. The new Cyclones manager was Howard Johnson. Bobby Ojeda returned as pitching coach and Donovan Mitchell was the new hitting coach. Kelly Sharitt, who worked 14-hour days and did a quietly outstanding job managing the Cyclones' clubhouse, was back at his former job in Florida — managing the clubhouse at the Mets' minor league complex. Mike Herbst, the Cyclones' trainer in their first year, received a promotion to assistant trainer with the New York Mets. Not counting those players who briefly played for the Cyclones on injury rehabilitation, like Shinjo and Tom Martin, the first Brooklyn Cyclone to make the major leagues was their trainer.

In the New York–Penn League, the Pittsfield franchise was replaced by the Tri-City Valley Cats, whose headquarters were in Troy, New York. The Utica franchise was replaced by a new Baltimore Orioles' affiliate in Aberdeen, Maryland. The Aberdeen team was owned by Cal Ripken, Jr.

When spring training began, most of the Brooklyn players from the inaugural season were back in Florida, but a few were not. Brett Herbison, the 24-year-old pitcher on injury rehab who was trying to come back from shoulder surgery, was released. Leandro Arias was released. David Abreu, who on June 19 had been the first player to bat for Brooklyn in 44 years, was released.

In early April, squads were selected for the Mets' full season A clubs: Low-A Capital City and High-A St. Lucie. Brett Kay was assigned to St Lucie, as was fellow catcher Mike Jacobs. Also assigned to St. Lucie were two infielders who had played in Brooklyn's first season: Sean Pittman and Danny Garcia. Later, Australian Matt Gahan, the accountant with the 95 Mph fastball, was added to St. Lucie's roster. Joel Zaragoza, a Brooklyn infielder in the initial season, was given his release.

The Capital City Bombers opened the season at home. On Opening Night, the Capital City fans were unfamiliar with the players, and there was none of the hysteria associated with Brooklyn's initial home opener.

Before an announced crowd of 2,350, Capital City started a lineup that included eight former Brooklyn players. Capital City won 4–1. This time there was no press contingent on the field after the game, no packed stands screaming and yelling, no storybook finish. After the game, outside the Capital City clubhouse in right field, there were no police barriers restraining 200 fans and friends. Here in Columbia, only two fans were waiting for the players.

Down in Florida, the St. Lucie Mets shutout the visiting Jupiter club 8–0. The game was played before 3,401, and the evening was uneventful.

While the full season clubs in the Mets' system were beginning their seasons in April, a number of the Met minor leaguers were left in Florida to continue their practicing as part of extended spring training. If these players weren't eventually assigned to one of the full season clubs, they would either go to Brooklyn or to Kingsport, or they would be released. Brooklyn alumni included: Noël Devarez, the power hitting outfielder; catcher Francisco Sosa, who in limited action hit .389 in Brooklyn; popular infielder Vladimir Hernandez; Australian pitcher Wayne Ough; and Opening Day Brooklyn hero, third baseman Edgar Rodriguez.

Hanging over the heads of the players in "extended" was the upcoming First-Year Player Draft on June 4 and 5. In the draft, the Mets would select nearly fifty players, sign many of them quickly, and assign the players to their spring "mini-camp" to compete with the players in extended spring training.

The Mets would assemble their second season Brooklyn squad and send them up to Brooklyn for a few days of workouts before opening the new season.

Before the Brooklyn squad was assembled, longtime baseball fans received sad news when they learned of the passing of Joe Black, star Brooklyn Dodger hurler. Black was the National League Rookie of the Year in 1952 when he went 15–4 as a reliever, and then became the first black pitcher to win a World Series game when he beat the Yankees 4–2 in that year's Series opener. Later he was a teacher, and then an executive with the Greyhound Corporation, and as an Arizona resident was an active supporter of the World Champion Arizona Diamondbacks.

Brooklyn had earlier lost another long time Dodger fan when Irwin Brandon passed away. A successful corporate headhunter, Brandon in his youth had been an occasional ticket taker at Ebbets Field. Brandon had been so affected by the Dodger move to Los Angeles that he had not seen a professional baseball game in 44 years. "I am the last angry man," stated Brandon in describing his feelings about the loss of the Dodgers. He finally saw another game when he attended a Brooklyn Cyclones game in August.

On June 15, the Mets were beginning to arrive in Brooklyn. The players would be staying in downtown Brooklyn in the new dorms of Brooklyn Polytechnic College. Howard Johnson noted that it was his job to calm the new players down, and it was their job as new professionals to stop calling him "coach."

One of the players not back for the Cyclones was Joel Zaragoza. After his April release, he had hooked on with the independent Atlantic League, playing for the Pennsylvania Road Warriors. They were called the Road Warriors because they had no home field, playing all their games on the road. After years of litigation, their anticipated stadium near Allentown, Pennsylvania, remained unfinished, and the Atlantic League operated the team with younger players, in effect loaned to the Road Warriors from other teams in the league. Zaragoza, not deterred after being cut loose from an affiliated team, endured his permanent life on the road. Once Zaragoza left his clothing bag in the compartment of the team bus and the bus company switched buses and he lost most of his clothes. He stated how he was able to keep going. "You have to forget about being on the road and concentrate on baseball."

As Zaragoza orbited from Atlantic City to Newark to Bridgeport, in a homeless odyssey around the fringes of New York City, at KeySpan Park the Brooklyn farmhands still lucky enough to be on a team affiliated with the majors were engaged in their initial workout on June 15. Then they had several more workouts before the season opened. The roster for the second year Cyclones showed six pitchers who had pitched for Brooklyn in the team's first year: Chad Bowen, Yunior Cabrera, Rylie Ogle, Wayne Ough, Ryan Olson, and Chris Sherman.

The lone returning infielder was Edgar Rodriguez, back to share time at third base. Noel Devarez was a returning outfielder, and Tyler Beuerlein, on an injury rehab, was back as a catcher, first baseman, and outfielder. Not back for Brooklyn was Vladimir Hernandez, who had just been released. Also not returning to Brooklyn was catcher Francisco Sosa, who had erroneously believed he was going to be released and who had the left the Met organization.

On June 18, both Capital City and St. Lucie were on their leagues' all-star break between the leagues' first and second halves. Capital City had won the last five games in the first half to finish in a tie for first place. Because of the tightness of minor league scheduling, the South Atlantic League decided that a July 14 second half game between Cap City and South Georgia (Albany) would count as both a playoff game to determine the first half championship of their division and a regular season game in the second half.

At Cap City, Wayne Lydon had improved his switch-hitting and was batting .308 with an outstanding 43 stolen bases in a half season. Angel Pagan was also lighting things up, hitting .310 with 34 stolen bases. Justin Huber, who had gone hitless in nine at bats for Brooklyn last season, was tearing up the South Atlantic League, hitting .331 with 10 home runs and 66 RBI. Huber was named to the Futures All-Star game to be played in the major league All-Star weekend, a great honor.

Joe Jiannetti had missed a large part of the first half with injuries, and was struggling at .241. Frank Corr, no longer living in his aunt's Brooklyn basement, was at .286 with four home runs. Jay Caligiuri had sprained his ankle in spring training and was in effect taking his spring training in real games, and for the first time in his life was having difficulty with hitting, batting only .218.

Huber, Pagan, and pitcher Blake McGinley were Brooklyn alumni named to the South Atlantic League All-Star team. Harold Eckert's recovery from his "Tommy John" arm surgery was complete. After a winter of rest, exercise and throwing, his arm was healthy and strong. He had a 6–2 record with a 4.14 ERA.

Describing life at Capital City, Mike Cox said, "The minor leagues are dog eat dog. But the guys who played at Brooklyn last year had to learn to stick together and that special bond is still there."

Cox was still his creative self. Last year, it was practical jokes. This year, he had created the Capital City Bombers' Championship belt — like a wrestler's belt, made of cardboard and Velcro. In daily clubhouse contests, players competed to wear the belt for a day. Cox had lost the honor of wearing the belt when Forrest Lawson won a challenge by seeing who could hold his breath longer with his head in a bucket of water.

At St. Lucie, there were fewer players from the inaugural Brooklyn team. St. Lucie had finished their first half tied with Lakeland in their division with records of 42–30, but Lakeland was awarded the first half championship because they, at 6–2, had a better record head to head against St. Lucie. Danny Garcia was at second base batting .275 and was named to the Florida State League's All-Star team. Mike Jacobs was sharing the catching with Brett Kay. Jacobs was at .207 with two home runs and Kay was at .228 with four homers. Kay admitted that for the first time in his life he was struggling with baseball.

After the Cyclones' second year home opener, there were many events to come. Next week would bring the 75th anniversary of Coney Island's Cyclone ride. On July 24, the Brooklyn Dodger Hall of Fame would officially open its gallery at KeySpan Park. Marty Adler and his Brooklyn Dodger Hall of Fame staff had constructed a gallery of Brooklyn baseball, with exhibits ranging from the Nineteenth Century Atlantics through the Twentieth Century Dodgers to the Twenty-First Century Cyclones. Ensconced in the gallery were: the spikes Carl Erskine wore when he pitched his second no-hitter, the one against the New York Giants; the glove Mickey Owen wore when his dropped third strike led to a rally that helped the Yankees win the World series against the Dodgers; and a Brooklyn uniform worn by a Dodger outfielder named Casey Stengel. Former Brooklyn Dodgers Duke Snider, Gene Hermanski, Al Gionfriddo, Tommy Holmes, Johnny Podres, and possibly Ralph Branca were expected to attend. July 24 was also Duke Snider Night. It would be Duke's first ever appearance at the new ballpark, but Snider was well aware of the new Brooklyn team. In fact, though residing on the other coast, he was already a fan. The Duke noted, "I have a Brooklyn Cyclones hat at home that I wear around the house."

In a minor league signing that went nationally unnoticed but that pleased the new Brooklyn faithful, Cuban defector Vladimir Hernandez was given another baseball life as he signed with the Montreal Expos' affiliate in Clinton, Iowa.

As the new Cyclone season began, Brooklyn Dodger connections were still part of the New York Mets. Brooklyn Dodger pitcher Ralph Branca is married to Dearie Mulvey, the daughter of a former part owner of the Brooklyn Dodgers. Ralph and Dearie Branca's daughter is married to former Los Angeles Dodger (as well as former Met) Bobby Valentine, the New York Mets' manager. Meanwhile, at the time the Cyclones opened their second season, the parent New York Mets were hovering around the .500 mark. Before the season began, the author asked Ralph Branca if while sitting around at a family dinner he ever gave baseball advice to his son-in-law, Bobby Valentine. Branca replied, "He doesn't need it. He knows more baseball than I do anyway."

Meanwhile Bobby Ojeda, who had learned the change-up from Brooklyn Dodger Johnny Podres, was teaching his new Brooklyn charges how to throw it. From former Brooklyn Dodger to former LA Dodger (and Met) to current Cyclone — again, the threads went all the way back to Brooklyn.

Later in the Cyclones' second season, there would be a statue erected at the entrance to KeySpan Park. The statue would show Dodger greats Jackie Robinson and Pee Wee Reese. Clem Labine was on the committee to choose the design of the statue. He noted, "Last year, only a few weeks before September 11, my wife and I, who were on the committee to choose the statue along with Ralph Branca, and Rachel Robinson and Jackie's daughter, all met in an office in the World Trade Tower to view the proposed statues. The models of the statues were all wonderful. No matter which one they choose, it would be fitting. My wife and I hope to make it to KeySpan Stadium for the unveiling of the statue."

For a span of 44 years, the Brooklyn baseball past was embodied in events concerning the Dodgers. And now, somehow, there were two pasts: that of the Dodgers and now that of the original Brooklyn Cyclones. The Dodgers' golden years from 1947–1957 were remembered for players like Hodges, Robinson, Reese, Cox, Snider, Furillo, Campanella, Newcombe, Branca, Black, Labine, and Erskine. Now there were names from a new past: Caligiuri, McIntyre, Bacani, Rodriguez, Jiannetti, Pagan, Devarez, Lawson, Corr, Jacobs, Kay, Portobanco, Peeples, Eckert, and Cox (not Billy, but Mike).

The Brooklyn Dodgers will be forever remembered on a grand scale. On a smaller scale, so would the original Cyclones. Perhaps only a few would have major league careers, but they all had hope. For their fans, these new Brooklyn players held a special place. They were the ones who brought baseball back to Brooklyn. That they were talented players who achieved the best record in the league was a bonus. More essential for Brooklyn fans was that while the Cyclones were playing fine baseball, these young men were having the time of their lives. And they were sharing their joy with the fans, who were also having the time of their lives. These original Cyclones signed autographs galore, joked with the fans, had dinner with the fans, made friends with the fans.

And when the new season began, they were missed by the fans. It was not enough to root for a Brooklyn uniform. The fans wanted to root for their original Cyclones — and most of them were gone.

Fans could follow the original Cyclones as they tried to work their way up the ladder to the majors. Some of the original Cyclones were still with Brooklyn. Fans might again see some of the initial Cyclones when those players made the major leagues. But Brooklyn fans might see some of them again in other ways. It seemed (because of KeySpan's fine new facilities and the proximity of the ballpark to the New York Mets' offices and team doctors) that the New York Mets would be using Brooklyn as a spot to rehab injured players in their farm system. From time to time past Cyclone players on rehab might return for brief encores in Brooklyn. Cyclone players might return to Brooklyn in another way. Rumors still abounded that the Brooklyn Cyclones would eventually become a full season team, perhaps in Double-A baseball.

In that case, the original Cyclones who had success could climb their way up to Double-A and return for a reunion to Brooklyn, an idea that the players and fans eagerly anticipated.

But while some of original players might return, the inaugural season of the Brooklyn Cyclones was over. The first Brooklyn Cyclones season was now like a cherished gift, placed in a jewelry box and put on the top shelf of a closet with other family heirlooms. And from time to time, this gift of a season could be taken down from the shelf, the jewelry box opened and the season could be lived again — that time when baseball returned to Brooklyn.

Meanwhile, baseball not only had a new Brooklyn past and a promising future, it also had a day-to-day present. There were new Cyclones: the extroverted Kevin Deaton; the "Big Dog," talented first baseman Andres Rodriguez; Alhaji Turay, the outfielder with so many tools; and Chase Lambin, a second baseman who could add excitement. No longer was baseball in Brooklyn a hope or even an object of wonder. It was a reality. It had become an accepted part of everyday Brooklyn life.

As the official Brooklyn Dodger historian, Tom Knight, had said after witnessing the first-ever Brooklyn Cyclones home opener, "For the first time in 44 years, people are asking 'How did Brooklyn make out?'"

Appendix

Official Brooklyn Cyclones Statistics, 2001

W–L Record: 52–24

Player	AVG	G	AB	R	H	2B	3B	HR	RBI	BB	SO	SB	CS	SLG	OBP	E
#Abreu, Dave, 2B	.182	4	11	1	2	0	0	1	1	0	2	0	0	.455	.182	1
Arias, Leandro, 2B	.241	36	112	12	27	7	1	3	11	10	31	2	2	.402	.303	3
Bacani, David, 2B	.295	23	95	13	28	6	0	0	9	5	12	5	4	.358	.340	2
#Beuerlein, Tyler, C	.253	21	75	10	19	5	0	0	6	8	26	0	1	.320	.341	4
Caligiuri, Jay, 1B	.328	66	238	38	78	14	3	5	34	26	31	4	2	.475	.403	6
Corr, Frank, OF	.302	61	212	38	64	21	1	13	46	14	32	6	6	.594	.365	3
Coyne, Anthony, DH	.000	1	2	0	0	0	0	0	0	0	1	0	0	.000	.000	0
Devarez, Noel, OF	.250	54	188	30	47	10	0	10	33	10	63	3	3	.463	.296	3
Garcia, Daniel, 2B	.321	15	56	10	18	2	0	1	6	4	10	3	2	.411	.387	3
Hernandez, Vlad, 2B	.245	15	49	2	12	1	1	0	4	2	7	2	2	.306	.269	1
Huber, Justin, C	.000	3	9	0	0	0	0	0	0	0	4	0	0	.000	.000	0
*Jacobs, Mike, C	.288	19	66	12	19	5	0	1	15	6	11	1	1	.409	.364	3
Jiannetti, Joseph, 3B	.348	41	158	24	55	13	0	3	29	18	29	8	5	.487	.420	10
Kay, Brett, C	.311	49	180	28	56	13	0	5	18	16	28	2	1	.467	.380	6
Lawson, Forrest, OF	.280	49	164	18	46	6	2	1	15	6	23	7	4	.360	.314	0
#Lydon, Wayne, OF	.246	21	57	12	14	1	1	0	1	7	18	10	1	.298	.348	1
McIntyre, Robert, SS	.197	67	233	35	46	10	1	8	35	18	67	7	5	.352	.263	24
#Pagan, Angel, OF	.315	62	238	46	75	10	2	0	15	22	30	30	18	.374	.388	4
*Piercy, Mike, PH	.000	3	1	0	0	0	0	0	1	1	0	1	0	.000	.500	0
#Pittman, Richard, SS	.333	5	12	0	4	0	0	0	0	1	5	0	0	.333	.385	2
Rodriguez, Edgar, 3B	.239	27	92	8	22	5	0	5	13	4	23	0	0	.457	.287	4
Shinjo, Tsuyoshi, OF	.286	2	7	0	2	0	0	0	1	1	2	0	0	.286	.375	0
Sosa, Francisco, C	.389	24	72	12	28	3	1	1	8	2	7	2	4	.500	.421	6
*Todd, Jeremy, 1B	.182	17	44	4	8	1	0	0	3	7	13	0	1	.205	.291	0
Toner, John, OF	.258	38	124	10	32	8	1	1	16	8	33	3	4	.363	.326	2
#Zaragoza, Joel, 3B	.170	28	53	5	9	2	0	0	1	3	16	1	1	.208	.228	3
All Others	.000	0	0	0	0	0	0	0	0	0	0	0	0	.000	.000	22
Total-All Batters	.279		2548	368	711	143	14	58	321	199	524	97	67	.414	.343	113

* = Left-handed batter
\# = Switch-hitter

Pitcher	W–L	ERA	G	GS	CG	SHO	SV	IP	H	R	ER	HR	HB	BB	SO	WP	OPP AVG
Bowen, Chad	1–2	4.82	3	2	0	0	0	9.1	14	5	5	0	0	3	11	0	.359
*Braswell, Bryan	1–0	2.08	5	2	0	0	0	13.0	12	3	3	1	0	2	13	0	.235
Byard, David	3–1	1.46	22	0	0	0	9	37.0	21	7	6	0	1	11	32	1	.164
*Cabrera, Junior	0–0	3.00	1	0	0	0	0	3.0	4	1	1	0	0	2	4	1	.308
*Cox, Mike	6–1	2.91	13	7	0	0	0	52.2	40	25	17	2	2	41	73	6	.213
*DiNardo, Lenny	1–2	2.00	9	5	0	0	0	36.0	26	10	8	0	1	17	40	4	.200
Eckert, Harold	9–1	3.34	13	11	0	0	0	70.0	51	31	26	4	6	21	75	9	.200
Gahan, Matt	4–1	1.99	10	3	0	0	4	40.2	29	16	9	1	1	7	42	2	.187
Herbison, Brett	0–2	6.75	6	5	0	0	0	12.0	15	11	9	0	1	6	9	1	.294
*Martin, Tom	0–0	0.00	1	1	0	0	0	1.0	2	0	0	0	0	0	0	0	.500
Mattox, David	1–0	0.90	2	2	0	0	0	10.0	5	2	1	0	0	3	12	0	.147
*McGinley, Blake	5–0	1.94	18	0	0	0	4	46.1	30	12	10	3	3	11	59	3	.182
*Ogle, Rylie	0–1	1.26	6	0	0	0	0	14.1	15	3	2	0	0	5	14	0	.278
*Olson, Ryan	0–1	2.16	7	1	0	0	2	25.0	15	6	6	0	0	9	22	3	.169
Ough, Wayne	0–1	6.48	7	3	0	0	0	16.2	11	12	12	1	1	17	19	2	.180
*Peeples, Ross	9–3	1.34	16	15	1	1	0	80.1	63	19	12	1	1	29	67	4	.214
Peterson, Matt	2–2	1.62	6	6	0	0	0	33.1	26	7	6	0	3	14	19	2	.217
Portobanco, Luz	5–3	2.04	13	12	0	0	0	70.2	51	20	16	1	13	29	52	3	.210
Roman, Orlando	1–1	5.03	9	0	0	0	2	19.2	14	13	11	1	2	8	18	0	.192
Scobie, Jason	3–0	0.89	18	0	0	0	7	40.1	22	4	4	2	2	8	32	0	.161
Sherman, Chris	0–0	3.72	3	0	0	0	1	9.2	10	4	4	1	0	5	6	1	.286
*Walker, Brian	1–2	2.57	13	1	0	0	2	28.0	26	11	8	2	1	12	24	1	.236
All Others	0–0	4.50	1	0	0	0	0	2.0	3	1	1	0	0	1	1	0	.375
Total-All Pitchers	52–24	2.37	202	76	1	1	31	671.0	505	223	177	20	38	261	644	43	.207

* = Left Hander

New York–Penn League Leaders, 2001

Batting Top 10 (Minimum 205 Plate Appearances)

Batter	Club	AVG	G	AB	R	H	HR	RBI
Francia, Juan	ONE	.340	47	191	30	65	0	8
Gonzalez, Edgar	HDV	.332	73	277	49	92	9	34
Caligiuri, Jay	BRK	.328	66	238	38	78	5	34
Rabelo, Mike	ONE	.325	53	194	27	63	0	32
Rifkin, Aaron	STA	.318	69	245	41	78	10	49
Youkilis, Kevin	LOW	.317	59	183	52	58	3	28
Duffy, Chris	WPT	.317	64	221	50	70	1	24
Pagan, Angel	BRK	.315	62	238	46	75	0	15
Griffin, John-Ford	STA	.311	66	238	46	74	5	43
Kent, Mailon	JAM	.310	50	187	26	58	2	27

Pitching Top 10 (Minimum 61 IP)

Pitcher	Club	W–L	ERA	IP	H	BB	SO
*Peeples, Ross	BRK	9–3	1.34	80	63	29	67

Pitcher	Club	W–L	ERA	IP	H	BB	SO
Oquendo, Ian	WPT	7–0	1.39	65	55	10	56
Arnold, Jason	STA	7–2	1.50	66	35	15	74
Ungs, Nick	UTI	3–1	1.62	61	57	0	40
Miner, Zach	JAM	3–4	1.89	91	76	16	68
Rodriguez, Juan	WPT	8–2	1.89	81	61	15	58
Portobanco, Luz	BRK	5–3	2.04	71	51	29	52
*Rodaway, Brian	PTF	7–3	2.34	88	76	11	56
Flinn, Chris	HDV	3–4	2.36	69	54	21	72
Wilson, Mike	BAT	4–4	2.58	80	89	23	51

Individual Top 5

Home Runs

Corr, Frank	BRK	13
Young, Walter	WPT	13
Morton, Rickie	MHV	12
Several Players Tied at		10
Several Players Tied at		7

Wins

Peeples, Ross	BRK	9
Eckert, Harold	BRK	9
Rodriguez, Juan	WPT	8
Manning, Charlie	STA	8

RBI

Camacho, Juan	STA	51
Self, Todd	PTF	49
Rifkin, Aaron	STA	49
Reece, Eric	HDV	48
Young, Walter	WPT	47

Saves

Miller, Jeff	WPT	15
Bustillos, Oscar	HDV	13
Romero, Felix	AUB	12
Barry, Kevin	JAM	12
Russ, Chris	STA	12

Stolen Bases

Duffy, Chris	WPT	30
Pagan, Angel	BRK	30
Cuello, Domingo	WPT	28
De Aza, Modesto	PTF	27
Money, Freddie	LOW	27

Strikeouts

Manning, Charlie	STA	87
Julianel, Ben	NJY	86
McGowan, Dustin	AUB	80
Delossantos, Carlos	WPT	80
Eckert, Harold	BRK	75

Hits

Gonzalez, Edgar	HDV	92
McCarthy, Bill	JAM	84
Self, Todd	PTF	79
Rifkin, Aaron	STA	78
Caligiuri, Jay	BRK	78

Games

Barry, Kevin	JAM	29
Merrigan, Josh	NJY	29
Clark, Ryan	STA	29
Khoury, Josh	UTI	29
Wood, Brandon	PTF	29

Doubles

Durazo, Ernie	AUB	22
Corr, Frank	BRK	21
Walsh, Sean	BAT	20
Reece, Eric	HDV	20
Several Players Tied at		19

Complete Games

Kim, Il	BAT	2
Wood, Bobby	STA	2
Arnold, Jason	STA	2
Several Players Tied at		1

Triples

Raburn, Ryan	ONE	8
De Paula, Luis	HDV	6
Kolodzey, Chris	ONE	5

Shutouts

Kim, Il	BAT	2
Peeples, Ross	BRK	1
Rodriguez, Jose	JAM	1

Triples

| Rifkin, Aaron | STA | 5 |
| Conrad, Brooks | PTF | 5 |

On-Base Percentage

Youkilis, Kevin	LOW	.512
Duffy, Chris	WPT	.440
Moylan, Dan	NJY	.424
Shelton, Chris	WPT	.415
Griffin, John-ford	STA	.413

Slugging Percentage

Corr, Frank	BRK	.594
Rifkin, Aaron	STA	.559
Gonzalez, Edgar	HDV	.527
Morton, Rickie	MHV	.521
Young, Walter	WPT	.509

Extra-Base Hits

Corr, Frank	BRK	35
Rifkin, Aaron	STA	34
Raburn, Ryan	ONE	33
Gonzalez, Edgar	HDV	32
Morton, Rickie	MHV	30

Runs Scored

Youkilis, Kevin	LOW	52
Self, Todd	PTF	52
Duffy, Chris	WPT	50
Gonzalez, Edgar	HDV	49
Several Players Tied at		46

Shutouts

| Johnson, Jeremy | ONE | 1 |
| Arnold, Jason | STA | 1 |

Innings Pitched

Miner, Zach	JAM	90.2
Rodaway, Brian	PTF	88.1
Roberson, Brandon	PTF	87.0
Julianel, Ben	NJY	85.1
Mayfield, James	BAT	85.0

Losses

Dischiavo, John	HDV	8
Generelli, Daniel	LOW	8
Fulchino, Jeff	UTI	8
Kleine, Victor	MHV	8
Several Players Tied at		7

Walks

McGowan, Dustin	AUB	49
Stephenson, Eric	AUB	44
Cox, Mike	BRK	41
Peguero, Radhame	HDV	40
Mitchell, Tom	VMT	39

Home Runs Allowed

Colton, Kyle	JAM	9
Mattison, Corey	NJY	8
Marceau, Pierre-Luc	VMT	8
Searles, Jonathan	WPT	8
Lewis, Jeremy	ONE	8

Team Statistics

Team Batting	AVG	AB	R	H	HR	BB	SO	SB	CS
Brooklyn	.279	2548	368	711	58	199	524	97	67
Staten Island	.265	2561	383	678	46	265	498	71	30
Williamsport	.262	2432	374	637	36	243	489	132	36
Oneonta	.258	2450	327	631	25	244	597	73	48
Hudson Valley	.257	2700	352	694	41	210	579	41	23
New Jersey	.257	2545	330	653	29	325	580	89	52
Lowell	.252	2594	354	653	28	315	578	86	35
Pittsfield	.251	2492	398	625	35	290	600	133	55
Jamestown	.247	2452	292	606	26	217	511	68	35
Batavia	.241	2565	323	617	28	229	581	58	41
Auburn	.239	2547	306	610	33	206	507	94	40
Utica	.237	2479	297	588	38	244	649	41	26
Mahoning Vly	.226	2487	292	561	48	257	554	38	43
Vermont	.208	2432	264	506	21	232	638	66	38

Team Pitching	W–L	ERA	H	CG	SHO	SV	HR	BB	SO
Brooklyn	52–24	2.37	505	1	6	31	20	261	644

Team Pitching	W–L	ERA	H	CG	SHO	SV	HR	BB	SO
Williamport	48–26	2.91	550	2	5	23	34	229	567
Staten Island	48–28	3.22	556	4	5	22	34	240	633
New Jersey	35–41	3.27	630	0	5	24	44	234	621
Batavia	37–39	3.44	686	4	3	17	37	209	471
Pittsfield	45–30	3.47	644	1	4	18	23	260	564
Jamestown	39–36	3.48	603	1	3	20	43	242	556
Oneonta	37–37	3.53	630	3	6	18	27	223	529
Utica	27–47	3.82	598	0	3	14	35	231	458
Lowell	33–43	3.90	666	1	2	16	37	259	518
Hudson Valley	39–37	3.91	669	2	1	20	38	295	544
Auburn	32–42	3.96	631	0	5	14	39	306	685
Mahoning Vly	26–49	4.25	722	0	4	18	41	250	568
Vermong	28–47	4.45	680	1	1	12	40	237	527

New York–Penn League Standings and Highlights, 2001

Standing of Clubs Through Games of 9/05/01

Division Standings McNamara Division	W	L	PCT	GB	Last Streak	Last 10
#Brooklyn	52	24	.684	W	1	5–5
Staten Island	48	28	.632	4.0	L 1	7–3
Pittsfield	45	30	.600	6.5	L 1	7–3
Hudson Valley	39	37	.513	13.0	W 1	3–7
New Jersey	35	41	.461	17.0	W 1	6–4
Lowell	33	43	.434	19.0	W 2	7–3
Vermont	28	47	.373	23.5	L 9	1–9

Pinckney Division	W	L	PCT	GB	Last Streak	Last 10
#Williamsport	48	26	.649	W	3	6–4
Jamestown	39	36	.520	9.5	W 1	6–4
Oneonta	37	37	.500	11.0	L 1	6–4
Batavia	37	39	.487	12.0	L 1	4–6
Auburn	32	42	.432	6.0	W 1	3–7
Utica	27	47	.365	21.0	L 2	4–6
Mahoning Valley	26	49	.347	22.5	L 1	4–6

&— Clinched Playoff Spot #— Clinched Division Title

Attendance Report (Unofficial-Based on Game Report Information)

	Total to Date	Openings	Average
Brooklyn	289,381	37	7,821
Lowell	185,000	37	5,000
Staten Island	188,127	38	4,951
Mahoning Valley	181,170	37	4,896
Hudson Valley	160,858	37	4,348
New Jersey	130,103	38	3,424
Vermont	115,560	36	3,210

	Total to Date	*Openings*	*Average*
Williamsport	72,258	36	2,007
Jamestown	63,069	36	1,752
Pittsfield	56,747	36	1,576
Oneonta	52,688	34	1,550
Auburn	54,994	36	1,528
Utica	45,123	34	1,327
Batavia	43,257	37	1,169

2001 Brooklyn Cyclones Roster

Abreu, David, #23 — Infielder; Age 21 from SP de Macoris, DR; switch hitter; throws right; height is 6'0" and weighs 160; High School: Gaston Deligne.

Abreu was the first batter to hit for Brooklyn in 44 years when he led off the first game at Jamestown. He hit .182 in 4 games for Brooklyn and then asked for and was granted his release.

Alfonzo, Edgar — The manager of the Cyclones spent 13 years as a minor league player. The brother of the Mets star second baseman, Edgar Alfonzo.

After coaching for two years in the Mets system, he was named the initial Brooklyn Cyclones manager. He's from Venezuela.

Arias, Leandro, #8 — Second Baseman; Age 20 from Santo Domingo, DR; bats right; throws right; height is 5'10" and weighs 160. High school: Melinda Giral.

Born in April of 1981, he hit .241 for Brooklyn.

Bacani, David, #31 — Second Baseman; Age 22 from Long Beach, CA; bats right; throws right; height is 5'8" and weighs 165. College: Cal Sate Fullerton.

Bacani was a sparkplug. Always hustling, he played fine defense and hit .295 after being called up from Kingsport.

Beuerlein, Tyler, #13 — Catcher; Age 22 from Cave Creek, AZ; switch hitter; throws right; height is 6'3" and weighs 230. College: Grand Canyon University.

A catcher who can also play first base or the outfield, he's a switch-hitter with power. He was hit by a pitch and hurt his arm in August and lost some time. He hit .235.

Bowen, Chad, #34 — Right-handed Pitcher; Age 19 from Hendersonville, TN; bats rights; throws right; height is 6'4" and weighs 205. High school: Gallatin.

For Brooklyn, Bowen went 1–2 with a 4.82 ERA.

Brantley, Mickey — The Mets minor league hitting coordinator, Brantley traveled throughout the farm system, spending time with all the clubs on a rotating basis. Serious about his instruction, he also has a good sense of humor and has learned some Spanish to help his instruction.

Braswell, Brian — Pitcher; Age 26 from Springboro, Ohio; bats left; throws left; height is 6' 1" and weighs 200; College: Toledo.

A lefthander, Braswell has been in minor league ball since '96, reaching as high as the Double-A Texas League. He spent part of 2001 on injury rehab assignment with Brooklyn.

Byard, David, #40 — Right-handed Pitcher; Age 23 from Mount Vernon, OH; bats right; throws right; height is 6'3" and weighs 235; High School: Mt. Vernon Nazarene.

Known as "Big Bird," he pitched in relief for the Cyclones, often closing out games and had an outstanding season. Also, was the driver of the team van, resident humorist, excellent dart shooter and a tough competitor.

Cabrera, Yunir— Pitcher; Age 21 from Dominican Republic; bats left; throws left; height is 6'0" and weighs 166; School: San Pedro de Macoris High School.

A lefthander from the Dominican Republic, he saw only limited action with Brooklyn. He allowed 1 earned run in 3 innings.

Caligiuri, Jay, #43 — First Baseman; Age 21 from Camarillo, CA; bats right; throws right; height is 6'0" and weighs 190; College: Cal State.

The California resident started off the year at third base and then switched to first base. He was outstanding at each position. An excellent hitter for average, he received, along with Ross Peeples, the Mets Doubleday Award as the outstanding player from Brooklyn in the Mets' farm system. A high average hitter, he led Brooklyn with a .328 batting average, good for third in the league.

Carter, Gary— A catcher who should by all accounts be in Major League Baseball's Hall of Fame, Carter helped to coach Brooklyn on a few occasions as he traveled about coaching in the Mets' farm system. He also coached in a game at first base for the Cyclones, so he might be the first Cyclone to reach the Hall of Fame.

Corr, Francis, #29 — Left Fielder; Age 22 from Daytona Beach, FL; height is 5'9" and weighs 195; bats right; throws right; College: Stetson University.

Corr started off the year as Francis. Within a few days nobody called him his real name, everyone said Frank. But when the Cyclones arrived in Brooklyn, the Brooklyn fans made his name "Frankie." An outfielder who is capable of catching, Corr even came in to a game and pitched effectively in relief. By any name, Corr was an exciting power hitter who plays with a world of enthusiasm. Although only 5'9", Corr is very strong. He likes to quote his father, who says, "If you can play, you can play. Forget size." Corr can play.

Cox, Mike, #26 — Pitcher; Age 22 from Pasadena, TX; bats left; throws left; height is 5'11" and weighs 195.

Cox was the shortest pitcher on the Cyclones. A lefty, his friendly nature made him a fan favorite. Showed his potential when he once struck out 14 batters in only six innings. A practical joker. He was 6–1 with a 2.91 ERA for Brooklyn.

Coyne, Anthony, #13 — Infielder; Age 22 from Huntington, MD; bats right; throws right; height is 5'10" and weighs 190; School: Yale University.

An infielder from Yale University, this Maryland resident spent part of the 2001 season at Pittsfield and was back in the league again with Brooklyn. He didn't play much in the first week of the season and he asked and was granted his release. A personable player, he was attempting to find another team to play with for the 2002 season.

Devarez, Noel, #38 — Outfielder; Age 19 from San Francisco de Macoris, DR; bats right; throws right; height is 6'0" and weighs 175; High School: San Francisco de Macoris, DR.

A power hitting outfielder, Noel got off to a great start, but then tailed off as pitchers fed him a steady diet of curves and change-ups instead of his beloved fastballs. Howard Johnson worked with him and changed his stance so that Devarez was showing improvement near the end of the season. With Brooklyn, he hit .250 with 10 home runs.

DiNardo, Lenny, #17 — Pitcher; Age 21 from High Springs, FL; bats left; throws left; height is 6'4" and weighs 188; College: Stetson University.

DiNardo pitched for Team USA. He came to the Cyclones with a tired arm after pitching in college but has high potential, having been drafted in the third round.

Eckert, Harold, #15 — Right-handed Pitcher; Age 23 from Edison, NJ; bats right; throws right; height is 6'3" and weighs 215; College: Florida International.

When the season began, Eckert was attempting to come back from a baseball absence of two years because of surgery to his pitching elbow. His comeback was a fine success as he stayed injury free and was an effective pitcher all year. He lost only one game — on his birthday. The most local of the Cyclones, he lived in his boyhood home in Edison, New Jersey, only a forty minute drive from Coney Island. Thrilled to be back pitching, he usually had about 30 to 40 friends and family members at each home game. He tied Peeples for the league lead in wins (Eckert was 9–1) and had an ERA of 3.34. He was fifth in the league in strikeouts with 75.

Gahan, Matt, #12 — Pitcher; Age 25 from Agonellaban, NSW, Australia; bats right; throws right.

An Australian, Gahan was 25 years old during the season. He was outstanding and at mid-season was moved up a level to Capital City.

Garcia, Danny, #13 — Second Baseman; Age 21 from Anaheim, CA; bats right; throws right; height is 6'0" and weighs 180; School: Pepperdine.

A second baseman from Pepperdine, Garcia had played for the U.S. National team. Outstanding in baseball fundamentals such as bunting, the hit and run, taking out runners on a slide, etc., he was an effective hitter and fielder and was moved up to Capital City in July. He hit .321 for Brooklyn.

Herbison, Brett, #45 — Right-handed Pitcher; Age 24 from Elgin, IL; bats right; throws right; height is 6'5" and weighs 208; High School: Burlington Central.

A right-handed pitcher, Herbison has been in minor league baseball for seven years. Coming back from a serious arm injury, he spent about a month at Brooklyn on injury rehab.

Hernandez, Vladimir, #39 — Second Baseman; Age 24 from Havana, Cuba; bats right; throws right; height is 6'0" and weighs 180; High School: Ho-Chi-Minh High School.

Vladimir went to Ho Chi Min High School in Havana, Cuba. This speedy infielder escaped Cuba and spent a year and a half hiding in Mexico. He returned to baseball this summer with the Cyclones; hit .245 and was sent to Capital City near the end of August.

Huber, Justin — Catcher; Age 20 from Emerald, Victoria, Australia; bats right; throws right; height is 6'2" and weighs 190; School: Beacon Hills College.

A catcher from Australia, Justin played on their national team. He is a top catching prospect. He started the year at Kingsport and was promoted to Brooklyn in August.

Jacobs, Mike, #17 — Catcher; Age 20 from Chula Vista, CA; bats left; throws right; height is 6'2" and weighs 200; School: Grossmont JC.

A catcher, this Californian was one on the heroes of Brooklyn's home opener as he drove in the winning run in the tenth inning. He received a mid-season promotion to Capital City. He is a left-handed hitting catcher with power.

Jiannetti, Joe, #44—Third Baseman; Age 19 from St. Petersburg, FL; bats right; throws right; height is 6'0" and weighs 190; College: Daytona Beach, CC.

Joe was only 19 during the season. From St. Petersburg, Florida, Jainnetti is a hard-nosed former high school football star who never let his diabetes get in the way of a hustling performance. A standout hitter, he played third for the Cyclones, but could wind up playing second base, the outfield or even catching. He has good speed and plays smart.

Johnson, Howard—The Cyclones' hitting coach in 2001 and newly named manager for 2002, Johnson was a 30/30 man three times in the major leagues, meaning he hit at least thirty home runs and stole at least thirty bases both in the same season three times in his career. Soft spoken, he helped the Cyclones to lead the New York–Penn League in hitting.

Kay, Brett, #3 — Catcher; Age 21 from Villa Park, CA; bats right; throws right; height is 6'1" and weighs 190; College: Cal State Fullerton.

Kay played in the College World Series. A crafty player, he hits for average and power, runs well, and is an outstanding bunter. Always plays all-out and plays well in big games. Kay hit .311.

Lawson, Forrest, #2 — Outfielder; Age 20 from Puyallup, WA; bats right; throws right; height is 6'3" and weighs 195; High School: Rogers.

An outfielder from the State of Washington, Lawson plays all the outfield positions and works hard. He had a hot second half of the season, winding up at .280.

Lydon, Wayne, #11—Outfielder; Age 20 from Jessup, PA; bats right; throws right; height is 6'2" and weighs 190; High School: Valley View High School.

Lydon started the season at Kingsport. He was learning to bat left-handed to become a switch hitter. Although batting under .200 at Kingsport, he was called up to the Cyclones for the second half of the season. Extremely fast, he can be electrifying in his base running.

Martin, Tom—Left-handed Pitcher; Age 31 from Charleston, SC; bats left; throws left; height is 6'1" and weighs 200.

Martin is a pitcher that the New York Mets sent to Brooklyn for a brief appearance in a rehab start.

Mattox, Tommy—Right-handed Pitcher;

A right-handed pitcher, Mattox was called up from Kingsport in August and was impressive in brief appearances, finishing with a 0.90 ERA in 10 innings, with 12 strikeouts and a .147 opponents' batting average.

McGinley, Blake, #33 — Left-handed Pitcher; Age 22 from Bakersfield, CA; bats left; throws left; height is 6'1" and weighs 170; College: Texas Tech.

McGinley pitched in relief and was effective all season. For Brooklyn, he was 5–0 with a 1.94 ERA. He struck out 59 in 46.1 innings.

McIntyre, Robert, #1 — Shortstop; Age 20 from Tampa, FL; bats right; throws right; height is 5'10" and weighs 170; High School: Hillsborough.

He showed good power for a middle infielder at Brooklyn, but had an off season in the field. He hit .197, but was third on the Brooklyn club with 8 home runs and was second in RBI with 35.

Miller, Rich—NY Mets Assistant Field/Outfield/Baserunning, Coordinator

Miller was a roving instructor who briefly worked at Brooklyn.

Ogle, Rylie, #34 — Left-handed Pitcher; Age 23 from Seal Beach, CA; bats left; throws left; height is 6'3" and weighs 185; College: UC Santa Barbara.

Ogle had an ERA of 1.26 in 14.1 innings for the Cyclones.

Ojeda, Bobby — Ojeda was the Cyclones' pitching coach in 2001 and will serve the same role in 2002. Known as "Bobby O.," he tutored the Cyclone pitchers, with an emphasis on both the physical and mental aspects of pitching. His charges finished first in the league in pitching, and Ojeda gave a boost to all of the careers. As a player, Ojeda led the Mets to the 1986 World Series win over the Boston Red Sox.

Olson, Ryan, #46 — Left-handed Pitcher; Age 21 from Oakdale, CA; switch hitter; throws left; height is 6'5" and weighs 187; College: UNLV.

Olson was a relief pitcher for Brooklyn. He had a 2.16 ERA in 25 innings.

Ough, Wayne, #27 — Right-handed Pitcher; Age 22 from Vinceni Townsville, Australia; bats right; throws right; height is 6'2" and weighs 205; College: Trinidad State Junior College.

A big, strong Australian, he was one of three Aussies on the Cyclones.

Pagan, Angel, #35 — Outfielder, Age 20 from Rio Piedras, PR; switch hitter; throws right; height is 6'1" and weighs 175; College: Republic de Columbia.

Pagan started the season at Capital City. Even though he was playing well there, he was sent to Brooklyn where he could play regularly, and the speedy center fielder hit .311 as a switch hitter. From Puerto Rico, Pagan was a favorite "matinee idol" with the female fans. He tied for first in stolen bases in the New York–Penn League with 30.

Peeples, Ross, #18 — Left-handed Pitcher; Age 21 from Cordele, GA; bats left; throws left; height is 6'4" and weighs 196; College: Middle Georgia.

The big lefthander starter shared the New York Mets Doubleday Award with Jay Caligiuri. Displaying outstanding control, the Georgia native pitched well all year and went 9 and 3 in the regular season and won a game in the playoffs.

Peterson, Matthew, #10 — Right-handed Pitcher; Age 19 from Alexandria, LA; bats right; throws right; height is 6'5" and weighs 185; School is Rapides High School.

Peterson pitched effectively in the first part of the season and then was promoted to Capital City. He was a second round draft pick in 2000.

Piercy, Mike, #4 — Outfielder, Age 25 from Hillside, NJ; bats left; throws left.

The outfielder from New Jersey was, at 25, old for Class-A ball and only played briefly before being released. The popular and loquacious Piercy hooked on with an independent league team.

Pittman, Sean — Infielder

An infielder called up from Kingsport in late August, Pittman played well in limited appearances, hitting .333 in 12 at-bats.

Portobanco, Luz, #47 — Right-handed Pitcher; Age 21 from Granada, Nicaragua; bats right; throws right; height is 6'3" and weighs 205; College: Miami Dade, CC.

Originally from Nicaragua, Luz is now a Miami, Florida resident, with a 94 miles per hour fastball. The right-hander spent 2000 working on his curve and change-up and showed marked improvement, having an excellent season. He was known as the "Yankee Killer" because he beat the Cyclones' rival, the Staten Island Yankees, three times in the regular season.

Rippelmeyer, Ray—NY Mets' Minor League Pitching Coordinator

A pitching instructor in the Mets' system, Rippelmeyer worked with the Cyclones' pitchers as part of his duties, roving throughout the Mets' minor league clubs. Rippelmeyer pitched in the majors and in limited at bats hit .500 (4 for 8) in the major leagues.

Rodriguez, Edgar, #22 — Third Baseman; Age 21 from San Pedro de Marcoris; bats right; throws right.

A third baseman, Edgar was only 19 in the Cyclones' inaugural season. He hit the first Cyclones' home run, in the opening game at Jamestown, and was an Opening Day hero when he hit a two-out home run in the bottom of the ninth to tie up the game. He broke his hand when he was hit by a pitch and missed a good part of the season, returning in late August. From the Dominican Republic, Edgar is the cousin of New York Mets' closer Benetiz.

Roman, Orlando, #12 — Right-handed Pitcher; Age 22 from Vaja Baja, DR; bats right; throws right; height is 6'2" and weighs 205; College: Indian Hills CC.

A right-handed pitcher from the Dominican Republic, Roman was a relief pitcher who appeared in 9 games, pitching up 2 saves.

Scobie, Jason, #28 — Right-handed Pitcher; Age 22 from Austin, TX; bats right; throws right; height is 6'1" and weighs 190; College: LSU.

At Louisiana State University, Scobie was used to pitching before large, enthusiastic crowds in college. He was outstanding out of the bullpen, going 3–0 with an ERA of 0.89 and 7 saves.

Sherman, Chris—A right-hander, Sherman saw limited action with the Cyclones. He finished with a 3.72 ERA.

Shinjo, Tsuyoshi—Outfielder; Age 29 from Fukuoka, Japan; bats right; throws right; height is 6'1"; weighs 185.

A New York Mets outfielder, Shinjo played two games for the Cyclones while he was on injured rehabilitation. Shinjo, regarded with the fame of a rock star in his native Japan, created quite an international media stir with his Brooklyn Cyclone appearances.

Sosa, Francisco, #21— Catcher; Age 20 from Esperanza, DR; bats right; throws right; height is 5'11" and weighs 180.

A catcher in his third season in the Mets farm system, Sosa is from the Dominican Republic and no relation to Sammy Sosa. Bothered by a sore arm, he still hit .389 for Brooklyn in 72 at-bats and handled pitchers well. He is an excellent bunter and can steal a base.

Teufel, Tim—NY Mets Infield Coordinator

Teufel, an former infielder and another member of the New York Mets 1986 World Series winners, was an infield instructor throughout the Mets' minor league system.

Todd, Jeremy, #25 — First Baseman; Age 23 from West Frankfurt, IL; bats left; throws right; height is 6'2" and weighs 210; School: Gaston Deligne High School.

Todd, a first baseman, was playing in his second year in the New York–Penn League. He got off to a slow start, and since he was one of the older Cyclones, he was released. He was trying to hook on with another team.

Toner, John, #9 — Outfielder; Age 21 from St. Joseph, MI; bats right; throws right; height is 6'3" and weighs 210; College: Western Michigan.

A power-hitting outfielder, Toner had a strong second half and played well in the playoffs. From Michigan, he suffered an ankle sprain in mid-season, but came back strong. He finished at .258.

Walker, Brian, #23 — Left-handed Pitcher; Age 21 from Miami, FL; bats left; throws left; height is 6'3" and weighs 210; College: University of Miami.

A left-hander from the University of Miami, winner of the 2001 College World Series, Walker came to the Cyclones with a tired arm. A fourth round draft pick, he had a 2.58 ERA for Brooklyn.

Zaragoza, Joel, #24 — Second Baseman/Shortstop; Age 22 from Bayamon, PR; bats right; throws right; height is 6'1" and weighs 190; College: Berthune-Cookman.

Zaragoza is a slick fielder, playing any infield position. He played for Kingsport in 1999 and Pittsfield in 2000.

Sources

Much of the material for this book was gathered from interviews I conducted with past and current Brooklyn players, with fans, announcers, club officials, umpires, scouts, etc. The bulk of these interviews were conducted at both KeySpan Stadium in Brooklyn, and at each of the ballparks that the Cyclones visited during the 2001 season. Most of the Brooklyn Cyclones were interviewed during the course of the season. Other interviews were conducted after the season, particularly during the Instructional League in Florida. Manager Edgar Alfonzo and coaches Bobby Ojeda and Howard Johnson were interviewed numerous times. Players Jay Caligiuri, Frank Corr, Mike Cox, Harold Eckert, Vladimir Hernandez, Joe Jianetti, Brett Kay, and Luz Portbanco, also contributed numerous interviews. Fan Mark Lazarus was a key contributor via his interviews.

In addition, a number of interviews with the Brooklyn Dodgers were conducted at Dodgertown in Vero Beach, Florida, particularly interviews with Duke Snider, Clem Labine, and Ralph Branca. Tommy Holmes was interviewed at KeySpan Stadium as was Al Gionfriddo. Joe Pignatano was interviewed in a Brooklyn restaurant near his Bay Ridge home. Carl Erskine was interviewed in Manhattan, Brooklyn (twice) and in Vero Beach.

Guy Conti, the New York Mets Minor League Field Coordinator, was particularly helpful in interviews at Vero Beach, at Port St. Lucie, and at Augusta New Jersey. Warner Fusselle was especially helpful through his recollections and impressions. His meticulous scorebooks helped to recreate all the key games. Warner also generously provided the tapes of his pre-game interviews. Material from his interviews with Mike Jacobs, Frank Corr, Lynn and Barbara Caligiuri, and Howard Herman were invaluable. Umpire John Blackburn helped through his interview in Brick, New Jersey. Rudy Riska was helpful both in an interview and through his friendships with so many in baseball. Marty Adler, president of the Brooklyn Dodger Hall of Fame, was a key source of information and so was Tom Knight, the official Brooklyn Dodger historian, and a columnist for the *Brooklyn Eagle* and the *Staten Island Record*.

A number of texts were particularly helpful with the history of Brooklyn baseball.

Brooklyn's Dodgers, by Carl Prince, was a valuable source for information on Jackie Robinson's career. Mr. Prince's book also provided much of the information on the Dodger haunts of the golden era (1947–57) as the thoroughly researched chapter on Brooklyn's baseball taverns was the near exclusive source for material on the Dodger players' and fans' haunt habits.

Bums, by Peter Golenbock, was particularly helpful in its portrayal of the history of the Dodgers, and was the source of much information on the early years of the Dodgers.

The Boys of Summer, by Roger Kahn, is a modern classic in its portrayal of the Dodgers' golden era in Brooklyn, particularly in conveying the history of the team and in the book's verbal portraits of the Brooklyn Dodgers. *The Boys of Summer* was a valued resource.

Jackie Robinson, by Arnold Rampersad, was very helpful, particularly as a source for Jackie Robinson's initial spring training with the Brooklyn organization in 1946.

Jackie Robinson 1947, by Tot Holmes, was a source for Jackie Robinson's first two seasons (1946–47) in the Brooklyn Dodger organization, and this source was very helpful with details of Jackie Robinson's first two spring trainings with Montreal and the Dodgers.

Selected Bibliography

Golenbock, Peter. *Bums — An Oral History of the Brooklyn Dodgers*. New York: Putnam, 1984.

Holmes, Tot. *Jackie 1947*. Gothenburg, Nebraska: Holmes Publishing, 1997.

Kahn, Roger. *The Boys of Summer*. New York: Harper-Collins, 2000.

Manbeck, John B., consulting ed. *The Neighborhoods of Brooklyn*. New Haven: Yale University Press, 1998.

Milazzo, Joe. *New York–Penn League Media Guide*. New York–Penn League Office, Utica, New York, 2001.

Prince, Carl. *Brooklyn's Dodgers*. Oxford University Press, 1997.

Rampersad, Arnold. *Jackie Robinson*. New York: Ballantine Books, 1997.

Index

Numbers in **bold** represent photographs.